The Impact of Directive 2005/29/EC on Polish Law on Combating Unfair Competition

Ius, Lex et Res Publica
Studies in Law, Philosophy and Political Cultures

Edited by Barbara Janusz-Pohl

Volume 42

Jakub Kępiński

The Impact of Directive 2005/29/EC on Polish Law on Combating Unfair Competition

PETER LANG

Berlin · Bruxelles · Chennai · Lausanne · New York · Oxford

Bibliographic Information published by the Deutsche Nationalbibliothek
The Deutsche Nationalbibliothek lists this publication in the Deutsche Nationalbibliografie; detailed bibliographic data is available online at http://dnb.d-nb.de.

Library of Congress Cataloging-in-Publication Data
Names: Kępiński, Jakub author
Title: The Impact of Directive 2005/29/EC on Polish Law on Combating Unfair Competition / Jakub Kępiński.
Description: First edition. | Berlin ; New York : Peter Lang, 2025. | Series: Ius, lex et res publica, 2191-3250 ; vol. 42 | Includes bibliographical references. | Summary: "Polish law on combating unfair competition is influenced by EU law. This influence is so significant that it requires a new and comprehensive look at Polish solutions. The aim of the conducted research was to analyse the problems encountered in Polish law, in particular in relation to the implementation of Directive on unfair commercial practices"-- Provided by publisher.
Identifiers: LCCN 2025020182 (print) | LCCN 2025020183 (ebook) | ISBN 9783631933480 hardback | ISBN 9783631933497 pdf | ISBN 9783631940730 epub Subjects: LCSH: Competition, Unfair--Poland | Competition, Unfair--European Union countries | Antitrust law--Poland | Antitrust law--European Union countries | International and municipal law--Poland | International and municipal law--European Union countries | Court of Justice of the European Union
Classification: LCC KKP1234 .K47 2025 (print) | LCC KKP1234 (ebook) | DDC 343.43807/21--dc23/eng/20250428
LC record available at https://lccn.loc.gov/2025020182
LC ebook record available at https://lccn.loc.gov/2025020183

The monograph is a translated and revised version of the publication "Wpływ prawa Unii Europejskiej na polskie prawo o zwalczaniu nieuczciwej konkurencji ze szczególnym uwzględnieniem sprzedaży premiowanej" published in C.H. Beck in 2019. Translated by Iwona Grenda

The project is co-financed by state budget funds granted by the Minister of Education and Science under the Programme 'Doskonała Nauka II' (Polska).

Minister of Science and Higher Education
Republic of Poland

ISSN 2191-3250
ISBN 978-3-631-93348-0 (Print)
ISBN 978-3-631-93349-7 (ePDF)
ISBN 978-3-631-94073-0 (ePUB)
DOI 10.3726/b23050

Published by Peter Lang GmbH, Berlin (Germany)
info@peterlang.com

This publication has been peer reviewed.

www.peterlang.com

Table of Contents

Introduction

"Polish law against unfair competition has been influenced by international law and, in recent years, primarily by EU law. The impact of EU law is so significant that it requires a new and comprehensive look at Polish law on combatting unfair competition, particularly since it may be expected that in the near future the regulations on unfair competition in Member States will undergo further harmonisation. With this being the case, the Polish legislator is likely to face the not very easy task of proper implementation of EU legislative acts in the national legal system. As the experience of recent years shows, all to date implementations of various pieces of legislation, including in particular Directive 2005/29/EC on unfair commercial practices,[1] have posed a major challenge. Implementations in Poland were carried out hastily, without the necessary consultation with legal scholars (and the academic community), and lacked a holistic view of the entire system of protection against unfair competition. This publication is an attempt to present the major problems that continue to exist in Polish law against unfair competition.

The considerations begin with a presentation (in chapter 1) of the sources of law that have had a fundamental impact on the issues discussed in the book and that provide a foundation for further discussion. The catalogue of

---

1 Directive 2005/29/EC of the European Parliament and of the Council of 11 May 2005 concerning unfair business-to-consumer commercial practices in the internal market and amending Council Directive 84/450/EEC, Directives 97/7/EC, 98/27/EC, and 2002/65/EC of the European Parliament and of the Council, and Regulation (EC) No 2006/2004 of the European Parliament and of the Council (OJ L 149, 2005, pp. 22–39).

the sources of law against unfair competition presented in this work is not exhaustive. The purpose of the analysis of the legislative acts cited was to place the discussed issues in a specific legal context to draw readers' attention to the fact that despite various actions taken at the international and EU level, the law on combatting unfair competition in EU Member States, although basically built on the same legal foundations, has not yet been fully harmonised and differs from one Member State to another.

The basic piece of international law is the Paris Convention for the Protection of Industrial Property of 20 March 1883,[2] which has had a significant impact on the shape of the law against unfair competition in the EU Member States today. Article 1(2) of the Convention places combatting unfair competition among the objects of industrial property law.

Another international convention that, indirectly, relates to the law against unfair competition is the Agreement on Trade-Related Aspects of Intellectual Property Rights (TRIPS).[3] Although TRIPS does not mention combatting unfair competition among its objectives, it does refer to the Paris Convention, and its provisions on geographical indications and undisclosed information influence the solutions adopted in EU Member States.

Among the international material worthy of inclusion in the discussion are the model provisions on protection against unfair competition developed by the World Intellectual Property Organisation (WIPO).[4] While their adoption is not mandatory, they may provide a point of reference for developing countries wishing to establish an effective system aimed at the protection of fair competition.

---

2 The Stockholm text is now in force, the Stockholm Act amending the Paris Convention for the Protection of Industrial Property of 20 March 1883, as amended in Brussels on 14 December 1900, Washington on 2 June 1911, The Hague on 6 November 1925, London on 2 June 1934, and Lisbon on 31 October 1958, drawn up at Stockholm on 14 July 1967 (Dz.U.1975 No. 9, item 51).

3 TRIPS is an annex to the 1994 Marrakesh Agreement Establishing the WTO. See Notice of the Minister of Foreign Affairs of 12 February 1996 on the publication of annexes to the Agreement Establishing the World Trade Organization (WTO) (Dz.U. No. 32, item 143).

4 Model Provisions on Protection against Unfair Competition. Articles and Notes, Publikacja WIPO Nr 832(E), ISBN 92-805-0642-0. Publication available on the WIPO website: <https://tind.wipo.int/record/28768/files/wipo_pub_832.pdf> (accessed on: 1.2.2025).

Other instruments of international law cited in the literature have been omitted from consideration[5] as a source of law against unfair competition. This is because their scope of application is limited only to certain specific, albeit discrete, issues (designations, trademarks, appellations of origin, or advertising) and not to issues of a fundamental nature.

Among the EU acts relating to the law against unfair competition, Directive 2005/29/EC plays a key role for any deliberations, as it introduced a new approach to the way in which the law against unfair competition is to be transposed. Unlike previous acts that were based on the adoption of a minimum standard of protection,[6] the Directive adopted a maximum standard and left Member States with little leeway in its implementation. Moreover, since a regulation of unfair competition more restrictive than that anticipated in Directive 2005/29/EC is not allowed, Member States had to carry out an overall revision of their respective legislation in that respect. This, in turn, has led to multiple doubts of interpretation also with regard to the existing national regulations intended to protect the interests of traders.

Doubts arise primarily because Directive 2005/29/EC does not harmonise the entirety of the law against unfair competition but only addresses unfair business-to-consumer (B2C) commercial practices. Harmonisation has thus proved to be only partial and has created confusion as to the interplay between national rules on business-to-business (B2B) relations and harmonising (at least partially) rules on B2C relations. The difficulty of these relationships stems from the model adopted in EU law. Commercial practices are divided according to the criterion of the trader's relationship with other parties, i.e. with the trader (B2B) and with the consumer (B2C). However, the division does not take into account the person to whom these practices cause or are likely to cause harm. A practice addressed to a consumer may also harm the trader, while a practice addressed to the trader may harm the consumer,[7] and this means that the effects that commercial practices may produce, regardless of whether they are applied in a B2B or B2C relationship, will

---

5 *J. Szwaja, A. Kubiak-Cyrul*, in: *J. Szwaja, J. Kępiński* (eds.), Ustawa o zwalczaniu nieuczciwej konkurencji. Komentarz, Warszawa 2024, p. 26–28.

6 OJ EU L 250 of 1984 r., p. 17, as amended.

7 *M. Namysłowska*, Nieuczciwe praktyki handlowe między przedsiębiorcami w prawie Unii Europejskiej, in: *T. Skoczny* (ed.), Prawo konkurencji. 25 lat, Pierwszy Polski Kongres Prawa Konkurencji, Warszawa 2016, p. 604.

affect the interests of traders and of consumers. This unsatisfactory legal status is, to some extent, due to the failure of a successful completion of the 2001 EU Regulation on Sales Promotion.[8] The aim of the Regulation was to establish common rules for sales promotion and commercial communication rules to ensure the proper functioning of the internal market and a high level of consumer protection. The work on Directive 2005/29/EC and on the Regulation was carried out in parallel and formed a single, interlinked harmonisation project. The adoption of only one of the acts means that not only has harmonisation not been carried out in its entirety to the extent envisaged, but, what is more, the focus of the measures taken has been on the protection of consumer interests. A closer look at the solutions adopted in the proposed Regulation and its main objectives is important for several reasons. In the solutions proposed at the EU level, we also note the spirit of the draft Regulation. Therefore, we may expect that the EU legislator will, when making new proposals, refer to previous solutions that have not even been adopted but that have nevertheless already been discussed and thought through. The proposals adopted in the draft Regulation should also be taken into account when considering further attempts to harmonise sales promotion regulations. They may certainly provide a point of reference for legislators in individual Member States seeking to modernise national regulations on sales promotions.

In Poland, there is an ongoing discussion on the future shape of Polish law against unfair competition. The need for discussion arose as a result of the implementation of Directive 2005/29/EC into Polish law against unfair competition in the form of a separate Act of 23 July 2007 on Counteracting Unfair Market Practices.[9] This Act introduced new solutions to the law

---

8 Proposal for a Regulation of the European Parliament and of the Council concerning sales promotions in the internal market of 2 October 2001, COM(2001) 546 final, 2001/0227 (COD), <http://www.europarl.europa.eu/meetdocs/committees/envi/20020226/01-546_en.pdf> (accessed on: 1.2.2024). The whole legislative process is available at: <https://eur-lex.europa.eu/procedure/EN/2001_227> (accessed on: 1.2.2024). *The Green paper on European Union* Consumer *Protection*, COM (2001) 531 final, was also published on the same date. Both legislative proposals are compared by *H-W. Micklitz*, A General Framework Directive on Fair Trading, in: *H. Collins* (ed.), The Forthcoming EX Directive on Unfair Commercial Practices, Contract, Consumer and Competition Law Implications, The Hague – London–New York 2004, pp. 47–49.

9 Dz.U. 2017 item 2070.

on combatting unfair competition, which were not coherent with the then-existing legislation (the Act on Combatting Unfair Competition). As a consequence, currently there exist two key legislative acts in Poland, both governing the law against unfair competition, but which are not properly interrelated.

One is the Act on Combatting Unfair Competition. At the time of its enactment in 1993, it was a state-of-the-art act, and for many subsequent years, it effectively protected honest traders against acts of unfair competition, as shown in the numerous judgements delivered by common courts in matters concerning various acts of unfair competition. Depending on the factual situation in Poland, some of the provisions have been applied extremely frequently, attracting the interest of courts and doctrine representatives. Others, on the other hand, have not received much interest and have been seldom referred to in adjudications and have triggered little academic attention or interpretation.

The other is the Act of 23 July 2007 on Counteracting Unfair Market Practices. Its adoption stirred great interest among academics but encountered severe criticism. Needless to say, too, that this Act has very little practical significance. Consumers, as actively entitled persons, generally do not assert any claims under its provisions, and there have only been a few court decisions known to have been delivered.

In order to propose possible solutions to the current situation of the Polish law against unfair competition, it was necessary to examine, in Chapters II and III, the scope and objectives of both legislative acts. In the course of the research, many issues were discussed extensively. Studying them in depth was necessary because some pertained to key questions, which, being controversial both in the literature and in the judicial decisions, had to be addressed and solved. The main problem was finding an answer to the questions of whether the implementation of Directive 2005/29/EC in a new, separate act was a proper and justified implementation, or whether it would have been better to transpose the Directive into the Act on Combatting Unfair Competition already in force, taking into account the Polish tradition of protection against unfair competition. These doubts are also outlined in the Polish literature. On the one hand, it has been argued that, in connection with the implementation of the Directive, the two above-mentioned Acts should be repealed and replaced with a single new Act that would comprehensively cover the issue of honesty in business dealings.[10] On the other hand, the idea of repealing the Act on Combatting Unfair Competition and introducing protection of traders' interests against unfair competition into the Act on Counteracting Unfair Market Practices was criticised. It was assessed that such actions would result in the rejection of the case law and doctrine developed on the basis of the Act on Combatting Unfair Competition and would disrupt the functioning of the market economy in Poland.[11]

In order to demonstrate that separating the scope of the two Acts may be a difficult task and that certain solutions available under Polish law may be in conflict with EU law, in Chapter IV the prohibition of bonus sales as regulated in Article 17a of the Act on Combatting Unfair Competition is analysed in detail.[12] That prohibition was added to the Act on 5 July 2002. Pursuant to this provision, it is an act of unfair competition to 'sell goods or services to consumers if their sale is combined with the granting to all or some of the buyers of a free bonus in the form of goods or services different from those constituting the object of sale'. Article 17a(2) of the Act on Combatting Unfair Competition provides for certain exceptions to this prohibition. And so, a bonus sale will not amount to an act of unfair competition if it is a good or service: '(1) of small value or a sample of goods; (2) a winning in a promotional lottery organised under gambling regulations or competitions whose outcome does not depend on chance." This prohibition was introduced in order to protect small and medium-sized traders who, as economically weaker market participants, were

---

10 *M. Namysłowska*, O konieczności uchylenia ustawy z dnia 16 kwietnia 1993 r. o zwalczaniu nieuczciwej konkurencji, in: *J. Ożegalska-Trybalska, D. Kasprzycki* (eds), Aktualne wyzwania prawa własności intelektualnej i prawa konkurencji. Księga pamiątkowa dedykowana Profesorowi Michałowi du Vallowi, Warsaw 2015, pp. 399–400; *A. Tischner*, Miejsce implementacji dyrektywy 2005/29/WE do prawa polskiego, in: *E. Nowińska, D. Kasprzycki* (eds), Nieuczciwe praktyki rynkowe. Ocena regulacji, Kraków 2012, pp. 62–63. *A. Tischer* is of the opinion that a thorough reform of the Polish law on the fairness of market behaviour is necessary, which should consist in the integration of the Act on Counteracting Unfair Market Practices and the Act on Combatting Unfair Competition into a single act.

11 *R. Skubisz*, Cele i zakres zastosowania ustawy o zwalczaniu nieuczciwej konkurencji. Dylematy trudnego sąsiedztwa z ustawą o przeciwdziałaniu nieuczciwym praktykom rynkowym, in: *T. Skoczny* (ed.), Prawo konkurencji 25 lat. Pierwszy Polski Kongres Prawa Konkurencji, Warszawa 2016, p. 578.

12 Act of 5 July 2002 amending the Act on Combatting Unfair Competition (Dz.U. of 2002, No. 126, item 1071), see art. 1 point 4 of the Act.

unable to compete with larger ones by granting free bonuses in sales contracts with consumers. In principle, the prohibition should therefore be limited to B2B relationships. However, as clearly reads from Article 17a of the Act on Combatting Unfair Competition, that prohibition applies to the sale of goods and services to consumers, a practice used in B2C relationships. In view of this interesting relationship between the purpose of the prohibition introduced and the relationships to which it actually applies, it was necessary to examine what role the introduced prohibition plays. After all, if it has no impact on the economic interests of consumers but concerns only and exclusively the interests of traders, it is outside the scope of Directive 2005/29/EC. If this is not the case, however, the prohibition must be looked at through the prism of that Directive. Alternatively, the consumers' interest can be found in the assumption that the latter should make informed choices based on rational premises. On the other hand, the common commercial practice adopted by traders, which consists of adding various types of free bonuses in transactions with consumers, may have a significant impact on the decisions the consumers make. Consequently, considerations concerning the prohibition of bonus sales are relevant not only to the attempt to seek justification for maintaining or repealing Article 17a of the Act on Combatting Unfair Competition, but also to the entire Polish system of combatting unfair competition. For if it turns out that Article 17a, although enacted to protect the interests of entrepreneurs, at least indirectly applies to the protection of the interests of consumers, its interpretation should be considered in the light of the provisions of Directive 2005/29/EC. In this respect, the applicable provisions would have to be in line with the provisions of that Directive. It may therefore turn out that the prohibition of bonus sales, although originally intended to protect traders, is incompatible with Directive 2005/29/EC and, accordingly, will have to be amended or repealed.

It should be added that the conceptual scope of 'bonus sales' itself is also unclear. In case law and in the literature, there are other, comparable terms that are also used, such as a premium sale or a combined sale. In defining these terms, it was necessary to refer to the case law of the Court of Justice of the European Union.[13]

---

13 This concerns the case law of the Luxembourg-based Court of Justice of the European Union and, more specifically, one of its judicial organs, the ECJ, which deals with

Thus, the most important judgements of the CJEU relating to this kind of commercial practice have been analysed in Chapter V. In a relatively large number of rulings, the Court considered the issue of the admissibility of bonus sales and combined sales, as well as the interpretation of the basic concepts (commercial practice, trader) and issues (prohibition of making provisions and the role of national courts) of Directive 2005/29/EC. The analysis of CJEU rulings made it possible to assess the compliance of the Polish prohibition of bonus sales with EU law, in particular with Directive 2005/29/EC.

The purpose of the conducted research was to analyse the problems that occur in the Polish law against unfair competition, which are partly a consequence of the impact of EU law. Finding a single solution for all Member States is a major challenge not only for the EU legislator but even more so for national legislators, who have to 'adjust' the adopted compromise solutions to their respective existing systems of combatting unfair competition, encapsulated by case law and doctrinal views. It should not be forgotten either that these systems have developed in countries with different levels of economic development and different economic experiences. The creation of a single, one-size-fits-all, harmonised system today is extremely difficult, as illustrated by the issues presented in the publication.

references for a preliminary ruling sent to it by national courts, certain complaints and appeals. More on the CJEU website: <https://curia.europa.eu/jcms/jcms/Jo2_7024/en/> (accessed on 1.02.2025).

Chapter I

Sources of European law and an Attempted Harmonisation of European Law against Unfair Competition Practices

§ 1. The Paris Convention

I. Introductory Remarks

The main international piece of legislation that affects the law against unfair competition of the EU Member States is the Paris Convention for the Protection of Industrial Property of 20 March 1883. The purpose of the adopted Convention was to ensure international protection of industrial property as well as to combat unfair competition. As stated in Article 1(2) of the Paris Convention, it has as its objects 'patents, utility models, industrial designs, trademarks, service marks, trade names, indications of source or appellations of origin, and the repression of unfair competition'. As of 2024, it has 180 contracting parties, including all EU Member States. Under its Article 10 bis, the parties to the Convention are obliged to ensure effective protection against unfair competition for natural and legal persons. An act of unfair competition is to be understood as every act of competition contrary to honest practices in industry and commerce.

Article 10 bis of the Paris Convention, as originally drafted, was added in 1900 at a conference in Brussels.[14] As a result of subsequent revisions of the Paris Convention,[15] Article 10 bis was extended to cover the definition of an act of unfair competition and provide a number of examples of delicts of unfair competition.[16] The Stockholm Conference of 1967 amended Article 10 bis, which now consists of 3 clauses. They are: (1) 'The countries of the Union are bound to assure to nationals of such countries effective protection against unfair competition'; (2) 'Any act of competition contrary to honest practices in industrial or commercial matters constitutes an act of unfair competition', while clause (3) lists exemplary acts (delicts) of unfair competition, such as (i) all acts of such a nature as to create confusion by any means whatever with the establishment, the goods, or the industrial or commercial activities, of a competitor; (ii) false allegations in the course of trade of such a nature as to discredit the establishment, the goods, or the industrial or commercial activities, of a competitor; (iii) indications or allegations the use of which in the course of trade is liable to mislead the public as to the nature, the manufacturing process, the characteristics, the suitability for their purpose, or the quantity, of the goods.

In addition, the Paris Convention, as provided for in Article 10 ter clause 1,[17] obliged countries, members of the Union,[18] 'to undertake to assure to nationals of the other countries of the Union appropriate legal remedies effectively

---

14 See *G.H.C. Bodenhausen*, Guide d'application de la Convention de Paris pour la protection de la propriété industrielle, Telle que revisée a Stockholm en 1967, Geneva 1968, pp. 148–149.

15 Article 10 bis was added in 1900 and read: *Les ressortissants de la Convention (art. 2 et 3), jouiront, dans tous les Etats de l'Union, de la protection accorde aux nationaux contre la concurrence deloyale*. It is emphasised in the literature that this provision is a compromise between the continental and the common law systems. See *F. Henning-Bodewig*, International Unfair Competition Law, in: *R.M. Hilty*, *F. Henning-Bodewig* (eds), Law Against Unfair Competition, Berlin–Heidelberg 2007, p. 55. The provision was revised and amended in 1911 in Washington, in 1925 in the Hague, in 1934 in London and in 1958 in Lisbon. See: <http://www.wipo.int/treaties/en/ip/paris/> (accessed on 1.02.2025).

16 See The Hague Act of the Paris Convention of 1925 <https://www.wipo.int/wipolex/en/treaties/textdetails/12992> (accessed on 1.02.2025).

17 Art. 10 ter of the Paris Convention was added in the Hague in 1925.

18 Pursuant to Article 1(1) of the Paris Convention 'The countries to which this Convention applies constitute a Union for the protection of industrial property'.

to repress all the acts referred to in Articles 9, 10, and 10 bis'. Further in the same Article, members of the Union were obligated to undertake and provide measures to permit federations and associations representing interested industrialists, producers, or merchants, provided that the existence of such federations and associations is not contrary to the laws of their countries, to take action in the courts or before the administrative authorities, with a view to the repression of the acts referred to in Articles 9, 10, and 10bis, insofar as the law of the country in which protection is claimed allows such action by federations and associations of that country."

Currently, the relevance of Article 10 bis of the Paris Convention is limited for developed countries, as most of the parties to it, including EU Member States, have much more elaborate systems for combatting unfair competition than what is provided for in the Convention. This does not mean, however, that Article 10 bis has now lost its relevance altogether. Indeed, it is submitted that it remains important for developing countries that have not yet created their own sufficient system of protection against unfair competition.[19] The Paris Convention is also the primary source for current regulations on combatting unfair competition applied in developed countries. The solutions adopted by member states in the field covered by the Convention must be compatible with the provisions of the Convention. The great importance that Article 10 bis(2) and (3) has had on the legislation and practice of the European countries, especially in the first half of the 20th century, is also emphasised.[20]

II. Acts of Unfair Competition under the Paris Convention

The catalogue set out in Article 10 bis(3) of the Paris Convention may be divided into three basic categories of acts of unfair competition:

1) acts likely to cause confusion about the competitor;

---

[19] *F. Henning-Bodewig*, International Unfair Competition Law, p. 58. The author stresses that currently Article 10 bis of the Paris Convention, which was last amended in 1958, should be adapted to the current situation, including the role of the consumer in the law against unfair competition.

[20] *R. Skubisz*, Klauzule generalne w prawie zwalczania nieuczciwej konkurencji, Annales Universitatis Mariae Curie-Skłodowska 2016, No 2, vol. LXIII, Sectio G, p. 76.

2) acts likely to discredit a competitor by communicating false information about the competitor;
3) acts using indications or information likely to mislead the public about the products.

This catalogue contains only examples of acts of unfair competition[21] and authors agree that the list of acts of unfair competition may be supplemented by the internal rules of the EU Member States which have also been left free to classify certain acts (as well as omissions to act) as acts of unfair competition.[22]

Consequently, various sales promotion practices, although not listed in the Paris Convention, may also be classified as acts of unfair competition in the individual laws of the Member States. This is also in line with the assumptions adopted in the Convention. This follows, *inter alia*, from the very definition of an act of unfair competition provided for in Article 10 bis(2), according to which it is an act of competition contrary to honest practices in industrial and commercial matters. Thus, if an act to promote sales and a competitor's behaviour is contrary to 'honest practices in industrial or commercial matters', then, although not expressly defined in Article 10 bis(3) of the Paris Convention, it may be qualified as a violation of the principles of fair competition.

The concept adopted in Article 10 bis(2) that competition should comply with honest practices in industry or commerce refers to good practice that is generally accepted and followed by all market participants, not only businesses.[23] It may therefore be the case that a certain behaviour commonly accepted by traders is detrimental to other market participants and therefore inconsistent with the fair custom clause.

---

21 In doing so, it is emphasised that the very catalogue of acts of unfair competition adopted in Article 10 bis(3) of the Paris Convention has been adopted in many countries. Nowadays, although states have developed much more elaborate regulations against unfair competition, the roots of these regulations can be sought in Article 10 bis of the Paris Convention (*F. Henning-Bodewig*, International Unfair Competition Law, p. 58).

22 *E. Nowińska, M. du Vall, A. Adamczak, A. Szewc* (eds), Konwencja paryska o ochronie własności przemysłowej. Komentarz, Warszawa 2008, p. 287, Nb 1 and p. 293, Nb 5.

23 See: *E. Nowińska, M. du Vall*, in: *A. Adamczak, A. Szewc* (eds), Konwencja paryska, p. 286.

However, it is argued in the literature that defining a 'fair custom' clause may be difficult. Indeed, the interpretation of this concept may vary depending on the country in which protection is sought. Certain clues are offered in the Convention itself and may allow for a proper interpretation of this clause and minimise possible differences in its interpretation. The first indication is provided by the examples of acts of unfair competition listed in Article 10 bis(3), and these types of practices must be considered unfair with fair custom. The second clue will be the reference in Article 10 bis(2) to the standard of fair industrial and commercial custom. These should therefore be certain generally accepted and currently applied practices in industry and commerce,[24] which may nevertheless change over time.

However, it will not always be possible to adopt a uniform interpretation of this clause. As an example, in some countries the issue of fairness in industrial and commercial matters will be assessed mainly from the point of view of consumer interests, and in others from the point of view of other interests, including entrepreneurs' interests. Thus, a problem with the interpretation of the 'fair trade' clause may arise when an act of unfair competition is committed not just in one country (where the clause is uniformly interpreted), but in relationships between countries, where the clause could be examined through the prism of the interests of different market participants.[25]

It must be emphasised here that the main purpose of Article 10 bis of the Paris Convention was not to protect consumers but to protect honest traders.[26]

F. Henning-Bodewig notes that the original purpose of Article 10bis was to strengthen the position of the entities that enjoyed exclusive rights concerning industrial property goods.[27] Hence, it would not be appropriate to assume that under the Paris Convention consumers' interests are given priority. As a matter of fact, the interests of consumers are placed on an equal footing with the interests of traders and the public interest, and the most important

---

[24] See: *F. Henning-Bodewig*, International Protection Against Unfair Competition, in: *F. Henning-Bodewig* (ed.), International Handbook on Unfair Competition, Monachium 2013, p. 24, Nb 46–47.

[25] See: *F. Henning-Bodewig*, International Unfair Competition Law, p. 57; and International Protection Against Unfair Competition, p. 24, Nb 50.

[26] *E. Nowińska, M. du Vall*, in: *A. Adamczak, A. Szewc* (eds), Konwencja paryska, p. 287, Nb 5.

[27] *F. Henning-Bodewig*, International Protection Against Unfair Competition, p. 20.

consideration therefore will be whether a given practice is consistent with honest or fair practices. Whether it violates the interests of the trader or the consumer is of lesser significance because these interests are most often interrelated.[28]

At the same time, it is argued in the literature that the acts referred to in Article 10 bis (2) and (3) can only be committed by an entrepreneur, while the victim of an act of unfair competition does not have to be solely a competitor entrepreneur; he may also be another entrepreneur or a consumer. Neither does it follow from the wording of Article 10 bis that protection in the event of an act of unfair competition is conditional on the existence of a competition relationship.[29] The existence of a competition relationship could possibly be derived from Article 10 bis (3)(1) and (2). This is because these provisions expressly mention that they refer to acts directed against a competitor. On the other hand, such a requirement does not arise from the general clause (Article 10 bis(2) or Article 10 bis(3)(3). Thus, it would have to be assumed that the Paris Convention does not make the commission of an act of unfair competition or the possibility of pursuing a claim conditional on the existence of a competitive relationship in every case. It has been emphasised in the literature that, as the years have passed and the competitive struggle has intensified, the premise of a direct competition relationship is no longer required. It is sufficient for the act to violate the market position of another market participant, and in some countries, including Poland, even the existence of potential competition is not required.[30]

Article 10 ter obliges countries to introduce appropriate legal measures to effectively combat acts of unfair competition (listed in Article 10 bis). However, the Convention does not regulate what type of measures these should be. Indeed, countries are entirely free to do so, provided that the measures are 'appropriate' and 'effective'. They may thus be civil law, criminal law or administrative law measures.[31] It is also argued in the literature that Article 10 ter of the Paris Convention confers no rights on natural or legal persons.

---

28 *Ibidem*, pp. 20–21.

29 *E. Nowińska*, *M. du Vall*, in: *A. Adamczak*, *A. Szewc* (eds), Konwencja paryska, p. 287, Nb 5.

30 *Ibidem*, p. 318, Nb 2.

31 *F. Henning-Bodewig*, International Protection Against Unfair Competition, p. 28.

What is more, Article 10 ter (2) of the Paris Convention obliges the members of the Union to provide measures enabling federations and associations representing industrialists, producers or merchants concerned and whose existence is not contrary to the legislation of their country to appear before the courts or administrative authorities—in order to combat the acts provided for in Articles 9, 10, and 10 bis—to the extent that the legislation of the country in which protection is sought allows the federations and associations of that country to take such action.

§ 2. Agreement on Trade-Related Aspects of Intellectual Property Rights (TRIPS)

Another piece of legislation addressing the issue of unfair competition is the Agreement on TRIPS. The concept of 'intellectual property' defined in it is to be understood as all categories of intellectual property that are the subject of the regulations of Sections 1 to 7 of Part II of TRIPS, i.e. copyright and related rights, trademarks, geographical indications, industrial designs, patents, mask designs (topographies) of integrated circuits, and protection of undisclosed secrets.

As can be seen, TRIPS does not see the law against unfair competition as an element of intellectual property law. What is mentioned in the definition is the protection of undisclosed secrets, which in some legislations is considered part of the law against unfair competition. Thus, it is assumed that 'combatting unfair competition is not explicitly mentioned among the objectives of TRIPS'.[32] On the other hand, however, it is emphasised that the aim of TRIPS is to promote competition, which also follows from its Article 7, according to which 'the protection and enforcement of intellectual property rights should contribute to the promotion of technical innovation and to the transfer and dissemination of technology, to the mutual advantage of producers and users of technical knowledge, in a manner conducive to social

---

[32] *J. Szwaja*, *A. Kubiak-Cyrul*, Introduction, in *J. Szwaja*, *J. Kępiński* (eds), Law on Combatting Unfair Competition, Warszawa 2024, p. 27, Nb 31. As *C.M. Correra* points out, this may be due to the fact that not all countries, including primarily the United States, consider combatting unfair competition as a separate discipline. *C.M. Correra*, Trade Related Aspects of Intellectual Property Rights, A Commentary on the TRIPS Agreement, New York 2007, pp. 38–39.

and economic welfare and to a balance of rights and obligations'. Therefore, it is in TRIPS where one may seek solutions that could shape the law against unfair competition.

This position is justified by Article 2(1) of TRIPS, which refers to Article 10 bis of the Paris Convention. Indeed, Article 2(1) provides that, in respect of Part II (Standards on the Availability, Scope and Exercise of Intellectual Property Rights), Part III (Enforcement of Intellectual Property Rights) and Part IV (Acquisition and Retention of Intellectual Property Rights and Dispute Procedures Relating to Those Matters) of this Agreement, Members shall comply with the requirements of Articles 1–12 and 19 of the Paris Convention. This is undoubtedly a reference to the regulations on combatting unfair competition.

Article 2(2) provides that 'nothing in Parts I to IV of this Agreement shall derogate from the existing reciprocal obligations of Members under the Paris Convention, the Berne Convention, the Rome Convention and the Intellectual Property Treaty with respect to integrated circuits'. Thus, Member States are not relieved of their obligations under the Paris Convention, including the need to secure effective measures to protect fair competition.

However, in view of the solutions so adopted in TRIPS, doubts have arisen in the literature as to the mutual relationship between TRIPS and the Paris Convention.[33] Their source may be found in the formulation adopted in Article 2.1, the provision of which does not directly refer to Articles 1–12 and Article 19 of the Paris Convention but only 'within the scope of Parts II, III and IV' of TRIPS. The wording used in this provision, 'to the extent of', is questionable, as none of the Parts listed in TRIPS regulate combatting unfair competition. It is only in Articles 22 and 39 of Part II that there is a direct reference to Article 10 bis of the Paris Convention. Article 22(2)(b) on geographical indications provides that 'with respect to geographical indications, Members shall create legal means for interested parties to prevent: (...) 2) (b) any use which is an act of unfair competition within the meaning of Article 10 bis of the Paris Convention (1967)'. On the other hand, Article 39 of TRIPS, which deals with the protection of undisclosed information, regulates that 'in order to provide effective protection against unfair competition, as provided for in Article 10 bis, Members shall protect undisclosed information

---

33 *F. Henning-Bodewig*, International Protection Against Unfair Competition, pp. 33–36.

in accordance with paragraph 2, as well as data submitted to a government or government agencies in accordance with paragraph 3'.

This raises doubts as to whether the reference in TRIPS to Article 10 bis of the Paris Convention is limited only to the regulation of geographical indications and the protection of undisclosed information or whether it also covers other cases. Opinions are divided on this point; however, the prevailing view in the literature is that only a violation of Article 10 bis related to geographical indications and undisclosed information will also constitute a violation of TRIPS.[34] *F. Hennig-Bodewig* adds that the problem with the interpretation of Article 2(1) of TRIPS should be dealt with through the prism of the ruling in *Havana Club*,[35] in which it was argued that in the case of trade names, which are neither listed in Part II of TRIPS but are protected by Article 8 of the Paris Convention, Article 2(1) should be interpreted broadly. But even so, there is no clarity as to whether the general reference in Article 2(1) TRIPS refers to Article 10 bis of the Paris Convention or whether it applies only to acts of unfair competition relating to geographical indications and undisclosed information (Articles 22 and 39 TRIPS).

A guideline for the interpretation may be found in the CJEU ruling in the joined cases of *Parfums Christian Dior SA v. Tuk Consultancy BV* and *Layher Germany v. Assco Gerüste GmbH*,[36] in which the CJEU commented on the concept of 'intellectual property.' The need to interpret this concept arose in relation to the admissibility of the provisional measures provided for in Article 50(1) TRIPS and the direct application of the TRIPS provisions. In both disputes, the national courts referred a question to the CJEU for a preliminary ruling, which the Court limited to 3 main issues.[37] Of material importance for the present deliberations is the resolution of one of them,

---

[34] See: *ibidem*, p. 34 and the literature indicated in it. *C.M. Correra* is of the opinion that a reference to Paris Convention in art. 2.1 of Trips means that TRIPS must be in accordance with the Paris Convention *C.M. Correra*, Trade Related Aspects, pp. 38–39.

[35] Appellate Body Report, United States–Section 211 Omnibus Appropriations Act of 1998, pp. 139–148, WT/DS176/AB/R <https://www.wto.org/english/tratop_e/dispu_e/cases_e/ds176_e.htm> (accessed on: 1.2.2025). See: *F. Henning-Bodewig*, International Protection Against Unfair Competition, pp. 34–36.

[36] CJEU judgment of 14 December 2000 , C-300/98 and C-392/98, *Parfums Christian Dior SA v. TUK Consultancy BV i Assco Gerüste GmbH i Rob van Dijk v. Wilhelm Layher GmbH & Co. KG* i *Layher BV*, Zb.Orz. 2000, p. I-11307, ECLI:EU:C:2000:688.

[37] CJEU judgment C-300/98 and C-392/98, point 30, p. I-11356.

namely, 'whether the possibility of asserting rights under the general rules in connection with unlawful acts, in particular those which may constitute acts of unfair competition, in order to protect an industrial design in the form of an exclusive right against its copying may be classified as an "intellectual property right" within the meaning of Article 50(1) TRIPS?'.

In other words, the question is whether the law against unfair competition, which protects an industrial design from copying, may be qualified as an element of intellectual property right within the meaning of TRIPS. It should be clarified that such a problem does not exist when protection for an industrial design is granted in the form of an exclusive right conferred under separate, specific legislation. Such protection qualifies as part of an intellectual property right (TRIPS allows for this possibility in Articles 25–26 TRIPS).[38]

In resolving the doubts of national courts, the CJEU held that the protection of an industrial design from being copied may qualify under the general provisions on unfair competition as an intellectual property right within the meaning of Article 50(1) TRIPS[39] and stated further that TRIPS leaves to its Members the task of specifying, in their legal systems and particularly in private law, the interests that will be protected in TRIPS as intellectual property rights. Members are also left free to choose how to protect these interests. This protection must be effective, and, in particular, must protect, in the case of industrial designs, against trading in counterfeit goods. At the same time, it must not lead to distortion or constitute an obstacle to international trade.[40]

Taking into account the above considerations, it may be assumed that despite the absence of a general rule in this respect, TRIPS is, if only indirectly, relevant to the law on combatting unfair competition and, in particular, to the protection of geographical indications and undisclosed information.

---

[38] CJEU judgment C-300/98 and C-392/98, point 52–54, p. I–11362.

[39] *Ibidem*, point 62, p. I–11365.

[40] *Ibidem*, point 63, p. I–11365.

§ 3. WIPO model provisions on Protection Against Unfair Competition

I. Preparatory work

For examination of issues relating to combatting unfair competition and sales promotion, reference should be made to the work carried out between 1994 and 1995 by the WIPO—(WIPO with the aim of developing model provisions regulating protection against unfair competition.

First, an extensive analysis was carried out, and its results were published in 1994 under the title Protection Against Unfair Competition: Analysis of the Present World Situation.[41]

It was then emphasised that the existing regulations on the protection of unfair competition must be retained,[42] and the legal grounds justifying that protection were to be further identified. Although the analysis was prepared more than 20 years ago and referred to the factual situation existing at that time, the presented views are, to some extent, still valid today.[43]

In the analysis, three basic models for the protection of fair competition were distinguished. The first model featured protection based primarily on specific legislation on the protection of competition. In the second model, protection was assumed to be based on the general law of delict (the law of tort) and the law relating to the institution known in the common law system as passing off and trade secrets. In the third model, on the other hand, protection was based on a combination of the above 2 solutions, i.e. general tort law, case law and specific legislation.[44]

It was emphasised that the catalogue of acts of unfair competition adopted in Article 10 bis (2) of the Paris Convention was not exhaustive and that other acts, including, most notably, violations of trade secrets as well as the

---

41 WIPO publication No 725(E), ISBN 92-805-0484-3 <https://tind.wipo.int/record/20405?v=pdf> (accessed on 1.2.2025), hereinafter referred to as Analysis.

42 Analysis, Chapter I, "The need for Protection," pp. 11–23.

43 However, some assumptions and trends in the law against unfair competition have changed. Thus, it is argued that the model rules should be revised. See: *M. Höpperger, M. Senftleben*, Protection Against Unfair Competition at the International Level, p. 75.

44 Analysis, Chapter II, "Legal grounds of protection," pp. 19–21.

so-called free riding and comparative advertising, may also be classified as acts of unfair competition.

It was further added that apart from the three mentioned, there also existed a category of other acts of competition that were contrary to honest practices. They include, among other things, sales promotion consisting of adding bonuses and gifts to the products sold, or lotteries.[45] It was highlighted that such marketing techniques could constitute a new and efficient distribution channel and could also stimulate competition. On the other hand, however, these techniques can divert the consumer's attention away from the main object of sale or service and thus induce them to buy something that is not worth the price or that they do not need. This is particularly evident in the situation of games, lotteries or other competitions where consumers' predisposition to gamble is exploited for advertising purposes.[46] Finally, the differences regarding the use of those techniques in different countries were highlighted. It was also concluded that in most countries when assessing the admissibility of such sales promotions, the courts take into account the circumstances under which a given practice occurred. They examine whether the consumer was under psychological or other pressure and whether the prizes were exceptionally valuable and thus more tempting. Thus, it will depend on the specific circumstances whether even an accepted sales promotion practice turns out to be contrary to fair industrial and commercial customs.[47]

II. Content of the Model Provisions

1. General Principles

In February 1996, WIPO presented the Model Provisions on Protection against Unfair Competition. Articles and Notes.[48]

It must be noted that the model provisions are neither binding law nor a soft law instrument and do not entail any legal consequences. They merely provide a model that may serve as an example for legislative initiatives to

---

45 Analysis, Chapter III, "Acts of unfair competition," p. 66.

46 *Ibidem*, pp. 66–67.

47 *Ibidem*, p. 67.

48 *Model Provisions on Protection against unfair competition. Articles and Notes*, WIPO No 832(E), <https://tind.wipo.int/record/28768?v=pdf> (accessed on 1.2.2025).

be taken by states.[49] It is generally agreed that they are in compliance with both Article 10 bis of the Paris Convention and Article 2 of TRIPS.[50] It is also accepted in the literature that the model solutions, although referring to Article 10 bis, are not merely an interpretation of that Article but an extension of the protection provided by the Paris Convention.[51] Accordingly, for an act to qualify as contrary to good practice, there does not have to be a 'competition relationship between the parties'. Article 1(1)(a) of the model provisions simply states that it is 'any act or practice in the course of an industrial or commercial activity that is contrary to honest practices'. The underlying rationale of the model provisions emphasises that these provisions will also apply to situations where there is no direct competition between the entity committing an act of unfair competition and the party whose interests the unfair act has affected. The argument in favour of such a solution is the assumption that even in a situation where an act of unfair competition is not directly targeted at a competitor of the entity committing the unfair competition act, such an act may still affect competition in the market by increasing the competitiveness of that entity in relation to its competitors. It was emphasised that the adopted solution also constituted consumer protection.[52]

Furthermore, Article 1(1)(a) of the model provisions refers to the concept of 'honest practices' as a premise that must be assessed by national courts. It was explained that in the case of traders coming from different countries, the examination of this premise should not be limited to the honest practices

---

49 See: *F. Henning-Bodewig*, in: *F. Henning-Bodewig* (ed.), International Handbook on Unfair Competition, Munchen 2013, p. 29.

50 For more on the legal status of the model provisions see: *M. Höpperger, M. Senftleben*, Protection Against Unfair Competition at the International Level—The Paris Convention, the 1996 Model Provisions and the Current Work of the World Intellectual Property Organisation, in: *R.M. Hilty, F. Henning-Bodewig* (ed.), Law Against Unfair Competition, Berlin–Heidelberg 2007, p. 72–73; Model Provisions, p. 14.

51 See: *F. Henning-Bodewig*, in: *F. Henning-Bodewig* (ed.), International Handbook, p. 29. It is pointed out though that the model solutions repeat more or less *verbatim* Article 10 bis of the Paris Convention. See: *H.W. Micklitz* (ed.), The Feasibility of a General Legislative Framework on Fair Trading, p. 13, <http://ec.europa.eu/comm/consumers/cons_int/safe_shop/fair_bus_pract/green_pap_comm/studies/sur21_vol1_en.pdf> (accessed on 13.6.2017, currently unavailable).

52 Also see: Model Provisions, point 1.10, p. 12. It emphasises that consumers and their unions will also be able to bring claims under Article 1(1)(b) of the Model Provisions.

accepted in the country where the unfair competition act was committed, but there should be adopted a concept of honest practices in international trade.[53]

The relationship between Article 1(1)(a) of the model provisions, treated as a general clause, and the specific delicts of unfair competition was also explained and analysed. It was taken that Articles 2 to 6 of the model provisions described specific acts of unfair competition, which *per se* constitute an act of unfair competition and do not need to be proved. It was further argued in the literature that Articles 2 to 6 are not limited to 'acts of competition' but will also apply in situations where there is no competitive relationship between the entity committing an act of unfair competition and the entity whose interest has been violated.[54]

It is also emphasised that compared to Articles 10 bis and 10 ter of the Paris Convention, Article 1(1)(b) of the model provisions provides for more detailed solutions with respect to claims. Although the model provisions do not set out in detail the provisions governing the enforcement of rights, it was assumed that a claimant may be 'any natural person or legal entity damaged or likely to be damaged', as well as consumers or their unions.[55] The concept of damage should be understood in its broadest sense to include instances where the defendant has gained or was likely to gain unjust enrichment at the expense of the claimant.

It was also clarified that Article 1(1)(c) sets out the relationship between the provisions on protection against unfair competition and the provisions on protection of intellectual property rights. It was assumed that the provisions of Articles 1–6 should apply independently of the provisions on the protection of specific intellectual property rights because protection against unfair competition is complementary, or additional, to the protection granted by specific intellectual property rights. Thus, the protection granted by exclusive

---

53 Model Provisions, p. 6.

54 *M. Höpperger, M. Senftleben*, Protection Against Unfair Competition at the International Level, p. 70.Also see: *F. Henning-Bodewig*, International Protection Against Unfair Competition, p. 20.

55 This is a proposal that goes beyond the solutions adopted in Article 10 ter of the Paris Convention. See: *M. Höpperger, M. Senftleben*, Protection Against Unfair Competition at the International Level, p. 69.

ign, trademark, and copyright protection) does not prevent f the provisions on combatting unfair competition.[56]

2. Sales Promotions in Model Provisions

Model Provisions regulate to a certain extent acts or practices that could be qualified as being related to sales promotions. First of all, these will be the acts or practices set out in Article 4 of the Model Provisions.

Article 4.1 sets out the general principle that an act or practice that misleads or is likely to mislead the public as to the enterprise or its activities, and in particular as to the products or services offered by such enterprise, is an act of unfair competition.

Article 4(2) sets out examples of misleading practices. It is thus mentioned that misleading conduct may arise in connection with advertising or promotion and may occur in particular in relation to:

1) the manufacturing process of a product. This includes the provision of misleading information relating to product safety, configuration, assembly of components or other technical details;
2) the suitability of a product or service for a particular purpose. Misrepresentation may occur not only when misleading information is provided as to the suitability of the product in question, but also when the information provided is limited in scope or not at all existent;[57]
3) the quality and quantity or other characteristics of a product or service. This includes misleading advertising or claims as to the durability of the product, its production process or the specific characteristics it should have, as well as the tests carried out to prove the quality of the product or its safety for humans and animals;[58]
4) the geographical origin of a product or service. In such a situation, as a consequence of the mislabelling, a misleading impression is created that the product or service in question originates from a particular country or place;[59]

---

56 Model Provisions, p. 14.
57 *Ibidem*, p. 36.
58 *Ibidem*.
59 *Ibidem*, p. 38.

5) the conditions under which the product or services are offered or provided. An example would be an avalanche sale in which the buyer has to introduce new buyers. In such a situation, the buyer is misled as to the real reasons for the sale. Other examples would be advertisements where the information provided is misleading, as well as incomplete or false claims relating to the contract being concluded;[60]
6) the price of a product or service or the manner in which it is calculated. The way the price, which is one of the decisive factors in choosing a product or service, is calculated should be clear and transparent. This will also include situations where a good is claimed to be on a special price offer, whereas in reality its price is the regular price.[61]

The solutions adopted in the Model Provisions refer to the assumptions described in Article 10 bis (3)(3) of the Paris Convention. It is argued in the literature that the wording of the formulated prohibitions contained in Article 10 bis(3) determines their purpose, which was to protect primarily honest entrepreneurs and not consumers. The protection of the public interest was merely a 'reflection' of the protection of fair competition rules.[62] The current trend is, as can be seen, to equalise the interests of all market participants. Already from the rationale of the model provisions, it may be clearly understood that misleading actions, although directed at consumers and not directly against competitors, may be classified as acts or practices of unfair competition. Such acts or practices may take different forms and may result from different methods of communication.[63]

There is no doubt that the examples presented above refer to different types of sales promotion methods. As can be seen from the model provisions, those acts or practices used by traders should not be misleading. Giving incomplete, untrue or missing information regarding various aspects of the purchased products or services should be qualified as an act of unfair competition. And

---

60 *Ibidem*.

61 *Ibidem*, p. 40.

62 *E. Nowińska, M. du Vall*, in: *A. Adamczak, A. Szewc* (ed.), Konwencja paryska, p. 287, Nb 6. Also see: *F. Henning-Bodewig*, in: *F. Henning-Bodewig* (ed.), International Handbook, Nb 75, p. 29.

63 Model Provisions, p. 30.

it is irrelevant whether or not those acts are directed directly at consumers and not at competitors.

§ 4. EU law against Unfair Competition

I. Harmonisation

The legislation of the EU Member States is shaped by EU law. Likewise, the law against combatting unfair competition is no exception. However, it has only been harmonised to a certain, rather limited extent. The lack of attempts at comprehensive harmonisation is a consequence of the great disparities in the regulations on combatting unfair competition in the individual Member States. As emphasised in the literature, the very concept of 'unfair competition' may be understood differently in individual EU Member States.[64] The concepts and assumptions of protection systems in different states also differ. In some countries (Austria, Belgium, Denmark, Spain, Germany, Poland, and Sweden), there is an integrated model of protection against unfair competition, in which the protection of consumers' and traders' interests is considered equal and is regulated in the same piece of legislation. In other countries (France, Italy), the protection of consumers and the protection of business interests have been separated (to form a so-called 'dual protection model'). In this model, the interests of traders are protected under civil law, while the interests of consumers are protected under criminal or administrative law. Under common law that prevails in the United Kingdom or Ireland, the legal systems only recognise certain tortious acts [passing-off, libel or slander] as grounds for raising claims for unacceptable competitive behaviour (the so-called common law model with a passing-off complaint).[65] Other differences occur in procedural matters that shape the fair competition model).[66]

---

64 *A. Kur, T. Dreier*, European Intellectual Property Law. Text, Cases and Materials, Cheltenham–Northampton 2013, p. 412.

65 *F. Henning-Bodewig*, Der Schutzzweck des UWG und die Richtlinie über unlautere Geschäftspraktiken, GRUR 2013, p. 240, and *R. Skubisz*, Cele i zakres zastosowania ustawy, pp. 564–565. For more see: *S. Augenhofer*, European Union, in: *F. Henning-Bodewig* (ed.), International Handbook, Munchen 2013, pp. 44–72.

66 *A. Kur, T. Dreier*, European Intellectual Property Law, p. 412.

The consequence of the existing differences is a lack of overall harmonisation of the law against combatting unfair competition in the European Union, while those differences are responsible for the serious difficulties when attempts are made to harmonise certain areas of the law combatting unfair competition. An example may be the problems with the implementation of Directive 2005/29/EC.

As a result, there has only been fragmentary, piecemeal harmonisation achieved so far. The most harmonised provisions are those relating to advertising. In this area, Directive 2006/114/EC of the European Parliament and of the Council of 12 December 2006 on misleading and comparative advertising is now codified and binding.[67] As stated in Article 1 of this Directive, its purpose is 'to protect traders against misleading advertising and its adverse effects and to lay down the conditions under which comparative advertising is permitted'. The literature[68] cites other regulations and directives on advertising and marketing, in which regulations on pharmaceuticals,[69] foodstuffs,[70] tobacco products,[71] or consumer goods have been provided.[72]

---

67 OJ EU L 376 of 2006, pp. 21–27. The Directive replaced Council Directive 84/450/EEC of 10 September 1984 concerning misleading advertising (OJ EU L 250 of 1984, p. 17 as amended).

68 *A. Kur, T. Dreier*, European Intellectual Property Law, p. 414, and in detail in: *J. Dudzik, R. Skubisz*, in: *J. Szwaja, J. Kępiński* (eds), Ustawa o zwalczaniu nieuczciwej konkurencji, Warszawa 2024, Kom. do art. 16, p. 527, Nb 7.

69 See Articles 86–100 of Directive 2001/83/EC of the European Parliament and of the Council of of 6.11.2001 on the Community code relating to medicinal products for human use (OJ EU L 311 of 2001, pp. 67–128 as amended). These articles regulate the advertising of medicinal products.

70 *Regulation (EU) No 1169/2011 of the European Parliament and of the Council of 25.10.2011 on the provision of food information to consumers, amending Regulations (EC) No 1924/2006 and (EC) No 1925/2006 of the European Parliament and of the Council, and repealing Commission Directive 87/250/EEC, Council Directive 90/496/EEC, Commission Directive 1999/10/EC, Directive 2000/13/EC of the European Parliament and of the Council, Commission Directives 2002/67/EC and 2008/5/EC and Commission Regulation (EC) No 608/2004* (Official Journal of the EU L 304 of 2011, pp. 18–63, as amended).

71 *Directive 2003/33/EC of the European Parliament and of the Council of 26.5.2003 on the approximation of the laws, regulations and administrative provisions of the Member States relating to the advertising and sponsorship of tobacco products* (OJ L 152 of 2003, pp. 16–19). As a general rule, tobacco advertising is significantly restricted or prohibited.

72 *Directive (EU) 2019/771 of the European Parliament and of the Council of 20 May 2019 on certain aspects concerning contracts for the sale of goods, amending Regulation* (EU)

Another harmonising act is Directive 2005/29/EC. The purpose of this Directive is to 'contribute to the proper functioning of the internal market and achieve a high level of consumer protection by approximating the laws, regulations and administrative provisions of the Member States relating to unfair commercial practices harming consumers' economic interests' (Article 1).

An example of an unsuccessful attempt to harmonise the law against unfair competition in relation to sales promotion measures is the Proposal for a European Parliament and Council Regulation concerning sales promotions in the Internal Market.[73] It is necessary to recall this project and the individual solutions, as the regulation, together with the enacted Directive 2005/29/EC, was intended to be of complementary character,[74] which was also stressed in Recital 7 of the first draft of Directive 2005/29/EC.[75] It stated that the directive was intended to complement the Community *acquis* applicable to commercial practices that affected consumers' interests, in particular the regulation on sales promotions. According to the European Commission, the two legislative initiatives (one on the protection of traders and the other on the protection of consumers) were intended to complement each other. The regulation on sales promotions, which was intended to ensure a high level of protection of the public interest (including consumers' interests), was to coexist with the proposed legislation that was to follow the legislative process initiated by the publication of the Green Paper on Consumer Protection.[76] Eventually, only Directive 2005/29/EC was enacted, and the work on the

---

2017/2394 and Directive 2009/22/EC, and repealing Directive 1999/44/EC (OJ L 136 of 2019, pp. 28–58 as amended).

73 *Proposal for a Regulation of the European Parliament and of the Council concerning sales promotions in the internal market of 2.10.2001*, COM(2001) 546 final, 2001/0227 (COD) <https://eur-lex.europa.eu/legal-content/EN/ALL/?uri=CELEX:52001PC0546> (accessed 1.2.2025). The whole legislative process is available at: <https://eur-lex.europa.eu/procedure/EN/2001_227> (accessed 1.2.2025).

74 *A. Mokrysz-Olszyńska*, Swoboda promocji a ochrona przez nieuczciwymi praktykami w projektach prawa Unii Europejskiej, Państwo i Prawo (PiP) 2005, No 2, p. 51.

75 *Proposal for a Directive of the European Parliament and of the Council concerning unfair business-to-consumer commercial practices in the Internal Market and amending directives 84/450/EEC, 97/7/EC and 98/27/EC* (the Unfair Commercial Practices Directive), COM (2003) 356 final.

76 *Proposal to the European Parliament and the Council on sales promotion in the internal market*, COM(2001) 546 final, 2001/0227 (COD), p. 3.

regulation concerning sales promotions in the internal market had never been completed and was officially withdrawn in 2005.[77] Certain legislative works intended to harmonise B2B relationships were later again initiated and have been going on since 2012.[78]

II. Work on the Proposal for a Regulation Concerning Sales Promotions in the Internal Market

1. The Concept of Sales Promotions and Sales Communication

Sales promotion, as explained by the European Commission in its Communication,[79] is the key tool for the sale of goods and services and may take different forms depending on the circumstances. These forms include discounts, premium offers, free gifts, or promotional contests and games. Sales promotion may also be tailored to circumstances such as the launch of an innovative product, stimulation of customer loyalty or a short-term competitive action, as a response to losses incurred, or for efficient stock management. Such forms of sales promotion are included in the broader concept of commercial communication, which, as the Commission explains, should be understood as all types of advertising, direct marketing, sponsoring, sales promotion and public relations promoting a product or service.[80]

---

77 The work relates to unfair business-to-business commercial practices in the food and non-food supply chain (see Green Paper, COM(2013), 37 final) and the protection of traders against misleading marketing practices (see Commission Communication the, COM(2012) 702 final).

78 See: *Commission Communication on Sales Promotion in Internal Market*, 52001DC0546, p. 3, <http://eur-lex.europa.eu/legal-content/EN/TXT/?uri=COM:2001:0546:FIN> (accessed 1.2.2025). Also *Z. Okoń*, Czyny nieuczciwej konkurencji w działalności promocyjnej, in: *E. Traple* (ed.), Prawo reklamy i promocji, Warszawa 2007, p. 731.

79 See: *Commission Communication on Sales Promotion in Internal Market*, p. 3, <http://eur-lex.europa.eu/legal-content/EN/TXT/?uri=COM:2001:0546:FIN> (accessed on 1.2.2025).

80 See: *Green Paper on Commercial Communication*, p. 2 [*Executive Summary*], COM 1996, 192 (final) <https://aei.pitt.edu/1181/> (accessed on: 1.2.2025).

2. Legislative Work

Initially, the legislative work was intended to harmonise the provisions in force in individual EU Member States governing commercial communication. In 1996, the 'Green paper on commercial communication'[81] was published and was followed by the publication in 1998 of 'The follow-up to the Green Paper on Commercial Communication in the Internal Market'.[82] As emerged from the Green Paper and its follow-up, there existed significant differences in legislation in the Member States with regard to sales promotions, and those differences could constitute an obstacle, in particular to the provision of services within the internal market. Therefore, the Commission took action to ensure that sales promotion communications could be used across borders.[83]

The first Proposal for a regulation concerning promotional sales (COM/2001/546) was presented on 2 October 2001[84] and was then followed by opinions of the Economic and Social Committee[85] and the European

---

81 *Green Paper on Commercial Communication*, COM 1996, 192 (final) <http://aei.pitt.edu/1181/> (accessed on 1.2.2025).

82 *Communication from the Commission to the Council, the European Parliament and the Economic and Social Committee, The follow-up to the Green paper on Commercial Communications in the Internal Marke*t, COM(1998), 121 final, <http://aei.pitt.edu/977/1/commercial_communications_gp_follow_COM_98_121.pdf> (accessed on 1.2.2025).

83 See: *Communication from the Commission on sales promotions in the Internal Market*, p. 3 <http://www.europarl.europa.eu/meetdocs/committees/envi/20020226/01-546_en.pdf> (accessed on 1.2.2025).

84 Proposal for a regulation of the European Parliament and of the Council on sales promotion in the internal market of 2.10.2001, COM(2001 546 final, 2001/0227 (COD) <http://www.europarl.europa.eu/meetdocs/committees/envi/20020226/01-546_en.pdf> (accessed on 22.11.2024). The whole legislative process available at: <http://eur-lex.europa.eu/procedure/EN/2001_227> (accessed on 13.1.2019).On the same day the *Green paper on European Union Consumer Protection was published* COM (2001) 531 final. Both proposals have been compared by *H-W. Micklitz*, A General Framework Directive on Fair Trading, in: *H. Collins* (ed.), The Forthcoming EX Directive on Unfair Commercial Practices, Contract, Consumer and Competition Law Implications, The Hague– London–New York 2004, pp. 47–49.

85 *Opinion of the Economic and Social Committee on the 'Proposal for a European Parliament and Council Regulation concerning sales promotions in the Internal Market'* (COM(2001) 546 final—2001/0227 (COD)) "OJ" - official journal as well Nr as No C Nr 221 of 2002, pp. 73–80, <http://eur-lex.europa.eu/legal-content/EN/TXT/?uri=celex:52002AE0689> (accessed on 1.2.2025).

Parliament.[86] After that, an amended draft (COM/2002/0585) was prepared,[87] and submitted to the European Council and the Parliament. Between 2003 and 2004 the Proposal was discussed[88] to be eventually withdrawn officially in 2005 despite quite advanced legislative work devoted to it.[89]

It is still worthwhile to quote the main reasons underlying the drafting of the regulation because similar considerations were taken into account by the Polish legislator when enacting the Polish draft of Article 17a of the Act on Combatting Unfair Competition in 2002.[90] The arguments used first in the Green Paper and then in the Proposal for a regulation concerning promotional sales appear in the explanatory memorandum to the Polish amendment. However, since the Proposal for a regulation provided a comprehensive and much broader rationale for the need to unify the provisions on sales promotion than the Polish explanatory memorandum, it is necessary to refer to the considerations made in the work on the regulation. The

---

86 *European Parliament legislative resolution on the proposal for a European Parliament and Council regulation on sales promotions in the Internal Market* (COM(2001) 546—C5-0475/2001—2001/0227(COD)),O.J.EU C No 272E of 2003 pp. 397–405, <http://eur-lex.europa.eu/legal-content/EN/TXT/?uri=celex:52002AP0400> (accessed on 2.2.2025).

87 *Amended proposal for a European Parliament and Council Regulation concerning sales promotions in the Internal Market (presented by the Commission pursuant to Article 250 (2) of the EC Treaty)*, COM/2002/0585 final – COD 2001/0227, <http://eur-lex.europa.eu/legal-content/EN/TXT/?uri=celex:52002PC0585> (accessed on 1.2.2025).

88 Discussions took place on 19 May 2003 (<http://europa.eu/rapid/press-release_PRES-03-140_en.htm?locale=en>), 18 May 2004 (<http://europa.eu/rapid/press-release_PRES-04-140_en.htm?locale=en>, accessed on: 13.1.2019) and 24 September 2004 (<http://europa.eu/rapid/press-release_PRES-04-269_en.htm?locale=en>, accessed on 13.1.2019). There was no agreement at the last meeting and it was felt that the draft should be returned to the Permanent Representatives Committee for further consideration.

89 In 2005, all pending legislative proposals were scrutinised from the point of view of their compatibility with the Commission's political priorities and whether there was still a need, under the changed circumstances, to continue the work that had been started. As a result of this analysis, it was concluded that the draft Sales Promotion Regulation (along with a number of other drafts) should be withdrawn. See: *Communication from the Commission to the Council and the European Parliament, Outcome of the screening of legislative proposals pending before the Legislator*) of 27.9.2005, COM(2005) 462 final, p. 2 and p. 9, <http://eur-lex.europa.eu/LexUriServ/LexUriServ.do?uri=COM:2005:0462:FIN:EN:PDF> (accessed on: 1.2.2025).

90 Article 17a to the Act on Combatting Unfair Competition was added in 2002.

reasoning adopted there may be used in the current discussion on the need to amend or repeal Article 17a.

The Green Paper highlighted the importance of commercial communications because of its link to the potential for jobs and growth and because of its relevance to European businesses and nonprofit organisations wishing to place their products and services on the EU market.[91]

The initiative to undertake further work arose from the European Commission's concern that differences in national laws on commercial communication services could constitute a barrier to traders wishing to offer their services across national borders. It was also feared that these differences could pose a problem for consumers seeking redress for the provision of unlawful commercial communication services. The aim of the Commission's action was to ensure that in the future, as commercial communication services develop in the Internal Market, there are no obstacles to the cross-border provision of such services.[92]

As can be seen from the above, the scope of the Commission's work was very broad and covered all forms of commercial communication.

3. Project

Although initially the work on commercial communication was broad, it was later limited to one of its forms—sales promotion. This limitation of the scope of work was reflected in the Proposal to a European Parliament and Council Regulation concerning sales promotions in the Internal Market of 4 October 2001.[93] The Proposal for a regulation was preceded by an analysis of the situation[94] and was published together with a communication

---

91 See: *Communication from the Commission to the Council, the European Parliament and the Economic and Social Committee, The follow-up to the Green paper on Commercial Communications in the Internal Market*, COM (1998), 121 final, <http://aei.pitt.edu/977/1/commercial_communications_gp_follow_COM_98_121.pdf> (accessed on 1.2.2025).

92 See: *Green Paper on Commercial Communication*, pp. 1–2 [*Executive Summary*].

93 Proposal presented by the Commission 4.10.2001. 'Proposal for a European Parliament and Council concerning sales promotion in the internal market, COM(2001) 546 final—2001/0227(COD).

94 *Analytical Report: Sales Promotions in the Internal Market, Internal working paper*, DG Markt. Report, published but currently unavailable.

in which the Commission outlined its principle rationale.[95] It was found that there was a lack of legal certainty in cross-border relations concerning sales promotion services and that there were substantial divergences among national legislations. The solutions adopted were outdated and needed to be modernised.[96] The aim of the regulation was to ensure the proper functioning of the internal market by establishing clear, modern and legally secure rules to enable faster development of cross-border activities and also allow different forms of commercial communication in cross-border relations in sales promotion. The aim was also to increase the level of protection for consumers, minors and public health. The work on consumer protection was going on in parallel with the work on a regulation on sales promotions. As the Commission explained, the two initiatives were complementary, as the aim of the regulation was to ensure transparency in trade and in communication with potential customers.[97]

After the first draft had been presented for discussion,[98] the next one, of 25 October 2002, entitled the Amended Proposal to the European Parliament and the Council Regulation on sales promotions in the Internal Market, was published with account taken for certain amendments.[99] The considerations outlined below relate to the revised version of the Proposal for a regulation.

---

[95] See: *Communication from the Commission on sales promotions in the Internal Market* <http://www.europarl.europa.eu/meetdocs/committees/envi/20020226/01-546_en.pdf> (accessed on: 1.2.2025).

[96] *Communication from the Commission on sales promotions in the Internal Market* 52001DC0546, p. 3.

[97] *Ibidem*.

[98] In the course of the discussions, opinions were expressed, also by the Economic and Social Committee, which considered that the Commission should amend the proposed draft in its entirety, taking into account, *inter alia*, the discussion arisen in connection with the issuing of the Green Paper on consumer protection (see <http://eur-lex.europa.eu/legal-content/EN/TXT/?uri=celex:52002AE0689>, accessed on: 1.2.2025), and by the European Parliament, which approved the draft with amendments (see *European Parliament legislative resolution on the proposal for a European Parliament and Council regulation on sales promotions in the Internal Market* (COM(2001) 546—C5-0475/2001—2001/0227(COD)) (O.J.EU C 272E of 2003 pp. 397–405).

[99] *Amended Proposal for a European Parliament and Council Regulation concerning sales promotions in the Internal Market* (COM(2002)585 final, 2001/0227(COD), <http://eur-lex.europa.eu/legal-content/EN/TXT/PDF/?uri=CELEX:52002PC0585&from=EN> (accessed on: 1.1.2025). The European Parliament proposed 57 amendments to the

The Proposal for a regulation comprised 8 Articles and an Annex to its Article 4 setting out the scope of information to be provided in connection with the use of sales promotions.

Article 1 as well as the preamble, provided a precise definition of the purpose of the regulation, which was 'to lay down rules for the use of sales promotions and rules of commercial communication with regard to sales promotions in order to ensure the proper functioning of the internal market and a high level of consumer protection'.[100] The extensive preamble, and particularly recitals 1–6, emphasised that the internal market consisted of areas without internal barriers in which the free movement of goods, services and freedom of establishment was ensured, and within which it was crucial to develop sales promotion to increase cross-border activity.[101] It was recognised that sales promotion was important for the development of all industries in the Community as it contributed to their growth and development, stimulating competition and thus allowing consumers to choose from a wider range of offers and competitive prices. Sales promotion is also an important tool that contributes to the development of small and medium-sized enterprises.[102]

Article 2 clarified the terms contained in it. The broadest term referred to in the regulation was 'commercial communication', which was to be understood as 'any form of communication designed to promote, directly or indirectly, the goods, services or image of a company, organisation or natural person pursuing an economic, industrial or craft activity or exercising a regulated profession'. What was excluded from the scope of this concept was information allowing direct access to the activities of a business, organisation or natural person, in particular a domain name and an e-mail address, as well as communications relating to the goods, services and image of the business, organisation or natural person developed in an independent manner, in particular without financial consideration.

---

draft regulation at first reading. Of these, the Commission accepted 40 amendments in full, 7 in part and 10 were rejected. For details of the Commission's position, see Explanatory Memorandum, in: Revised draft Regulation, pp. 2–4.

[100] The second stated objective, i.e. 'a high level of consumer protection,' was added during the work on the first draft of the regulation. In the original draft, Article 1 lacked such a term.

[101] See Recital 1 of the Preamble to the draft Regulation.

[102] *Ibidem* recital 2 .

Another broad definition referred to the concept of sales promotions, according to which 'sales promotion' was an offer of:

1) discount, by which is meant a price reduction, an additional quantity of a product or service identical to the product or service purchased not involving additional costs for the purchaser a voucher or coupon entitling the purchaser of a product or service to a price reduction on a subsequent purchase of identical goods and services;
2) a free gift, which is defined as a temporary offer that enables one to receive a good or service at no extra charge, independently of any obligation to purchase an identical good or service;
3) a premium, which is defined as a temporary offer to receive a good or service that is not identical to the good or service offered for purchase;
4) the opportunity to take part in a promotional contest, which is defined as a temporary offer that allows participation in a contest in which participation may be dependent on the prior purchase of a good or service and the outcome of which depends mainly on the skill of the winner, or in a promotional game, which is defined as a temporary offer that allows participation in a game in which victory depends mainly on chance. Participation in the game is independent of the payment of a fee or the prior purchase of a product or service. Such a game does not, however, include gambling activities consisting of betting with monetary values in games of chance, including lotteries and betting.

It should be added that the Proposal for a regulation referred to short-term as well as long-term sales promotions, including loyalty and mileage accumulation programmes for flights.[103]

Article 3 was key to defining its purpose. It further specified that Member States or non-public regulatory bodies[104] should not impose:

[103] See *Ibidem*, recital 7.

[104] By which, according to Article 2(m), is meant an organisation or association not governed by public law which, within the scope of its legal autonomy, exercises supervision in a collective manner over economic activities.

1. a general prohibition on the use of sales promotions or related commercial communications, unless required by Community law. A general prohibition should be understood to mean a prohibition that does not refer to a particular type of promoted goods or services;[105]
2. limitations on the value of sales promotions, with the exception of discounts on fixed-price products or sales below cost;
3. a prohibition on discounts preceding a seasonal sale;
4. a requirement for prior authorisation or other requirements having an equivalent effect for the use of or commercial communication of a sales promotion.

Furthermore, Member States and non-public regulatory bodies should not restrict either the freedom to provide services or the free movement of goods on the grounds of the use of sales promotions and references to them in commercial communications (Article 3.2).

The proposed rules were not intended to affect national and Community competition law or national rules on sales below cost (Articles 3.2. and 3.3). Nor were they intended to apply to medicinal products.[106] Although, according to the preamble, the Regulation applied without prejudice to Community and national competition law, which contained specific provisions applicable to the press.[107]

Article 4 of the Proposal for a regulation also provided for extensive information obligations in respect of sales promotions and stated that it was assumed that the rules of sales promotions should be transparent and that interested persons should be capable of easily obtaining all important information.[108] All information must be presented in a clear and unambiguous manner. Thus, a high level of consumer protection was assumed, while its scope was to be specified in the Annex under the title 'Information to be provided in relation to the use and commercial communication of sales promotions'.

---

[105] It follows that certain restrictions may be introduced with regard to sales promotion. However, this cannot be a general prohibition. This position is also confirmed by recital 15 of the draft Regulation.

[106] *Ibidem*, recital 16.

[107] *Ibidem*, recital 10.

[108] *Ibidem*, recital 14.

Article 5 provided for the protection of children and adolescents[109] and stated that the organiser of a promotional sale should not, with certain exceptions, collect personal data from children. Also, granting children gifts, bonuses or services that, by their nature, could be harmful to their health was prohibited. Above all, prohibition concerned alcoholic products. Restrictions also applied to tobacco products. However, in this respect, the Proposal referred to the provisions on advertising and sponsorship of tobacco products.[110]

Article 6 of the Proposal regulated the issue of redress. First of all, the obligation to provide evidence as to the accuracy of the information required by Article 4 had been shifted to the organiser of the sales promotion, on whom there were also imposed additional obligations, including those relating to the complaint procedure (ensuring that complaints were free of charge and preparing appropriate measures for this) and responses (obligation to reply in writing within 4 weeks). It was further provided that for out-of-court agreements, domestic law was to apply. In the event of a sales promotion being carried out from another Member State, the organiser was obliged to specify under which national law the sales promotion was organised.

The above provisions aimed at ensuring that if the organiser failed to comply with an obligation, the complainant could find out who the organiser was and easily seek redress.[111] Out-of-court settlements were also allowed.[112] What is more, they would be carried out free of charge.[113]

Although this Proposal for a regulation on sales promotions had never been adopted, it came to the attention of not only Polish scholars.[114] In German literature, it was noted that had the sales promotions as proposed

---

[109] See also recitals 19 and 20 of the preamble to the draft Regulation.

[110] See recital 20 and the reference there to the 2001 draft Directive COM/2001/0283 final – COD 2001/0119 (OJ EU C 270E of 2001, pp. 97–100).

[111] *Ibidem*, recital 21.

[112] *Ibidem*, recital 22.

[113] Article 7 of the draft Regulation provided that an evaluation report on the application of the Regulation together with proposals for amendment would be presented 2 years after its entry into force. In turn, Article 8 of the draft Regulation was to specify the date on which its provisions would come into force.

[114] See. *A. Mokrysz-Olszyńska*, Swoboda promocji, pp. 49–63; *Z. Okoń*, Czyny nieuczciwej, p. 731.

been allowed in Germany, their scope and extent could have been carried out to a greater extent than under German law then applicable.[115]

The project was based on a so-called information model according to which discounts, bonuses and contests with prizes were allowed, provided that the organiser (advertiser) complied with the extensive information obligations imposed.[116] It was argued that those information obligations listed in the Annex complemented the provisions of the previously adopted Directive 84/450/EEC on misleading advertising.[117] While failure to comply with the obligations of the proposed regulation would be tantamount to a breach of the prohibition on misleading information contained in Directive 84/450/EC. It was alleged, however, that the information obligation alone might not be sufficient, for example, in the case of children and adolescents. Sales promotions targeting this group of consumers, as being particularly susceptible to this type of behaviour, should be subject to different criteria than for adults.[118] It may be noted that, although Article 5 of the Proposal for a regulation introduced some specific obligations in relation to children and adolescents, in principle it allowed the same sales promotion measures as for adults.

It is rightly noted that the proposed regulation envisaged the protection of the consumer's right in B2C relations, with the aim of strengthening consumer confidence in sales promotions within the internal market. Importantly, the protection of consumer rights was not the only objective of the proposed regulation, as its aim was also to protect businesses in relations with other businesses (B2B).[119] This was also made clear in the preamble to the Proposal for a regulation (Recital 6), as well as in the definition of a 'consumer' understood as a company, organisation or individual who purchases goods or services promoted by the organiser.

---

[115] *A. Beater*, Europäisches Recht gegen unlauteren Wettbewerb – Ansatzpunkte, Grundlagen, Entwicklung, Erforderlichkeit, ZEuP 2003, No 11, p. 33.

[116] *A. Ohly*, Das neue UWG – Mehr Freiheit für den Wettbewerd?, GRUR 2004, issue 11, p. 890.

[117] Directive 84/450/EEC which was replaced by Directive 2006/114/EC.

[118] *A. Beater*, Europäisches Recht, p. 33.

[119] *P.W. Heermann*, Lauterkeitsrechtliche Informationspflichten, p. 142 where the author discusses mainly the information obligations provided for in § 4 No 4 UWG.

The solutions, and primarily those concerning information obligations, adopted in the Proposal influenced subsequent legislative solutions and were later reproduced basically *verbatim* in Articles 5 and 6 of Directive 2000/31/EC adopted in 2000 on certain legal aspects of information society services, in particular electronic commerce, in the Internal Market (Directive on electronic commerce).[120] This Directive aimed to ensure the proper functioning of the internal market by securing the movement of information society services[121] between Member States. The trend of imposing numerous information obligations on businesses was also maintained in subsequent EU legislation.[122]

There is no doubt that the obligation to provide certain information under EU law applies in particular to the trader–consumer relationship. However, this should not mean that incorrect labelling of products or omission of certain indications cannot be qualified as a delict of unfair competition also in relations between traders. Mislabelling certain features of a product, failure to disclose certain features of a product, or failing to comply with certain packaging or labelling obligations could, under Polish law, constitute an infringement of Article 10 of the Act on Combatting Unfair Competition or its Article 3(1) or lead to criminal liability if regulations

---

120 OJ EU L 178 of 2000, pp. 1–16.

121 Information society services should be understood as [in accordance with Article 1(2) of Directive 98/34/EC as amended by Directive 98/48/EC (OJ EU L No. 217 of 1998, p. 18–26 as amended) and now with Article 1(2)(b) of Directive (EU) 2015/1535 of the European Parliament and of the Council of 9.9.2015 laying down a procedure for the provision of information in the field of technical regulations and rules on information society services (OJ EU L 241 of 2015, p. 1)], any service normally provided for remuneration, at a distance, by electronic means and at the individual request of a recipient of services. The Directive also further defines services provided: 'at a distance', 'by electronic means' and 'at individual request' of the recipient of services.

122 See *H. Köhler*, § 5a, in: *H. Köhler, J. Bornkamm, J. Feddersen* (eds), Gesetz gegen den unlauteren Wettbewerb mit PAngV, UKlaG, DL-InfoV Munchen, 2017, Nb 5.20–5.25, pp. 1042–1043. See also extensively on the grounds of Article 10 of the Act on Combatting Unfair Competition in relation to informing indications *M. Kępiński, J. Kępiński*, in: *J. Szwaja, J. Kępiński* (eds), Ustawa o zwalczaniu nieuczciwej konkurencji, Warszawa 2024, commentary to Article 10, pp. 305–337.

relating to the labelling of certain products are applicable (e.g. tobacco[123] or chemical substances).[124]

III. Unfair Commercial Practices Directive

1. Introductory Remarks

In parallel with the above-discussed Proposal for a regulation on sales promotions in the internal market, work was ongoing on solutions aimed (primarily) at consumer protection. In October 2001, the European Commission presented the Green Paper on EU Consumer Protection.[125]

The publication of the Green Paper was preceded by an extensive study documented in The Feasibility of a General Legislative Framework on Fair Trading, presented in October 2000.[126] The study focused on an issue that was narrower than those addressed later in the Green Paper and was limited to unfair commercial communication only, which it defined as 'any form of communication designed to promote, directly or indirectly, the goods, services or image of an undertaking, organisation or person engaged in a commercial, industrial or craft activity or engaged in a liberal profession'. However, the literature claims that it was also a prelude to the work on the Unfair Commercial Practices Directive,[127] which indeed contained an

---

[123] Article 12(7) of the Act of 9.11.1995 on health protection against the consequences of tobacco and tobacco products use (Dz.U. of 2024, item 1162, as amended).

[124] Articles 43–46 of the Act on Chemical Substances and their Mixtures (Dz. U of 2022, item 1816 as amended).

[125] COM(2001) 531 final. Green Paper, <https://eur-lex.europa.eu/legal-content/EN/ALL/?uri=CELEX%3A52001DC0531> (accessed on: 1.02.2025).

[126] <http://ec.europa.eu/comm/consumers/cons_int/safe_shop/fair_bus_pract/green_pap_comm/studies/sur21_vol1_en.pdf> (accessed on: 13 July 2017, currently unavailable). See: *H-W. Micklitz*, A General Framework Directive on Fair Trading, in: *H. Collins* (ed.), The Forthcoming EC Directive on Unfair Commercial Practices. Contract, Consumer and Competition Law Implications, The Hague 2004, pp. 43–90; *Ch. Wadlow*, The Case for Reclaiming European Unfair Competition Law from Europe's Consumer Lawyers, in: *S. Weatherill, U. Bernitz* (ed.), The Regulation of Unfair Commercial Practices under EC Directive 2005/29. New Rules and New Techniques, Oxford–Portland 2007, pp. 175–189, hereinafter referred to as Study.

[127] See: *Ch. Wadlow*, The Case for Reclaiming European Unfair, p. 180.

extensive analysis of the broad concept of honest trade and seemed to go beyond the mere issue of commercial communication.

In 2005, after almost 2 years of legislative work, the Unfair Commercial Practices Directive was enacted in its final version as Directive 2005/29/EC, and Member States were obliged to implement it by 12 June 2007 at the latest.[128] The implementation of the Directive took different forms in different States.[129] In Poland, it was implemented in the form of a new legislative act adopted on 23 August 2007 known as the Act on Counteracting Unfair Market Practices,[130] which had practically taken over the entire text of the Directive.

At the moment, it is difficult to grasp the interdependence, or mutual relation, of the two Acts currently in force in Poland, i.e. the Act on Combatting Unfair Competition of 1993 and the Act on Counteracting Unfair Market Practices of 2007 implementing Directive 2005/29/EC. This is because the European Commission's Proposal for a regulation on sales promotions concerning (B2B) relations had eventually been withdrawn, and the only solutions that were adopted concerned basically consumer protection in B2C relations.

2. Green Paper on Consumer Protection in the EU

The document in which the Commission presented the consumer protection issues that needed to be regulated at the EU level was the Green Paper on EU Consumer Protection, published in October 2001.

The main reason why it was published was to initiate a discussion at the EU level as to which direction the consumer protection in the European Union should take.[131] In the Commission's view, consumers would only be able to enjoy the benefits of the internal market when the goods and services offered and sold among Member States across borders were easily accessible. However, as long as the laws of the Member States on B2C commercial

[128] See: Article 19 of Directive 2005/29/EU

[129] See: <http://eur-lex.europa.eu/legal-content/PL/NIM/?uri=celex:32005L0029> (accessed on: 1.2.2025). Also *F. Henning-Bodewig*, Die Bekämpfung unlauteren Wettbewerbs in den EU-Mitgliedstaaten: eine Bestandsaufnahme, GRUR Int 2010, pp. 273–287.

[130] History of the legislative process the Polish Act on Counteracting Unfair Market Practices, <http://orka.sejm.gov.pl/proc5.nsf/opisy/1682.htm> (accessed on 1.2.2025).

[131] The Green Paper, Chapter 1 "*Consultation on EU consumer protection*" pp. 2–3.

practices differ, there will continue to be obstacles hampering the development of the internal market.[132]

To provide consumer protection, a regulatory system had to be developed that would:

1) ensure a high level of consumer protection at minimal cost to traders;
2) be as simple as possible but flexible enough to respond rapidly to market developments;
3) ensure legal certainty and effective means of enforcement, in particular in cross-border relations.[133]

Although there had already been a certain degree of consumer protection provided for in other Directives,[134] but their assessment confirmed that:

1) the adopted Directives did not provide a sufficient framework for the creation of a consumer protection scheme for B2C commercial practices, the main objective of consumer protection;
2) some of the Directives, particularly those relating to specific sectors, introduced very specific solutions that responded to specific problems at a specific time. Over the years they had become inadequate and were now limiting innovation or could be easily circumvented. Thus, they needed to be revised to match the level of technological development while maintaining the same level of consumer protection;
3) the resulting regulatory framework was complex and difficult to understand for both businesses and consumers;
4) the case law of the CJEU was also not a sufficient basis, as it was limited to the issue of the particular case;
5) the system of self-regulation that was developing in some Member States (Denmark, Sweden, Finland, the United Kingdom, Ireland and the Netherlands) was also insufficient at the EU level because, due to

---

132 The Green Paper, Chapter 2 "*Consumer protection in the internal market*" pp. 3–8.

133 *Ibidem*, point 2.1, pp. 3–4.

134 *Ibidem*, pkt 2.2, p 4. The Commission lists directives laying down general rules as well as those relating to specific sectors or sales methods, and a directive on the enforcement of consumer rights.

the differences between countries in this respect, it had to rely on the application of codes of conduct;[135]
6) due to the diversity of the markets, it was necessary to ensure greater expert participation in the regulatory solutions adopted.[136]

The national laws of the individual Member States also differed both in their foundations (substance) and application. Significant differences existed with regard to the applicable commercial practices in B2C relations, and they resulted from the diversity of national regulations or case law. The Commission also pointed out commercial practices used in sales promotions and announced that work on a regulation on sales promotions was underway.[137]

It was also pointed out that the existing differences in the legislation of individual Member States were likely to increase with the development of 'new economy' commercial practices, such as new advertising or marketing methods, which had not been foreseen in the regulations currently binding and which had therefore already been regulated but treated differently in the laws of the Member States.

In assessing this state of affairs, the Commission concluded that there was a need for specific action[138] and argued that the different ways of treating the same commercial practices were not only to the disadvantage of small and medium-sized companies but also to the detriment of consumers, who saw the lack of transparency and certainty as an important factor affecting their confidence and trust. A fully functioning consumer internal market could be important for the achievement of EU objectives, where traders would have easier access to national markets to boost up their competitiveness, and consumers would have more choice and better prices. And yet, the barriers to cross-border B2C relations meant that still a greater level of harmonisation was needed. Here, the Commission identified two possible solutions to achieve a further level of harmonisation:

1) a specific approach, meaning that further directives would be adopted;

---

135 *Ibidem*, point 2.2, p. 5 and point 2.3, p. 7.
136 *Ibidem*, point 2.2, p. 6.
137 *Ibidem*, point 2.3, pp. 6–8.
138 *Ibidem*, Chapter 3 – *The future direction of EU consumer protection*, pp. 9–12.

2) a mixed approach consisting of the adoption of a single, overarching framework directive, supplemented, where necessary, by targeted directives.[139]

Further issues considered in the Green Paper related to further consumer protection reform. It was argued that the Framework Directive should be based on a general clause on consumer-business relations, which would be complemented by a general test of integrity and specific rules aimed at eliminating differences in national legislation on commercial practices.[140] An alternative to the integrity test for commercial practice could be grounding the directives on a more restrictive concept such as misrepresentation or deceptive practice.[141]

In the last chapter of the Green Paper, the Commission also raised issues relating to the creation of appropriate structures to enable consumers to enforce their rights.[142]

3. The First Draft of the Directive

The result of the work published in the Green Paper on EU Consumer Protection and subsequently presented for further consultation was a draft Directive of the European Parliament and of the Council concerning unfair B2C commercial practices in the internal market and amending Directives 84/450/EEC, 97/7/EC, and 98/27/EC (Unfair Commercial Practices Directive) published by the European Commission on 18 June 2003.[143]

From the outset, it had been assumed that the Unfair Commercial Practices Directive would be based on the principle of full harmonisation. It was intended to fully harmonise EU requirements of unfair commercial practices and ensure 'an appropriately high level of consumer protection'. As the Commission explained, this approach would make it feasible to eliminate barriers in the internal market caused by divergent Member State legislation (harmonisation principle) and provide the necessary support to consumers

---

139 *Ibidem*, point 3.2, p. 10.
140 *Ibidem*, point 4.1, p. 13.
141 *Ibidem*, point 4.2, p. 13.
142 *Ibidem*, chapter 5 – *Enforcement in the EU today*, pp. 16–19.
143 COM/2003/0356 final – COD 2003/0134, <http://eur-lex.europa.eu/legal-content/EN/TXT/?uri=COM:2003:0356:FIN> (accessed on 1.2.2025).

in the mutual recognition of their rights relating to unfair commercial practices (the mutual recognition principle).[144] It is believed that by adopting its maximalist nature, the Directive represents a new stage in the development of consumer legislation and an erosion of the presumption of legality of national law stemming from the judgement in *Keck*.[145]

The supporters of the implementation of a maximalist nature directive were members of the team carrying out the feasibility study before the Green Paper was published, who believed that the best option would be adoption of a directive that would combine the solutions of a traditional directive with a new approach-type directive. This, however, would also implicate an adoption of a safeguard clause that would reflect the legitimate interest of the Member States and which would allow them to amend (or revise) the list of prohibited commercial practices. In this way, the general clause and the list of prohibited commercial practices would constitute a set of uniform standards. At the same time it was argued that the new approach[146] directive was not intended to be an alternative to the 'traditional' Directive, in which certain standards of honest trade had to be defined. The 'new approach' solutions could only complement the general clause and the list of prohibited commercial practices.[147]

An Explanatory Memorandum was also published alongside the draft directive and set out the key reasons underpinning the proposed amendment and outlining the legislative approach.[148]

First and foremost, it was emphasised that the proposed project was intended to benefit both consumers and the functioning of the internal market. The Commission's intention was that, as a result of the amendment, consumers would have greater access to goods and services whose movement

144 Draft Directive, Explanatory Memorandum, p. 5.

145 Judgement of the ECJ of 24 November 1993, *Criminal proceedings v. Bernard Keck and Daniel Mithouard*, joined cases C-267/91 and C-268/91, p. I-06097, ECLI:EU:C:1993:905.

146 See: Study part I, pp. 19–22; part 2, pp. 118–119.

147 See Study, part I, pp. 19–22; part 2, p. 118–119.

148 In the literature on the draft Directive, see: M. Namysłowska, Draft reform of the law against unfair competition of the EU Member States—material and legal issues, Monitor Prawniczy (MoP) 2004, No 3.

across borders would be ensured. In this way, they would also have access to innovative products not available on their own market.

Based on the report cited in the Explanatory memorandum,[149] the Commission stressed that the further development of the internal market depended on two factors, i.e. encouraging traders to advertise and trade across borders and stimulating consumers to buy across borders. The importance of achieving greater price convergence in the internal market was also pinpointed. This would be possible through further integration and ensuring competition, which would consequently benefit consumers and ensure the efficient functioning of the internal market.[150]

In its conclusions, the Commission stressed that action would have to be taken at the EU level, as unfair trading practices and their only fragmented regulation distort competition and constitute a significant barrier to the development of the internal market.[151]

It was also believed that the most effective solution would be an adoption of a directive based on full harmonisation.[152] An alternative to it would have been a number of specific directives or a mixed approach.[153]

In the second part of the Explanatory memorandum, the main principles upon which the Directive was founded were explained. They were:

1. the Directive defines the conditions that are decisive for recognising a given practice as unfair;
2. the Directive contains an internal market clause whereby traders must comply only with the conditions imposed in the country of origin. The clause is intended to prevent other Member States from imposing additional conditions on such traders;
3. The Directive fully harmonises EU laws relating to unfair B2C commercial practices and provides for an appropriate, high level of consumer protection;

---

149 Report on the functioning of Community product and capital markets, COM (2002) 743 final.

150 Explanatory memorandum pp. 3–4.

151 *Ibidem*, pp. 6–7.

152 *Ibidem*, p. 6, Nb 27.

153 *Ibidem*, p. 7, Nb 28 and 29. This issue was discussed earlier in the Green Paper, points 3.2–3.4, pp. 10–12.

4. The Directive introduces a general prohibition on the use of unfair commercial practices, thereby simplifying the legal environment for traders and consumers;
5. the Directive adopts the model of the average consumer developed in the CJEU case law;
6. the Directive discusses in detail two types of unfair commercial practices: misleading and aggressive. These practices are ipso facto considered to be unfair. All other practices must be assessed through the prism of the general clause, whether they are unfair or not;
7. the Directive takes over the provisions of the Misleading Advertising Directive[154] relating to B2C relations. Thus, the scope of the Misleading Advertising Directive was limited to advertising used in B2B relationships. The same applies to the provisions on comparative advertising;
8. the Annex to the Directive contains a blacklist of commercial practices that are in all circumstances unfair and therefore prohibited in all Member States.[155]

The Directive was to be divided into four chapters, and there was to be a rather extensive preamble preceding it, followed by 2 Annexes. The first Annex lists commercial practices that are considered unfair in all circumstances. The second contains the provisions of Community law setting out the rules for advertising and commercial communication. Such a structure, envisaged in the draft, was maintained, in principle without major changes, in the adopted text of the Directive. Following the publication of the draft Directive in 2003, further work on its final version continued for almost two years.

4. Completion of the Work on Directive 2005/29/EC

Eventually, the Unfair Commercial Practices Directive was enacted on 11 May 2005. The enacted Directive 2005/29/EC retains its original layout adopted in the draft. The Directive consists of a comprehensive preamble with 25 recitals, 21 articles divided into 4 chapters (Chapter 1—General provisions, Chapter 2—Unfair commercial practices, Chapter 3—Codes of conduct, Chapter

---

[154] Council Directive 84/450/EEC of 10.10.1984 concerning misleading and comparative advertising (OJ EU L 250 of 1984, p. 17). Directive as amended by Directive 97/55/EC of the European Parliament and of the Council (OJ EU L 290 of 1997, p. 18).

[155] Explanation of the draft directive, pp. 7–9.

4—Final provisions), and two extensive annexes (No. 1—Commercial practices and No. 2—Community legislation setting out rules for advertising and commercial communication).

First and foremost, the Directive was intended to safeguard directly the economic interests of consumers against unfair commercial practices by traders. Only indirectly was it intended to protect legitimate traders against those competitors who act contrary to its provisions. It was emphasised that there are commercial practices that do not harm consumers but that may harm competitors and customers. Therefore, it was proposed to examine and, if necessary, regulate issues in the sphere of unfair competition that do not fall within the scope of this Directive.[156] This involved any commercial practice that did not directly harm the economic interests of consumers but was likely to harm the interests of competitors and customers.

It must be thus inferred that the drafters of the Directive were aware of the need to adopt different regulations for the protection of consumers against practices of unfair commercial practices used in B2C relations and the protection of fair competition in B2B relations. It seems as well that what underlay the attempt to make a clear distinction between the protection of consumers' interests and the protection of traders' interests was the presumption that the provisions of the Directives concerning misleading advertising and comparative advertising, insofar as they applied to traders, were not affected by the Unfair Commercial Practices Directive.[157] It can be deduced from the above that as long as advertising does not mislead consumers, it does not fall within the scope of the Directives even if the interests of traders have been affected.

It was also further emphasised that the Directive applied to commercial practices having a direct effect on consumers' decisions. It would not apply, however, if the commercial practices were undertaken for other purposes, e.g. commercial communications aimed at investors (annual reports or promotional material).[158]

---

[156] Recital 8 of Preamble to Directive 2005/29/EC.
[157] *Ibidem*, recital 6.
[158] *Ibidem*, recital 7.

The primary objective of the drafters of the Directive was to achieve coherence with other Community acts; hence, there was a need to revise the existing legislation.[159] It was also important that it was complementary to the existing *acquis* on commercial practices harming the economic interests of consumers. And yet, harmonisation was intended to provide legal certainty not only for consumers but also for traders.[160]

It was taken that there were two categories of unfair commercial practices, i.e. misleading practices[161] and aggressive commercial practices.[162] As explained, the model of the average consumer should be taken as a benchmark when assessing the practice in question. The average consumer is sufficiently well-informed, sufficiently attentive and sufficiently cautious. At the same time, there are certain groups of consumers who are more susceptible to unfair commercial practices (e.g. the children and the sick). In such a situation, the practice in question should be assessed from the perspective of the average member of that group.[163]

According to the drafters of the Directive, the best way to eliminate the barriers to the functioning of the internal market that exist in national laws and to ensure a high, common level of consumer protection was to take action at Community level.[164]

The objective of Directive 2005/29/EC, which coincided with the initial objectives set out in the draft, is defined in Article 1 and is to 'contribute to the proper functioning of the internal market and achieve a high level of consumer protection by approximating the laws, regulations and administrative provisions of the Member States on unfair commercial practices harming consumers' economic interests'.

Article 3 regulated the scope of the Directive stating that, in principle, it should be applied in the event of 'unfair commercial practices within the meaning of Article 5 used by traders before, during and after a commercial transaction in relation to a product'.

---

159 The legislative acts are enumerated in recital 10 of the preamble to Directive 2005/29/EC.

160 *Ibidem*, recital 12.

161 *Ibidem*, recital 14.

162 *Ibidem*, recital 16.

163 *Ibidem*, recital 18–19.

164 *Ibidem*, recital 23.

A 'consumer' within the meaning of Article 2(a) is 'any natural person who, in commercial practices covered by this Directive, is acting for purposes which are outside his or her trade, business, craft or profession', and a 'trader' is 'any natural or legal person who, in commercial practices covered by this Directive, is acting for purposes relating to his trade, business, craft or profession and anyone acting in the name of or on behalf of a trader' (Article 2(b)). By contrast, 'business-to-consumer commercial practices' are to be understood as 'any act, omission, course of conduct or representation, or commercial communication, including advertising and marketing, by a trader, directly connected with the promotion, sale or supply of a product to consumers' (Article 2(d). Article 5(1) introduced a general prohibition of unfair commercial practices, and paragraph 2 defined a commercial practice as unfair if it:

'(a) was contrary to the requirements of professional diligence; (b) materially distorted or was likely to materially distort the economic behaviour with regard to the product of the average consumer whom it reached or to whom it was addressed, or of the average member of the group of consumers when a commercial practice was directed to a particular group of consumers'.

A significant 'distortion of consumers' economic behaviour' should be understood as 'using a commercial practice to appreciably impair the consumers' ability to make an informed decision, thereby causing the consumer to take a transactional decision that he or she would not have taken otherwise' (Article 2(e)).

Despite the general definition of unfair market practices, the Directive divided unfair market practices into two types of practices, i.e. (1) misleading and (2) aggressive commercial practices. A misleading practice may take the form of an action (Article 6) or an omission (Article 7). An action is meant to be the provision of false information that causes or is likely to cause the consumer to make a decision that he would not have taken had the information been true. Incorrect information may relate to: (1) the existence or nature of the product; (2) the main characteristics of the product; (3) the extent of the trader's commitments; (4) motives for using a given market practice or form of the sales process; (5) sponsoring; (6) pricing; (7) services, spare parts, replacement and repair; (8) the entrepreneur/trader (type, characteristics, and rights; 9) and consumer rights.

A misleading practice will also be (1) any marketing of products, including comparative advertising, that is likely to cause confusion as to the product, trademark, trade names or other distinctive signs of a competitor; (2) failure by traders to comply with the obligations contained in the codes of conduct.

Moreover, a commercial practice may be considered misleading in the event of an omission (Article 7), which may be (1) omission of material information for the consumer or (2) concealing or conveying in an unclear, unintelligible, ambiguous or untimely manner information that may be of material importance to the consumer.

Annex I of the Directive lists 23 misleading commercial practices that should in all circumstances be regarded as unfair.[165] The second category of unfair commercial practices listed in the Directive is aggressive commercial practices. Aggressive commercial practices are practices that, through harassment, coercion, also with the use of physical force, or undue influence significantly limit or are likely to significantly limit the average consumer's freedom of choice or conduct with regard to the product. Consequently, this causes or is likely to cause the consumer to take a decision that he or she would not have taken in the absence of the aggressive commercial practice.

Similarly, as was the case for misleading commercial practices, Annex I identifies 8 aggressive commercial practices that are always unfair, regardless of any circumstances.[166]

Article 11(1) contains provisions on the implementation of the Directive in national legal systems. And so, Member States are to ensure that the measures they implement to combat unfair commercial practices are adequate and effective. They are to be taken in the interest of consumers and must constitute appropriate legal provisions allowing persons or organisations with a legitimate interest in combatting unfair commercial practices, as well as competitors, to (i) initiate legal proceedings against unfair commercial practices and (ii) bring actions against such unfair commercial practices before administrative authorities.

Articles 11(2) and (3), 12 and 13 set out further obligations on Member States in relation to the transposition of the Directive into their legal systems.

---

165 See Annex I, paragraphs 1–23. Each of these practices is described by M. Namysłowska, Czarna lista nieuczciwych praktyk handlowych a granice prawa zwalczania nieuczciwej konkurencji w Unii Europejskiej. Analiza prawnoporównawcza, Warszawa 2014, pp. 322–482.

166 See, Annex I, point 24–31. These practices have been described by M. Namysłowska, in: Czarna lista nieuczciwych praktyk handlowych, Warszawa 2014, pp. 482–545.

In particular, it is left to Member States to decide which powers should be conferred on the courts or administrative authorities to effectively combat unfair commercial practices. An obligation is also imposed on Member States to lay down sanctions for infringements of national provisions implementing the Directive. These sanctions are to be effective, proportionate and dissuasive.

It was also the intention of the drafters of the Directive to emphasise (Article 10) the special role of the Codes of Conduct as an element of self-control for traders. And so, a 'code of conduct' is to be understood as 'an agreement or set of rules, not required by the laws, regulations or administrative provisions of a Member State, which defines the conduct of traders who undertake to be bound by the Code in relation to one or more particular commercial practices or business sectors'. The use of codes of conduct would ensure the effective application of the provisions of the Directive and provide a basis for assessing professional diligence in a particular sector.[167]

Although the Member States were obliged to implement the directive in their legal systems by 12 June 2007 at the latest, they were allowed, for a period of 6 years, to apply relevant national provisions that were more restrictive or prescriptive than those contained in this Directive and that implemented guidelines containing a minimum harmonisation clause. This deadline expired in 2013. According to the Commission Report[168] only five countries requested to maintain more restrictive or prescriptive national rules.[169] The Commission concluded that such a low number of applications was due to Member States' reluctance to repeal existing, national solutions. The Commission considered in its 2013 Report that the exemption provided for in Article 3(5) of the Directive should not be extended for a further period. It must therefore be recognised that it is currently unlikely that more

167 See recital 20 of the preamble of Directive 2005/29/EC.

168 Report of the Commission for the European Parliament, the Council and the Social-Economic Committee of 14 March 2013. The First Report on the application of Directive 2005/29/EC of the European Parliament and of the Council of 11 May 2005 concerning unfair business-to-consumer commercial practices in the internal market and amending Council Directive 84/450/EEC, Directives 97/7/EC, 98/27/EC and 2002/65/EC of the European Parliament and of the Council and Regulation (EC) No 2006/2004 of the European Parliament and of the Council ('Unfair Commercial Practices Directive'), COM(2013) 139 final, <https://eur-lex.europa.eu/legal-content/en/ALL/?uri=CELEX%3A52013DC0139> (accessed on 1.2.2025).

169 They were: Denmark, Finland, Ireland, Latvia and Sweden.

restrictive or prescriptive provisions on the basis of Article 3(5) of Directive 2005/29/EC can be maintained in national legislation'.

It should be added that due to its wide scope of application, the implementation of Directive 2005/29/EC was a difficult legislative challenge for the Member States. The delays with its implementation were caused by its maximal nature, which warranted a comprehensive review of the existing national systems that the Directive covered. As a result of the problems that arose, only some Member States (Belgium, Ireland, Malta, Poland, Slovakia and Slovenia) adopted Directive 2005/29/EC within the stipulated time. Spain was the last to implement it at the end of 2009, more than 2 years after the deadline.[170]

The Member States adopted different ways of implementing the Directive. One group of Member States (Austria, Denmark, Germany, and Spain) implemented Directive 2005/29/EC in the legal regulations that were already in force in their legislations. Those were primarily laws relating to the prevention of unfair competition, being part of their Civil Code provisions (the Netherlands), or other specific laws (Belgium, Finland and Sweden). The other group of countries adopted new laws in which they implemented the Directive almost *verbatim* (Cyprus, Estonia, Greece, Hungary, Ireland, Latvia, Lithuania, Luxembourg, Poland, Portugal, Romania, Slovakia, Slovenia and the United Kingdom).[171]

---

[170] Data from the Report of the Commission for the European Parliament, the Council and the Social-Economic Committee of 14 March 2013. The First Report on the application of Directive 2005/29/EC of the European Parliament and of the Council of 11 May 2005 concerning unfair business-to-consumer commercial practices in the internal market and amending Council Directive 84/450/EEC, Directives 97/7/EC, 98/27/EC and 2002/65/EC of the European Parliament and of the Council and Regulation (EC) No 2006/2004 of the European Parliament and of the Council ('Unfair Commercial Practices Directive'), COM(2013) 139 final, <https://eur-lex.europa.eu/legal-content/en/ALL/?uri=CELEX%3A52013DC0139> (accessed on 22.11.2024).

[171] Report of the Commission for the European Parliament, the Council and the Social-Economic Committee of 14 March 2013, p. 3. Also see: European Commission – DG Justice 'Study on the application of Directive 2005/29/EC on Unfair Commercial Practices in the EU. Part 1 – Synthesis Report' Final Report, Civic Consulting, 22.12.2011, <https://ec.europa.eu/info/sites/info/files/synthesis_on_application_of_directive_2012_en.pdf> (accessed on 13.1.2019).

5. Assessment of the Directive

The draft directive, and subsequently the Directive itself, was subject to extensive analysis in the literature.[172] And while the very idea of harmonising the rules on unfair commercial practices received a positive assessment and was seen as an important step towards the creation of a uniform law of fair competition, the Directive itself was criticised. F. Henning-Bodewig believes that by adopting the Directive in its proposed form, the opportunities to unify and simplify the European framework of fair competition law had been missed. This was mainly due to the narrowing of the scope of application of Directive 2005/29/EC to B2C relationships.[173]

However, the most serious criticism that appears to have emerged in the literature is that the drafters of Directive 2005/29/EC overlooked or did not take sufficient account of the fact that Member States already had different models of legal protection against unfair competition in place in their respective legal systems.[174] Over the years, many Member States had developed a well-functioning system for combatting unfair competition, and

[172] See: *S. Weatherill*, *U. Bernitz* (eds), The Regulation of Unfair Commercial Practices under EC Directive 2005/29. New Rules and New Techniques, Oxford–Portland 2007; *J. Glöckner*, Richtlinievorschlag über unlautere Geschäftspraktiken, deutsches UWG oder die schwierige Umsetzung von europarechtlichen Generalklauseln, Wettbewerb in Recht und Praxis 2004, pp. 936–945; *F. Henning-Bodewig*, Stellungnahme des Max-Planck-Instituts zum Vorschlag einer Richtlinie über unlautere Geschäftsprktiken vom 18.6.2003 und einer Verordnung über die Zusammenarbeit im Verbraucherschutz vom 18.7.2003, GRUR Int 2003, pp. 926–929; Die Richtlinie 2005/29/EG über unlautere Geschäftspraktiken, GRUR Int 2005, pp. 629–634. In Poland *J. Szwaja*, *A. Tischner*, Implementacja dyrektywy 2005/29/WE, pp. 1117–1122; Dokąd zmierza prawo zwalczania nieuczciwej konkurencji?, in: *J. Barta*, *A. Matlak* (eds), Prawo własności intelektualnej wczoraj, dziś i jutro, Prace Instytutu Prawa Własności Intelektualnej UJ 2007, issue 100, pp. 499–513; *A. Kukiel-Kryńska*, Implementacja dyrektyw opartych na zasadzie harmonizacji pełnej na przykładzie dyrektywy o nieuczciwych praktykach rynkowych, Monitor Prawniczy (MoP) 2007, No 18, p. 989 et seq.; *I.B. Nestoruk*, Europejskie prawo o zwalczaniu nieuczciwej konkurencji? (Prezentacja projektu dyrektywy o nieuczciwych praktykach handlowych), Prace Instytutu Prawa Własności Intelektualnej UJ, ZNUJ 2005, issue 89, pp. 139–171.

[173] *F. Henning-Bodewig*, Die Richtlinie 2005/29/EG, p. 634.

[174] See: *J. Stuyck*, The Unfair Commercial Practices Directive and its Consequences for the Regulation of Sales Promotion and the Law of Unfair Competition, in: *S. Weatherill*, *U. Bernitz* (eds), The Regulation of Unfair Commercial Practices under EC Directive 2005/29. New Rules and New Techniques, Oxford–Portland 2007, pp. 166–170.

the implementation of Directive 2005/29/EC entailed a partial rejection of the *acquis* of the courts and legal doctrine that had 'developed' over decades in the field of the law against unfair competition. As a consequence, the implementation of the Directive was easier in some countries and much more complicated in others.[175] F. Henning-Bodewig differentiated four principal models of regulation:

1) a model of integrated protection of competitors and consumers in which, in principle, it is left to those whose interests have been harmed to assert their rights (das Modell eines 'integrierten' Mitbewerber- und Verbraucherschutzes) (Austria, Belgium, Denmark, Spain, Germany, Poland and Sweden);
2) a dual protection model (das 'duale Modell'), in which the interests of competitors are protected in civil law (primarily the law of delict) and consumer protection is secured by solutions adopted in administrative or criminal law (France, Italy);
3) a unitary competition model (das Wettbewerbsmodell), in which there is a close link between fair competition law and antitrust law, and enforcement is mainly seen as a task of the State (mostly former socialist states);
4) a common law model, in which the market participants concerned have, in principle, a very limited possibility, apart from the narrowly provided remedies, to enforce their rights, but in which an element of self-control is important (Ireland and the United Kingdom).[176]

This is obviously an oversimplification. However, it allows us to understand that in those Member States where the integrated protection model existed, Directive 2005/29/EC was the most difficult to implement due to the separation of B2C and B2B relations. According to F. Henning-Bodewig, of all countries where the integrated model had been in place, only Sweden and Denmark managed to maintain the existing system of integrated protection and comply with the requirements of Directive 2005/29/EC. The remaining countries, including Poland, failed to transpose the Directive. Countries that

---

175 *R. Skubisz*, Cele i zakres zastosowania ustawy, p. 576.

176 *F. Henning-Bodewig*, Der Schutzzweck, p. 240. A similar division has been adopted by *R. Skubisz*, Cele i zakres zastosowania ustawy, pp. 569–571.

adopted the common law model were those that encountered the fewest problems with its transposition.

Another objection concerned the need to implement the casuistic Annex I, which contained a list of 31 unfair market practices. Member States faced a dilemma as to how this catalogue should be adopted. For example, in Germany it was argued that the practices listed in Annex I had already been partly regulated by German laws. Therefore, it was unclear whether the commercial practices listed in Annex I were to be merely mentioned in the explanatory memorandum of the law transposing the Directive but not to be included in the statutory provisions, or whether it would be more appropriate and safer to adopt them as an annex to the law. However, this would lead to an unnecessary repetition and would require the linguistic adaptation of Directive 2005/29/EC to the provisions of the German law.[177] And yet, it was not the implementation of Annex I that posed the biggest problems. The main criticism was that the EU legislator had imposed a casuistic catalogue of unfair commercial practices. One might ask whether the adoption of such a catalogue is justified today, given the rapidly changing market situation in the different Member States. A better solution would have been to adopt more abstract, general solutions. The main starting point for any consideration should therefore be the general clause in Article 5(1) of Directive 2005/29/EC prohibiting unfair commercial practices. It would then be for the national courts to assess each practice in the light of the Directive and the prohibition flowing from that clause. Annex I could only have an illustrative value to help national courts to assess the commercial practice in question.

The case-law of the CJEU (expressed in *Total Belgium*[178]) it follows, however, that Annex I is of greater importance. This is because it is the starting point for the assessment of all national solutions, and the Directive does not allow Member States to adopt different rules. J. Szwaja's and A. Tischner's assertion that prescriptive regulation of unfair commercial practices is an expression of 'distrust in judges to decide on cases of unfair market conduct is also

---

[177] See *R. Lutz*, Veränderungen des Wettbewerbsrechts im Zuge der Richtlinie über unlautere Geschäftspraktiken, GRUR 2006, pp. 910–911.

[178] Point 78–79 of the Opinion of the Advocate-General *V. Trstenjak* of 21.10.2008 in joint cases C-261/07 and C-299/07, *VTB-VAB NV v. Total Belgium NV* and *Galatea BVBA v. Sanoma Magazines Belgium NV*, ECLI:EU:C:2008:581.

correct'.[179] Moreover, the list of prohibited commercial practices in Annex I is a closed catalogue. Such a solution has raised serious doubts. Opponents of such a solution, as quoted by R. Stefanicki[180] argued that an exemplary rather than a closed list of unfair commercial practices would have a positive impact on the dynamism and development of examples of such practices. It would also encourage Member States to work on the list by updating and simplifying it, while with things being as they were, any change to the list of unfair commercial practices required an amendment to Directive 2005/29/EC. The proposed solution would certainly prolong the possibility to adapt Annex I to changing economic conditions and consumer needs.

It was also argued that the Directive was an example of bad legislation because it was vague, unclear and repeated provisions that had already been adopted.[181] It may be added here that the greatest difficulties in transposition were related to the insufficient reconstruction of individual concepts, including general clauses.[182] In specific cases, it was also difficult to correctly transpose the wording and definitions adopted in Directive 2005/29/EC, as their scopes no longer overlapped with the concepts and definitions already adopted and established in individual legislations.[183]

In assessing the Directive, one cannot overlook the fact that the adoption of the maximum character entailed numerous consequences for the Member States. The most serious consequence was the need for Member States to revise their existing systems for combatting unfair competition. Indeed, according to the CJEU case law, the Directive fully harmonises the rules at the Community level, and 'the Member States may not adopt more stringent measures than those laid down in the Directive, even if this were to ensure an even higher level of consumer protection'.[184]

---

179 *J. Szwaja, A. Tischner*, Implementacja dyrektywy 2005/29/WE, p. 1117.

180 *R. Stefanicki*, Prawo uczciwej konkurencji a ochrona konsumentów w świetle ustawy o przeciwdziałaniu nieuczciwym praktykom rynkowym, System Prawa Prywatnego 2011, No 2, p. 61.

181 *J. Szwaja, A. Tischner*, Implementacja dyrektywy 2005/29/WE, p. 1117.

182 See: *A. Kukiel-Kryńska*, Implementacja dyrektyw, p. 989.

183 *F. Henning-Bodewig*, Der Schutzzweck, p. 238, and *J. Szwaja, A. Tischner*, Implementacja dyrektywy 2005/29/WE, p. 1118.

184 Point 54 of the rationale to the judgment of 23.4.2009 in joint cases C-261/07 and C-299/07, *VTB-VAB NV v. Total Belgium NV, Galatea BVBA v. Sanoma Magazines Belgium NV*, OJ EU C 141 of 2009, pp. 3–4.

Such an assumption has far-reaching consequences. Indeed, if it is necessary to examine whether national provisions prohibiting certain commercial practices are permissible in light of the Unfair Commercial Practices Directive, it must first be determined whether the practice in question is one of the 31 practices listed in Annex I to the Directive. If not, it must be further examined whether the prohibition relates to a commercial practice that could be classified as misleading or aggressive (see General Clauses—Articles 6–9 of the Directive). If the national measures still do not fall into one of these categories, only then does the general clause of Article 5(1) apply. Even in this case, if the national provisions do not qualify for such a reference, the prohibition must be considered to be contrary to the Directive because it is more restrictive or prescriptive than the Directive provides for.[185]

To sum up, a commercial practice can only be prohibited if it falls into one of the categories of commercial practices, i.e. (1) it is listed in the Annex; (2) it is a misleading or aggressive practice; (3) it is contrary to the requirements of professional diligence or distorts customer behaviour. Member States cannot go further and prohibit other commercial practices. This was possible under the previous consumer protection directives, which were minimum harmonisation directives. There is an exception to the above rule where Member States may impose requirements of a more restrictive or prescriptive nature than those imposed by the Directive. This exception applies to financial services[186] and immovable property (Article 3(9).[187]

This way of examining national solutions raises certain doubts. H-W. Micklitz stressed the regulatory role of the Directive, which stems from the adoption of the principle of full harmonisation. However, he noted that

---

185 See: Points 78–79 of the Opinion of the Advocate-General *V. Trstenjak* of 21.10.2008, in joint cases C-261/07 and C-299/07, *VTB-VAB NV v. Total Belgium NV* and Galatea BVBA v. Sanoma Magazines Belgium NV, ECLI:EU:C:2008:581.

186 Financial services are defined in Directive 2002/65/EC of the European Parliament and of the Council of 23.9.2002 concerning the distance marketing of consumer financial services and amending Council Directive 90/619/EEC and Directives 97/7/EC and 98/27/EC (OJ L 271, 2002, p. 16–24, as amended). According to Article 2(b) of this Directive, 'financial service means any service of a banking, credit, insurance, pension, investment or payment nature'.

187 See also Recital 9 of the Preamble of the Directive and judgment of 18.6.2013, *Citroën Belux NV v. Federatie voor Verzekerings- en Financiële Tussenpersonen (FvF)*, ECLI:EU:C:2013:498.

Member States' commercial practices must first and foremost comply with the general fairness test set out in Article 5 of the Directive, and that the catalogue of prohibited commercial practices itself is of secondary importance. By applying the fairness test under Article 5, Member States could draw up their own list of prohibited commercial practices. In contrast, the way in which the CJEU proposed to review national solutions changes the principles of the whole system. In fact, the catalogue of prohibited commercial practices becomes the starting point, the core of the whole Directive, and the significance of Article 5 is reduced to a 'safety valve'. According to H.-W. Micklitz, this approach requires a revision of the Directive.[188]

It has been rightly pointed out in the literature that the adoption of the principle of full harmonisation also affects the existing interpretation of the general principles of EU law on the free movement of goods. C. Barnard cites the Keck case, which interprets the presumption of legality of national measures restricting or prohibiting certain selling methods, e.g. advertising or other promotional techniques such as free gifts. However, the situation has now changed following the adoption of the Directive. With regard to the practices covered by the Directive, where national rules restrict or prohibit such practices in a general manner, there is a presumption of incompatibility with EU law. Directive 2005/29/EC has changed the presumptions to the extent that it regulates them. The presumption of incompatibility can be rebutted after an assessment of whether a practice prohibited or restricted by national law is unfair under Articles 5–9 of the Directive. In other words, if the assessment shows that a commercial practice is also unfair under the Directive, national solutions prohibiting the practice are compatible with the Directive and therefore permissible. The above does not apply where the national rules concern practices listed in the Annex. Such rules are compatible with Directive 2005/29/EC.[189] The above considerations do not apply to commercial practices that fall outside the scope of the Directive.

---

188 *H.-W. Micklitz*, Full Harmonisation of Unfair Commercial Practices Under Directive 2005/29, International Review of Intellectual Property and Competition (IIC) 2009, No 4, pp. 371–372.

189 See: *C. Barnard*, The Substantive Law of the EU, p. 147. Also see: *G. Anagnostaras*, The Unfair Commercial Practices Directive in context: From legal disparity to legal complexity, Common Market Law Review 2010, No 47(1), pp. 156–160.

It is important to add that the above-mentioned development concerning presumptions has also been reflected in the case law of the CJEU (starting with the Total Belgium judgement). According to C. Barnard, if, in assessing the provisions of Belgian law in the case concerning the prohibition of tied offers examined in the *Total Belgium*[190] case, the existing interpretation set out in the Keck judgement were adopted, the provisions of national law assessed in that judgement would be compatible with EU law. However, if the assessment had been made on the basis of Directive 2005/29/EC, the result would have been different.

§ 5. Conclusions

Attempts have been made at various levels to harmonise European law against unfair competition. In international law, the Paris Convention remains the basic legal instrument. Its role has been significant and has had a major impact on the current shape of European unfair competition law. Today, its role is limited. Poland, as well as other EU Member States, has developed a much more elaborate system of protection against unfair behaviour (acts or omissions) by entrepreneurs in order to ensure fair competition. Those systems, in accordance with Article 10 ter of the Paris Convention, provide adequate remedies to effectively combat unfair competition. The Paris Convention does not directly address the issue of sales promotions. However, the conduct of a trader in relation to the promotion of goods or services may be a form of tort described in Article 10 bis (3) of the Paris Convention.

TRIPS is also of limited relevance as an element of harmonisation of European laws against unfair competition. Its role is limited to the protection of geographical indications and classified information. TRIPS does not apply to other acts of unfair competition. WIPO's work that culminated in the publication of the WIPO Model Provisions on protection against unfair competition is noteworthy. Of particular interest are the analyses that preceded the publication of these provisions. One has to agree with the view expressed in the literature that the model solutions presented in 1996 and drawn up on the basis of the 1994 analysis should now be revised, particularly because of

[190] Judgement in joined cases C-261/07 and C-299/07, *VTB-VAB NV v. Total Belgium NV, Galatea BVBA v. Sanoma Magazines Belgium NV*, pp. 3–4.

the changes in the approach to unfair competition law that have taken place in the European Union in recent years. To a large extent, they follow the implementation of Directive 2005/29/EC, which has necessitated changes in the basic concepts underlying the law against unfair competition in the EU Member States. Consequently, it is proposed to carry out a further analysis (research) of the legal situation of unfair competition law, which may shed new light on the model solutions presented so far.[191] It should be noted that such a position was already taken in the literature in 2007. Today it is even more justified. It seems that the solutions proposed by WIPO should be formulated differently and should also refer to the solutions adopted in EU law.

The failure to adopt a regulation on sales promotions should be seen as a major failure that could have had an impact on the current shape of EU law on unfair competition. It should be emphasised that while work on the regulation in question was underway, work on the draft Directive on Unfair Commercial Practices was going on in parallel. As it turned out, the chances of the regulation being adopted were slim, as many Member States rejected the proposed draft. An agreement was reached on the Directive, and the work was completed.

J. Stuyck noted that the scope of the enacted Directive 2005/29/EC is very broad, as can be seen from the definition of unfair commercial practices, and that although the draft regulation could not be enacted, the issues covered in it with regard to the consumer-to-consumer (B2C) relations were in fact covered by the Directive. The author argued that there was a contradiction between the solutions provided for in the proposal for a regulation and the Directive. On the one hand, the proposed regulation defined the conditions for the admissibility of sales promotions (Article 3), while on the other hand, the Directive lists commercial practices that are considered unfair in all circumstances (Annex I of Directive 2005/29/EC). Thus, even if any restrictions on sales promotions regulated by national law were allowed under the provisions of the proposed regulation (Article 3(2)), in the absence of their qualification as unfair commercial practices under Directive 2005/29/EC, it

---

191 *M. Höpperger, M. Senftleben*, Protection Against Unfair Competition at the International Level, pp. 74–76.

could not be argued that these restrictions are justified in B2C relations. This is due to the maximum nature of the Directive.[192]

However, one may wonder whether the proposal for a regulation did not, nevertheless, identify some general trends in sales promotions that should have been taken into account during the legislative work at the national level. The current case law of the CJEU is precisely moving towards a liberalisation of the rules on the applicability of sales promotions, including bonus sales. This position was, as shown above, also adopted in the work on the proposal for a regulation.

In parallel to the work on the proposal for a regulation and Directive 2005/29/EC, work was also underway on amendments to the Polish law on combatting unfair competition. In 2002, a draft amendment of the Act on Combatting Unfair Competition was presented. In the explanatory memorandum to the amendment, it was emphasised that the French solutions found in Article L 121-35 of the *Code de la consomation* had served as a model for the Polish amendment.[193] Those solutions placed a ban on promotional sales (*vente ou offere*), in the event when the free bonus was not the same as the main object of sale.

The fact that the legislator did not take into account the scope of the proposed regulation when amending the Polish Act on Combatting Unfair Competition must be viewed negatively. In 2002, Poland was not yet an EU Member State, but the prospect of its accession to the EU was already imminent. It would therefore have been reasonable to take into account the legislative work in progress in the Union. This was important because the solutions adopted by the Polish legislator in the amendment turned out to be fundamentally different from those proposed and considered by the EU legislator. If certain EU trends had been taken into account even then, today's discussion on whether to repeal the provisions on bonus sales in the Polish Act on Unfair Competition would be pointless.

It should be added that Polish scholars were familiar with the proposal for the regulation. It was easy to see that 'Polish legislation differs from the

---

192 See: *J. Stuyck*, The Unfair Commercial Practices, p. 171.

193 See Explanatory Memorandum to the draft law in the Government draft law on amending the Act on combatting unfair competition. Parliamentary paper of the 4th term No 375 of 10.4.2002 p. 4, <http://orka.sejm.gov.pl/proc4.nsf/opisy/375.htm> (accessed on 1.2.2025).

proposed Community solutions. The amendment to the Act on Combatting Unfair Competition (...) introduced changes that limited the possibility of carrying out promotions and prohibited them in certain situations'.[194] At the same time, it must be noted that Poland's situation with regard to sales promotions was different from that of other Member States, which had banned sales promotions many years before the proposal for a Regulation. This is because 'it was only after the period of political transformation and the introduction of a free market economy that Poland came to grips with the phenomenon of sales promotions and associated with them aggressive practices of traders'.[195] It is also pointed out that in Poland in 2001 the existing legislation allowed a purchase to be rewarded with a gift or a promotional gift to be given. This, however, as is argued, threatened the functioning of fair market rules and the interests of consumers.[196]

It seems that the different factual situation in Poland, where the institution of sales promotions was just taking shape, led to different legislative assumptions. When liberalisation of sales promotion regulations was being considered at the EU level and in the Member States, the Polish legislator introduced regulations that strictly regulated the permissibility of sales promotions, including bonus sales.

---

194 See *J. Wrona*, Promocje sprzedaży, in: *C. Banasiński* (ed.), Standardy wspólnotowe w polskim prawie ochrony konsumenta, Warszawa 2004, p. 120.

195 Zob. *ibidem*, p. 119.

196 Zob. *R. Stefanicki*, Prawne granice swobody przedsiębiorcy w odniesieniu do reklamy "wartościowej", Prawo Spółek 2001, No 3, p. 45.

Chapter II

The Subject Matter and Scope of the Act on Combatting Unfair Competition

§1. Sources of the Polish Act on Combatting Unfair Competition

I. Introductory Remarks

The first legislation addressing unfair competition in Poland was the Act of 2 August 1926 on combatting unfair competition,[197] subsequently replaced by the Act of 16 April 1993 on Combatting Unfair Competition. The provisions of the latter Act (the 1993 Act) constitute the basic, albeit not the only[198] source of the regulations of laws against unfair competition in force in Poland today.

When Directive 2005/29/EC on unfair commercial practices came into force, Poland, already then a Member of the European Union, was under the

---

[197] Dz.U. No 9, item 559, as amended. The Act was intended to unify regulations on unfair competition throughout Poland. On the need to introduce the Act on Combatting Unfair Competition see also *M. Mayzel*, O zwalczaniu nieuczciwej konkurencji, Przegląd Prawa Handlowego (PPH) 1926, No 5, pp. 193–201; and by the same author O zwalczaniu nieuczciwej konkurencji (Dokończenie), PPH 1926, No 8, pp. 339–345.

[198] There are also other laws that apply to combatting unfair competition. See *J. Szwaja, A. Kubiak-Cyrul*, in: *J. Szwaja, J. Kępiński* (eds), Ustawa o zwalczaniu nieuczciwej konkurencji, Warszawa 2024, p. 32–33, Nb. 56 in which the authors distinguish 5 groups of regulations.

obligation to implement it in the Polish legal system. Consequently, the Act on Counteracting Unfair Market Practices implementing the Directive was adopted in 2007, prompting discussions among scholars on the relationship between the two Acts, i.e. the Act on Combatting Unfair Competition of 1993 and the Act on Counteracting Unfair Market Practices of 2007.[199]

There were doubts as to the subject matter and the scope of both Acts[200] as well as their purpose. The considerations undertaken here are an attempt to resolve the controversies raised in the literature.

II. Historical outline

The first Polish law addressing unfair competition was the Act of 2 August 1926 on combatting unfair competition. Its adoption was preceded by a draft of the 'Act on the Rights on Business Enterprises and on Combatting Unfair Competition'[201] drawn up by F. Zoll, who claimed that it was to be 'a full realisation of the civil law approach to the fight against unfair competition – an approach based on the recognition of an entrepreneur's subjective right'. Initially, the Act met with criticism, which was primarily directed at the changes introduced in the legislative process by the Senate. As a result of the criticism, certain modifications were made and implemented by the Regulation of the President of the Republic of 17 September 1927.[202] The amended Act entered into force 14 days after its promulgation, on 10 October 1926. With its entry into force, the German legislative Act of 7 June 1909 on unfair competition ceased to be binding.[203] The Act of 1926 remained

---

[199] See *R. Skubisz*, Cele i zakres zastosowania ustawy, pp. 563–579, *M. Namysłowska*, O konieczności uchylenia ustawy, pp. 382–400; *T. Targosz*, Ustawa o przeciwdziałaniu nieuczciwym praktykom rynkowym – model ochrony, zasady, zakres ochrony, implikacje dla systemu prawa konkurencji i konsumentów, in: *E. Nowińska*, *D. Kasprzycki* (eds), Nieuczciwe praktyki rynkowe. Ocena regulacji, Kraków 2012, pp. 29–52; *A. Tischner*, Miejsce implementacji dyrektywy, pp. 53–63, and *J. Szwaja*, *A. Tischner*, Dokąd zmierza prawo zwalczania nieuczciwej konkurencji, pp. 499–513.

[200] See *B. Giesen*, Przedmiot ochrony przewidzianej ustawą o zwalczaniu nieuczciwej konkurencji, Monitor Prawnicy (MoP) – dodatek 2014, No 6, pp. 34–38, and *F. Henning-Bodewig*, Der Schutzzweck, p. 238.

[201] For more, see: *M. Mayzel*, O zwalczaniu nieuczciwej konkurencji, No 8, pp. 339–345.

[202] Dz.U. No 84, item 749.

[203] For more on the legislative work on the Act on combatting unfair competition of 1926, see *T. Dolata*, The Fight Against Unfair Competition in Poland in the Years

in force until 1939.[204] After WW2, when under the new regime socialised entrepreneurs did not compete, the Act, although in force, was never referred to or applied.[205]

Worth mentioning here is the resolution of the Constitutional Court (*Trybunał Konstytucyjny*) of 23 January 1991,[206] which repealed Articles 6–12 of the 1926 Act, thus ending definitely the dispute on the applicability of its remaining articles. Of particular importance was the fact that the Court rejected the opinion that the whole Act had been repealed by *desuetude*, which points out the doubts before the Constitutional Court as to the clarity of the legal situation then in force and its compatibility with the international standards. This was even more important because the Treaty with the United States of 21 March 1990[207] imposed far-reaching obligations on Poland in terms of protection against unfair competition, particularly with respect to manufacturing and trade secrets. The Court's resolution was not, however, without flaws, since it had left room for a prejudgment that criminal law provisions of the repealed Articles 6–12 of the Act remained nevertheless enforceable under civil law. It must be admitted, however, that the overall content of the Constitutional Court's resolution corresponded to the postulates of the doctrine on the validity of this Act.

1918–1939, Wroclaw Review of Law, Administration & Economics 2012, vol. 2, No 1, pp. 16–27.

[204] See *M. Kępiński, J. Kępiński*, Z historii prawa nieuczciwej konkurencji – międzywojenne orzecznictwo Sądu Najwyższego, in: *A. Matlak, S. Stanisławska-Koc* (eds), Spory o własność intelektualną. Księga jubileuszowa dedykowana Profesorom Januszowi Barcie i Ryszardowi Markiewiczowi, Warszawa 2013, pp. 443–463.

[205] See *J. Szwaja, A. Kubiak-Cyrul*, in: *J. Szwaja, J. Kępiński* (eds), Ustawa o zwalczaniu nieuczciwej konkurencji, Warszawa 2024, pp. 28–30.

[206] Resolution of the Constitutional Court of 23.1.1991 (W 4/90, Legalis) regarding the interpretation of Article V of the Act of 19.4.1969—provisions introducing the Penal Code. See *M. Kępiński*, Problemy ogólne ustawy o zwalczaniu nieuczciwej konkurencji, Ruch Prawniczy Ekonomiczny i Socjologiczny (RPEiS) 1994, No 2, pp. 1–12. The author refers to the Court's resolution of 23.1.1991 in which it was determined that Article V of the 1969 Act had not repealed the Act of 1926 in its entirety but only repealed the articles that provided for criminal liability.

[207] The Treaty on Trade and Economic Relations between the Republic of Poland and the United States of America, drawn up in Washington on 21.3.1990 (Dz.U. 1994 No 97, item 467).

The judgement of the Supreme Court of 14 June 1988,[208] delivered prior to the resolution of the Constitutional Court, also needs attention, as it had been the first time in the post-war period that the Supreme Court held that the Act of 1926 on combatting unfair competition had not been repealed by the Provisions introducing the Criminal Code.[209] In particular, it was explained that Article 2 of the 1926 Act remained in force and the operative part of the Supreme Court's ruling was based on this provision and on the provisions of the Paris Convention. In this way, the Supreme Court rightly pointed out that international obligations binding Poland required an extensive system of protection against unfair competition.

The Act of 1926 on combatting unfair competition was eventually repealed with the entry into force of the still-binding Act of 1993 on Combatting Unfair Competition. As it was emphasised, a new regulation was necessary because the Act of 1926 was an obsolete piece of legislation that did not meet the modern needs. It was also argued that the earlier Act fostered the interests of entrepreneurs only, ignoring consumers' interests, and failed to take into account a handful of conducts that also classified as acts of unfair competition, and, what was more, it failed to provide for sanctions under criminal law.[210] Also, the international obligations undertaken by Poland required an amended regulation.[211] However, as it is pointed out in literature, efforts were made to nevertheless preserve in the new regulation the spirit of the provisions of the former Act.[212]

---

[208] Judgement of the Supreme Court of 14.6.1988, II CR 367/87, OSP 1990, No 9, item 328.

[209] Article V § 1 and 2 of the Act of 19.4.1969—Provisions introducing the Penal Code. Pursuant to Article V § 1 specific legislative acts issued before 5.9.1939 and other legislation having the force of an Act and providing for criminal liability has been repealed.

[210] Explanatory memorandum to the draft Act, Druk sejmowy I kadencji No 278 of 18.5.1992, p. 2, biblioteka.sejm.gov.pl, hereinafter referred to as Rationale for the draft Act of 1993.

[211] First and foremost it was the adoption of the Treaty on Trade and Economic Relations between the Republic of Poland and the United States of America, drawn up in Washington on 21.3.1990 (Dz. U. 1994, No. 97, item 467) and the Interim Agreement on Trade and Trade-related Matters between the Republic of Poland and the European Economic Community and the European Coal and Steel Community, drawn up in Brussels on 16.12.1991 (Dz.U. of 1992 No 17, item 69).

[212] *M. Kępiński*, Problemy ogólne nowej ustawy, p. 3.

The legislative work aimed at the modernisation of the existing provisions began in 1991, and in May 1992, a government bill on the 'prevention and combatting unfair competition'[213] was tabled. Eventually, on 16 April 1993, the new Act on Combatting Unfair Competition was adopted, and it has remained in force to this day, together with several amendments.[214] When implemented, it was considered as a modern piece of legislation, drawn up to contemporary European standards.[215]

The Act of 1993 belongs to the group of Germanic laws, but its final form was also influenced by the laws of Switzerland and Spain. In the Germanic model, in addition to the individual delicts of unfair competition (Articles 5–17), a general clause is included (Article 3).[216]

The other basic legislative Act currently shaping Polish competition law since 21 December 2007 is the Act on Counteracting Unfair Market Practices as amended, implementing Directive 2005/29/EC.

§ 2. The Subject Matter and Scope of the Acts on Combatting Unfair Competition of 1926 and 1993

I. The Act on Combatting Unfair Competition of 1926

1. The Subject Matter

The Act on combatting unfair competition of 1926 concerned the protection of the rights of entrepreneurs under civil law (Articles 1–5) and criminalised certain acts of unfair competition (Articles 6–12).[217]

---

[213] Explanatory memorandum, Druk sejmowy Nr 278, biblioteka.sejm.gov.pl. About legislative process See *J. Szwaja*, *A. Kubiak-Cyrul*, in: *J. Szwaja*, *J. Kępiński* (eds), Ustawa o zwalczaniu nieuczciwej konkurencji, Warszawa 2024, pp. 28–30.

[214] See *J. Szwaja*, Ostatnie nowelizacje ustawy o zwalczaniu nieuczciwej konkurencji, part I, MoP 2002, No 24; and of the same author, Ostatnie nowelizacje ustawy o zwalczaniu nieuczciwej konkurencji, part II, MoP 2003, No 1; and Kolejne nowelizacje ustawy o zwalczaniu nieuczciwej konkurencji (between 2003–2013), in: *J. Szwaja* (ed.), Dwadzieścia lat ustawy o zwalczaniu nieuczciwej konkurencji, MoP-dodatek 2014, No 6, pp. 3–8.

[215] *M. Kępiński*, Problemy ogólne nowej ustawy, p. 12.

[216] For more see: *ibidem*, pp. 3–5.

[217] Uwagi na temat ZNKU1926 *A. Peretz*, Z powodu ustawy o zwalczaniu nieuczciwej konkurencji (Głos kupca), PPH 1926, No 9, pp. 396–410.

The fundamental aim of the Act was to protect the entrepreneur. Pursuant to Article 1(1), 'an entrepreneur has the right to demand that another entrepreneur (competitor) does not penetrate his clientele by any act capable of creating the misleading impression in the persons to whom he offers his products, goods or services that they originate from the first entrepreneur'.

It was also pointed out that acts of unfair competition might turn against consumers. However, in such a case, customers usually suffered only minor damages, and therefore taking legal action was considered impractical. Protection could be sought under criminal law instead.[218] Already in the comments to the Act, it was explained that its provisions were intended to 'keep an eye on both, the rights of entrepreneurs and of consumers'. In the case of the latter, however, it was assumed that their interest should be protected by criminal law provisions, hence the adoption of Articles 6, 7, and 8.[219] Although, as explained in the explanatory memorandum to the draft Act, Article 6 covered acts of unfair competition with respect to which an entrepreneur could rely on Article 1 to pursue certain claims under civil law, the difference between the provisions of those two articles concerned the protected interest. While Article 6 concerned unfair competition acts against public interest and thus protected the public, the consumers, and the customers, the protection of an entrepreneur was to be sought by reference to the provisions of Article 1.[220] M. Mayzel also emphasised that the civil law sanctions provided for in the Act were predominantly in the interest of the harmed entrepreneur (competitor), while the criminal law sanctions were intended first and foremost to protect the interest of the consumer, i.e. the public interest.[221] On the other hand, in the situation of a violation of

---

218 *A. Kraus, F. Zoll*, Polska ustawa o zwalczaniu nieuczciwej konkurencji, pp. 24–25.

219 See: Explanatory memorandum to the draft Act of 1926, Druk sejmowy No 2448 of 7.5.1926, p. 7, and also *A. Kraus, F. Zoll*, Polska ustawa o zwalczaniu nieuczciwej konkurencji, p. 93.

220 Explanatory memorandum to the Act of 1926, Druk sejmowy No 2448 of 7.5.1926 r., p. 14.

221 *M. Mayzel*, O zwalczaniu nieuczciwej konkurencji, No 5, pp. 193–201; by the same author O zwalczaniu nieuczciwej konkurencji, No 8, p. 342. As an example, the reasons for adopting Article 6 of the Act of 1926, may be referred to as it follows from them that its provisions were to foster 'the interest of the public, the recipients and the consumers and therefore the public interest and not the interest of the harmed entrepreneur or entrepreneurs'. See *A. Kraus, F. Zoll*, Polska ustawa o zwalczaniu

competitors' rights, protection under criminal law should be of an auxiliary nature, limited only to gross infringements (Articles 9 and 10). As pointed out in the explanatory memorandum, the offences listed in Articles 9 and 10 did not apply to consumers but to entrepreneurs. Hence, the public interest was considered second in importance, and criminal proceedings could be initiated at the request of the injured party. However, where protection of an entrepreneur against unfair competition was at stake, the solutions available under civil law, i.e. claims on grounds of a failure to act and address the damages, were to be resorted to.[222]

A. Krause and F. Zoll proposed a subjective entrepreneur's right to the enterprise.[223] In this concept, the enterprise was treated as an intangible good, to which an entrepreneur had an absolute title. They argued that the good protected was an enterprise as such, in the broadest sense of the term, that is to say 'each distinct economic unit separated from the entrepreneur's person as an object of property, organised for the purpose of providing services to various persons (recipients, consumers, customers) against payment (in particular, the supply of goods and products)'.[224] An enterprise was therefore an object of rights, while the subject of the law was an entrepreneur (a natural or legal person).

The two authors also explained that the Act of 1926 was not limited to instances in which an entrepreneur could be distinguished from an enterprise but also covered the so-called liberal professions, i.e. a sphere in which someone personally, in a professional manner, and for a profit satisfied the needs of others. Moreover, when doing so, a member of the liberal profession was not obliged to have a separate establishment with which the clientele would be connected and which could be sold as an enterprise. The provisions

---

nieuczciwej konkurencji, p. 255, and also Explanatory memorandum to the Act of 1926, Druk sejmowy No 2448 of 7.5.1926. p. 7.

222 See, together with the explanatory notes in *A. Kraus, F. Zoll*, Polska ustawa o zwalczaniu nieuczciwej konkurencji, p. 25.

223 Explanatory memorandum to the draft Act of 1926, Druk sejmowy No 2448 of 7.5.1926, pp. 8–9. Also see *J. Dauman*, O "nieuczciwej konkurencji" *de lege ferenda*, Miesięcznik Prawa Handlowego i Wekslowego 1937, No 5–8, pp. 152–155. This approach was challenged by *M. Kępiński*, Problemy ogólne nowej ustawy, pp. 9–10, who argued that protection under the Act of 1996 was of delict nature even if the event of certain delicts certain absolute subjective rights were capable of being created.

224 See *A. Kraus, F. Zoll*, Polska ustawa o zwalczaniu nieuczciwej konkurencji, pp. 28–31.

of the Act could also be applied to entrepreneurs without an enterprise, in which case there is no enterprise, but there is an entrepreneur. Hence, based on the Act of 1926, it was possible to construct the 'absolute property rights of an entrepreneur'.[225]

And yet, certain liberal professions had nevertheless been excluded from its scope, and as stated in Article 13, the Act did 'not apply to combatting unfair competition in respect of liberal professions which have a statutorily regulated organisation allowing to punish unfair competition by means of disciplinary measures'.[226]

It must be added that to the extent that international agreements[227] did not otherwise regulate it (Article 14), the Act also protected, within the scope of the existing reciprocity, foreigners whose enterprises had no registered offices in the Republic of Poland.

2. The Scope of the Act

It was emphasised in the literature on the subject that the concept of unfair competition was defined very broadly and therefore was capable of covering various spheres of life, including social, political, and even family life. The Act itself, however, referred only to 'free competition in gainful activity, and

225 General explanatory memorandum to the draft Act of 1926, Druk sejmowy No 2448, p. 7. Also see *A. Kraus, F. Zoll*, Polska ustawa o zwalczaniu nieuczciwej konkurencji, p. 40. Decision of the Supreme Court of 10.1.1936, C. III 520/34, in: Orzeczenia Izby Cywilnej 1936, issue VI, item 450 where it was determined that a commercial agent/broker exercising a liberal profession was an entrepreneur.

226 The exclusion was done at the request of the Bar. This does not mean, however, that a lawyer cannot take action against a non-lawyer when the non-lawyer has committed the tort of unfair competition. *A. Kraus, F. Zoll*, Polska ustawa o zwalczaniu nieuczciwej konkurencji, pp. 40–41. See also judgement of the Supreme Court of 25.5.1931, III 2 N. 50/31, OSP 1932, vol. XI, item 252 concerning the disciplinary responsibility of a patent agent.

227 The literature on the subject explained that a legislative act of international law could be the Paris Convention of 1883, or the commercial treaty concluded between Poland and France in 1925. It was also clarified that protection against unfair competition was to be enjoyed by foreign nationals in the same way as Polish nationals, regardless of whether protection against unfair competition had already been introduced in their country of origin under Article 10 bis of the Paris Convention. See *A. Kraus, F. Zoll*, Polska ustawa o zwalczaniu nieuczciwej konkurencji, pp. 320–323.

only insofar as the wage-earner in his own name, and not as an employee of another person, satisfies the needs of the clientele'.[228]

Adopting the construction of an absolute property right on an enterprise, two categories of acts of unfair competition were distinguished. One included acts involving misappropriation (in various ways) of the enterprise's attractive power and, consequently, of its clientele (Articles 1 and 2), which consisted of misrepresentation as to the origin of goods and services from another entrepreneur.

The other category of acts was defined in Article 3 of the Act. Those acts did not involve misappropriation of the attractive power of an enterprise or penetration of the clientele of another entrepreneur but causing damage to the entrepreneur through acts contrary to the binding legal regulations or good practice (business integrity).[229] Examples of such acts included dissemination of false information about the enterprise, encouraging personnel to abstain from fulfilling their duties, or disclosing company secrets.[230]

It was presumed further that the protection arising from Article 3 was not conditional on whether the action of the person harming the entrepreneur was intended to pursue competitive objectives.[231]

Article 4, on the other hand, regulated unfair misrepresentation (creating the impression) as to the origin of the goods or services from a certain geographical area or the entrepreneur's membership of an association of entrepreneurs. Such an act was considered unfair if the 'power of attraction to the enterprise' resulted from the fact that certain goods or services offered by the entrepreneur originated from a certain geographical area or that the entrepreneur belonged to a certain association of entrepreneurs, while in

---

228 *Ibidem*, p. 39.

229 The decision of the Supreme Court of 8.5.1992 may be recalled (I ACr 273/92, Legalis) in which the Court determined that pursuant to Article 3 of the Act of 1926 unfair advertising must be assessed in the light of its provisions.

230 For more extensive comments on Article 3 see: *J. Namitkiewicz*, Uwagi nad polską ustawą o zwalczaniu nieuczciwej konkurencji, PPH 1926, No 6, pp. 241–245.

231 See judgements of the Supreme Court of 10.1.1936, C III 520/34, in Zb.Orz. SN 1936, vol. XIII, item 450. Whereas in the judgment of 20.5.1932 (I C 2564/31 in Zb.Orz. SN 1932, vol. 1, item 111) the Court held that the condition necessary to apply Article 3 is 'is not only the existence of an economic advantage enjoyed by one competitor over another, which is in itself a normal course of business and not prohibited by law, but the use of that advantage with the intention of driving the competitor to ruin'.

reality the goods or services were not related to a geographical area or the entrepreneur did not belong to an association of entrepreneurs. Provision of false information to entrepreneurs belonging to certain associations of entrepreneurs or the disclosure of their trade secrets was also considered an act of unfair competition.[232] Legal action could be brought by entrepreneurs operating in the same geographical district who manufactured products of the same kind, their joint representations, as well as any entrepreneur selling such products.

It was further argued the Act also covered infringements of copyright and industrial property rights. However, it was considered that there was a *lex specialis-lex generali* relationship between the provisions of the Act of 1926 and provisions of other legislative acts adopted to address other infringements of rights. Therefore, individual acts of violation were first assessed based on the specific provisions of other relevant legislation, and only when impossible to be qualified within their scope, they were recognised in the light of the provisions of the Act of 1926.[233]

The scope of the Act was broad and concerned acts of unfair competition in various forms of economic activity, including farming, forestry and mining, as well as agriculture, forestry, and mining.[234]

The primary objective of the Act was to protect the attractive power of an enterprise, i.e. the ability of an enterprise to attract and win customers or recipients owing to its organisation, its characteristics or successful advertising. Both the attractive power of the enterprise as such and the attractive power of the enterprise resulting from the geographical region of its origin or its membership in certain associations were to be protected.

The legislative objective of the Act of 1926 was primarily to prevent acts of unfair competition (unfairness of competition) by one entrepreneur directed against another entrepreneur. As emphasised in the literature, 'repression of

---

232 *A. Kraus, F. Zoll*, Polska ustawa o zwalczaniu nieuczciwej konkurencji, p. 41 and pp. 33–38; *M. Mayzel*, O zwalczaniu nieuczciwej konkurencji, No 5, pp. 193–201 and by the same author, O zwalczaniu nieuczciwej konkurencji, No 8, p. 340.

233 *A. Kraus, F. Zoll*, Polska ustawa o zwalczaniu nieuczciwej konkurencji, p. 41 and pp. 92–111. Different forms of the convergence of different legislative acts have been presented in it.

234 The adopted regulation arose from the scope of the German Act on combatting unfair competition of 1909.

unfair competition that will be vigorous, strong and comprehensive should become one of our primary tasks'.[235] It was also explained that an act of unfair competition occurred when 'competition exceeds the boundaries set by the general interest and infringes the economic freedom and interests of other individuals by using methods contrary to accepted good practices in a given environment'.[236] In this way, an entrepreneur whose rights to the enterprise (its attractive power) were violated by another entrepreneur (a competitor) was granted protection against such an act of unfair competition. The power of these provisions under criminal law was of an auxiliary character and was also considered as a form of customer protection.[237] Such an interpretation of the Act also transpires in the case law of the Supreme Court, in which a number of judgements, delivered between 1919 and 1939, may be found and which involved a variety of disputes between business competitors subsequently settled under civil law regulations. Criminal law provisions were referred to rather occasionally, and never in matters involving the protection of consumer rights. The Act clearly served to protect fair competition among entrepreneurs.

It is currently being raised in the literature that the Act of 1926 was initially intended exclusively to protect the interests of entrepreneurs operating in the market rather than the customers or consumers' interests. And yet, already in the 30s of the 20th century, first among German legal scholars, there emerged views that the law against unfair competition was not only to protect particular interests of an entrepreneur but also had a social role of protecting fair competition considered as a good in itself. Consequently, placing an entrepreneur in the central position would be contrary to the very

---

235 *Ibidem*, p. 16.

236 *J. Dauman*, O "nieuczciwej konkurencji," p. 153. Also see *M. Mayzel*, O zwalczaniu nieuczciwej konkurencji, No 8, p. 339.

237 Judicial decisions concerning the interpretation of criminal provisions related to the violation of Articles 6, 9 and 10 of the Act of 1926 of: 4.4.1932, of 20.10.1932, of 23.1.1933, and of 16.4.1936. The Supreme Court confirmed in the reasons for the judgement that 'The driving idea behind the Act was to protect the entrepreneur from the competition of another entrepreneur for the sake of all, even future customers', see judgment of the Supreme Court of 20.10.1932, II 3 K 748/32.

essence of competition because protection also lies in the interest of other participants of the economic life.[238]

J. Szwaja and A. Kubiak-Cyrul claimed that also the Act of 1926 focused on the protection of competitors, and as the competition law developed in Poland, it was established that indeed the provisions of the Act on combatting unfair practices adopted in 1926 were intended not only to protect the entrepreneur but also the consumer and the general public.[239]

Thus, it should be kept in mind that, albeit incidentally, the Act of 1926 noted the need to protect the consumer whose interest was identified with the public interest. Consequently, although the Polish legislator had provided first and foremost for the possibility to protect the interest of entrepreneurs, he also sought to ensure that competition was seen to have a positive impact on the entire economic turnover. In this way, the situation of the consumer would also be fair. Having said that, it is still clear that the main purpose of the Act was to ensure protection of the entrepreneur (or the attractive power of an enterprise).[240]

As a consequence of this, the Act granted active legitimation (standing) only to the entrepreneur, not his clientele or consumers. Article 1(2) and (3) of the Act of 1926 provided that in a situation of a violation of rights, the aggrieved entrepreneur could apply for the cessation of wrongful acts, the elimination of causes likely to create confusion on the part of the public, the surrender of unjust enrichment, or compensation and damages in the event of malice or obvious negligence. Moreover, some scholars argued that in a situation described in Article 4 (geographical indications), entrepreneurs' collective standing (*actio popularis*) was allowed as well. Indeed, claims for the protection of 'collective exclusivity' could be brought by the manufacturers, their joint representation (if it had the capacity to sue), and any entrepreneur selling the products in question.[241]

---

238 See *B. Giesen*, Przedmiot ochrony przewidzianej ustawą, pp. 35–36 and the literature quoted therein.

239 See *J. Szwaja, A. Kubiak-Cyrul*, in: *J. Szwaja, J. Kępiński* (eds), Ustawa o zwalczaniu nieuczciwej konkurencji, 2024, pp. 71–73.

240 A view expressed by *F. Zoll – M. Szydło*, Introduction in: *M. Zdyb, M. Sieradzka* (eds), Ustawa o zwalczaniu nieuczciwej konkurencji. Komentarz, Warszawa 2016, p. 31.

241 *A. Kraus, F. Zoll*, Polska ustawa o zwalczaniu nieuczciwej konkurencji, p. 128 and pp. 232–235.

The passive legitimation was primarily for entrepreneurs (competitors) referred to in Article 1 as 'entrepreneurs wrongdoers' who had fraudulently encroached on the clientele of another entrepreneur or who had participated in the unlawful encroachment on the clientele of the wronged party.[242] In such a situation, their liability was joint and several.

II. The Act on Combatting Unfair Competition of 1993

1. The Purpose of the Act

Right from the onset of the legislative work on the draft[243] of the 1993 Act on Combatting Unfair Competition (the Act of 1993), it was proposed that it also prohibit unfair competition in economic activity, including in particular industrial and agricultural production, construction, trading, and services, in the interests of the public, entrepreneurs, and customers, and especially consumers. These proposals were adopted in their original wording as drafted and are now contained in the text of the new Act enacted in 1993.

It is evident from the Explanatory memorandum to the draft Act of 1993 that the goal of the legislator was to secure a place for fair competition as a main principle governing the economy and to ensure the fair nature of competition. Accordingly, the new law was intended to eliminate unfair practices that might exist in economic activity and that otherwise would lead to its deformation and adulteration. It was argued that Article 1 expressed 'the thought of comprehensiveness of the proposed regulation by having taken into account the general, business, and consumer interests. Therefore it implies that a violation of any of the listed interests is of equal importance for the recognition of an action as an act of unfair competition'.[244] As can be seen, when creating the Act, the legislator had in mind the public interest, the interest of entrepreneurs, and the interest of customers and consumers in particular.

---

[242] However, the catalogue of claims was limited because the harmed entrepreneur could not sue on grounds of unjust enrichment.

[243] Explanatory memorandum to the Act of 1993, Druk sejmowy I kadencji No 278 of 18.5.1992.

[244] Explanatory memorandum to the Act of 1993, Druk sejmowy I kadencji No 278 of 18.5.1992, p. 3.

However, in consequence of the coming into force of the Act on Counteracting Unfair Practices,[245] the phrase 'and consumers in particular' contained in Article 1 of the Act on Combatting Unfair Competition of 1993 was deleted. Thereby, now, according to the literal wording of its Article 1, the Act of 1993 aims to protect the public interest, the interest of entrepreneurs, and the interest of customers. This raises the fundamental question of what impact this legislative amendment should have on the objectives and interpretation of its provisions.

It has been argued in the literature that the above amendment does not have a significant impact on the scope of protection, as the broad understanding of the notion of 'customer' allows it to include in it consumers as well, and even other entities in the trade.[246] Such an interpretation is justified because, despite the amendment of Article 1, the Act retains other regulations that also directly refer to acts of unfair competition having the potential of harming the interests of consumers. The best example of this is Article 17a, which is the only one that directly refers to consumers (i.e. the sale of goods and services to consumers in combination with the granting of a bonus) and in which the phrase 'consumer' is used. The other provisions, although not specified in wording, also indirectly refer to ensuring that the consumer is not misled. This provision may be interpreted as the obligation to properly label a business (Articles 5–7), to present accurate information as to the origin of goods and services (Articles 8 and 9), to ensure the specific characteristics of goods or services (Article 10), or to not be allowed to copy finished products (Article 13). It also means extensive regulations on advertising (Article 16). Hence, the assumption that in the Act of 1993 the consumer's interest is indirectly protected is correct.

On the other hand, it may be argued that the deletion of the phrase 'and consumers in particular' expresses the legislator's intention to determine clearly and in a manner that does not leave room for ambiguity which or

---

245 See Article 18 of Act on Counteracting Unfair Practices (original text Dz.U. of 2007 No 171, item 1206).

246 *B. Giesen*, Przedmiot ochrony przewidzianej ustawą, p. 36, also *A. Tischner*, Cele i zakres zastosowania ZNKU, in: *M. Kępiński* (ed.), System Prawa Prywatnego, vol. 15, Prawo konkurencji, Warszawa 2014, p. 104.

whose interests are to be protected under the adopted Act.[247] However, such an interpretation is not fully justified, as in my view all protected interests are equally important and treated equally in the Act of 1993. The deletion of the phrase 'consumers in particular' can only indicate that consumer interests are as important as the interests of other customers, i.e. non-consumers (see further below). Thus, one may formulate a thesis that the legislator did not see the need, as regards the Act on Combatting Unfair Competition of 1993, to emphasise the special importance of consumer protection, as consumers' interest is protected on an equal footing with the interest of other market participants. Under current legislation, consumers are not a particularly privileged group.

2. The Subject Matter of the Act. Protected Interests

A. Public Interest

One of the objectives of the Act on Combatting Unfair Competition identified in the first place is to protect the public interest.[248] The Act leaves the concept of 'public interest' undefined. An attempt to clarify it is therefore necessary.

According to the dictionary definition, the term 'public' means 'pertaining to the whole of society or a certain collectivity'. Thus, the public interest should concern the entire community and collectivity, and not the interest of individual entities (entrepreneurs or customers).

It is also argued that pursuant to the Act in question, the public interest 'consists in the preservation of competition being one of the "flywheels" of the economy, and in its proper and effective, as well as lawful, fair and unadulterated operation'.[249] Other scholars have expressed opinions, when referring to the case law of the antitrust court, that the public interest must

---

[247] See *J. Szwaja*, *A. Kubiak-Cyrul*, in: *J. Szwaja* (ed.), Ustawa o zwalczaniu nieuczciwej konkurencji. Komentarz, Warszawa 2016, p. 78.

[248] *A. Tischner* notes that the Act on Combatting Unfair Competition is a private-law regulation, and therefore, it is questionable whether under its provisions the protection of the public interest is justified. Furthermore, she argues that the Act does not provide for measures to directly protect the public interest. The public interest is primarily protected in the Act on Competition and Consumer Protection. *A. Tischner*, Cele i zakres zastosowania ZNKU, p. 100, Nb 20.

[249] *J. Szwaja*, *A. Kubiak-Cyrul*, in: *J. Szwaja*, *J. Kępiński* (eds), Ustawa o zwalczaniu nieuczciwej konkurencji, 2024, p. 79, Nb 32.

be understood broadly, as 'the interest of the many unidentified entities factually affected by the offender's behaviour'.[250] Similar opinions are shared by courts of law that base their judgements on the provisions of the Act on Competition and Consumer Protection,[251] arguing that the public interest consists in ensuring proper conditions for the market operation and that it applies to the public in general, not only an individual or a selected group of entities. The Supreme Court, on the other hand, determined in reference to the Act on Competition and Consumer Protection that the public interest is violated 'when the effects of certain actions are of a general nature, affecting all potential actors on a given market, and not only a strictly defined group. The public interest is violated when the prohibited actions restrict the proper conditions for the functioning of the market which otherwise enable competition to emerge and develop, where competition is understood as a phenomenon characterising the functioning of the economy'.[252]

The public interest in the Act on Combatting Unfair Competition should therefore be identified as an interest aimed at the development of the economy as a whole, based on lawful competition and built on reciprocal fairness. The opinion expressed in the literature that, when assessing the interests of the entrepreneur and the interests of the customer, the public interest should also be taken into account as a common point of reference when it comes to the assessment of individual interests of different entities is right.[253] This is because the interests of entrepreneurs and customers are coupled with the public interest. One may therefore agree that in a situation where there is a need to resolve a collision between the interest of entrepreneurs or customers and the public interest, the public interest should be given decisive importance. Thus, theoretically, on the grounds of protecting the public interest,

---

[250] *M. Sieradzka*, in: *M. Zdyb*, *M. Sieradzka* (eds), Ustawa, Commentary to Article 1, p. 51, Nb 21.

[251] Dz.U. of 2024 item 1616 as amended.

[252] Ruling of the Supreme Court of 20.4.2017, III SK 21/16, Legalis. The case concerned practices restricting competition. Also see the ruling of the same Court of 16.10.2008 (III SK 2/08, Legalis) concerning what was still the Act on Counteracting Monopolistic Practices and Protection of Consumer Interests. (Dz.U. of 1995 No 80, item 405 as amended).

[253] *A. Tischner*, Cele i zakres zastosowania ZNKU, p. 100, Nb 20.

certain acts might be qualified as permissible, even though infringing on the entrepreneur's interest.

It should be added here that the Act on Combatting Unfair Competition as such does not provide for any special measures to protect the public interest. The public interest is primarily protected under the Act on Competition and Consumer Protection,[254] which follows from its Article 1(1), which provides that the Act 'defines the conditions for the development and protection of competition and the rules for the protection of the interests of entrepreneurs and consumers undertaken in the public interest'.

B. Entrepreneur's Interest

The basic concept defined under the Act on Combatting Unfair Competition is that of an 'entrepreneur'.

In Article 2 of the draft Act, it was proposed that the Act should apply 'to natural and legal persons and organisational units without legal personality which, in the course of their gainful or professional activity, participate in the economic activity (of entrepreneurs)'. Article 2(2) of the draft clarified that the Act was also to apply:

1) to other legal persons and organisational entities without legal personality to the extent that they participated in economic activity. According to the Explanatory memorandum of the draft, this included such entities as, inter alia, trade unions, foundations, establishments of higher education, scientific and research institutes, and registered associations, as long as they were involved in economic activities;
2) to natural persons who are not consumers, in instances set out in Articles 11 (Business Secrets), 28–31 (Criminal Provisions), and 33–35 (Amendments to Existing Provisions).

---

[254] According to Article 1(2) of the Act on Competition and Consumer Protection, the Act 'regulates the principles and procedures for counteracting practices restricting competition, practices infringing the collective interests of consumers and the use of prohibited contractual terms and conditions, as well as for counteracting anti-competitive concentrations of entrepreneurs and their associations, if these practices, the use of prohibited terms and conditions or concentrations produce or may produce effects on the territory of the Republic of Poland'.

However, the final wording of Article 2 was different when the Act was adopted. Only the concept of 'entrepreneur' was defined, with no mention of other entities to which the Act should also apply, and eventually in the enacted version, entrepreneurs were denoted as 'natural persons, legal persons and organisational units without legal personality, which, even if only incidentally, engaged in gainful or professional activity'.

The adopted definition should be understood as autonomous, and it may be interpreted differently from the concept of an entrepreneur adopted under other laws. In particular, this will apply to the definition of an 'entrepreneur' contained in Article 4(1) of the Act on Competition and Consumer Protection, Article 43^1 of the Polish Civil Code, Article 4 of the Act of 6 March 2018—Entrepreneurs' Law,[255] as well as Article 2(1) of the Act on Counteracting Unfair Market Practices.

It seems that an enactment of the solutions proposed in the draft Act would have been better and helped to avoid the ambiguities in the interpretation of the provisions of the adopted and binding Act that currently arise. It was apparent from the wording of the draft Act that, in principle, it was to be applied in disputes between businesses or entrepreneurs. However, in certain cases (listed in Article 2(2) of the draft Act), the Act could also be applied to natural persons who are not entrepreneurs. An adoption of a more extensive definition would have resolved doubts about who precisely the addressees of its provisions were and that the Act included entities other than entrepreneurs as well.

To illustrate what is meant here, let us recall doubts that arose prior to the amendment added in 2018 when it was necessary to determine the addressees of the prohibitions flowing from Article 11 of the Act on Combatting Unfair Competition.[256] This provision stated that the obligation not to disclose a business secret was binding also upon a person who provided work pursuant to a contract of employment or another legal relationship. The obligation of secrecy lasted for 3 years after the termination of the employment

---

255 Dz.U. of 2024 item 236, 1222, 1871 as later amended. The Act came into force on 30.4.2018. Earlier, the term entrepreneur was defined in Article 4 of the Act of 2.7.2004 on the freedom of economic activity (Dz.U. of 2016 item 1829 as amended). This Act was repealed by the Act of 6.3.2018—Entrepreneurs' Law.

256 The Act of 5.7.2018 on the amendments to the Act on Combatting Unfair Competition and certain other Acts (Dz.U. of 2018 item 1637) which came into force on 4.9.2018.

relationship, unless the contract provided otherwise or the state of secrecy had ceased. In the literature, some authors considered that the defendant under Article 11 could only be an entrepreneur, while others argued, which was the prevailing view, that it could be anyone potentially capable of violating another person's business secret, including a person who was not an entrepreneur (e.g. an employee of the entrepreneur).[257] The amendment to this Article introduced in 2018 deprived employees of passive standing (legitimation).[258] It must be added, however, that regardless of the amendment, a natural person who was not an entrepreneur was entitled to passive legitimation in cases regulated in Articles 12[259] and 14 of the Act.[260]

Generally, there are no doubts that the criminal law provisions currently listed in Articles 23–26 apply to offenders who have committed unpermitted

---

257 More in *S. Sołtysiński, S. Gogulski*, in: *J. Szwaja* (ed.), Ustawa o zwalczaniu nieuczciwej konkurencji, 2016, p. 423, Nb 10 and in the ruling of the Court of Appeal in Katowice which explained in the reasons for its decision of 15.2.2012 (V ACa 5/12, OSA 2012, No 11, item 30, p. 36), that 'as a rule, the Act on Combatting Unfair Competition regulates relations between entrepreneurs, which leads to the conclusion that entities capable of committing acts of unfair competition are, in principle, entrepreneurs (with the exception of the regulation under Article 11, which does not apply in this case)'.

258 Such solutions were criticised. Leaving the norm concerning liability for violation of business secrets was postulated, for example, by the Centre for Research, Studies and Legislation of the National Council of Legal Advisers in its Opinion of 30.1.2018 to the draft Act of 5.12.2017 on amendments to the Act on Combatting Unfair Competition and certain other Acts, pp. 6–7, <http://obsil.pl/aktualnosci/opinia-obsil-krrp-projektu-ustawy-5-grudnia-2017-r-o-zmianie-ustawy-o-zwalczaniu-nieuczciwej-konkurencji-oraz-niektorych-innych-ustaw/> (accessed on: 13.1.2019, currently unavailable).

259 See *M. Kępiński, J. Kępiński*, in: *J. Szwaja, J. Kępiński* (eds), Ustawa o zwalczaniu nieuczciwej konkurencji, 2024, p. 416, Nb 24–25.

260 See *E. Nowińska, M. Du Vall*, Ustawa o zwalczaniu nieuczciwej konkurencji. Komentarz, Warszawa 2013, p. 450, Nb 7. There are however certain doubts regarding Art. 14. See *M. Kępiński, J. Kępiński* in: *J. Szwaja, J. Kępiński* (eds), Ustawa o zwalczaniu nieuczciwej konkurencji, 2024, p. 455–456, Nb 6. According to the author, the one who performs an act of unfair competition will primarily be a competing entrepreneur (but it may also be a non-competing entrepreneur). It may also be the entrepreneur's client and his employee. In certain situations, according to the author, it may be possible to sue organisational units not conducting business activity, e.g. foundations or associations. In principle, the possibility for a trader to sue a consumer is excluded.

acts, including natural persons who are not entrepreneurs or employees of an entrepreneur.[261]

The Explanatory memorandum to the draft Act on Combatting Unfair Competition emphasises that the Act deliberately fails to use the term 'business entity', using the term 'entrepreneur' instead. This procedure was intended to prejudge that the Act did not only cover 'business entities within the meaning of the Act of Economic Activity[262] but also all persons and organisations participating in the business activity by running their own gainful or professional activity'.[263] Running a business does not have to be the main purpose of the entrepreneur; it is sufficient that the business activity is carried out incidentally,[264] nor does it need to be carried out for a profit.[265]

[261] This may include: (1) a person who owes a duty to an entrepreneur to keep a business secret (Art. 23); (2) any person who copies the external form of a product (Art. 24), 3) any person who organises or directs an avalanche sales scheme (Article 24a). It is accepted in the literature that this is a universal offence and may be committed by any entity capable of incurring criminal liability (see *J. Raglewski*, in: *M. Zdyb*, *M. Sieradzka* (eds), The Act, p. 1175, Nb 7); 4) any person who marks goods in a misleading manner (Art. 25). It is argued, however, that the qualification of this offence to the category of common or individual forbidden acts depends on the form of the causative act. Depending on this, it may be a common or individual forbidden act, see *ibidem*, p. 1185, Nb 7. However, it appears that in practice the wrongdoer as described in Article 25 will usually be the entrepreneur; 5) any person who disseminates false or misleading information about an enterprise (Article 26(1). In addition, Article 26(2) provides that it may be a person associated with the entrepreneur. This follows from the use in the provision of the phrase 'to the entrepreneur's enterprise'.

[262] It concerned the Act of 23.12.1988 on economic activity (Dz.U. No 41, item 324 as amended),according to which (Art. 2(2)) 'an economic entity may be a natural person, a legal person, as well as an organisational unit without legal personality, established in accordance with the provisions of the law, if its objects include the conduct of economic activity'. The Act was repealed due to the entry into force of the Act of 19.11.1999. – Economic Activity Law (Dz.U. No 101, item 1178 as amended).

[263] Explanatory memorandum to the draft Act of 1993, Druk sejmowy I kadencji No 278 of 18.5.1992, p. 4.

[264] The phrase 'incidentally' was added in the final version of the Act of 1993; it was not in its draft version. This solution broadens the circle of entrepreneurs within the meaning of the Act.

[265] In the ruling of 22.10.2003 (II CK 161/02, OSNC 2004, No 11, item 186, p. 115) The Supreme Court held that an entrepreneur within the meaning of the Act on Combatting Unfair Competition would also be the Association of Estate Satellite Television 'Rad Sat 2' in Łódź, despite the fact that it was not operating for profit. The

The term 'business activity' was very broadly defined, and pursuant to Article 1, that activity includes any industrial production, agriculture, construction, trade, and services. In the explanatory memorandum to the draft Act, it was explained that, unlike in the Act of 1926 on combatting unfair competition, the Act of 1993 will also be capable of being applied to the so-called liberal professions to the extent that their representatives, as themselves or organised businesses, act as entrepreneurs in business activities.[266]

In consequence, the Act of 1993 will apply to all Polish entities conducting business activities.[267] Pursuant to its Article 4, foreign natural and legal persons enjoy the rights under the provisions of the Act pursuant to the provisions of international agreements binding the Republic of Poland or on the basis of reciprocity. At the same time, there is no doubt that these

---

Supreme Court argued that the definition of an entrepreneur under the Act is broadly construed—more broadly than, for example, the concept of an entrepreneur within the meaning of the Act of 19.11.1999. Economic Activity Law (Dz.U. No. 101, item 1178 as amended), in which the profit-making nature of the activity is a necessary characteristic of an entrepreneur. According to the Supreme Court, entrepreneurs within the meaning of the Act may therefore also be entities carrying out professional, not-for-profit activities. In doing so, the Supreme Court emphasised that the Act in question uses the concept of 'participation' in economic activity. This concept is semantically capacious. According to the Supreme Court, 'a certain entity may therefore, when carrying out professional activities, participate in economic activities, although it does not act for profit. Participation in economic activity is a wide range of behaviours that may affect the current or future results of the entrepreneurs' activity or the interests of customers. Whether such participation occurs is determined not only by the will of the entity in question, but above all by an objective assessment of the nature and extent of its activities. These features may cause the entity in question, while not acting for profit itself, to affect a certain economic sphere'. E. Nowińska, M. Du Vall, Ustawa o zwalczaniu nieuczciwej konkurencji, are critical of the verdict of the Supreme Court., p. 47,as well as *K. Szczepanowska-Kozłowska*, in *E. Nowińska*, *K. Szczepanowska-Kozłowska*, Ustawa o zwalczaniu nieuczciwej konkurencji. Komentarz, Warszawa 2022, p. 51, Nb 8.

266 On the subject of the liberal professions, as well as other actors involved in the economic turnover (local authorities, municipalities, universities, farmers, etc.), see. *J. Szwaja*, *A. Kubiak-Cyrul*, in: *J. Szwaja* (ed.), Ustawa o zwalczaniu nieuczciwej konkurencji, 2016, pp. 112–118, Nb 41–63.

267 On the possibility of recognising a legal entity with its registered office outside the territory of the Republic of Poland as an entrepreneur, see.*J. Dudzik*, Legitymacja czynna na podstawie przepisów ustawy o zwalczaniu nieuczciwej konkurencji—aktualne problemy, in: *T. Skoczny* (ed.), Prawo konkurencji 25 lat. Pierwszy Polski Kongres Prawa Konkurencji, Warszawa 2016, pp. 642–648.

entities, when pursuing business in the territory of Poland, must do it in accordance with its provisions.

C. Customer's Interest

The interests of the customer are placed on an equal footing with those of the entrepreneur and the public interest. These interests interpenetrate one another and cannot be clearly separated. Thus, it does not seem appropriate to assume that one particular interest should be given preferential treatment. Each is of equal importance and is protected under the Act of 1993.

Furthermore, Article 3 of the Act provides that an action or an omission to act that threatens or prejudices the interest of another entrepreneur or of a customer is an act of unfair competition. This leads to the conclusion that it will suffice that a customer's interest is threatened or violated for an act to qualify it as a delict of unfair competition. At the same time, for the application of Article 3, it is not necessary that the interest of another entrepreneur is violated. It is not a prerequisite for the application of the Act that an entrepreneur's interest is threatened or violated; it is sufficient that the interest of the customer has been threatened or violated. In such a situation, however, the issue of standing or legitimation remains relevant (see further below).

The notion of a 'customer' is also mentioned in other provisions of the Act defining individual acts of unfair competition (Articles 5, 6, 10, 12, 13, 15, and 16) and prohibited acts (Articles 24 and 25).

Despite the use of the term, the Act on Combatting Unfair Competition does not provide the definition of the term. It is noted in the literature that the concept of a customer should be understood broadly. A customer may be not only a consumer as defined in Article 22^1 of the Civil Code, i.e. a natural person concluding a legal transaction with an entrepreneur, which transaction is not directly related to the person's economic or professional activity.[268] Customers may also be other entrepreneurs who purchase means

---

[268] On the concept of a 'consumer' in the Civil Code see e.g. *M. Gutowski*, in: *M. Gutowski* (ed.), Kodeks cywilny. Comments to Articles 1–449,[11] vol. 1, Warszawa 2021, pp. 180–183. The author explains that the definition of 'consumer' in the civil code constitutes *lex specialis* and is applicable to consumer regulations contained in other laws. It is also correct to assume that the concept of 'consumer' under the Act

of production or services or goods for further resale (indirect purchasers) as well as entities that are the final recipients but cannot be included in any of the previous categories, and they include associations, schools, courts, hospitals, offices, and the like. For the purposes of the Act on Combatting Unfair Competition, a customer is any market participant to whom actions of other entities participating in the trade (entrepreneurs) offering various goods or services to the customer are addressed, regardless of whether the customer is an entrepreneur or a consumer. The decisive factor is being the entrepreneur's customer. Consequently, the amendment of 2007[269] to Article 1 of the Act of 1993 that consisted of a deletion of the term 'consumers in particular' did not constitute a change in the scope of the Act. This treatment may only affect the interpretation of its provisions and the assumption that the consumer's interest does not deserve special consideration, as it is protected on an equal footing with the interests of all customers. Nor is there any justification for the position that the protection of the consumer's interest is outside its scope. And yet, under the Act in question, although consumers are not protected as a weaker group of market participants that need protection,[270] they still do receive protection as customers of entrepreneurs' customers.[271]

Thus, a doubt may arise as to whether, in connection with the entry into force of the Act on Counteracting Unfair Market Practices, reference may be made when assessing a given action on the grounds of the Act on Combatting Unfair Competition to the model of the average consumer, which has been developed in the case law of the CJEU and is now defined in the Act on Counteracting Unfair Market Practices. Pursuant to its Article 2(8), an average

---

on Combatting Unfair Competition understood in the same way as under other laws, including in particular the Act on Competition and Consumer Protection *J. Szwaja*, *A. Kubiak-Cyrul*, in: *J. Szwaja*, *J. Szwaja* (eds), Ustawa o zwalczaniu nieuczciwej konkurencji, 2024 p. 82, Nb 42.

269 In connection of the adoption of Act on Counteracting Unfair Market Practices.

270 First and foremost, this will concern the so-called consumer law, which aims at the need to balance the position of entrepreneurs and consumers in their mutual relationship regarding contracts (see *A. Wędrychowska-Karpińska*, *A. Wiercińska-Krużewska*, in: *A. Stawicki*, *E. Stawicki* (ed.), Ustawa o ochronie konkurencji i konsumentów, Warszawa 2011, comments to Art. 24, p. 529 and 534. The consumer, as a weaker party requiring special protection, is recognised in the Act on Competition and Consumer Protection and the Civil Code.

271 *A. Tischner*, Cele i zakres zastosowania ZNKU, p. 104, Nb 26.

consumer means 'a consumer who is reasonably well-informed, observant and prudent; the assessment is to be made taking into account social, cultural, and linguistic factors and the consumer's membership of a particular consumer group, by which is meant a clearly identifiable group of consumers who are particularly vulnerable to a market practice or to the product to which the market practice relates because of particular characteristics, such as age or physical or mental disability.[272] The adoption of such a model is, in the view of the EU legislator, in line with the principle of proportionality and is intended to allow the effective application of the protection measures contained in Directive 2005/29/EC.[273]

As unreservedly expressed in the literature,[274] in an assessment of whether a given behaviour was likely to mislead or otherwise influence a consumer's decision, reference should be made to the model (pattern) of the average consumer.[275] Actions that may threaten or harm the interests of the customer-consumer should therefore be assessed through the prism of the average consumer. Hence, it does not seem reasonable to apply a similar model, i.e. that of the average entrepreneur, and use this model with regard to the customer–entrepreneur relationship.

3. The Scope of the Act

A. Introductory Remarks

The protection of the public interest, as well as the protection of entrepreneurs and customers, will be guaranteed if unfair competition in economic activity is combatted and prevented. Accordingly, the starting point for deliberations with regard to the provisions of the Act on Combatting Unfair Competition is the assumption that competition is to be fair. All manifestations of unfair

---

[272] On the definition 'average consumer' see documents of the European Commission Guidance on the Implementation/Application of Directive 2005/29/EC on Unfair Commercial Practices) of 25.5.2016, COM(2016) 320, pp. 41–46.

[273] See Recital 18 of Directive 2005/29/EC.

[274] *J. Szwaja, A. Kubiak-Cyrul*, in: *J. Szwaja. J. Kępiński* (eds), Ustawa o zwalczaniu nieuczciwej konkurencji, 2024, p. 81, Nb 39; *A. Tischner*, Cele i zakres zastosowania ZNKU, p. 104, Nb 26, and of similar opinion was *M. Sieradzka* in *M. Zdyb, M. Sieradzka* (eds), Ustawa, Comments to Art. 1, pp. 58–62.

[275] For more, see *M. Sieradzka*, in: *M. Zdyb, M. Sieradzka* (eds), Ustawa, pp. 60–62, Nb 28–29; *A. Tischner*, Cele i zakres zastosowania ZNKU, p. 105, Nb 27.

competition (delicts of unfair competition) should be combatted and possible dangers detected in advance (prevention). This principle is also expressed in the Constitution of the Republic of Poland,[276] and as stated in its Article 76, 'public authorities shall protect consumers, users and lessees (...) from unfair market practices'. In principle, the Act concerns market participants who, due to their weaker position in the market, require protection against unfair market practices. The concept of 'unfair market practices' referred to in Article 76 of the Constitution should be understood more broadly than the concept of unfair market practices in the Act on Counteracting Unfair Market Practices, in which such practices may refer to all types of unfair behaviour, not only those defined in the Act on Counteracting Unfair Market Practices.

Moreover, according to Article 20 of the Constitution of the Republic of Poland, the economic regime in Poland is a social market economy based on freedom of economic activity, private property and solidarity, and a dialogue and cooperation of social partners. And although the Constitution does not mention the fairness of competition as one of the pillars of the economic regime,[277] it is emphasised in the literature that free and fair competition is the driving force underlying the development of a free market economy, which the state is expected to ensure by creating institutional guarantees conducive to 'the functioning of a market based on competition, and therefore guarantees designed to effectively protect entrepreneurs from interference with their economic freedom by other actors competing in ways that may violate equality of opportunity in the broad sense and fair play and competition for customers'.[278]

Also in Article 9 of the Act—the Entrepreneurs' Law adopted in 2018[279]—it is unambiguously provided that 'an entrepreneur pursues business in accordance with principles of fair competition, respect for good practice and the

---

[276] Dz.U. No 78, item 483.

[277] As noted in the literature, constitutions of some countries contain an express prohibition of unfair competition or an obligation to protect fair competition. Examples here are: Article 74(3) in the Slovak Constitution, Article 19(1) of the Bulgarian Constitution or Article 135 of the Rumanian Constitution. See: *K. Zaradkiewicz*, in: *M. Safian*, *L. Bosek* (eds), Konstytucja RP. Komentarz do art. 1–86, vol. 1, Comments to Art. 20, Legalis 2016.

[278] *K. Zaradkiewicz*, in: *M. Safian*, *L. Bosek* (eds), Konstytucja RP. Komentarz do art. 1–86, vol. 1, Comments to Art. 20, Legalis 2016 and literature quoted therein.

[279] This Act entered into force on 30 April 2018.

legitimate interests of other entrepreneurs and consumers, as well as with respect for and protection of human rights and freedoms'.

The concept of 'competition' has not been defined in the Act on Combatting Unfair Competition, while its dictionary definition provides that it is 'rivalry between persons or groups interested in achieving the same goal'.[280]

B. A Delict of Unfair Competition in the General Clause of the Act

Article 3(1) of the Act on Combatting Unfair Competition, which is a general clause,[281] defines an act of unfair competition. It further provides that an act of unfair competition is an act contrary to the law or contrary to morality if it threatens or prejudices the interests of another entrepreneur or the customer/client of that entrepreneur. It is also argued that a failure to act may constitute an act of unfair competition as well.[282] In order for an act or an omission to act to qualify as an act of unfair competition, the behaviour in question must be contrary to the law or morality and be undertaken in connection with the conduct of a business activity (as follows from Article 1), as well as it must threaten or violate the interest of the entrepreneur (entrepreneurs) or customer (customers).

It should be noted, however, that Article 3(1) ignores the public interest mentioned in Article 1. One may wonder whether such an exclusion entails consequences for the interpretation of Article 3(1). An act of unfair competition will be an act that threatens or prejudices the interest of an entrepreneur or a customer of an entrepreneur. Such an act will also indirectly prejudice the general (public) interest. It is in the interest of all market participants that competition be fair. Thus, the acts or omissions of entrepreneurs should be assessed from the perspective of the public interest. Public interest is also the focus of attention of the Act on Combatting Unfair Competition,

---

280 Dictionary definition PWN, <https://sjp.pwn.pl/slowniki/konkurencja.html> (accessed on: 1.2.2025).

281 Broadly on general clauses in the law on counteracting unfair competition writes *R. Skubisz*, Klauzule generalne, pp. 71–92.

282 See *J. Szwaja*, *A. Kubiak-Cyrul*, in: *J. Szwaja*, *J. Kępiński* (eds), Ustawa o zwalczaniu nieuczciwej konkurencji, 2024, p. 128, Nb 41. This statement is also reflected in the Act on Combatting Unfair Competition, from which it follows that also the absence of certain actions may constitute an act of unfair competition, e.g. the failure to label a good or service (Art. 10).

the purpose of which is also 'to prevent and combat unfair competition (...) in the public interest'. However, pursuant to this Act, public interest will be protected indirectly in a situation where an entrepreneur seeks to protect his interest or the interest of a customer where such interest has been violated or threatened by the action of another entrepreneur. When interpreting Article 3(1), one should therefore take into account the public interest that may be prejudiced by an act of unfair competition threatening or violating the interest of entrepreneurs or their customers. In a situation where the public interest is threatened, it will be the Act on Competition and Consumer Protection adopted in 2007 and not the Act on Combatting Unfair Competition that will be the appropriate basis for seeking protection. The Act on Competition and Consumer Protection, as is aptly emphasised in the literature, serves direct protection of the public interest, and protection of this interest 'constitutes the basic justification for the protection of consumers and entrepreneurs'.[283]

As can be seen from the explanatory memorandum to the draft Act on Combatting Unfair Competition, its general clause (Article 3(1)) was intended to be of fundamental importance. This is because when, in a certain business activity, there emerges a new act that is contrary to the law or fairness but is not included in the catalogue of acts expressly prohibited by the Act, and where such an act harms the interest of the public, the entrepreneurs, or the customers, the courts may, pursuant to the general clause, declare such an act to be also prohibited and apply to it sanctions as provided for in the Act on Combatting Unfair Competition.[284]

In turn, Article 3(2) is an attempt to define in general terms acts of unfair competition, which are 'the most serious and occurring most frequently in practice'.[285] An illustrative, non-exhaustive catalogue of unfair competition acts includes:

[283] *A. Tischner*, Cele i zakres zastosowania ZNKU, p. 101, Nb 21.

[284] Explanatory memorandum to the draft Act of 1993, Druk sejmowy I kadencji No 278, p. 6. On the specific role of general clauses see: *M. Kępiński*, Problemy ogólne nowej ustawy, p. 5.

[285] Explanatory memorandum to the draft Act of 1993, Druk sejmowy I kadencji No 278, p. 5.

1) misleading designation of an enterprise;
2) false or fraudulent indication of the geographical origin of goods or services;
3) misleading designation of goods or services;
4) violation of a business secret;
5) inducement to dissolve or not to perform a contract;
6) imitating products;
7) slander or unfair praise;
8) obstructing access to the market;
9) bribery of a person holding a public function;
10) unfair or prohibited advertising;
11) organising an avalanche sales scheme;
12) conducting or organising a business in a consortium system.

The above catalogue of unfair competition acts coincides with the catalogue of unfair competition delicts referred to specifically in Articles 5–17f of Chapter 2 of the Act of 1993. However, such a legislative solution causes doubts as to the mutual relation between the provisions of Article 3 and the delicts contained in Articles 5–17f of the same Act.

C. The Relationship between the General Clause (Article 1(3)) and Specified Delicts (Articles 5–17f)

On the one hand, there are views that Article 3(1) does not introduce any additional prerequisites for qualifying each act or omission to act described in Articles 5–17f as an act (delict) of unfair competition. If that is the case, then not every act of unfair competition referred to in Chapter 2 of the Act must be examined in the light of the provisions of Article 3(1).

M. Kępiński argued that Article 3(1) may not, in particular, lead to an abrogation of the application of the provisions on specified delicts, as these provisions formulate delicts that by definition are capable of an independent application. If, therefore, a factual situation fulfils the characteristics of a specified delict, the provisions of Chapter 2 must be applied. Only if there occur exceptional circumstances may the behaviour of the wrongdoer be assessed negatively in the light of good practice.

The court itself must not extend the list of delicts of unfair competition by adding the prerequisites referred to in Article 3(1). In the case of an act not listed in Chapter 2, Article 3(1) may be applied as a supplementary measure.

It seems that this view is shared by M. Szpunar, who considers that the effect of the general clause on special provisions is limited to two cases. In the first case, within the corrective function, the general clause serves to fill the gaps in the provisions on specified delicts. Some, but not all, of these provisions are formulated in such a way that they require assessment in light of the criteria of the general clause. In the second case, by invoking the general clause, a protection may be denied to an entrepreneur who makes a claim asserting that an act of unfair competition described in Articles 5–17f has been committed by another entrepreneur but who himself violates good practice (incapacitating function).[286]

On the other hand, an opposite view is presented, according to which 'in each case, also in the event of the application of the provisions of Chapter 2 of the Act on Combatting Unfair Competition, it is necessary to demonstrate the general prerequisites for determining liability for an act of unfair competition, and those prerequisites are listed in Article 3(1).[287] In other words, in a situation where a delict of unfair competition, including delicts referred to in Chapter 2, is established, it is necessary to demonstrate its conflict with the law or good practice, as well as to demonstrate a violation of the entrepreneur's or customer's interest.

Rulings delivered by courts are, however, also inconsistent in this respect. For example, the Supreme Court once argued that Article 3(1) fulfils different functions: that of defining, supplementary, and corrective. Referring to the corrective function, the Supreme Court assumed that 'in a situation where a certain behaviour falls under the hypothesis of any of the provisions of Chapter 2 of the Act, but it is not conduct contrary to the law or good practice, it is not an act of unfair competition'.[288] It follows from the above that, in the opinion of the Supreme Court, irrespective of demonstrating the prerequisites for the delicts under Articles 5–17, it is also necessary to demonstrate their inconsistency with the law and good practice. Consequently, the courts conclude that 'it is always necessary to subject the behaviour in question to

---

[286] *M. Szpunar*, Pojęcie czynu nieuczciwej konkurencji – zagadnienia wybrane, in: *M. Pyziak-Szafnicka* (ed.), Odpowiedzialność cywilna. Księga pamiątkowa ku czci Profesora Adama Szpunara, Kraków 2004, p. 707.

[287] See: *M Zdyb*, in: *M. Zdyb*, *M. Sieradzka* (eds), Ustawa, p. 175, Nb 125.

[288] See the ruling of the Supreme Court of 9.12.2011, III CSK 120/11, Legalis.

its assessment from the point of view of Article 3(1)'.[289] It has been argued in the literature that this view emphasises the corrective function of the general clause of the provisions of the specific part and that the corrective function here does not consist of examining the claims from the point of view of good practice but imposes an additional prerequisite necessary to establish an act of unfair competition.[290] The above-mentioned relationship seems to have been noted by the Supreme Court, which explained that 'when determining that an act fulfils the hypothesis of one of these provisions [Articles 5–17 – J.K.], recourse to Article 3 is in fact unnecessary, unless there is a case of a cumulative application of the provisions or there is a need to assess its application as part of a corrective function'.[291]

Ultimately, it should be taken that the corrective function of Article 3(1) ought to be resorted to in very few cases only. These would be situations in which the adjudicating court doubted, taking into account the principles of equity, that the entrepreneur, by his or her action, had violated the principles of good practice, even though that action did not fulfil the prerequisites of the delicts specified in the detailed part of the Act. Another situation could be finding by the court that, although a delict of unfair competition was committed, such an act was not contrary to good practice and thus the assertion of certain claims would have no effect.

Some courts also accept that Article 3 constitutes a *lex generalis* in relation to delicts from Chapter 2 of the Act.[292] Other courts express an opinion that

---

289 Ruling of the Supreme Court in Warszawa of 30.6.2016, I ACa 1349/15, Legalis; Ruling of the Supreme Court in Warszawa of 5.6.2017, I ACa 529/16, Legalis.

290 *M. Kępiński*, Stosunek art. 3 ust. 1 ustawy, p. 11.

291 Ruling of the Supreme Court of 28.10.2010, II CSK 191/10, OSNC 2011, No 6, item 71, p. 66. And ruling of the Supreme Court in Warszawa of 19.12.2007 (I ACa 209/06, LEX No 516551), according to which 'competing acts should be examined first of all in the light of the prerequisites specified in the provisions of Articles 5–17 and only if they do not fall within the scope of any of these provisions are they subject to assessment according to the general clause Art. 3'.

292 Ruling of the Supreme Court in Warszawa of 27.7.2017 (I ACa 445/16, Legalis), in which the S.C. invoked the ruling of the Regional Court which stated that 'the general clause in Article 3(1) constitutes a *lex generalis* not only for acts listed in Article 3(2) and defined in its Chapters 2 and 4, but also in relation to acts of unfair competition which are or will be specified in other acts. Individual acts of competition should be examined first of all in the light of the prerequisites specified in the provisions of

there is no such dependence[293] and are of an opinion that in each case, also in the event of the application of the specific provisions from Chapter 2 of the Act, it is necessary to demonstrate the general prerequisites of Article 3(1). Thus, Article 3(1) seems to be treated by the courts as *lex specialis vis-à-vis* the provisions of the specific part, which constitute *lex generalis.*[294]

Such an understanding of the relationship between these provisions has been criticised in the literature as being contrary to the construction of the Act on Combatting Unfair Competition.[295] We must agree with this criticism, as in relation to the delicts listed in Chapter 2, the provision of Article 3(1) might be regarded as *lex generalis* and not *lex specialis*. Furthermore, Article 3(1) may, on par with the specific acts of unfair competition, be an equivalent basis for the assertion of claims. Indeed, the behaviour of the person committing an act of unfair competition may fulfil both the prerequisites of an act of unfair competition under Article 3(1) and the provisions of Chapter 2. In such a situation, it is not possible to speak of a relationship of *lex generalis–lex specialis*.

Articles 5-17, and only when they do not fall within the scope of any of these provisions are they subject to assessment in the light of the general clause of Article 3'.

293 See Ruling of the Supreme Court of 30.5.2006, I CSK 85/06, OSP 2008, No 5, item 55, p. 377 where the Supreme Court determined that there were 'no grounds to recognise that there occurs a *leges speciales–lex generalis* relationship between the provisions of Chapter 2a and Art.3(1) and only when it is not possible to qualify a given behaviour as a specified act of unfair competition is it possible to assess that behavior through the prism of the general clause in Article 3(1)'. Also, see ruling of the Court of Appeal in Warszawa of 5.12.2007, I ACa 1053/07, Legalis; ruling of the Court of Appeal in Katowice of 13.2.2008, V ACa 256/07, LEX No 519350.

294 See Ruling of the Supreme Court of 5.1.2005 II CK 329/04, Legalis. The Supreme Court stated that 'although the relationship between the general clause (Article 3) and the provisions creating the named acts of unfair competition (Articles 5-17) is not uniformly perceived in the literature, it is assumed in the case law that it is similar to the one characterising the relationship *lex specialis–lex generalis* (compare the reasons given in the ruling of the Supreme Court of 21.2.1997, II CKN 70/96, OSN 1997, N 8, item 113). This means that if a delict covered by a specific part of the Act is committed, the relevant provision must be applied in the first instance. Only if it cannot be fully used can the general rule – Article 3(1) – be resorted to as supplementary'.

295 *M. Kępiński*, Stosunek art. 3 ust. 1 ustawy, p. 12.

D. Functions of the General Clause

With reference to the above considerations, we should now look at the role of the general clause and the functions it fulfils. The literature emphasises the momentous and significant role of Article 3(1) in the application of the Act on Combatting Unfair Competition.[296] According to *R. Skubisz*, all general clauses 'fulfil a fundamental role in the legal systems (...) of the European Union Member States, and enable, due to their general nature, taking action against all market activities carried out by an entrepreneur which are, broadly speaking, of an unfair nature'.[297]

There is no doubt that general clauses fulfil the **corrective function** and, as mentioned earlier, allow the correction of the hypotheses of specific delicts of unfair competition. Such a correction may be made in two situations. In one, the corrective function allows limiting the reference to specified delicts when, although the prerequisites of relevant provisions have been met, good practice has not been violated.[298]

In doing so, it is argued that the application of the corrective function of Article 3(1) should only take place when the interpretation of a specific provision raises doubts.[299]

Another function of the general clause is supplementary. Thanks to it, it is possible to fill gaps in the existing provisions that regulate specific torts. It has been explained in the literature that 'if an act does not fall within the catalogue of acts expressly recognised as unfair in the law (Chapter 2), the courts may, based on the general clause in the event of a simultaneous threat to or violation of the interest of another entrepreneur, declare a specific act to be prohibited and apply sanctions (...)'.[300] The Supreme Court shares the same opinion, stating that 'the supplementary function consists in adding to the catalogue of acts of unfair competition, since it is not possible to catalogue and specify all behaviours that may be qualified as infringing the principles of fair trading; behaviours which do not fall under the provisions

---

296 *Ibidem*, p. 11; also *R. Stefanicki*, Klauzula generalna w ZNKU, in: *M. Kępiński* (ed.), System Prawa Prywatnego, vol. 15, Prawo konkurencji, Warszawa 2014, pp. 108–113, Nb 2–8.

297 *R. Skubisz*, Klauzule generalne, p. 72.

298 *M. Kępiński*, Stosunek art. 3 ust. 1 ustawy, p. 10.

299 *M. Szpunar*, Pojęcie czynu nieuczciwej konkurencji, p. 703

300 *R. Stefanicki*, Klauzula generalna w ZNKU, p. 121, Nb 20.

of Chapter 2 of the Act but are contrary to the law or good practice and at the same time threaten or violate the interest of another entrepreneur or customer also constitute an act of unfair competition as defined in Article 3 of the Act'.[301] Owing to this function, certain acts of unfair competition may be included in the scope of the Act on Combatting Unfair Competition even though they do not fulfil the prerequisites of a delict of unfair competition from its Chapter 2. As the Supreme Court noted in this respect, Article 3(1), as a general provision, and specified delicts (as specific provisions) are complementary and may be applied cumulatively. An act of unfair competition may thus meet the prerequisites of Article 3(1) of the Act and the prerequisites of Chapter 2 of the same Act. It may also be the case that a given behaviour may be qualified as an act fulfilling the prerequisites of Article 3(1) while not fulfilling the prerequisites arising from the provisions of Articles 5–17f. It has been argued in the literature that the supplementary function should not result in any widening of the boundaries of the acts (delicts) that have already been named and described (as typical). Indeed, Article 3(1) may constitute the basis for creating an unnamed act of unfair competition. It should not, however, broaden the scope of the named acts.[302] *R. Skubisz* rightly points out that in each case of unnamed acts of unfair competition, the entrepreneur's behaviour is contrary to accepted principles of good practice, and he stresses that defining the concept of good practice is crucial for the practice.[303]

The defining function of the general clause, on the other hand, makes it possible to define, using general terms and in particular by making a reference to good practice, what an act of unfair competition is. This permits recourse to certain extra-legal criteria that may be understood and interpreted differently at different times. In this way, the provisions of the Act on Combatting Unfair Competition can also be interpreted flexibly. As stated by the Supreme Court, this function 'consists in determining, and therefore defining, an act of unfair competition. An act of unfair competition is an act contrary to the law or good practice if it threatens or infringes the interest of another entrepreneur or customer. This does not affect, in principle, the typified,

[301] Judgement of the Supreme Court of 9.12.2011, III CSK 120/11, Legalis.
[302] *M. Czajkowska-Dąbrowska*, Przesłanki, zakres zastosowania i funkcje klauzuli generalnej.
[303] *R. Skubisz*, Klauzule generalne, p. 83.

specific acts of unfair competition listed in Articles 5-17f (and referred to for example, in Article 3(2)) and their definitions, but, as a general clause, it makes it possible to read them correctly'.[304]

Some also distinguish **the adaptive function** of Article 3(1), which allows adapting the provisions of the Act on Combatting Unfair Competition to the changing social and economic situation.[305] As with the defining function, this function is also intended to provide flexibility in the application of the provisions of the Act. However, it seems rather unnecessary to distinguish an adaptive function since general clauses as a rule are treated as those that refer to something existing outside the legal system[306] and therefore also to the changing social, economic, or other relationships.

Others distinguish an **incapacitating function** as well.[307] *M. Szpunar* believes that 'the use of the general clause may be similar to the prohibition of an abuse of law'. He points out that such a role is also fulfilled by Article 5 of the Civil Code; however, he believes that Article 3(1) better corresponds to the specificity of claims for an act of unfair competition. According to M. Szpunar, the difference between the corrective and the incapacitating function is that in the case of the incapacitating function, the application of the general clause will make it possible to 'incapacitate' the claims of an entrepreneur that are grounded on the provisions regulating specific delicts of unfair competition in the event when this entrepreneur's behaviour violates good practice. The role of the corrective function will be to fill in the interpretative gaps.[308] While *M. Kępiński* argues that, although also in his view the general clause serves to incapacitate claims that would be contrary to good practice, such 'incapacitation' constitutes part of the corrective function of the general clause.[309]

---

304 Judgement of the Supreme Court of 9.12.2011, III CSK 120/11, Legalis.

305 *R. Stefanicki*, Klauzula generalna w ZNKU, p. 119, Nb 17.

306 See *M. Zieliński*, Wykładnia prawa. Zasady, reguły, wskazówki, Warszawa 2012, p. 132, Nb 223.

307 See *M. Szpunar*, Pojęcie czynu nieuczciwej konkurencji, pp. 703–705, also *M. Kępiński*, *J.Kępiński*, Przedmowa do Artykułu 5, in: *J. Szwaja*, *J.Kępiński* (eds), Ustawa o zwalczaniu nieuczciwej konkurencji, 2024, pp. 221, Nb 5.

308 *M. Szpunar*, Pojęcie czynu nieuczciwej konkurencji, p. 703.

309 *M. Kępiński*, Stosunek art. 3 ust. 1 ustawy, p. 10.

E. Conflict with the Law

The entrepreneur's behaviour may be claimed to be contrary to the general clause if the committed act or an omission to act is unlawful and infringes or threatens the interests of the entrepreneur or the customer. As rightly argued by E. Nowińska and M. du Vall, the entrepreneur's behaviour may be classified as contrary to the law if it is undertaken in connection with the conducted business activity.[310] This limitation arises from Article 1 of the Act, which clearly defines its scope, i.e. preventing and combatting unfair competition in business activities.

Unlawfulness is to be understood broadly as any conduct of an entrepreneur that violates the provisions of the law. In the literature, for example, the following are listed as being contrary to the law: acts that are prohibited or threatened with a criminal sanction, acts that are prohibited by disciplinary sanctions, acts that are prohibited by provisions of administrative law or public economic law, acts that are prohibited under civil law acts that are contrary to the precepts of civil law or administrative law.[311] M. Kępiński is of the opinion, however, that the Act on Combatting Unfair Competition is about a conflict with the law, which gives the infringing entrepreneur a competitive advantage over other entrepreneurs. Therefore, not every conflict with the law will give rise to liability under this Act.[312]

Unlawfulness will also occur in a situation where an entrepreneur, by an act or an omission to act, commits an act of unfair market practice as defined in Articles 4–11 of the Act on Counteracting Unfair Market Practices. In that respect, M. Namysłowska notes that Article 3 of the Act on Combatting Unfair Competition could be a substantive legal basis for pursuing claims when an entrepreneur commits a delict of unfair market practice. In her opinion, 'a violation of the Act on Counteracting Unfair Market Practices would have to be considered as an act contrary to the law, and such violation

---

310 *E. Nowińska, M. du Vall*, Ustawa o zwalczaniu nieuczciwej konkurencji, Comments to Art. 3, p. 53, Nb 4; also *E. Nowińska*, in: *E. Nowińska, K. Szczepanowska-Kozłowska*, Ustawa o zwalczaniu, Comments to Art. 3, p.75. Also *M. Kępiński*, Problemy ogólne nowej ustawy, p. 6.

311 *M. Zdyb*, in: *M. Zdyb, M. Sieradzka* (eds), Ustawa, Comments to Art. 3, p. 99, Nb 47. Also *J. Szwaja, K. Jasińska*, in: *J. Szwaja, J. Kępiński* (eds), Ustawa o zwalczaniu nieuczciwej konkurencji, 2024, Comments to Art. 3, p. 130, Nb 52.

312 *M. Kępiński*, Problemy ogólne nowej ustawy, p. 6.

would be an act of unfair competition if it threatened or violated the interest of another entrepreneur. Only in the event of a market practice prohibited in all circumstances under Articles 7 and 9 of the Act on Counteracting Unfair Market Practices, a presumption of a threat to an interest would be irrebuttable. No judge could determine that a given market practice is consistent with good practice or with the law, or that it does not violate the consumer's interest'.[313] Of a different opinion is J. Dudzik, who argues that a violation of the provisions of the Act on Counteracting Unfair Market Practices will not constitute grounds for the claim of a delict of unfair competition as being contrary to the law in the understanding of Article 3 of the Act on Combatting Unfair Competition. The author argues that the content of the delicts under the Act on Counteracting Unfair Market Practices overlaps to a fundamental extent the content of the regulation of the Act on Combatting Unfair Competition, which concerns acts of unfair competition consisting in contravening good practice. Thus, in his opinion, it would not be correct to formulate a claim of delict of unfair competition consisting of a contravention of the Act on Counteracting Unfair Market Practices, because the determination of such a contravention would still need to be assessed through the premise of compliance with good practice.[314]

In principle, we may agree with M. Namysłowska, who argued that pursuant to Article 3(1), a commission of an act of unfair market practice may be found unlawful. However, it cannot be prejudged that this will always constitute an act of unfair competition. A situation may arise in which, as a result of the use of an unfair market practice, the interest of the entrepreneur or the customer has not been violated or threatened. The cumulative prerequisite for the application of Article 3(1) is that it is contrary to the law or good practice and that it threatens or infringes the interest of an entrepreneur or customer.[315] By contrast, the prerequisites for the application of Article 4(1) of the Act on Counteracting Unfair Market Practices include

---

313 *M. Namysłowska*, O konieczności uchylenia ustawy, p. 397.

314 *J. Dudzik*, Legitymacja czynna, p. 642.

315 See *P. Podrecki*, Dyrektywa o nieuczciwych praktykach handlowych i jej implementacja do prawa polskiego, ZNUJ 2007, No 4, pp. 365–386. *P. Podrecki* states that 'any behaviour constituting an unfair market practice which is prohibited and unlawful may, in principle, constitute an act of unfair competition if it threatens or prejudices the interests of another entrepreneur'.

inconsistency with good practice and a significant distortion or potential significant distortion of the market behaviour of the average consumer, but it ignores the premise of illegality altogether. As can be seen, the premises for the application of the general clause in the two Acts are different. On the other hand, however, it might be argued that, since a given practice has been found to be capable of distorting the behaviour of a consumer, the interest of the consumer has also been violated.

On the other hand, we must agree that one needs to be particularly vigilant when assessing the practices included in Annex I to Directive 2005/29/EC (Articles 7 and 9 of the Act on Counteracting Unfair Market Practices). Such practices are unfair in all circumstances. To consider that they are not acts of unfair competition would contradict the premise and purpose of Directive 2005/29/EC. It is also necessary here to apply a pro-EU interpretation of the provisions of the Act on Combatting Unfair Competition.

Moreover, it should be borne in mind that even if an entrepreneur's act or omission may be qualified as an unfair market practice and an act of unfair competition, in order to effectively pursue claims under Article 18 of the Act on Combatting Unfair Competition, the entrepreneur will have to demonstrate that his or her interest has been threatened or violated. In a situation where only the consumer's interest has been affected as a result of an unfair market practice, it will in principle be impossible for the entrepreneur to pursue claims under the Act on Combatting Unfair Competition.

F. Conflict with Good Practice

The general clause will apply when the entrepreneur's conduct is contrary to good practice and infringes or threatens the interest of another entrepreneur or customer.

Article 3(1) of the Act on Combatting Unfair Competition makes reference to good practice but does not define this concept. It is therefore necessary to resort to literature and case law in this regard. In the course of work on the Act on Combatting Unfair Competition, a possible use of the term 'principles of social co-existence' in the general clause was considered, but ultimately it was decided that using it would be too risky for the further fate of the Act in the event of a departure from this clause in the Civil Code. Consequently, it was decided to keep the good practice clause as used in the Act of 1926 on combatting unfair competition. Nonetheless, it Hs been argued that 'good practice' should be understood as similar to the 'principles of social co-existence'[316] as those principles, these are 'moral norms customarily present in economic activity'. They may therefore refer to other social relationships and be different from the typical rules of social coexistence under the Civil Code." It is accepted in the literature that two criteria may be adopted for the assessment of good morals, i.e. a moral-ethical criterion and an economic-functional criterion.[317] According to the first criterion, in assessing the elements of good practice, one should be guided by 'the sense of integrity of the general public, thinking justly and rightly'. The measure adopted will thus be the general, average moral level present in business dealings. On the other hand, adopting the economic-functional criterion, the assessment 'will be oriented towards ensuring operation of fair and unadulterated competition that is not distorted by price and other characteristics of the goods or services offered to customers'.[318] The prevailing view today is that the assessment should be made in the light of the economic-functional criterion.[319] It is also true that separation of moral/ethical and economic/functional assessments will often be difficult to carry[320] and despite recourse to economic/functional assessments, it will be necessary to make moral and ethical ones as well.[321]

Thus, the ruling of the Supreme Court regarding the dispute between the producers of Vegeta and Kucharek seasonings is correct. The court stated that 'good commercial practice constitutes other than legal norms of conduct to be

---

[316] These two terms are also are equated with each other. See the verdict of the Court of Appeal in Warszawa of 21.1.2010, I ACa 1032/09, LEX No1120050. The court held that 'a breach of good practice is the same as a breach of the principles of social co-existence which limit the principle of freedom of contract expressed in Article 3531 of the Civil Code'. Doubts are pointed out by *E. Nowińska*, *M. du Vall*, Ustawa o zwalczaniu nieuczciwej konkurencji, comments to Art. 3, p. 70, Nb 17; *E. Nowińska*, in: *E. Nowińska*, *K. Szczepanowska-Kozłowska*, Ustawa o zwalczaniu, comments to Art. 3, pp. 73–75.

[317] More on that: *J. Szwaja*, *K. Jasińska*, in: *J. Szwaja*, *J. Kępiński* (eds), Ustawa o zwalczaniu nieuczciwej konkurencji, 2024, Comments to Art. 3, pp. 139–143, Nb 95–106.

[318] *Ibidem*, p. 139, Nb 97.

[319] *E. Nowińska*, *M. du Vall*, Ustawa o zwalczaniu nieuczciwej konkurencji, Comments to Art. 3, p. 61, Nb 11; and *E. Nowińska*, in: *E. Nowińska*, *K. Szczepanowska-Kozłowska*, Ustawa o zwalczaniu, Comments to Art. 3, p. 87, Nb 12.

[320] *M. Zdyb*, in: *M. Zdyb*, *M. Sieradzka* (eds), Ustawa, comments to Art. 3, p. 118, Nb 92.

[321] See *R. Stefanicki*, Wymogi staranności zawodowej przedsiębiorcy (w świetle dyrektywy o nieuczciwych praktykach handlowych), PiP 2010, No 4, p. 61.

followed by entrepreneurs. Their content cannot be defined in an exhaustive manner, as they are shaped by human attitudes conditioned by moral values and associated with them economic goals and practices of economic life. All of these are subject to change in the wake of changing political and socio-economic ideologies and moral revaluations. In economic relationships, which allow for competitiveness of actions, the criterion of harm, which usually marks the boundary between permissible and impermissible behaviour in other interpersonal relations, cannot be the basis for judgements in terms of right and wrong. The essence of economic activity is the pursuit of economic benefits. The appearance of a competitor on the market is generally to the detriment of another entrepreneur in terms of less profit or, in any case, the risk of losing its existing position, and this is inherent in the very principle of competition. Therefore, it is not the mere fact of threatening or creating a loss on the part of another entrepreneur, but the manner in which the mechanism of competition between competitors is implemented that must be considered when assessing competitive acts from the point of view of being contrary to good practice (Article 3(1) of the Act on Combatting Unfair Competition). This manner should be verified each time in the circumstances of a specific place and time, taking into account the usual ways in which entrepreneurs achieve economic benefits, provided those ways deserve approval in the light of moral and ethical norms'.[322]

4. A Threat to or Violation of the Entrepreneur's or Customer's Rights

Article 18 of the Act on Combatting Unfair Competition contains a catalogue of claims actionable under civil law that may be made when a delict of unfair competition has been committed. For such claims to be made, two general conditions must be met. First, an act of unfair competition must have been committed. Secondly, the act must threaten or violate the interests of the entrepreneur or the customer. Thus, an entrepreneur who files a claim under the Act on Combatting Unfair Competition will have to prove that the act or omission of another entrepreneur not only constituted a delict of unfair competition but also that his or her interest was threatened or violated as a result of such behaviour. Alternatively, he will have to prove that his client's

---

[322] Judgement of the Supreme Court of 2.1.2007, V CSK 311/06, Legalis.

interests have been threatened or violated. According to the Explanatory Memorandum of the draft Act of 1993, the introduction of the criterion of 'threatened or interest' was necessary because the Act does not require the existence of a competitive relationship as a premise for protection. According to the drafters, 'an unfair act threatens or infringes the interests of the right holder when both entrepreneurs produce, sell or provide the same or substitute goods or services in the same territory and at the same time'.[323]

The normative basis for an entrepreneur to demonstrate a violation or threat to his or her interest will be Article 18 and not Article 3(1) of the Act on Combatting Unfair Competition. Hence, we must take it that as a general rule, pursuant to Article 18, in order to demonstrate the standing (active legitimation) to raise certain claims, it will be necessary to demonstrate the existence of a so-called concrete competition relationship.[324] The actual, concrete competition relationship (*konkretes Wettbeverbsverhältnis*) is defined in German law (pursuant to the UWG[325]) Competitors are in a concrete competitive relationship when they have the same circle of customers and their product range limits each other (*gegeneseitg behindern können*). In this type of competition relationship, entrepreneurs offer goods and services of the same type and seek to sell them to the same circle of end customers. They must also operate in the same product, territorial, and temporal market.[326] Such an interpretation adopted in German law corresponds to the justification of 'threatening or violating the interest of the entitled person' under Polish law on combatting unfair competition presented above.

A concrete competition relationship must be distinguished from a so-called abstract competition relationship (*abstraktes Wettbeverbsverhältnis*) in which

---

323 Explanatory memorandum to the Act on Combatting Unfair Competition, Druk sejmowy I kadencji No 278, p. 7.

324 *A. Walaszek-Pyzioł*, *W. Pyzioł*, Czyn nieuczciwej konkurencji (analiza pojęcia), PPH 1994, No 10, p. 7.

325 *Gesetz gegen den unlauteren Wettbewerb in der Fassung der Bekanntmachung vom 3. März 2010 (BGBl. I S. 254), das zuletzt durch Artikel 21 des Gesetzes vom 6. Mai 2024 (BGBl. 2024 I Nr. 149) geändert worden ist.* An act against unfair competition in its wording as of the date of announcement on 3.3.2010, recently amended by Art. 21 of the Act of 6.3.2024 (BGBl. 2024 I No. 233).

326 See *O. Sosnitza*, § 2 Konkretes Wettbewerbsverhältniss, in: *A. Ohly*, *O. Sosnitza* (eds), UWG, Gesetz gegen den unlauteren Wettbewerb. Kommentar, München 2023, Rn 65–77, Beck-online.

it will be sufficient that there exists a possibility of an infringement of the interests of entrepreneurs who may have standing, even if the probability of such an infringement is practically low.[327] The Polish literature on the subject interprets the above to mean that an act of unfair competition may also be committed when it threatens or violates the interests of an unspecified circle of entrepreneurs or customers. A combined case is also possible, i.e. an act or omission that will violate both the interest of a specific entrepreneur and the interest of unspecified entrepreneurs or customers.[328]

It has also been noted with regard to Article 18 of the Act on Combatting Unfair Competition that it is not clear how the existence of a threat to or violation of the entrepreneur's interest is to be proved at a trial, i.e. how to demonstrate actual damage to the claimant's assets. This premise should thus be interpreted liberally. Consequently, also according to the case law, the claimant would be relieved of the obligation to provide this evidence in a situation where there is a competitive relationship between the claimant and the defendant and it is clear from the very nature of the act of unfair competition that such act was aimed at taking over the claimant's clientele.[329] A good example of such an assumption may be the verdict of the Court of Appeal in Poznań, which held that 'in the light of undisputed findings as to the subject of activity of the claimants and the defendant and the area of the market for their products, there is no doubt that the parties are in competition with each other. If so, it would be detached from the principles of life experience and logic to assume that the defendant's use of unfair advertising in attracting customers is indifferent to the interest of the competing entrepreneur. At the very least, that interest is jeopardised by the possible loss of

---

[327] *Ibidem*, Nb 66.

[328] *A. Walaszek-Pyzioł, W. Pyzioł*, Czyn nieuczciwej konkurencji, p. 7. Also *R. Kasprzyk, B. Pietrzak*, Abstrakcyjny stosunek konkurencji, Palestra (Pal.). 1994, No 38(11), pp. 21–27. The authors deliberate whether, pursuant to Article 3 of 1993 Competition a competitive relationship must exist between the injured trader and the trader causing the damage. Referring to extensive case law of domestic as well as foreign courts, they come to the conclusion that liability under Art. 3 requires an assumption of an abstract, rather than a concrete, competition relationship.

[329] *J. Dudzik, R. Skubisz*, in: *J. Szwaja, J.Kępiński* (eds), Ustawa o zwalczaniu nieuczciwej konkurencji, 2024, Nb 14, p. 702, and the case-law quoted therein.

the sales market due to unfair advertising by the competitor'.[330] In a similar vein, the Supreme Court held that it was wrong to dismiss the application of Article 3(1) by the adjudicating court on the grounds that the prerequisite of a threat to the interests of the entrepreneur seeking protection had not been demonstrated. The Supreme Court found that the defendant had violated good practice by exploiting the claimant's trademark's reputation, which resulted in the dilution of the claimant's trademark and loss of its distinctive character and, consequently, of the attractive power of the enterprise and, subsequently, of its commercial value. According to the Supreme Court, the threat to the claimant's interests was evident,[331] and consequently, further-reaching evidence was not, in the actual state of affairs, necessary.

In contrast, the case is different when the claimant and the defendant are not in direct competition on the market. It has been argued in the literature that in such a situation, the claimant would have to prove that the defendant's conduct affected his interests (threatened or violated them). Thus, the claimant would have to prove at a trial that the acts or omissions of another market participant constituted a threat to or a violation of his or her own personal interest.[332] However, in many situations such evidence may be difficult to obtain and will thus limit the ability to pursue a claim.

5. Competition Relationship as the Basis for Active Legitimacy

Although it is accepted in the literature that the concept of a competition relationship should be understood broadly,[333] its definition is not straightforward.

[330] Judgement of the Court of Appeal in Poznań of 10.10.2005, I ACa 221/05, LEX Nr 519299. The appellant alleged that the Court of First Instance breached Article 18(1) by making an arbitrary assumption that the claimants are entrepreneurs whose interests have been prejudiced by the actions of the respondent and, consequently, on the assumption that they were entitled to legal standing.

[331] Judgement of the Supreme Court of 14.10.2009, V CSK 102/09, Legalis.

[332] *J. Dudzik*, *R. Skubisz*, in: *J. Szwaja*, *J. Kępiński* (eds), Ustawa o zwalczaniu nieuczciwej konkurencji, 2016, Nb 14, p. 702, and also *J. Rasiewicz*, in: *M. Zdyb*, *M. Sieradzka* (eds), Ustawa, p. 1038, Nb 69, which considers that the concept of an entrepreneur whose interest has been violated or threatened should be understood broadly. It stresses, however, that the scope of the claims made must be directly related to the interest of the entrepreneur with active legal standing.

[333] See *J. Szwaja*, *A. Kubiak-Cyrul*, in *J. Szwaja*, *J. Kępiński* (eds), Ustawa o zwalczaniu nieuczciwej konkurencji, 2024, p. 83, Nb 52 and the rulings quoted therein.

According to court rulings, entrepreneurs who operate in the same geographic and product market and compete for the same customers[334] are likely to be in a competitive relationship. Despite this approach, it has been held by the courts that there is also a competitive relationship between entrepreneurs even if they do not carry out the same type of activity[335]or if they do not operate in the same field.[336] The Supreme Court stated that 'the concept of a competing enterprise must be understood broadly and include not only competing enterprises in the strict sense, i.e. those operating in the same or similar sphere of production, services or trade, but also all cases in which the designation of an enterprise may mislead customers as to its identity with another enterprise. The risk of confusion as to the identity of enterprises may also arise when enterprises operate in different territories and have different objects of their activity'.[337]

In some situations, it may be difficult to establish whether traders are in a competitive relationship with each other. There are numerous examples of lawsuits concerning charges collected by traders for accepting goods for sale (Article 15(1)(4) of the Act on Combatting Unfair Competition, in which the courts adopted a view that in such cases the interests of suppliers of the goods were violated even if the traders (distributors) were not in a

---

334 Judgement of the Supreme Court of 25.11.2008, II CSK 343/08, Legalis.

335 Judgement of the Court of Appeal in Białystok of 29.6.1995, I ACr 114/95, OSA 1995, No 9, item 60, p. 12.

336 Judgement of the Supreme Court of 17.6.2004, V CK 550/03, Legalis. The dispute concerned a claim by Zakład Usług Informatycznych (IT Services) 'Novum' Sp. z o.o. for violation of the right to a name by the defendant who ran the Post-Secondary School of Informatics and Economics and the Post-Secondary School of Informatics and used the word 'Novum' in their name. The Supreme Court held that even though the claimant was not engaged in teaching activities, there was still a competition relationship between the entrepreneurs.

337 Judgement of the Supreme Court of 9.12.2011, III CSK 120/11, Legalis and its verdict of 11.3.2010 (IV CSK 379/09, Legalis), in which the Supreme Court, resolving a dispute on the basis of Article 5, held that a condition for the application of Article 5 is the existence of a competition relationship between enterprises in the broad sense of the term. The Supreme Court reasoned that the risk of confusion as to the identity of enterprises may also arise in relation to enterprises that are not competitive in the strict sense of the term and stated that the establishment of a competition relationship does not necessarily mean that in every such case there exists a possibility of misleading customers as to the identity of the enterprises.

direct competition relationship with one another). It seems that in a situation where the supply of goods to the distributor was not exclusive because the supplier also supplied its goods to other customers (distributors), there nevertheless remained a broadly understood competitive relationship with the distributor. If, on the other hand, the supplier supplied the goods only to the distributor, the two were operating at different levels of business activity and, in this sense, also only remained in an economic relationship that was partly competitive.[338] This type of relationship between the distributor and the supplier was sufficient to consider that the two were in a competitive relationship, and, therefore, the suppliers had active legitimation to make claims under Article 18 of the Act on Combatting Unfair Competition. A similar situation occurred when certain tenants of commercial premises in shopping centres were favoured at the time of calculating the shared costs. Although there was no direct competition relationship between the tenant (entrepreneur) and the landlord (entrepreneur-owner of the shopping centre), they undoubtedly remained in such business relations that could justify claims under the Act on Combatting Unfair Competition. This is because undoubtedly, favouring one trader over another trader affects the interests of the discriminated one.

Establishing the existence of a competition relationship may be necessary not only for the determination of those actively entitled to make specific claims, but also for the assessment of the existence of an act of unfair competition.[339]

There is a debate in the literature whether, under the Act on Combatting Unfair Competition of 1993, the occurrence of an act of unfair competition depends on the existence of a competition relationship. As a matter of fact, the requirement of the existence of a competition relationship was already provided for in the Act of 1926 and followed, *inter alia*, from the content of its Articles 1 and 2.[340]

---

338 See *J. Kępiński*, Pobieranie innych niż marża handlowa opłat za przyjęcie towaru do sprzedaży po wyroku TK z 16.10.2014 r., MoP 2016, No 15, pp. 796–803.

339 Also *B. Giesen*, Pojęcie konkurencji, in: *M. Kępiński* (ed.), System Prawa Prywatnego, vol. 15, Prawo konkurencji, Warszawa 2014, p. 69, Nb 18.

340 Article 1 of the Act of 1926 states that 'a trader has the right to demand that another trader (competitor) does not encroach on his clientele (...)'. Thus as can be seen from this provision it made a reference to a competitor. Also, Article 2 of the Act of 1926

Currently, the prevailing view is that the existence of a competition relationship is not a condition necessary for the determination of the existence of an act of unfair competition (a competition relationship is therefore not a premise for the application of the Act.)[341] Supporters of this view argue that most (albeit not all[342]) delicts of unfair competition may be committed by anyone, not only a competitor of the harmed entrepreneur. The same conclusion, they claim, will also be reached under the assumption that for the application of the Act on Combatting Unfair Competition, it will be sufficient to determine the existence of an abstract competition relationship. What is more, it will not be necessary that there occur a concrete competition relationship in which a certain act of one trader violates or threatens another trader directly.

On the other hand, it is argued that the premise of the competition relationship is valid with regard to those regulations of the Act on Combatting Unfair Competition that are directed at protecting entrepreneurs from the violation of their property interests by their competitors acting unfairly.[343] This view is supported by B. Giesen, who argues that the competition relationship is a condition necessary for establishing liability for a delict committed by a trader causing damage to another trader (competitor). However, as she

referred to the concept of a 'competing enterprise', and provided that 'The designation of an enterprise must not be such as to mislead the public as to its identity with another competing enterprise (...)'. See also *A. Kraus, F. Zoll*, Polska ustawa o zwalczaniu nieuczciwej konkurencji, p. 66. The authors repeatedly emphasise that claims under the 1926 Act arise as a result of the acts (or omission) of a competitor. It seems that the premise of a 'competition relationship' was unquestionable in the grounds of the Act of 1926. See also *B. Giesen*, Pojęcie konkurencji, p. 68, Nb 17.

341 See *J. Szwaja, A. Kubiak-Cyrul*, in: *J. Szwaja, J. Kępiński* (eds), Ustawa o zwalczaniu nieuczciwej konkurencji, 2024, p. 83, Nb 52, and also *E. Nowińska, M. du Vall*, Ustawa o zwalczaniu nieuczciwej konkurencji, comments to Art. 1, p. 36, Nb 5 and the case-law quoted therein, also *E. Nowińska*, in: *E. Nowińska, K. Szczepanowska-Kozłowska*, Ustawa o zwalczaniu, Comments to Art. 3, p. 74, Nb 4.

342 E.g. comparative advertising, imitation of a finished product.

343 *B. Giesen*, argues that, since the Act of Combatting Unfair Competition pursues various objectives, not only the protection of individual interests of competitors, it is necessary to diversify the nature of the individual norms, *B. Giesen*, O 'stosunku konkurencji' w prawie o zwalczaniu nieuczciwej konkurencji, in: Wyzwania dla ochrony konkurencji i regulacji rynku. Księga jubileuszowa dedykowana profesorowi Tadeuszowi Skocznemu, Warszawa 2017, p. 650.

further claims, for setting the framework for legal measures aimed to protect other entities, and in particular consumers or a concretised intangible asset, the condition of a competition relationship is not necessary, and the determination of a mere violation of such values is sufficient[344] and she adds that the existence of a competition relationship implies the applicability of Article 3 of the Act.[345]

It is also worth mentioning that Article 19 of the Act on Combatting Unfair Competition grants certain entities a right to make a claim under the Act even if they are not in a direct competition relationship with the entrepreneur who has committed an act of unfair competition. These are, currently, national or regional organisations whose statutory purpose is to protect the interests of entrepreneurs in general. They are not, however, established to protect the interests of a particular entrepreneur.

6. Active Legal Standing

Although the Act on Combatting Unfair Competition aims to prevent and combat unfair competition in the interest of the public, entrepreneurs, and customers, currently only entrepreneurs have standing to bring claims[346] and,

---

344 *B. Giesen*, O "stosunku konkurencji" w prawie, p. 647.

345 *Ibidem*, s. 649, and also *B. Giesen*, Pojęcie konkurencji, p. 74, Nb 29. See also verdict of the Supreme Court of 25.11.2008 (II CSK 343/08, Legalis), in which legal protection was denied to a claimant because as was claimed 'remaining in a competition relationship is relevant for the application of Articles 3 and 5 of the Act of 1993'. The adjudicating courts held that the parties were not competing on the same market because the claimant had ceased her business activity in 2004 and, what is more, between 2001 and 2002, two entities with a similar business name operated on the same market, with the claimant being the second to start using the disputed name. The reasoning of the Supreme Court was that this finding resulted 'not only from the substantive scope (Article 1 of the Act) and its purpose, but also from the categorisation of the prohibited acts defined, as in the case of Article 5, as acts of unfair competition ... the narrowing down of the protection of an enterprise's business name to cases of the use of the same or similar business name by competitors, i.e. persons competing for the same clientele, results from the reservation included in this provision which stipulates the possibility of misleading clients as to the identity of the enterprise. In the case at hand, it was established that the claimant has never rendered services in the area of organising tourist events in Poland, and as of since 2004 her activity in this sector has been ceased altogether'.

346 Judgement of the Supreme Court of 29.11.2013, I CSK 756/12, OSNC-ZD 2015, No 1, item 11 in which it was emphasised that 'in order to confer standing on an entity seeking

to some extent, a national or regional organisation whose statutory objective is to protect the interests of traders. A natural person that is not an entrepreneur, and therefore also a consumer, does not have such a possibility. According to the explanatory memorandum to the draft Act, active legal standing to take action is vested in the entrepreneur, and the Act does not provide for *actio popularis*. The individual customer (as a consumer) does not have standing but may assert his or her rights under other provisions, e.g. the Civil Code. Earlier, in a situation where an individual interest of a customer constituted an act of unlawful activity in a broader sense, a consumer organisation had standing to take action.[347] Today, however, a consumer organisation does not have active legitimation (to act).

Article 18 of the Act on Combatting Unfair Competition provides that when an act of unfair competition has been committed, the subject entitled to make certain claims is the entrepreneur whose interest has been threatened or violated. A national or regional organisation, the statutory objective of which is to protect the interests of entrepreneurs, also has an active legal standing, but only to make certain claims (i.e. to discontinue the prohibited activities, to remove the effects of the prohibited activities, to make one or more statements of appropriate content and form, and to award an appropriate sum of money for a specific social purpose related to the promotion of Polish culture or protection of national heritage). However, such an organisation cannot make these claims in the situation in respect of acts of unfair competition specified in Articles 5–7, 11, 14, and 15a.

It should be added that the catalogue of entities entitled to bring claims has changed over the period.[348] After the initial expansion of the list, as of the amendments to the Act of 5 July 2002,[349] the number of subjects entitled to make claims has been limited.

---

to obtain legal protection to pursue the claims provided for therein, it is necessary to establish that the entity has the status of an entrepreneur within the meaning of Article 2 of the Act on Combatting Unfair Practices'. See also the judgment of the Court of Appeal in Poznań of 19.12.2013, I ACa 978/13, Legalis.

347 Explanatory memorandum to the draft Act of 1993, Druk sejmowy I kadencji No 278, p. 7.

348 See *J. Szwaja*, *A. Tischner*, Legitymacja w sprawach zwalczania nieuczciwej konkurencji, in: *M. Kępiński* (ed.), System Prawa Prywatnego, vol. 15, Prawo konkurencji, Warszawa 2014, p. 629, Nb 105–108.

349 See: Act of 5.7.2002 (Dz. U. No 129, item 1102).

Initially, in addition to entrepreneurs, organisations whose statutory purpose was the protection of consumer interests or the protection of the interests of entrepreneurs were also entitled. Gradually, their number was increased, and the President of the Office of Competition and Consumer Protection (UOKiK President) and the district (municipal) consumer ombudsman also acquired standing. After successive amendments in 2003 and 2007, the only entity entitled to bring claims under the Act, apart from the entrepreneur, remained a national or regional organisation whose statutory objective is to protect the interests of entrepreneurs. The latter, however, may only file certain claims. This is because in the case of acts of unfair competition consisting of misleading identification of an enterprise (Articles 5–7), violation of business secrets (Article 11), dissemination of false or misleading information (Article 14), and bribery of a person holding a public function (Article 15a), the sole claimant is the entrepreneur whose interests have been threatened or violated.

It should be explained that entities that have so far been able to bring claims under the provisions of the Act on Combatting Unfair Competition may also do so under the provisions of other Acts and to the extent regulated in them. There is also a view in the literature that, despite the repeal of Article 19(1)(1) and (4), the entities it mentioned [consumer organisations and the district (municipal) consumer ombudsman] may bring unfair competition claims before the court. According to J. Szwaja and A. Kubiak-Cyrul, they may, in consumer protection cases, bring actions in favour of natural persons on the basis of the general rules of civil procedure (Articles 61–63 KPC[350]).[351] Active standing may also be due to the President of the UOKiK who pursuant to Article 26 of the Act on Competition and Consumer Protection may issue a decision determining a certain practice as violating the collective interests on consumers, and therefore order to stop in the event of a violation of the prohibition set out in Article 24 (practices infringing the collective interests of consumers),[352] or, according to *J. Szwaja* and *A. Kubiak-Cyrul* and

[350] The Act of 17 November 1964 – Code of Civil Procedure *(Kodeks postępowania cywilnego)* Dz.U. of 2024 item 1568 as amended).

[351] *J. Szwaja, A. Kubiak-Cyrul*, in: *J. Szwaja, J. Kępiński* (eds), Ustawa o zwalczaniu nieuczciwej konkurencji, 2024, pp. 801–802, Nb 4 and p. 804, Nb 11.

[352] Pursuant to Article 24(2) of the Act on Competition and Consumer Protection, a 'practice infringing the collective interests of consumers shall be understood as any

pursuant to Article 25, when it is determined that "a single instance of an unfair market practice requires intervention on account of a general interest of consumers, existing or potential, which is distinct from the sum of the individual consumer's interests."[353]

This view, expressed by J. Szwaja and A. Kubiak-Cyrul, is not shared by other authors who express an opinion that the Act on Combatting Unfair Competition explicitly defines who has the right of action. Consequently, entities not expressly mentioned in the Act have no legal standing.[354] Neither are there any rulings based on Article 19 that would address this issue. It can only be inferred from the judgement of the Court of Appeal in Białystok that the courts, following the views expressed in the literature,[355] do not apply an expansive interpretation. This court ruled, admittedly on the basis of Article 19(1)(2), that the claims listed in Article 18 clause 1, points 1–3 and 6, may be brought by a national or regional organisation whose statutory goal is to protect the interests of entrepreneurs. However, local organisations are not entitled to these rights. Therefore, since in this respect the courts refer to the literal wording of the provision, the view that only entities that have been listed in the Act on Combatting Unfair Competition should be granted standing is justified.

In addition, consumer organisations, which, following the 2003 amendment, have lost their active legal standing under the Act on Combatting Unfair Competition, may now bring claims under the Act on Counteracting Unfair Market Practices. Under Article 12(2)(3), the claims referred to in point

behaviour of a trader contrary to the law or morality, in particular: (1) (repealed); (2) breaching the obligation to provide consumers with fair, truthful and complete information; (3) unfair market practices or acts of unfair competition; (4) proposing to consumers the purchase of financial services that do not correspond to the needs of those consumers determined taking into account the information available to the trader regarding the characteristics of those consumers or proposing to purchase such services in a manner inappropriate to their nature'.

353 *J. Szwaja, A. Kubiak-Cyrul*, in: *J. Szwaja, J. Kępiński* (eds), Ustawa o zwalczaniu nieuczciwej konkurencji, 2024, s. 803, Nb 8. The authors are of an opinion that the prosecutor also has an active standing (Articles 55–60 of the Code of Civil Procedure).

354 See: *E. Nowińska, M. du Vall*, Ustawa o zwalczaniu nieuczciwej konkurencji, Comments to Art. 19, p. 449, Nb 2; *J. Rasiewicz*, in: *M. Zdyb, M. Sieradzka* (eds), Ustawa o zwalczaniu nieuczciwej konkurencji, Comments to Art. 19, p. 1073, Nb 10, p. 1075, Nb 14–15.

355 *J. Szwaja, A. Kubiak-Cyrul*, in: *J. Szwaja* (ed.), Ustawa o zwalczaniu nieuczciwej konkurencji, 2016, p. 868, Nb 15.

1 ('stopping the practice'), point 3 (making one or more statements of appropriate content and form), and point 5 (awarding an appropriate sum of money for a specific social purpose) may also be brought by a national or regional organisation whose statutory goal is to protect the interests of consumers, or a district (municipal) consumer advocate, and now, additionally, by the Ombudsman and the Financial Ombudsman. All of these entities are entitled to bring claims if, in the event of an unfair market practice, the consumers interests have been threatened or violated. However, the catalogue of the claims they can make is still limited and does not extend to the President of the Office of Competition and Consumer Protection either, who may only file claims under the Act on Competition and Consumer Protection in the event of a violation of collective interests of consumers.

Such a legislative procedure, clearly separating the standing of certain entities on account of the basic purpose of their activities (the entrepreneur's interest and the consumer's interest), may justify the legislator's intention to also separate the scope of the subject matter of the two Acts. Indeed, the purpose of the Act on Combatting Unfair Competition is to protect first and foremost the interests of entrepreneurs, and thus the entities with standing are primarily entrepreneurs and organisations that are supposed to protect their interests. On the other hand, the primary objective of the Act on Counteracting Unfair Market Practices is to protect the interests of consumers, and therefore the entities with standing are primarily consumers and public entities whose objective is to protect the interests of consumers.

7. Passive Legal Standing

Passive legal standing under the Act on Combatting Unfair Competition is held by a person[356] who has committed an act of unfair competition, as a result of which the interest of another entrepreneur is violated or threatened.

As a rule, an act of unfair competition may be committed by an entrepreneur, in particular a competitor of the entrepreneur whose interest has been threatened or violated.[357] However, an entrepreneur who is not a competitor

---

356 Also see the judgment of the Court of Appeal in Gdańsk of 24.2.2012 (V ACa 43/12, Legalis).

357 It follows from the hypotheses of some provisions that they may be committed exclusively by an entrepreneur. See:. *A. Walaszek-Pyzioł*, *W. Pyzioł*, Czyn nieuczciwej konkurencji, p. 6. The authors consider those acts be those referred to in Articles 5–10,

of the harmed entrepreneur may also be sued (in the event of committing a delict under Article 12[358] or Article 14[359]).

Article 17 extends the circle of entrepreneurs with passive standing. If an act of unfair competition in the field of advertising is committed, the advertising agency or other entrepreneur who prepared the advertisement may also be liable. It has been explained in the literature that the basis is the liability of the advertising party (Art. 16), but due to the importance of advertising, Article 17 serves as a warning to other entities involved in the creation of advertisements. They must be aware that when an advertisement is created in contravention to Article 16, they too may be liable for committing an act of unfair competition.[360]

On the other hand, the granting of passive standing to non-entrepreneurs should be considered as a derogation (exception) from this rule and should be sought 'among the named delicts of unfair competition which provide (*expressis verbis* or implicitly) for the possibility of committing acts of unfair competition by entities other than entrepreneurs'.[361] The literature underlines that some of the acts of unfair competition can be committed by anyone, so also by a non-entrepreneur, such as a client or customer (Articles 12[362] and 14[363]). It is further assumed that acts of unfair competition may be committed

---

Article 13, Article 14 point 3 and Article 15 points 1 and 3 of the Act on Combatting Unfair Competition. Also see the verdict of the Court of Appeal in Katowice of 15.2.2012, V ACa 5/12, Biul.SAKa 2012, No 2, items 30–31.

358 See Article 12 of the Act on Combatting Unfair Competition, *M. Kępiński, J. Kępiński*, in: *J. Szwaja, J. Kępiński* (eds), Ustawa o zwalczaniu nieuczciwej konkurencji, 2024, p. 417, Nb 24.

359 *J. Sroczyński, M. Mioduszewski*, in: *M. Zdyb, M. Sieradzka* (eds), Ustawa, Comments to Art. 14, pp. 577–578, Nb 32

360 *E. Nowińska, M. du Vall*, Ustawa o zwalczaniu nieuczciwej konkurencji, Comments to Art. 17, p. 388, Nb 1; *M. Sieradzka*, in: *M. Zdyb, M. Sieradzka* (eds), Ustawa, Comments to Art. 17, p. 956, Nb 6.

361 *J. Rasiewicz*, in: *M. Zdyb, M. Sieradzka* (eds), Ustawa, Comments to Art. 178, p. 1041, Nb 74.

362 *M. Kępiński, J. Kępiński*, in: *J. Szwaja, J. Kępiński* (eds), Ustawa o zwalczaniu nieuczciwej konkurencji, 2024, p. 418, Nb 25.

363 E.g. *A. Walaszek-Pyzioł, W. Pyzioł*, Czyn nieuczciwej konkurencji, p. 6, although this view is questioned. See: *J. Rasiewicz*, in: *M. Zdyb, M. Sieradzka* (eds), Comments to Art. 178, p. 1041, Nb 74.

by a person related in some way to the entrepreneur, e.g. an employee of the entrepreneur (see Articles 12 and 14).

The situation of an entrepreneur's employee is particularly peculiar, as the Act on Combatting Unfair Competition allows, in certain cases, an entrepreneur to sue an employee who acted to his or her detriment.[364] However, two situations must be distinguished here. In the first one, the employee commits an act of unfair competition, but the liability lies with the employer.[365] In such a situation it is not possible to sue the employee. In the other situation, an employee commits a delict of unfair competition and may himself be liable for its commission.[366]

Employee's liability was highlighted in the repealed Article 11(2)[367] which provided that not only employees, but also other legal persons, such as contractual partners or market participants who are neither entrepreneurs nor natural persons, such as associations or foundations, could be sued for breach of confidentiality.[368] Currently, Article 11 does not give employees passive procedural capacity.

An employee may be sued for committing an act of unfair competition, such as inducing those who provide work for the entrepreneur based on an employment or other legal relationship to not perform or improperly perform their employment or other contractual obligations, or inducing the entrepreneur's clients or other persons to terminate a contract with the entrepreneur or to not perform or improperly perform a contract with the entrepreneur, in order to benefit themselves or third parties or to harm the

---

364 See *B. Antczak*, Nieuczciwa konkurencja pracownika – wybrane zagadnienia, MoPP 2016, No 11, pp. 572–578. The author notes that there are disputes on the grounds of the Act on Combatting Unfair Competition regarding the possibility of suing the employee himself or the entrepreneur on whose behalf the entrepreneur acts. These disputes arise on the basis of Articles 12, 14 and Article 3 of the said Act.

365 *M. Gersdorf, M. Raczkowski*, Odpowiedzialność za pracowniczy czyn nieuczciwej konkurencji, PiZS 2005, No 1, p. 9.

366 To those belong, as it is believed, acts listed in Article 12 and Article 14 of the Act on Combatting Unfair Competition.

367 Article 11 of the Act on Combatting Unfair Competition has been changed by the Act of 5.7.2018 (Dz.U. of 2018 item 1637) which came into force on 4 September 2018.

368 *E. Nowińska, M. du Vall*, Ustawa o zwalczaniu nieuczciwej konkurencji, komentarz do art. 11, p. 192, Nb 10–11; also see: *E. Nowińska*, in: *E. Nowińska, K. Szczepanowska-Kozłowska*, Ustawa o zwalczaniu, 2018, Comments to Art. 11, p. 237, Nb 10–11.

entrepreneur (Article 12(1) and (2)). It is accepted in the literature that the subject of a breach of contractual relations can be anyone and thus also an employee.[369] When an unfair competition act of that type is committed by an employee, such behaviour will also qualify as a breach of the employee's duties (caring for the welfare of the workplace), which is, however, irrelevant to liability under the Act in question.[370]

It is also permissible to sue an employee of an entrepreneur in a situation where an act of unfair competition involves dissemination of untrue or misleading information about the entrepreneur's business or another's business, with the aim of benefiting or causing damage. As argued in the literature on the subject, although 'the provision of Article 14 does not explicitly single out natural persons as wrongdoers, the stylistic nature of the provision, in particular the introduction of two different concepts, one of "one's entrepreneur" and one of "one's enterprise" dictates that the wrongdoers mentioned in the provision may not only be entrepreneurs, but also their employees'.[371] However, the above view is sometimes contested in the literature on the subject. Some argue that there is no competition relationship between the employee and the employer, and therefore one cannot argue that 'the linguistic formulation of Article 14 justifies extending its hypothesis also to the employees of an entrepreneur'.[372]

Another doubt arises as to whether a consumer who disseminates false or misleading information, for example on the Internet, may be sued. As a rule, consumer liability under the Act on Combatting Unfair Competition

369 *E. Nowińska*, in: *E. Nowińska, K. Szczepanowska-Kozłowska*, Ustawa o zwalczaniu nieuczciwej konkurencji, Comments to Art. 12, p. 289, Nb 11–12.

370 *M. Kępiński, J. Kępiński*, in: *J. Szwaja* (eds), Ustawa o zwalczaniu nieuczciwej konkurencji, 2024, p. 417, Nb 24.

371 *E. Nowińska, M. du Vall*, Ustawa o zwalczaniu nieuczciwej konkurencji, Comments to Art. 14, p. 235, Nb 5; and also *E. Nowińska*, in: *E. Nowińska, K. Szczepanowska-Kozłowska*, Ustawa o zwalczaniu nieuczciwej konkurencji, Comments to Art. 14, p. 333, Nb 9. Also, the verdict of the Court of Appeal in Kraków of 24.7.2014, I ACa 575/14, Legalis. A different opinion has been expressed by *J. Sroczyński, M. Mioduszewski*, in: *M. Zdyb, M. Sieradzka* (eds), Ustawa o zwalczaniu nieuczciwej konkurencji, kom. do art. 14, p. 577, Nb 32.

372 *J. Sroczyński, M. Mioduszewski*, in: *M. Zdyb, M. Sieradzka* (eds), Ustawa, Comments to Art. 14, p. 578, Nb 32.

is excluded.[373] On the other hand, it would be possible to file claims against organisational units that do not engage in a business activity, for example, foundations or associations that disseminate such information. The latter might also include an entrepreneur who is not a competitor of the harmed entrepreneur, e.g. a press publisher disseminating untrue information.[374]

It is also questioned in the literature whether an employee may be liable under the general clause (Article 3(1)) in the event of committing an unnamed act of unfair competition.[375] *E. Nowińska* and *M. du Vall* note that in connection with the interpretation of Article 3, the relationship between that Article 3 and the provisions that provide for the possibility of a delict being committed by other entities must be resolved.[376] They propose three possible solutions. Firstly, they argue that an act of unfair competition can be committed only by an entrepreneur; secondly, that it may be committed by both an entrepreneur and an entity that does not have the status of an entrepreneur; and thirdly, that it may be committed by an entrepreneur and, exceptionally, by another entity as indicated in the Act.

The third view is to be favoured. This interpretation allows for the employee's passive standing, which, as shown above, is possible. However, the possibility of suing an employee under the Act on Combatting Unfair Competition

---

373 *E. Nowińska, M. du Vall*, Ustawa o zwalczaniu nieuczciwej konkurencji, Comments to Art. 14, p. 235, Nb 5; also *E. Nowińska*, in: *E. Nowińska, K. Szczepanowska-Kozłowska*, Ustawa o zwalczaniu, Comments to Art. 14, p. 333–334, Nb 9; *M. Kępiński, J. Kępiński* in: *J. Szwaja, J. Kępiński* (eds), Ustawa o zwalczaniu nieuczciwej konkurencji, 2024, p. 456, Nb 6 and *J. Sroczyński, M. Mioduszewski*, in: *M. Zdyb, M. Sieradzka* (eds), Ustawa o zwalczaniu nieuczciwej konkurencji, kom. do art. 14, p. 572, Nb 26.

374 *M. Kępiński, J. Kępiński* in: *J. Szwaja, J. Kępiński* (eds), Ustawa o zwalczaniu nieuczciwej konkurencji, 2024, p. 455–456, Nb 6; also *J. Sroczyński, M. Mioduszewski*, in: *M. Zdyb, M. Sieradzka* (eds), Ustawa o zwalczaniu nieuczciwej konkurencji, kom. do art. 14, pp. 577–578, Nb 32.

375 *M. Gersdorf, M. Raczkowski*, Odpowiedzialność za pracowniczy czyn, pp. 8–14 are of the opinion that one cannot qualify any action of an employee as an unnamed act of unfair competition (Article 3 of the Act on Combatting Unfair Competition). A similar opinion express *A. Walaszek-Pyzioł, W. Pyzioł*, Czyn nieuczciwej konkurencji, p. 6, but a different one is presented by *B. Antczak*, Nieuczciwa konkurencja pracownika, p. 574.

376 *E. Nowińska, M. du Vall*, Ustawa o zwalczaniu nieuczciwej konkurencji, kom. do art. 3, p. 71–72, Nb 18; also *E. Nowińska*, in: *E. Nowińska, K. Szczepanowska-Kozłowska*, Ustawa o zwalczaniu nieuczciwej konkurencji, Comments to Art. 3, p. 101, Nb 19.

should be regarded as an exception to the rule. It also seems that the employee's actions are not always related to business transactions. Indeed, some of the employee's actions should be treated as relating to the internal relationship of the business, i.e. the employer–employee relationship. However, it cannot be ruled out that some of the employee's actions will not fulfil the elements of the named acts of unfair competition. An example would be an employee of an entrepreneur persuading a potential employee or customer not to enter into a contract with the entrepreneur-employer. Such an act would not qualify as a delict under Article 12, as this provision relates to situations of interference with contracts already concluded. However, the employee's act could possibly constitute a delict under Article 3.[377] Above all, however, the conduct of an employee who, in the context of the employment relationship, persuades a potential client not to enter into a contract with the employer would constitute a breach of the employee's duties. In principle, however, the basis for the employee's liability in such a situation should be the provisions of the Labour Code, including the provisions related to the employee's duties (Article 100), as well as the prohibition of competition during and after the termination of the employment relationship (Articles 101^1–101^4).

Undue expansion of the sphere of application of the Act on Combatting Unfair Competition is unjustified, as in many situations the provisions of the Labour Law are sufficient. This does not mean, however, that the employee's liability under the Act on Combatting Unfair Competition can be fully separated from the liability under the Labour Code. An employee's liability under the Act on Combatting Unfair Competition should, however, be treated as an exception to the principle that it is the entrepreneur who is primarily liable for acts of unfair competition.[378]

8. The Nature of Claims under Article 18 of the Act on Combatting Unfair Competition

In the literature on the subject, as well as in the case law of the Supreme Court, doubts arise as to the nature of the pecuniary or non-pecuniary claims

---

[377] Also, *M. Kępiński*, *J. Kępiński*, in: *J. Szwaja*, *J. Kępiński* (eds), Ustawa o zwalczaniu nieuczciwej konkurencji, 2024, p. 418, Nb 25, and also *B. Antczak*, Nieuczciwa konkurencja pracownika, p. 575.

[378] *A. Walaszek-Pyzioł*, *W. Pyzioł*, Czyn nieuczciwej konkurencji, p. 6.

under Article 18 of the Act.[379] The prevailing view is that these claims are of a pecuniary nature. K. Szczepanowska-Kozłowska is of the opinion that claims provided for in Article 18(1) are purely pecuniary in nature because under Article 20 they are subject to the statute of limitations, and since they may prescribe, they are of a pecuniary nature.[380] Also, J. Szwaja and A. Tischner argue that due to the nature of the interests protected, these claims are of a pecuniary nature.[381] E. Nowińska shares this opinion.[382]

The Supreme Court made a similar statement regarding the pecuniary nature of claims seeking an injunction against prohibited acts,[383] arguing that 'when deciding for the purposes of determining the court fee whether a right is of a pecuniary or non-pecuniary nature, one should (...) be guided by whether the rights asserted in the case are directly conditioned by the economic interests of the entitled entity. A positive answer means recognition of the right as pecuniary, and a negative answer means recognition of the right as non-pecuniary'. In the justification, the Supreme Court also stated that the qualification of the claim for prohibition of prohibited acts, as well as for making an appropriate statement, as non-pecuniary claims has no legitimate basis. The court explained that the claims set out in the Act on Combatting Unfair Competition 'although, according to the prevailing view, are not based on an intangible good, which is the subject of an absolute property right, they are directly conditioned by the economic interests of the persons to whom they are entitled and thus have a pecuniary character due to the fact that the provisions of this Act, pursuant to Article 1, regulate the prevention and combatting unfair practices in the economic activity.

---

379 On the difficulty of classifying claims under Article 18 of the Act on Combatting Unfair Competition as either pecuniary or non-pecuniary *E. Nowińska, M. du Vall*, Ustawa o zwalczaniu nieuczciwej konkurencji, Comments to Art. 3, pp. 417–418, Nb 4.

380 See: *K. Szczepanowska-Kozłowska*, in: *E. Nowińska, K. Szczepanowska-Kozłowska*, Ustawa o zwalczaniu nieuczciwej konkurencji, kom. do art. 18, pp. 586–587, Nb 9.

381 *J. Szwaja, A. Tischner*, Odpowiedzialność cywilnoprawna za czyny nieuczciwej konkurencji, SPP 2009, No 2, p. 44.

382 See: *E. Nowińska*, Ochrona wyłączności korzystania, in: *E. Nowińska, K. Szczepanowska-Kozłowska* (eds), System Prawa Handlowego, vol. 3, Prawo własności przemysłowej, Warszawa 2015, p. 727.

383 Decision of the Supreme Court of 8.3.2007, III CZ 12/07, OSNC 2008, No 2, item 26, p. 72.

Also, the Act itself provides for the statute of limitations for claims for acts of unfair competition (Article 20).

However, in a later judgement, the Supreme Court expressed a different view and held that claims under the Act on Combatting Unfair Competition 'are of a varied nature: pecuniary (e.g. a claim for compensation for damage caused, the surrender of unfairly obtained benefits, a prohibition on marketing products), and non-pecuniary (a claim for the submission of an appropriate declaration)'.[384] It has been argued in the literature that a claim for an appropriate declaration may serve to protect both personal and pecuniary interests but will be mainly of a pecuniary nature. It is also possible that the entrepreneur will be concerned with compensation for the damage caused, which is available under Article 18 (1) (3) of the Act and Article 24 § 2 of the Civil Code.[385] In the literature the dominating view is that those rights are of a mixed character.[386] Some claims follow the model of protection of property and other subjective rights (claim for cessation, remedy, declaration). Others (claims for compensation for damage and surrender of unjustly obtained benefits) are based on tort protection and the institution of unjust enrichment.

To sum up the above, one must agree with the view on the pecuniary nature of the claims under Article 18(1). This is because at the heart of the Act on Combatting Unfair Competition lies the protection of the pecuniary (economic) and not the non-pecuniary interests of entrepreneurs.[387] This does not mean that the entrepreneur may not sue for non-pecuniary rights, primarily under the Civil Code. The catalogue of claims adopted in Article 18(1) does not preclude an entrepreneur from raising other claims. Notably, this situation occurs relatively often when an entrepreneur's actions violate provisions of other legislative acts, in particular the Act on Copyright and

384 Judgement of the Supreme Court of 9.1.2008, II CSK 363/07, Legalis.

385 *J. Szwaja, A. Kubiak-Cyrul*, in *J. Szwaja, J. Kępiński* (eds), Ustawa o zwalczaniu nieuczciwej konkurencji, 2024, Comments to Art. 18, p. 730, Nb 72.

386 *J. Szwaja, A. Tischner*, Odpowiedzialność cywilnoprawna za czyny nieuczciwej konkurencji, in: *M. Kępiński* (ed.), System Prawa Prywatnego, vol. 15, Prawo konkurencji, Nb 34, p. 596.

387 *K. Zawada*, Majątkowy charakter roszczeń określonych w art. 18 ust. 1 pkt 1 i 3 ZNKU i wynikające stąd konsekwencje dotyczące opłat sądowych, ZNUJ PIPWIUJ 2007, issue 10, p. 645.

Related Rights or the Industrial Property Law, in which case there occurs a cumulative protection.[388]

The consequence of accepting that such claims are pecuniary claims is the need to pay a proportional fee, not a fixed amount, when filing an action. A fixed fee is collected in cases concerning non-pecuniary rights and some pecuniary rights indicated in the Act, always in the same amount, regardless of the value of the object of dispute or the value of the object of appeal.[389] On the other hand, a proportional fee is charged in cases concerning pecuniary rights. It amounts to 5% of the value of the object of the dispute or the object of the appeal; however, it shall not be less than PLN 30 and no more than PLN 200,000.[390]

§ 3. Conclusions

Polish law on unfair competition has its roots in the Act of 1926 on combatting unfair competition, which was, at the time when enacted, a modern piece of legislation, and, as evidenced in the numerous court decisions and disputes pending at its time and preserved to this day, it was quite frequently applied. Many of the assumptions forming the basis for the resolution of the past disputes have remained relevant in modern times and may be used in support of the interpretation of today's provisions of the Act on Combatting Unfair Competition of 1993. The Act of 1926 addressed relationships between entrepreneurs, and its purpose was to protect them. However, since it was understood that delicts of unfair competition could also turn against consumers, if necessary, protection of their interests could be sought in its criminal law provisions.

The Act of 1993 is intended to protect the interests of the public, as well as of entrepreneurs and customers. That protection is to be guaranteed by preventing and combatting unfair competition in economic activities, while

---

388 *J. Szwaja, A. Tischner*, Odpowiedzialność cywilnoprawna, Nb 20, p. 589. On the cumulative protection on the example of industrial designs e.g. *J. Kępiński*, Wzór przemysłowy i jego ochrona w prawie polskim i wspólnotowym, Warszawa 2010, pp. 290–334.

389 Act of 28.7.2005 on court costs in civil law matters (Dz.U. of 2024 item 959,1237 as amended).

390 See Art. 13 of the Act of 28.7.2005 on court costs in civil law matters. More on that: *K. Zawada*, Majątkowy charakter roszczeń, pp. 643–652.

those interests overlap and cannot be separated. What is more, it would be inappropriate to assume that one of the interests should be given preferential treatment, as all of them are equally important.

Despite this assumption, under the currently applicable law, only the entrepreneur and, to a certain extent, a national or regional organisation whose statutory goal is to protect the interests of entrepreneurs will have standing, or active legitimation. If, however, the customer-consumer's interests are violated, no claims can be made under the Act on Combatting Unfair Competition since the legislator has not provided in the Act for customers' active legal standing. Consequently, if customers interests are violated by an entrepreneur's conduct amounting to an act of unfair competition, their assertion will be possible on the general principles of liability for prohibited acts or by claiming defects in the declaration of will.[391]

There is a dispute in the literature as well as in the judicial decisions as to the relationship between the general clause (Article 3(1)) and the specific delicts (Articles 5–17f) of the Act.

In my opinion, it is also incorrect to argue that it is always necessary, irrespective of the existence of premises that a specific delict has occurred, to also demonstrate the inconsistency with the law and good practice (Article 3(1)). The application of the corrective function of Article 3(1) should be exceptional and not constitute a rule that would allow courts to dismiss an action when these circumstances have not been established. I believe that the mere fulfilment of the prerequisites of acts of unfair competition listed in Chapter 2 should be sufficient to allow a claim, and recourse to the general clause should not consist in supplementing the content of a specific act with additional prerequisites flowing from Article 3(1).[392] It has been emphasised in the literature that the adoption of a different position (i) undermines the importance of singling out specific acts of unfair competition, (ii) limits the importance of the supplementary function of Article 3(1), (iii) raises the

---

391 See *J. Szwaja*, *A. Tischner*, Legitymacja w sprawach zwalczania nieuczciwej konkurencji, p. 629, Nb 105–108.

392 *M. Kępiński*, Stosunek art. 3 ust. 1 ustawy, p. 11. Also *R. Stefanicki*, Klauzula generalna w ZNKU, p. 125, Nb 26, in which he refers to the interpretation used by the ECJ with regards Directive 2005/29/EC. Also *R. Skubisz*, Klauzule generalne, p. 85.

importance of the corrective function of Article 3(1), (iv) and undermines the principle of legal certainty.[393]

M. Szpunar is correct when he argues that it is wrong to completely separate the general clause from the special provisions. This does not mean, however, that the disposition of each of these specific provisions has to be supplemented by elements contained in the general clause. Accordingly, in light of the above considerations, the justification of the judgement of the Regional Court appears to be erroneous.[394] According to the arguments presented by the Court, it is generally accepted in doctrine and case law that 'the requirements set out in the definition of Article 3(1) refer to acts listed in Articles 5–17, while the general clause has a corrective function in relation to special provisions. When a given factual situation, formally, meets the prerequisites of Articles 5–17, but in reality, the act in question does not exhibit any of the elements of Article 3(1) (unlawfulness, violation of good practice, etc.), such an act cannot be recognised as an act of unfair competition'. This standpoint of the Regional Court implies that the prerequisites listed in the general clause must be proved in each case. Such an assumption, as is evident from the literature and case law, is rather controversial and is not, as the Court argued, universally accepted. Indeed, the unlawfulness of a given act of unfair competition derives from the special provisions themselves. A corrective function may be exceptionally applied when the court considers that a given ruling would be contrary to good practice.

Another important issue addressed under the Act on Combatting Unfair Competition is the significance of the existence of a competition relationship. Demonstrating the existence of a competition relationship may be necessary for two reasons: firstly, to determine the occurrence of an act of unfair competition, and secondly, to determine the circle of persons actively entitled to bring specific claims. One should agree with the view prevailing in the literature that the existence of a competition relationship is not absolutely necessary for an act of unfair competition to arise. However, the essence of the premise of a competition relationship emerges

---

393 *R. Skubisz*, Klauzule generalne, p. 85.

394 See verdict of the Regional Court in Warszawa of 9.12.2017, XXII GWwp 5/16, Legalis.

from Article 18. Evidencing the existence of a competition relationship will be important for establishing the active standing of an entrepreneur, making him or her eligible to bring a claim. This is because an entrepreneur wishing to issue claims against another entrepreneur (who has committed an act of unfair competition) should demonstrate that the two remain in a broadly understood competition relationship. It thus appears that the opinion expressed by M. Sieradzka that 'an aggrieved entrepreneur is entitled to protection (of claims under Article18) despite the fact that there is no competitive relationship (bond) between the entrepreneur and the offender'[395] is oversimplified. As a rule, under the Act on Combatting Unfair Competition, it should be assumed that for making claims specified in Article 18, an entrepreneur must demonstrate that the competition relationship with the violator led to his or her interest being threatened or violated, which in turn justified the filing of specific claims in order to protect the entrepreneur's particular property interests. In other words, the entrepreneur has active legal standing to do so. Therefore, one must agree with B. Giesen that the existence of a competition relationship will, in principle, constitute a condition for delictual liability. At the same time, however, it will not be a condition for the qualification of an entrepreneur's conduct as an act of unfair competition.[396]

Yet, it could be argued that a competitive relationship does not always have to exist for the offender to be held liable for an act of unfair competition. Moreover, certain claims may be brought by an entrepreneur who is not in a competitive relationship with anyone but whose acts are aimed to protect the public's or customers interest. In such a situation, however, the catalogue of claims will be limited, as it will practically be impossible to prove damage. The most probable claims in such a case will be claims for failure to take a certain action (Article 18(1)(1)),[397] for filing a statement in a certain form and of a certain content (Article 18(1)(3), or the award of a certain sum for social purposes (Article 18(1)(6).

---

395 *M. Sieradzka*, in: *M. Zdyb*, *M. Sieradzka* (eds), Ustawa, kom. do art. 1, p. 45, Nb 10.

396 *B. Giesen*, O "stosunku konkurencji" w prawie, p. 651.

397 See: *J. Szwaja*, *A. Tischner*, System środków cywilnoprawnych, in: *M. Kępiński* (ed.), System Prawa Prywatnego, vol. 15, Prawo konkurencji, Warszawa 2014, p. 593, Nb 25.

Case law will play a special role in interpreting the premise of a competitive relationship as a basis for claims under the Act on Combatting Unfair Competition. The interpretation applied by the courts will determine how it should be interpreted. At the same time, it appears that it will not always be necessary to prove the existence of a competition relationship. This is because in many cases its existence is obvious and unequivocal and will not require any special proof. This will be true, among other things, for acts of unfair competition, which are always directed against a specific entrepreneur and include, for example, obstruction of sales, boycotts, defamation, discrimination, imitation, and exploitation of another's reputation. In such cases, there will be no need to prove the existence of a competition relationship.

Chapter III

The Scope and Objectives of the Act on Counteracting Unfair Market Practices

§ 1. Introductory Remarks

The underlying reason for the adoption of a legislative act intended to counteract unfair commercial practices was the obligation to implement into the Polish legal system Directive 2005/29/EC[398] on unfair commercial practices. The implemented Directive took the form of the Act on Counteracting Unfair Market Practices. Noteworthy, the implementation of the Directive was based on a so-called full harmonisation,[399] approach which, in turn, influenced the manner in which it was transposed to national legislations, as Member States were under the obligation to adopt precisely the solutions contained in the Directive. Thus, a reference must be made to the Directive and contained in it the Guidance of 2016 and 2021[400] on its implementation or application with regard to unfair commercial practices.

398 *T. Targosz*, Ustawa o przeciwdziałaniu nieuczciwym praktykom rynkowym, p. 29.

399 The intention of Directive 2005/29/EC was to regulate fully and comprehensively, and not only fragmentarily, issues relating to the combatting of unfair commercial practices (see Explanatory memorandum to the draft Act, p. 3, point 1.2).

400 Guidance on the Implementation/Application of Directive 2005/29/EC on Unfair Commercial Practices of 25 May 2016, COM(2016) 320, hereinafter referred to as the 'The Guidance (pl)'. The Polish version of the Guidance was used while working

The enactment of the Act on Counteracting Unfair Market Practices was preceded by legislative work that commenced in April 2007. Its first draft, entitled 'A government bill on counteracting unfair commercial (in the Polish original wording: market) practices', together with its rationale[401] was published in April 2007. The bill underwent only minor amendments[402] in the course of legislative work and was adopted in August the same year,[403] entering into force as provided for by law within three months after publication.[404] Since its adoption, the Act has been amended a number of times in order to comply with other legislative acts subsequently enacted,[405] but those amendments have not had any material impact on its binding contents.

---

on the publication. Pages in the Polish version of the guidelines differ from pages in other language versions. The purpose of the extensive Guidance (196 pages in the Polish version) was, as stated in the introduction, to facilitate the correct application of Directive 2005/29/EC. On 29 December 2021 a new 'Guidance on the interpretation and application of Directive 2005/29/EC of the European Parliament and of the Council concerning unfair business-to-consumer commercial practices in the internal market' has been published, hereinafter referred to as the 'The Notice'. The purpose of this Notice 'is to facilitate the proper application of the Directive. It builds upon and replaces the 2016 version of the Guidance'. The English version of the Notice was used while working on the publication.

401 History of the legislative work, Druk sejmowy, V kadencji No 1682. See: <http://orka.sejm.gov.pl/proc5.nsf/opisy/1682.htm> (accessed on: 1.2.2025).

402 Certain amendments were put forward by the Sejm (see: Druk sejmowy V kadencji No 1981 of 12.7.2007), subsequently partially adopted (Druk sejmowy V kadencji No 2021 of 21.8.2007).

403 Druk sejmowy V kadencji No 1981 of 12.7.2007.

404 The Act was published in the Polish Journal of Laws of 20.9.2007 (Dz. U. of 2007, No 171, item 1206) and therefore came into force on 21.12.2007.

405 In 2014—Act of 30.5.2014 on consumer rights (Dz. U. of 2014, item 827), in 2015—Act of 5.8.2015 on the handling of complaints by financial market entities and on the Financial Ombudsman (Dz. U of 2015, item 1348) and in 2016—Act of 23.9.2016 on out-of-court resolution of consumer disputes (Dz.U. of 2016, item 1823).

§ 2. Implementation of Directive 2005/29/EC in the Act on Counteracting Unfair Market Practices: Rationale and Criticism

The explanatory memorandum to the proposed draft implementing Directive 2005/29/EC largely echoed the recitals set out in it. First and foremost, it was stated that the premise of the proposed law was to 'regulate unfair commercial practices used by businesses towards customers'.[406] It was further explained that the Directive expressed the principle of 'no interference in the business to business (B2B) relations' and aimed to protect consumers, not entrepreneurs.[407]

The memorandum contained a list of examples of unfair commercial practices applied by entrepreneurs in Poland,[408] and their occurrence justified the implementation of the Directive. At the same time, attention was drawn to the fact that the source of unfair competition law in Poland was and continued to be the Act of Combatting Unfair Competition. It was also noted that the Act was originally intended to protect entrepreneurs against unfair trading behaviour of their competitors (other entrepreneurs), but over time, its provisions evolved to safeguard consumers as well and to protect them against unfair acts of entrepreneurs operating in the market. However, the Act on Combatting Unfair Competition was not free of certain weaknesses, namely:

1. consumer's interests are only indirectly protected, and the Act does not secure their adequate protection equivalent to that enjoyed by other market participants;
2. when an act of unfair competition is committed, the consumer has no legal recourse against the entrepreneur (no active legitimacy). As a result, in the event of an unfair commercial practice on the part of the entrepreneurs, of which there is a variety, the existing regulations on consumer protection do not adequately protect the latter.[409]

---

[406] Explanatory memorandum to the draft Act, Druk sejmowy V kadencji No 1981, p. 1.

[407] See Part I 'Basic assumptions, scope and methodology for the implementation of the Unfair Commercial Practices Directive', Explanatory memorandum to the draft law, Druk sejmowy V kadencji No 1981, pp. 3–7.

[408] Explanatory memorandum to the draft Act, Druk sejmowy V kadencji No 1981, pp. 8–11.

[409] *Ibidem*, pp. 12–14.

The proposed new law, whose main beneficiary was intended to be the consumer, was supposed to be the answer to these problems, while the protection of honest law-abiding entrepreneurs constituted only a 'reflexion of this protection'.[410] It was believed to be justified to adopt a separate piece of legislation implementing the provisions of Directive 2005/29/EC. It was also argued that 'the parallel functioning in the legal system of two legislative acts (the already existing Act on Combatting Unfair Competition and the Act Counteracting Unfair Market Practices), which largely regulated a similar subject matter and provided for an analogous catalogue of sanctions for actions specified in them, was justified by the fact of a different placement of the "centre of gravity" in terms of the group of entities benefitting from their regulations. In the case of unfair competition law, the centre of gravity was on the side of the entrepreneurs competing on the market, and only indirectly did it serve the protection of consumer interests, while in case of the unfair market practices law, it was on the side of consumers, serving entrepreneurs only in an indirect way'.[411] Both regulations ensured fairness in trade, and the drafters believed that such implementation of Directive 2005/29/EC would not require any change or modification of the existing catalogue of unfair competition acts that might occur between entrepreneurs, as those acts remained outside the scope of the Directive.[412] And yet, as it turned out, certain amendments to the Act on Combatting Unfair Competition were inevitable.

Further in the rationale (Part II—'Act on Counteracting Unfair Market Practices—discussion of the draft') the specific solutions to be adopted in the Act were discussed in detail. Attention should be drawn to some of them, in particular those concerning the general clause. In the rationale for the introduction of the general clause, it was emphasised that the main objective of the proposed legislative act was to counteract unfair commercial practices between a trader and a consumer. In view of the main objective of the Act thus adopted, it was proposed that a general clause should be adopted (Article 2)[413] and that it should specify the criteria (contrary to the accepted principles of good practice and material distortion of the average consumer's market

410 *Ibidem*, p. 14.
411 *Ibidem*, pp. 14–15.
412 *Ibidem*, p. 15.
413 The adoption of the general clause was, moreover, imposed by Directive 2005/29/EC (see Article 5 of the Directive)

behaviour) that would enable classification of a given practice as being unfair. In turn, Article 4(2) contained an exemplary catalogue of unfair practices, while in the final version of the Act on Counteracting Unfair Market Practices, Article 4.3 also referred to a consortium system as an example of an unfair commercial practice. The implementation of Directive 2005/29/EC to the national legal systems of Member States posed a number of difficulties and has also been discussed in the literature.[414] The reasons for that were, on the one hand, the full harmonisation principle, which left Member States little leeway in its implementation, and on the other hand, the requirement to maintain consistency between the new solutions and those already well-established and in force in Member States' legislation. The transposition of a Directive does not only involve adopting its solutions. It should be 'fitted', both linguistically and systemically, into the already existing laws against unfair competition in Member States. This was particularly difficult in countries that had already had a so-called integrated protection system in place, thus also in Poland.

The implementation of the Directive in Poland made in the Act on Counteracting Unfair Market Practices met with criticism in the Polish literature on the subject. The criticism concerned primarily the fact that the Directive had been implemented in a separate legislative act and was not connected to the existing provisions on combatting unfair competition or consumer protection. The inconsistency of the implemented provisions with the Directive was also raised.[415]

It was argued that the problems with the implementation of the Directive were also due to its poor legislative quality and numerous content-related doubts, while the Directive itself made no account for the national legal

---

414 *R. Stefanicki*, Prawo uczciwej konkurencji a ochrona konsumentów, p. 66.

415 *T. Targosz*, Ustawa o przeciwdziałaniu nieuczciwym praktykom rynkowym, p. 29–52; *A. Tischner*, Miejsce implementacji dyrektywy, pp. 53–63; *M. Strzelecki*, Nieuczciwe praktyki handlowe, pp. 51–67. Doubts have also been raised about the Directive itself and the problems that may be associated with its implementation see: *J. Szwaja, A. Tischner*, Implementacja dyrektywy 2005/29/WE, pp. 1118–1119; *A. Tischner*, Miejsce implementacji dyrektywy, pp. 53–63. Zob. *J. Szwaja, A. Kubiak-Cyrul*, in: *J. Szwaja, J. Kępiński* (eds), Ustawa o zwalczaniu nieuczciwej konkurencji, 2024, p. 72, Nb. 6.

system that had earlier adopted a model of integrated protection against unfair competition.[416]

Problems with the proper transposition of the Directive also arose, *inter alia*, from the need to align the Polish language version of the Directive with the legislation already in force, in which specific terminology had been adopted. The most conspicuous example is the different naming of practices. Indeed, the Polish version of the Directive uses the term 'commercial practices', while in the Polish Act on Counteracting Unfair Market Practices, the term 'market practices' is used. And although this distinction does not have any legal consequences, as both 'commercial practices'[417] and 'market practices'[418] are defined the same way,[419] this discrepancy highlights the linguistic problems faced by national legislators. In the German language, unfair commercial practices are translated as *unlautere Geschäftspraktiken*, and in French, *les pratiques commerciales déloyale*, whereas in English, *unfair commercial practices* sometimes are also known as *unfair trade* or *trading practices*. It seems that the term commercial practices would be more appropriate. And yet, the term 'market practice' in Poland denotes the concept of market practices referred to in Article 76 of the Constitution of the Republic of Poland,[420] in which this term is used in relation to unfair practices applied by market participants.

The inconsistencies of the current Polish Act on Counteracting Unfair Market Practices with the Directive also result from the attempt to align its solutions with certain concepts already well-established in the law on combatting unfair

---

416 *J. Szwaja*, *A. Tischner*, Implementacja dyrektywy 2005/29/WE, p. 1118. Also *R. Skubisz*, Cele i zakres zastosowania ustawy, p. 570.

417 According to Article 2(d) of Directive 2005/29/EC, 'commercial practices' means 'any act, omission, course of conduct or representation, commercial communication including advertising and marketing, by a trader, directly connected with the promotion, sale or supply of a product to consumers'.

418 Pursuant to Article 2(4) of the Act on Counteracting Unfair Market Practices, a market practice is 'an act or omission by a trader, a course of conduct, a statement or commercial communication, in particular advertising and marketing, directly related to the promotion or purchase of a product by a consumer'.

419 See Explanatory memorandum to the draft Act, Druk sejmowy V kadencji No 1981, p. 18, in which it is explained that, in order to avoid doubts of interpretation, it seems advisable to carry out a so-called mirroring procedure with Article 2 (d) Directive 2005/29 /EC.

420 See Explanatory memorandum to the draft Act, Druk sejmowy V kadencji No 1981, p. 14.

competition. For example, reference may be made to Article 5(2)(a) of Directive 2005/29/EC, according to which a 'commercial practice is unfair if it is contrary to the requirements of professional diligence(…)'. In making this transposition, the Polish legislator referred not to the 'requirements of professional diligence', but to the 'good practice' clause (see Article 4(1) of the Act on Counteracting Unfair Market Practices). The adoption of the 'good practice' clause makes it possible to refer to its interpretation developed on the grounds of the Act on Combatting Unfair Competition (Article 3(1)), although this raises doubts as to the correctness of the implementation made. The adoption of the 'good practice' clause allows recourse to the interpretation developed on the basis of the Act on Combatting Unfair Competition (Article 3(1)), but raises doubts as to the correctness of its implementation. It is clear from recital 13 of the preamble, which states that in order to achieve the objectives of the Community by eliminating barriers to the internal market, it is necessary to replace the existing divergent general clauses and legal principles operating in the Member States.

§ 3. The Scope and Objectives of the Act

I. Fundamental Principles

The process of implementing Directive 2005/29/EC into the Polish law was guided by the principle of consumer protection.

Already in the Explanatory memorandum to the draft Act on Counteracting Unfair Market Practices, a reference was made to the basic assumptions and scope of Directive 2005/29/EC, whose main principles aim at protecting consumers (a principle known as a 'consumer interest protection principle'). Pursuant to its provisions, consumer protection is to be achieved by ensuring that in dealings with consumers (B2C), traders behave fairly. The protection of consumer interests in this regard is independent of the contractual relationship between the consumer and the trader. It is also of no relevance to the assessment of the practice whether the trader has used the practice before, after, or during the contract (the so-called principle of independence of the Directive of the contractual relationship between the trader and the consumer).[421]

---

[421] See: Explanatory memorandum to the draft Act on Counteracting Unfair Market Practices, Druk sejmowy V kadencji No 1981, pp. 3–5.

It was also emphasised that the protection of traders' interests is secondary and that it merely mirrors the protection of consumers' interests. Therefore, Directive 2005/29/EC does not interfere in B2B relations (the so-called principle of non-interference in B2B relations).[422]

While drafting the Act, the Polish legislator also pointed out the then prevailing tendency to extend protection against unfair practices not only to other traders but also to consumers, who too must be protected. And yet, despite this tendency, the other legislative act, namely the Act on Combatting Unfair Competition, protects mainly the interests of entrepreneurs, while the interests of consumers are protected only indirectly 'through the functioning of a market characterised by sound competition'.[423] In other words, under the Act on Combatting Unfair Competition, neither the consumer nor the organisations established to protect consumers have any active legitimacy, and as a result, consumers are not protected to the same extent as other market participants are.

It was further emphasised that also the regulations of the Office of Competition and Consumer Protection failed to provide adequately for the protection of consumers' interests, and therefore not every unfair act on the part of an entrepreneur will trigger relevant sanctions. Thus, it might be stated that acts of unfair competition affecting individual interests of consumers or a group of consumers remain outside the scope of actions undertaken by the Office.

The purpose of the Act on Counteracting Unfair Market Practices was thus to fill in the gaps in consumer protection and, as a consequence, to improve the situation of consumers. It was clearly emphasised in the Explanatory memorandum to the draft that consumers, as the weakest players in trade, were to be the main beneficiaries of the proposed law. Moreover, consumer protection was meant to positively affect traders' interests. It was also made clear that under the Act on Counteracting Unfair Market Practices, the protection of the interests of honest traders was of secondary importance and merely a reflection of consumer protection.[424]

---

422 See *ibidem*, p. 3.
423 See *ibidem*, p. 12.
424 See *ibidem*, p. 14.

Taking into account the above remarks, the legislator decided to implement Directive 2005/29/EC into a piece of legislation separate from the Act on Unfair Competition, although it was emphasised that the subject matter of both Acts was similar and the catalogue of sanctions analogous. It was also explained that such a legislative procedure was aimed at emphasising who the beneficiaries of the existing (Act on Combatting Unfair Competition) and the proposed (Act on Counteracting Unfair Market Practices) acts were. The linking element between the two was to be the assumption of fairness in trading as a reflection of the public interest, while it would be in the interest of the latter to ensure fair and unadulterated competition reflected in the protection of consumers as the weakest participants in the market.[425]

The above assumptions were directly reflected in the provisions of the draft Act. In Article 1 of the draft Act on Counteracting Unfair Market Practices, it was explained that the Act shall define unfair market practices and specify how such practices will be combatted in the consumers interest and in the public interest, in business and professional activity.

In turn, Article 4(1) of the draft clarified the subject matter and scope of the Act, which was to apply to unfair practices (misleading and aggressive) used by traders against consumers. As explained in the explanatory memorandum, the subject of protection was the economic interests of consumers, 'which are at risk of being harmed by market practices directly influencing a consumer's decision concerning a business transaction'.[426]

According to the draft Act, consumers were to be granted active legal standing, allowing them to bring individual claims for unfair commercial practices. Pursuant to Article 12(1), in the event of an unfair practice, a consumer whose interest has been violated or threatened would be given a right to file specific claims. Active legal standing would also be vested in the Ombudsman, the Financial Ombudsman, a national or regional organisation whose statutory aim is to protect consumers' interests, and a district (municipal) consumer ombudsman. However, the catalogue of the claims that they could file would be limited.

[425] See *ibidem*, p. 15.
[426] See *ibidem*, p. 16.

II. Consumer as the Principal Beneficiary of the Implemented Solutions

As can be seen, based on the considerations so far, the main (but not only) beneficiary of the Act on Counteracting Unfair Market Practices is the consumer, who is the weaker party in the market trade. Further to this, also the whole community is or may be the beneficiary of the Act, whose aim is to protect public interest. Thus, indirectly, its provisions include traders as well, despite the fact that the latter are not granted active legal standing. In light of the above, saying that the Act on Counteracting Unfair Market Practices protects only and exclusively the interests of consumers would therefore be an oversimplification. The Polish legislator, when drafting the Act on Counteracting Unfair Market Practices, was most likely guided by the solutions adopted in the Act on Combatting Unfair Competition and equated the consumer's interest with the public interest (although who has been granted the right to seek redress is a different matter). Nevertheless, the overriding principle is that under the Act on Counteracting Unfair Market Practices, such practices are not allowed, and their prohibition lies in the interest of consumers as well as in the public interest.

Now, regarding the understanding of the concept of a consumer, pursuant to Article 2(2), the term consumer must be understood as defined in Article 22^1 of the Polish Civil Code.[427] However, it has also been argued that the reference to Article 22^1 of the Civil Code made in the Act on Counteracting Unfair Market Practices is not right because the definition of a 'consumer' in the Civil Code is defective under that Act. This being the case, the Act on Counteracting Unfair Market Practices must be amended in this respect.[428]

Under the Act on Counteracting Unfair Market Practices, the assessment of practices used by the traders should be made not from the perspective

[427] See *ibidem*, p. 18. Directive 2005/29/EC defines the term 'consumer' in Article 2(a). According to it, 'consumer' means any natural person who, in commercial practices covered by this Directive, is acting for purposes which are outside that person's trade, business, craft, or profession.

[428] See *A. Tischner*, Pojęcie 'przeciętny konsument' w ustawie o przeciwdziałaniu nieuczciwym praktykom rynkowym na tle prawa i orzecznictwa Unii Europejskiej, in: *E. Nowińska*, *D. Kasprzycki* (eds), Nieuczciwe praktyki rynkowe. Ocena regulacji, Kraków 2012, p. 126. However, the author does not explain what, in her opinion, the defect in the definition is.

of a consumer as such, but from the point of view of a so-called average consumer. The average consumer, as defined in Article 2(8), is one who is sufficiently well-informed, attentive and cautious and makes an assessment taking into account social, cultural, and linguistic factors. The choices that a consumer makes depend on the membership of a particular group understood as a clearly identifiable group of consumers who, because of particular characteristics that include age or physical or mental disability, are particularly vulnerable to exposure to a commercial practice or to a product that the commercial practice involves.[429] Such a model of an average consumer is based on the extensive case law of the CJEU that has been evolving since the 1960s.[430] As pointed out in the literature, the model of an average consumer reflects the worked-out compromise between the implemented principle of a free movement of goods and the need to protect consumers.[431]

It was stressed in the explanatory memorandum to the draft of Directive 2005/29/EC that notwithstanding the existence of a test of the 'average consumer' defined by the CJEU, there were Member States who failed to apply it and instead assessed the fairness of commercial practices taking into account their impact on the vulnerable consumer or a small percentage of consumers (10–15%).[432] In view of the above, one of the key premises underlying the draft

---

[429] The Explanatory memorandum of the draft of the Act on Counteracting Unfair Market Practices explains that Directive 2005/29/EC is based on the so-called principle of assessing an unfair market practice from the point of view of the average consumer. The Explanatory memorandum of the draft law (see Explanatory memorandum of the draft Act Druk Sejmowy V kadencji No. 1981, p. 21) explains that although the definition of the 'average consumer' was deleted from the Directive during the legislative work, it should be included in the glossary of the Act. It will provide courts and other authorities with guidance and direction on how to assess the facts under examination.

[430] See *A. Tischner*, Pojęcie "przeciętny konsument" w ustawie, pp. 92–100; and *A. Tischner*, Model przeciętnego konsumenta w prawie europejskim, KPP 2006, No 1, pp. 199–244.

[431] See *A. Tischner*, Model przeciętnego konsumenta, p. 213. As part of her analysis, the author reviews the CJEU case law relevant to the development of the 'average consumer' model (pp. 213–231).

[432] See Explanatory memorandum to the proposal for a 'Directive of the European Parliament and of the Council concerning unfair *business-to-consumer* commercial practices in the internal market and amending Directives 84/450/EEC, 97/7/EC and 98/27/EC (the Unfair Commercial Practices Directive)'. COM/2003/0356 final – COD 2003/0134, p. 5, Nb. 21 (hereinafter: Explanatory memorandum to Directive 2005/29/

Directive 2005/29/EC was adoption of a model of an average consumer. It was argued that this model is an expression of the principle of proportionality and applies when a commercial practice is aimed at, or affects, consumers in general. The 'average consumer' test may be modified when a commercial practice is targeted at a particular consumer group. The adoption of the 'average consumer' model allows certain standards to be determined to be applied by national courts, leading eventually to a significant reduction of the number of diverging assessments of the same practice in the EU. However, when assessing a given commercial practice, courts may take into account social, cultural, or linguistic differences, as those are relevant characteristics of specific consumer groups.[433]

The definition of the 'average consumer' was not included in Directive 2005/29/EC. This was a deliberate move. Although the definition was originally present in the draft Directive, the idea of its adoption was abandoned for fear that it would constitute an obstacle to the development of the concept of the 'average consumer' along with the development of the CJEU's case law. It was finally decided that it would suffice to refer to the concept of the 'average consumer' in Recital 18 of the Preamble to the Directive.[434]

Recital 18 states that 'In line with the principle of proportionality, and to permit the effective application of the protections contained in it, this Directive takes as a benchmark the average consumer who is reasonably well-informed and reasonably observant and prudent, taking into account social, cultural and linguistic factors, pursuant to the interpretation of the Court of Justice (...). The average consumer test is not a statistical test. In order to determine the typical reaction of the average consumer in a given case, national courts and administrative authorities will have to rely on their own judgement, taking into account the case-law of the Court of Justice'.

Thus, the starting point for the assessment of a commercial practice in the Act on Counteracting Unfair Market Practices and Directive 2005/29/EC is the 'average consumer' model. The Guidance explains that the 'average consumer' does not need a low level of protection, as he or she can always

EC) <http://eur-lex.europa.eu/legal-content/EN/TXT/?uri=COM:2003:0356:FIN> (accessed on: 1.2.2025).

433 See: Explanatory memorandum do the draft of Directive 2005/29/EC, p. 8.

434 Zob. *B. Keirsblick*, The New European Law of Unfair Commercial Practices and Competition Law, Oxford– Portland–Oregon 2011, pp. 281–282.

obtain the available information and make an informed decision based on it.[435] They also contain the results of a survey conducted by the European Commission on the customers' vulnerability to threats originating in the main markets.[436] According to the survey, the well-informed, average consumer 'feels relatively well-informed about prices, declares that he or she reads information on the Internet and communications from the bank and from energy suppliers (...), and claims not to rely solely on the information from advertisements'. The cautious and careful consumer, on the other hand, 'perceives himself or herself as rather cautious in dealing with people and in making decisions and as not very willing to take risks, (...) disagrees with the claim that advertisements present objective facts'[437] and, what is important, the concept of the average consumer may differ from Member State to Member State.[438]

The courts of each Member State will therefore have the task of defining the model of the average consumer in virtually every case assessed. Social, linguistic, and cultural factors will also have to be taken into account, as they may justify different interpretations of a commercial practice communicated by courts or national authorities.[439]

An analysis of rulings delivered by Polish courts shows that they skilfully interpret the premise of the 'average consumer' and correlate the degree of the consumer's attention and caution with the type of product or service or the characteristics of the provider of the product or service.[440]

Table 1 collects some individual rulings of the Polish Supreme Court, in which the model of the average consumer under the Act on Counteracting Unfair Market Practices has been reproduced. The judgements concerned practices infringing on, or violating, collective consumer interests, and the basis for their assessment was Article 24(2) of the Act on Competition and

---

435 See: The Guidance (pl) pp. 46–51 and Notice pp. 33–35.

436 Full report of 27 January 2016 '*Consumer vulnerability across key markets in the European Union*" of a survey conducted also in Poland, <https://op.europa.eu/en/publication-detail/-/publication/79b42553-de14-11e6-ad7c-01aa75ed71a1> (accessed on: 1.2.2025).

437 The Guidance (pl), p. 49.

438 The Notice, p. 34.

439 *Ibidem*, p. 51 and cited therein rulings of the CJEU. Also see: *B. Keirsblick*, The New European Law, pp. 284–289.

440 See judgement of the Court of Appeal in Warsaw of 20.04. 2017, VI ACa 67/16, Legalis.

Consumer Protection. In these rulings, the Court had to reconstruct the model of the average consumer, taking into account, *inter alia*:

1) the level of consumer's perception and attention, which varies depending on which product is affected by the commercial practice and under what circumstances the product is purchased;
2) the trading conditions and the realities of economic life;
3) the recipients of the contested practice.[441]

All the judgements of the Supreme Court presented in the Table concern a violation of the consumer collective interests. However, at the same time they are useful for establishing a model of the 'average Polish consumer' for the needs of the Act on Counteracting Unfair Market Practices, as they constitute one of the categories of practices infringing on the collective interests of consumers and must be referred to when it comes to their assessment under the laws in force.

Table 1. Model of the average consumer in rulings of the Supreme Court

Ruling	Good/Service/ Practice	Average consumer
I NSK 66/18[442]	Advertising flyers directed to everyone who visited a bank	**Customer of the Bank:** 1) **does not have** a higher than average knowledge of the financial services market 2) each customer has a different age, education, experience, etc. 3) does not have knowledge and skills specific to investors in the investment services market.

[441] See judgement of the Supreme Court of 6.12.2007, III SK 20/07, OSNAPiUS 2009, No 3–4, item 55, p. 166.

[442] Judgement of the Supreme Court of 23.10.2019, I NSK 66/18, Legalis.

Ruling	Good/Service/ Practice	Average consumer
III SK 67/15[443]	Mailing debt collection letters	**Debtor:** 1) **does not belong** to any specific group, 2) the practice used was not a marketing/advertising practice, and therefore no experience in the perception of advertising communications **could be assumed**, 3) neither could it be assumed that the consumer is aware of his or her rights, 4) **is not** sufficiently informed, reasonable, and rational and cannot possess legal knowledge pertaining to debt collection or recovery procedure, allowing him or her to ignore the letter (without anxiety or fear that someone will come to collect the debt as indicated in the letter), 5) **is not aware of the fact** that the terminology used in the letter, suggesting authority and powers, is untrue.
III SK 24/14[444]	Supplying electricity that is billed using different meters	**Recipient of electricity** who places a complaint and asks for a check-up if the meter installed by the energy supplier: 1) **understands that** the meter may not be accurate, 2) **knows** his or her rights to make a complaint, 3) **does not exclude** the possibility that the trader has misled him or her regarding the scope of his powers.

[443] Judgement of the Supreme Court of 30.11.2016, III SK 67/15, Legalis. See: also Judgement of the Supreme Court of 31.05.2022 r., I NSKP 1/22, Legalis.

[444] Judgement of the Supreme Court of 16.4.2015, III SK 24/14, OSNP 2017, No 5, item 64.

Ruling	Good/Service/ Practice	Average consumer
III SK 75/13[445]	Selling critical illness insurance (the insurer's definition of myocardial infraction)	**The insured** under a collective (group) insurance policy: 1) will agree to be covered by a group insurance, having first **become familiar** with the terms and conditions of the insurance policy, 2) **has read** and has properly **understood** the message aimed at making him or her choose and buy the product offered, 3) **has read** and in some way **understood** the detailed terms and conditions governing the product/service offered, as these are the elements that actually distinguish the offer and make it different from others, 4) **may be misled** as to the scope of the insurance cover because the definition of a myocardial infraction formulated by the insurer seems very professional and creates an impression that the insured is covered in all cases of an infraction, whereas in the actual fact he or she is not.
III SK 45/13[446]	Sales of goods in a hardware shop/ DIY store	**Customer in the DIY store** filling a complaint/ returning the purchase: 1) **cares for the quality or fitness for the purpose** of the good purchased, 2) **is aware of** consumer rights, 3) **may be misled** as to his or her rights to complain because of the trader's certain behaviour, 4) **knows** that his or her consent not to make a claim, as formulated in the form received, applies solely to the complaint made and accepted, and not to any other claims the consumer may have under consumer sales regulations, 5) **understands** terms such as 'validity date' or 'valid' placed on documents received in relation to the purchase,

[445] Judgement of the Supreme Court of 15.5.2014, III SK 75/13, Legalis.
[446] Judgement of the Supreme Court of 8.5.2014, III SK 45/13, Legalis.

Ruling	Good/Service/ Practice	Average consumer
III SK 34/13[447]	Advertising campaign involving the internet on a mobile	**Potential buyer of telecommunication services** advertised by the trader: 1) **has** certain knowledge of the services advertised, 2) **is aware of** the specificity of the operation of the telecommunication market, 3) **lacks** professional knowledge regarding the effects of the data compression technology used by the trader and the resulting possibilities to transfer the data using the advertised service (internet in a mobile phone), 4) **is aware** that the advertising message may not contain full information on the promotion campaign; however, the peculiarities of the language of advertising and the concise form of the message do not appear to a prudent consumer to suggest that the information on the essential characteristics of the good or service may not be true

Article 12 of the Act on Counteracting Unfair Market Practices provides that when an unfair market practice has been committed, the consumer may bring specific claims complaining that his or her interest has been threatened or infringed. However, an analysis of the case law shows that consumers relatively rarely rely on the provisions of this Act to bring such actions.[448]

[447] Judgement of the Supreme Court of 4.3.2014, III SK 34/13, Legalis, approved by M. Sieradzka in: Wzorzec przeciętnego konsumenta jako punkt odniesienia przy dokonywaniu oceny nieuczciwości praktyki rynkowej, Glosa do wyroku SN z 4.3.2014, III SK 34/13, Internetowy Kwartalnik Antymonopolowy i Regulacyjny 2014, No 6.

[448] Claims brought by borrowers against banks were omitted from consideration. This is due to their special nature and the high complexity of the disputes. See, e.g. judgement of the Court of Appeal in Katowice of 22.1.2016, I ACa 648/15, Legalis; decision of the Supreme Court of 2.6.2016, I CSK 119/16, Legalis; judgement of the Court of Appeal in Katowice of 24.6.2016, V ACa 562/15, Legalis; judgement of the Court of Appeal in Warszawa of 8.9.2017, I ACa 985/16, Legalis; judgement of the Court of Appeal in Warszawa of 28.9.2016, VI ACa 721/15, LEX No 2188851, decision of the Supreme Court of 2.6.2016, I CSK 119/16, Legalis and in the same matter judgement of the Court of Appeal in Warszawa of 3.6.2014, VI ACa 1382/13, Legalis.

In one of the few rulings, upon a claim filed by a consumer under Article 12(1) of the Act on Counteracting Unfair Market Practices, the District Court in Kamienna Góra[449] annulled the contracts for the sale and distribution of electricity concluded between that consumer and the energy seller (the entrepreneur). The ground for the judicial decision was that the defendant 'did not comply with the provisions of the Comprehensive Agreement, failing at the same time to note that there was a need to communicate on the subject with the claimant in order to obtain the statement of intent necessary for amending the contractual provisions'. Moreover, the defendant had no right to decide unilaterally that the binding provisions of the contract did not have to be complied with" and, therefore, in the Court's opinion, the consumer's claim was justified. Delivering the judgement, however, the Court did not explain the reasons for the ruling and why the entrepreneur's behaviour constituted an unfair commercial practice. Neither did the Court see it apt to refer to the average consumer model (to assess the claimant's behaviour).

In this particular case, it seems that it would have been more appropriate for the consumer to make a claim based on the provisions of the Civil Code and rely on improper performance of the contract, rather than rely on the Act on Counteracting Unfair Market Practices. However, this not being the case, the court attempted to demonstrate that the defendant's offer presented to the consumer was advertised as extremely favourable. Such an action might have been considered a misleading practice because, as could be drawn from the reasons accompanying the Court's ruling, the customer was made to believe in the assurances of the trader, but the reality turned out to be different. The consumer might also have been misled, believing that she was entering into a contract with a different trader. Yet, to establish this, the Court would have had to determine how the average consumer would have behaved and whether that behaviour would have been different from that of the claimant. As can be seen from this example, the assessment of practices used by traders is not always easy.

Another example where a consumer based his claims directly on the provisions of the Act on Counteracting Unfair Market Practices can be found

---

[449] Judgement of the District Court in Kamienna Góra of 15.9.2016, I C 152/16, LEX Nr 2133815.

in the ruling of the Court of Appeal in Warsaw.[450] The matter concerned a life insurance policy, and the essence of the dispute was the insurer's entitlement under the general terms and conditions of insurance to deduct from the total value of the policy the amount of liquidation fees corresponding to the accumulated funds. The court held that 'the defendant's offer was not addressed to a selected group of consumers with exclusive knowledge of the rules of marketing financial instruments, but had the character of an open offer addressed to a wide circle of consumers. Since the claimant was harmed as a result of unfair commercial practices pursuant to Article 12 of the Act, he could demand the removal of the effects of the prohibited actions'. Also noteworthy is the reasoning of the court of first instance, which held that the claimant was not the average consumer, as he 'had a university degree in law and had completed one of the professional legal internships, and therefore when signing the statement of having read and understood the agreement, he should have been aware of the meaning of the provisions contained therein. If the provisions were not precise or difficult to interpret unambiguously, he could have asked the agent (…), who presented the product to him, for an explanation'. Such an argument is incorrect. As the Supreme Court rightly stated, the offer was addressed to a wide consumer group and not to a group with some particular knowledge. The fact that the claimant had a legal education is irrelevant for the assessment of unfair commercial practices in the analysed facts. The first court's assumption, when assessing the trader's practices, that the claimant was not an average consumer on the insurance services market and thus the trader's actions could not have misled the claimant to such an extent that he would not have made a decision to conclude a contract, is incorrect. Indeed, the court should have examined who the average model addressee of the trader's practice was. This could have been anyone, a potential insured party who read and understood the terms of the contract being concluded and understood the insurance agent's explanations. He would have also understood, if that was the nature of the product offered, that it involved a certain financial risk. However, the average consumer would not have had any professional knowledge and therefore

[450] Judgement of the Court of Appeal in Warszawa of 28.9.2016, VI ACa 721/15, LEX No 2188851, see also Judgement of the Court of Appeal in Warszawa of 5.04.2019, VI Ca 1681/17, which relates to an agreement of group life insurance.

may have been misled as to the mechanism allowing 100% of all premiums accumulated by the consumer to be counted towards the liquidation fee in the event of termination of the insurance contract.

The fact that the claimant, as a lawyer, may have had more knowledge than the average consumer and was nevertheless misled should be an additional argument in support of the position that the average consumer would have been all the more misled by the commercial practice of the trader.

III. Entrepreneur Using Unfair Market Principles

The Act on Counteracting Unfair Market Practices concerns unfair practices (misleading and aggressive) performed by entrepreneurs towards consumers. As defined in its Article 2(1), an entrepreneur means 'natural persons, legal persons and organisational units without legal personality, conducting business or professional activities, regardless of whether such activities are of a primary or secondary nature, as well as persons acting in their name or on their behalf'. Unlike in the case of the 'consumer', when defining an 'entrepreneur', the Polish legislator did not refer to its definition in the Civil Code[451] but merely constructed a new (autonomous) definition for the purposes of the Act. Such a procedure is in line with Directive 2005/29/EC, which in Article 2(b) provides an autonomous definition of a 'trader'. The adoption by the Polish legislator of another autonomous definition of an entrepreneur has been criticised in the literature, which postulated that it referred to the definition of an entrepreneur as provided for in the Civil Code despite the fact that, as has been noted, its scope did not entirely coincide with the definition of an entrepreneur introduced in the Act on Counteracting Unfair Market Practices, which was broader than that in the Code.[452] Such postulates were not unusual in view of the fact that in other legislative acts

---

[451] Definition of an entrepreneur is contained in Article 43[1] of the Civil Code. Other definitions may be found in Article 2 of the Act on Combatting Unfair Competition, or Article 4 of the entrepreneurs' law. On different concepts of an entrepreneur see Rozdział II, § 8 Przedsiębiorca, in: *R. Hauser, Z. Niewiadomski, A. Wróbel* (eds), System Prawa Administracyjnego, vol. 8a, Publiczne prawo gospodarcze, Warszawa 2018, pp. 184–305.

[452] *R. Stefanicki*, Ustawa o przeciwdziałaniu nieuczciwym praktykom rynkowym, p. 102; *M. Wyrwiński*, Pojęcie przedsiębiorcy, in: *E. Nowińska, D. Kasprzycki* (eds), Nieuczciwe praktyki rynkowe. Ocena regulacji, Kraków 2012, p. 128; *M. Sieradzka*, Ustawa

references were also made to the Civil Code definition of an entrepreneur.[453] Thus, the solution applied by the Polish legislator in the Act on Counteracting Unfair Market Practices seems to be a frequent and common practice, as, true to form, an autonomous definition of an entrepreneur can be found in many other regulations.[454]

It follows from the explanatory memorandum to the draft Act on Counteracting Unfair Market Practices that the purpose of the adopted solution was to define very broadly the entities that should be deemed to be entrepreneurs. The decisive factor is to be the actual conduct of business activity and participation in business transactions on one's own behalf. At the same time, it is not of crucial importance whether this activity is conducted legally. An entrepreneur may also be considered person conducting business without a permit or concession or failing to comply with other formal conditions (e.g. entry in the register, etc.). To be considered an entrepreneur, it is sufficient to conduct some business activity only on an occasionally basis, not necessarily in a continuous or organised manner. Entrepreneurs under the Act on Counteracting Unfair Market Practices will therefore also include municipalities, schools, associations, foundations, and organisations of professional and business self-governing bodies.[455]

Under the same Act, entities acting in the name and on behalf of an entrepreneur are also considered to be entrepreneurs, so, for example, an entity that placed advertisements in the media on behalf and in the interest of another company is also an entrepreneur.[456] The Guidance on the interpretation and application of Directive 2005/29/EC devotes considerable attention to the issue of so-called disguised B2C sales. Such sales occur when 'natural persons appearing to be consumers selling products to other consumers are in fact traders or acting on behalf of traders'. Such a commercial practice is

---

o przeciwdziałaniu nieuczciwym praktykom rynkowym. Komentarz, Warszawa 2008, pp. 36–37.

[453] *J. Jacyszyn*, Przedsiębiorca w regulacjach prawnych, part 2, EP 2015, No 5, p. 47.

[454] See: *J. Jacyszyn*, Przedsiębiorca w regulacjach prawnych, part 1, EP 2015, No 4, pp 26–29; Przedsiębiorca w regulacjach prawnych, part 2, pp 42–47.

[455] Explanatory memorandum to the draft Act on Counteracting Unfair Market Practices, Druk sejmowy V kadencji No 1682, pp. 16–17, point 2.2.

[456] See The Guidance (pl), p. 37, The Notice, p. 27. See: *J. Szwaja*, *A. Kubiak-Cyrul*, in: *J. Szwaja*, *J. Kępiński* (eds), Ustawa o zwalczaniu nieuczciwej konkurencji, 2024, p. 94, Nb 16.

explicitly mentioned in point 22 of Annex I of Directive 2005/29/EC, in which commercial practices considered unfair in all circumstances are specified. The Commission made it clear that each case must be analysed on a case-by-case basis, taking into account different criteria. Thus, the Commission notes that a person whose main activity consists of a regular sale of products online, who first purchases some products in order to resell them at a higher price, could also be considered a trader.[457]

Following the Guidance, it should be considered that in the Act on Counteracting Unfair Market Practices, an entrepreneur is to be understood in a broad sense and may be any civil law entity that conducts business or professional activities.[458]

It may be argued that under the Act on Combatting Unfair Competition and the Act on Counteracting Unfair Market Practices, 'entrepreneur' should be interpreted identically, because even if the definitions in both Acts are literally different, they both refer to a wide range of entities as entrepreneurs. Being an entrepreneur within the meaning of these Acts does not depend on the fulfilment of formalities or the legality of one's activity. Neither is it necessary to conduct business in an organised and continuous manner or with the aim of making a profit. However, certain differences in the interpretation of the provisions may arise with respect to the premise of conducting business on one's own behalf. The Act on Counteracting Unfair Market Practices unequivocally states that persons acting on behalf of entrepreneurs or for their benefit are also entrepreneurs. Also, A. Michalak advocates a very broad understanding of the notion of a person acting on behalf of an entrepreneur as referred to in the Act on Counteracting Unfair Market Practices and expresses an opinion that 'an entrepreneur' may include an employee, legal counsel, contractor, agent, distributor, advertising agency, trustee, board member, etc. At the same time, he rightly observes that persons acting for and on behalf of an entrepreneur should be prudent when carrying out the orders of their principals and should always control whether the practices applied are not in breach of the Act on Counteracting Unfair Market Practices.[459]

---

457 The Guidance (pl), p. 38, The Notice, p. 27.

458 *J. Szwaja, A. Kubiak-Cyrul*, in: *J. Szwaja, J. Kępiński* (eds), Ustawa o zwalczaniu nieuczciwej konkurencji, 2024, p. 94, Nb 16.

459 *A. Michalak*, Przeciwdziałanie nieuczciwym praktykom rynkowym, p. 53.

It is worth noting that the Act on Combatting Unfair Competition does not stipulate that persons acting on behalf of entrepreneurs or for their benefit are also entrepreneurs. Article 17 of the Act provides for liability of an entrepreneur for actions of another entrepreneur, providing that an act of unfair competition may also be committed by an entrepreneur other than the entrepreneur who advertises his or her business, for instance, an advertising agency or another entrepreneur who developed the advertisement. And yet, undoubtedly, Article 17 applies only to entrepreneurs, i.e. the advertising agency and the entrepreneur who has developed the advertisement.

It should be stressed that an argument for adopting different definitions of an entrepreneur in the Act on Combatting Unfair Competition and the Act on Counteracting Unfair Market Practices may be the legislator's assumption during the legislative work on the amendment to the Act on Counteracting Unfair Market Practices. Initially, when drafting the Act, the legislator referred to the definition of an entrepreneur adopted in the Act on Combatting Unfair Competition. This approach was criticised by the Minister of Justice and an organisation representing entrepreneurs (Lewiatan Confederation), who argued, *inter alia*, that the intention was that the two Acts be independent of each other in practice and there was no substantive justification for duplicating the imprecise definition of an entrepreneur from the Act on Combatting Unfair Competition. The Confederation's comments were taken into account, and a new definition of an entrepreneur was duly formulated.[460]

In rulings concerning strictly claims made by consumers under the Act on Counteracting Unfair Market Practices against entrepreneurs, courts correctly assumed that the following were entrepreneurs: a mobile phone network operator,[461] a property developer,[462] a company providing services online,[463] a company conducting business activity consisting of extramural education

---

[460] Explanatory memorandum to the draft Act on Counteracting Unfair Market Practices, Druk sejmowy V kadencji No 1682, p. 46. See also *R. Stefanicki*, Ustawa o przeciwdziałaniu nieuczciwym praktykom rynkowym, p. 101.
[461] Judgement of the Court of Appeal in Katowice of 24.6.2016, V ACa 562/15, Legalis.
[462] Judgement of the Court of Appeal in Warszawa of 8.9.2017, I ACa 985/16, Legalis.
[463] Decision of the Supreme Court of 2.6.2016, I CSK 119/16, Legalis.

in the field of English language teaching,[464] or an insurer.[465] Similarly, the President of the Polish Office of Competition and Consumer Protection decided that an entrepreneur was, for example, a debt collector,[466] a supplier of electricity to consumers,[467] an insurer offering sickness insurance,[468] or a seller of consumer goods,[469] as well as a mobile network operator.[470] There have been hardly any rulings since the Act on Counteracting Unfair Market Practices came into force, where there would have been problems with determining whether the offender of an act of unfair competition was an entrepreneur or not.

IV. Protected interests

1. Consumer's interest

Pursuant to Article 1 of the Act on Counteracting Unfair Market Practices, the Act determines the principles of counteracting unfair market practices in the interest of consumers and in the public interest. Unlike the Act on Combatting Unfair Competition, the Act on Counteracting Unfair Market Practices does not mention the entrepreneur's interest. The latter is nevertheless protected, albeit indirectly, as part of the protection of the public interest, of which one element is also the interest of entrepreneurs.[471]

Directive 2005/29/EC distinguished between the protection of consumer interests in relations with businesses and the protection of the interests of businesses in relations with other businesses. Such distinction had not been known in Polish law against unfair competition,[472] as it had been a well-estab-

---

[464] Judgement of the Court of Appeal in Katowice of 22.1.2016, I ACa 648/15, Legalis.

[465] Judgement of the Court of Appeal in Warszawa of 28.9.2016, VI ACa 721/15, LEX No 2188851.

[466] Judgement of the Supreme Court in of 30.11.2016, III SK 67/15, Legalis.

[467] Judgement of the Supreme Court of 16.4.2015, III SK 24/14, OSNP 2017, No 5, item 64.

[468] Judgement of the Supreme Court of 15.5.2014, III SK 75/13, Legalis.

[469] Judgement of the Supreme Court of 8.5.2014, III SK 45/13, Legalis.

[470] Judgement of the Supreme Court of 4.3.2014, III SK 34/13, Legalis, and of 27.8.2014, III SK 80/13, Legalis.

[471] *A. Michalak*, Przeciwdziałanie nieuczciwym praktykom rynkowym, p. 49, Nb 5.

[472] For more on the discussion regarding the legitimacy or otherwise of such a separation, see. *M. Namysłowska*, Czarna lista nieuczciwych praktyk handlowych, pp. 73–76 and the literature cited therein.

lished principle that the Act on Combatting Unfair Competition protected the interests of entrepreneurs, the interests of customers, including consumers, and the public interest. These interests were, in principle, interrelated, and no distinctions were made between them. Thus, the Act on Combatting Unfair Competition regulated acts of unfair competition that concerned both B2B and B2C relationships. A characteristic example of the latter is Article 17a of the Act on Combatting Unfair Competition. However, other delicts of unfair competition, such as those under Articles 10 or 13 of the Act on Combatting Unfair Competition, also referred to relations with consumers.

Thus, we have to agree with T. Targosz, who observes that due to the fact that Directive 2005/29/EC covers only unfair practices in B2C relations, the problem arises of how to precisely distinguish such practices from practices relating to other relations, in particular practices in B2B relations. Such a distinction is difficult to make, as certain market behaviours may simultaneously violate the interests of various market participants. In addition, depriving entrepreneurs of legal standing in matters of unfair market practices only intensifies these difficulties.[473]

It seems that a strict distinction between B2B and B2C practices is not possible. The question arises whether it is really necessary to distinguish between them. As a result of such a distinction between the scope of the two Acts in Polish law (the Act on Combatting Unfair Competition and the Act on Counteracting Unfair Market Practices), when an entrepreneur commits a delict of unfair competition and uses an unfair market practice, the bases for pursuing claims will differ. In a situation of an entrepreneur's unfair market practice violating the consumer's interests, the consumer will be able to pursue claims under Article 12 of the Act on Counteracting Unfair Market Practices, whereas in a situation where the entrepreneur's interest is affected, the entrepreneur will be able to build a claim under Article 18 of the Act on Combatting Unfair Competition. The same Act will apply to unfair market practices violating consumer interests. Consequently, entrepreneurs may hypothetically be sued if their conduct fulfils the prerequisites of both an unfair market practice and the delict of unfair competition. This will be:

[473] *T. Targosz*, Ustawa o przeciwdziałaniu nieuczciwym praktykom rynkowym, pp. 45–46.

1) in connection with the use of an unfair market practice by:
   a) a consumer
   b) the Ombudsman
   c) the Financial Ombudsman,
   d) a national or regional organisation the statutory purpose of which is protection of consumer interests,
   e) a county (municipal) consumer ombudsman;

2) in connection with the commission of an act of unfair market practice by:
   a) the entrepreneur
   b) a national or regional organisation the statutory purpose of which is protection of consumer interests

Such a situation could arise, for example, in the case of labelling a product added to a purchase allegedly free of charge, while in reality it would be a product for which the consumer would have to pay a higher price than for the product itself without the add-on (Article 10 of the Act on Combatting Unfair Competition and Article 7(20) of the Act on Counteracting Unfair Market Practices). A broad spectrum of such unfair entrepreneurial behaviours could also concern various types of misleading advertising, e.g. disguised advertising (Article 16(1)(4) and Article 7(11), respectively).

The Act on Counteracting Unfair Market Practices protects the consumer's interest. That interest is to be understood in line with the interpretation of Article 1 of Directive 2005/29/EC, and therefore it is only the consumer's economic interests. This assumption is justified, *inter alia*, in recital 7 of the preamble to Directive 2005/29/EC, which states that the Directive 'applies to commercial practices directly related to influencing consumers' transactional decisions in relation to products. It does not apply to commercial practices carried out primarily for other purposes, including, for example, commercial communications intended for investors, including annual reports and promotional material for businesses. It does not address legal requirements relating to good taste and decency, which vary widely between Member States'.

Also, in the Guidance, the European Commission reiterates that Directive 2005/29/EC does not refer to national rules intended to protect non-economic interests. By practices of a non-economic character are meant commercial practices relating to health, safety, or environmental protection. Furthermore, the Directive does not affect national regulations relating to the protection of human dignity, the prevention of discrimination on grounds of sex, race, and religion, or the presentation of nudity, violence, or antisocial behaviour.[474]

On the other hand, however, if the protection of the economic consumers interests is combined with other interests (e.g. those of entrepreneurs[475]), they will still fall within the scope of Directive 2005/29/EC.

Although the Polish legislator does not expressly mention in Article 1 of the Act on Counteracting Unfair Market Practices that it concerns the protection of consumers' economic interests, given the assumptions underlying the Directive, such interests are at stake. This is in fact reflected in Article 4(1), pursuant to which an unfair practice is a practice that distorts or is likely to distort 'the average consumer's market behaviour'. This approach coincides with Article 5 of Directive 2005/29/EC, which refers to 'economic behaviour.' It is also emphasised in the Act on Combatting Unfair Competition that its purpose is to protect the economic interests of participants in economic transactions.[476] Customers, including consumers, are also participants in such transactions. Thus, the Act on Counteracting Unfair Market Practices and the Act on Combatting Unfair Competition will refer, albeit from different perspectives, to the economic consumers interests.

It is worth noting that the concept of 'consumers interests' is also present in Article 24 of the Act on Competition and Consumer Protection, which prohibits practices that violate the collective interests of consumers. The Act does not refer to the individual interests of consumers, but in the literature a distinction seems to be made between the interests of consumers in general and consumers economic interests. D. Miąsik emphasises that the premise of a violation of consumers interests cannot be treated 'as a premise correcting

---

474 See: The Guidance (pl), p. 10 and The Notice, p. 7.

475 These will include e.g. provisions on sales with additional extras—Judgment of the CJEU of 9.11.2010, C-540/08, *Mediaprint Zeitungs- und Zeitschriftenverlag GmbH & Co. KG v. Österreich-Zeitungsverlag GmbH*, Reports of Cases. 2010 I-10909, provisions allowing the announcement of a sale to be made subject to the approval of local authorities—Judgment of the CJEU of 17.1.2013, C-206/11, *Georg Köck v. Schutzverband gegen unlauteren Wettbewerb*, ECLI:EU:C:2013:14, or provisions concerning the admissibility of selling at a loss—Judgment of the CJEU of 19.10.2017, C-295/16, *Europamur Alimentación SA v. Dirección General de Comercio y Protección del Consumidor de la Comunidad Autónoma de la Región de Murcia*, ECLI: ECLI:EU:C:2017:782) etc.

476 See: *J. Szwaja*, *A. Kubiak-Cyrul*, in: *J. Szwaja*, *J. Kępiński* (eds), Ustawa o zwalczaniu nieuczciwej konkurencji, 2024, Comments to Art. 1, p. 76, Nb 23.

the application of a prohibition as a result of weighing whether the unlawful behaviour of an entrepreneur taking the form of depriving consumers of their lawful entitlements will or will not infringe their interests if other benefits are offered to them, and which, on balance, will justify a conclusion that as a result of the entrepreneur's unlawful behaviour the situation of consumers is – from an economic point of view – better than in the event of the entrepreneur's compliance with injunctions arising from the law'. And yet, as he points out, the Act protects consumers economic interests, too.[477] A violation of consumers interests may take the form, for example, of a pecuniary advantage obtained by an entrepreneur without a legal basis, at the expense of consumers, which, in the light of Article 405 of the Civil Code, should be regarded as unjust enrichment.[478] Thus, the concept of consumers' interests should be understood differently under the Act on Competition and Consumer Protection and differently under the Act on Counteracting Unfair Market Practices and the Act on Combatting Unfair Competition. The two latter ones are concerned with consumers economic interests.

2. Public interest

Article 1 of the Act on Counteracting Unfair Market Practices defines unfair market practices and the rules for counteracting these practices in the interest of consumers and in the public interest. It is argued in the literature that the consumer's interest is of primary importance and that the public interest should be taken into account only in the second place.[479] This, however, despite the first impression one may get, is not reflected in the construction of the Act, in which both the consumer and the public interests are given the same level of importance. What is different is the entities whose interests are to be protected and those with active legitimacy.

---

[477] *D. Miąsik*, in: *T. Skoczny* (ed.), Ustawa o ochronie konkurencji i konsumentów. Komentarz, Warszawa 2014, kom. do art. 24, p. 961, Nb 45.

[478] E.g. Decision of the President of the Office of Competition and Consumer Protection of 31.8.2011, DDK-5/2011, HDI – Gerling Życie Towarzystwo Ubezpieczeń Spółka Akcyjna z siedzibą w Warszawie, <https://decyzje.uokik.gov.pl> (accessed on: 1.2.2025).

[479] *A. Michalak*, Przeciwdziałanie nieuczciwym praktykom rynkowym, p. 49, Nb 5.

Interestingly, the public interest is not expressly mentioned in Article 1 of Directive 2005/29/EC,[480] which merely states that one of its objectives is also to 'contribute to the proper functioning of the internal market'. R. Stefanicki is of the opinion that, despite the omission of the phrase 'public interest' in Directive 2005/29/EC, the objectives of the Directive and the Act on Counteracting Unfair Market Practices are close.[481] This position is also confirmed by the explanatory memorandum to the draft Act on Counteracting Unfair Market Practices, in which we can read that the term 'public interest' should be understood as 'ensuring fair and unadulterated competition by protecting the primary interest of weaker market participants – consumers'.[482] This definition is too narrow. The public interest should not be viewed solely through the prism of the consumer. The reference to 'public interest', whose interpretation was developed on the grounds of the Act on Combatting Unfair Competition, allows the assumption that the public interest under both Acts should be interpreted in the same way. Indeed, their common element is assurance of fair and unadulterated competition, which entails the protection of the interests of all market participants. The fact that the Act on Counteracting Unfair Market Practices refers to unfair market practices in B2C relationships only affects the subject matter of protection[483] and its addressees. Protection may concern both the consumers interests and the public interest. In the case of unfair market practices, which violate the public interest, the entities with active legal standing will be primarily those listed in Article 12(2) of the Act on Counteracting Unfair Market Practices. However, an entrepreneur wishing to bring a claim in defence of the public interest will not have legal standing. While a consumer will be able to raise a claim in the public interest as specified in Article 12(1), but only if the unfair market practice will also violate or threaten his or her interests.

---

480 The concept of public interest, on the other hand, appeared in recital 5 of the preamble and in Article 11(2) of Directive 2005/29/EC.

481 *R. Stefanicki*, Ustawa o przeciwdziałaniu nieuczciwym praktykom rynkowym, pp. 97–98.

482 Explanatory memorandum to the draft Act on Counteracting Unfair Market Practices, p. 15.

483 See *M. Sieradzka*, Ustawa o przeciwdziałaniu nieuczciwym praktykom rynkowym, p. 21. However, the author further considers that 'the Act protects (...) only the economic interests of consumers from being threatened or infringed by unfair market practices'.

It should be added that although public interest is not mentioned in Article 1 of Directive 2005/29/EC, the EU legislator refers to it in the chapter under the title *'Enforcement'*. Pursuant to Article 11(2) of the Directive, Member States should, taking into account the interests of all concerned parties and in particular the public interest, provide the courts and administrative authorities with means (powers) enabling them to order abandonment of an unfair market practice or to institute appropriate proceedings enabling an order for abandonment of such practice or, if the practice has not yet been started, to issue an injunction against such practice or to institute appropriate proceedings for the prohibition of such practice. The requirement for such legislative solutions is (at least in part) reflected in the Act on Competition and Consumer Protection. This Act provides for the prohibition of practices that are against the collective interests of consumers. This protection is, however, of the administrative law nature.[484] On the other hand, neither the Act on Combatting Unfair Competition nor the Act on Counteracting Unfair Market Practices provides for similar competences to protect collective interests of consumers.

§ 4. Objectives of the Act

I. Draft Act on Counteracting Unfair Market Practices

According to the explanatory memorandum to the draft Act on Counteracting Unfair Market Practices, the Act is intended to counteract the use of unfair market practices by entrepreneurs against consumers. A market practice (Article 2(4) of the draft) was defined as an act or omission by an entrepreneur, an entrepreneur's behaviour, a statement or commercial information, and, in particular, advertising and marketing, directly related to the promotion or purchase of a product.

The drafters explained that market practices are unfair when they are contrary to good practice and are likely to materially distort or misrepresent the market behaviour of the average consumer (Article 4(1)). Unfair market

---

[484] See *A. Wędrychowska-Karpińska*, *A. Wiercińska-Krużewska*, in: *A. Stawicki*, *E. Stawicki* (eds), Ustawa o ochronie konkurencji i konsumentów. Komentarz, Warszawa 2016, p. 702.

practices were divided into subcategories, i.e. misleading practices, aggressive market practices, conducting and organising or arranging business in a consortium system, and applying an illegal code of good practices (Article 4(2) of the draft). Further in the draft Act, individual unfair market practices are also defined. The general definitions of misleading practices (by act or omission to act) and aggressive practices (contained in Articles 5(1), 6(1), and 8(1)) were supplemented by casuistic examples of unfair market practices (Articles 7 and 9). In this regard, the construction proposed in Directive 2005/29/EC had basically been taken over in its entirety.

Unfair misleading market practices were divided into practices of action (Article 5) and omission (Article 6). A market practice is misleading when the trader's action causes, or is likely to cause, the average consumer to make a contractual decision that otherwise would not have been taken.[485] In Article 7 of the draft, the legislator proposed to adopt a catalogue of unfair market practices that are misleading in all circumstances. The catalogue included 23 examples of such practices.[486]

On the other hand, market practices are deemed to be aggressive when, through unacceptable pressure (physical or mental coercion), the average consumer's freedom of choice or conduct with regard to the product is significantly impaired or is likely to be impaired and thereby causes or is likely to cause the consumer to take a contractual decision that would not otherwise have been taken. The Polish legislator, following the solutions of the EU legislator, adopted a catalogue of 'aggressive, unfair market practices in all circumstances'. The adopted catalogue lists 8 very precisely defined behaviours of an entrepreneur.[487]

It was added in Article 10 that an unfair market practice would also be running a business in the form of a consortium understood as an operation of a business involving the management of property pooled within a group with consumers, formed to finance the purchase of a product for the benefit of the participants of the group (Article 2(10)).

---

[485] Article 5(1) of the draft Act lists examples of misleading actions.

[486] These practices are the implementation of the commercial practices listed in Annex I of Directive 2005/29/EC 'Commercial practices regarded as unfair in all circumstances'.

[487] Like the catalogue of misleading practices, the catalogue of aggressive practices is also an almost identical copy of the catalogue contained in Annex I of Directive 2005/29/EC.

Article 11 provided that it was an unfair market practice to apply (as well as to create) a code of good practice with provisions contrary to the law. In accordance with the proposed definition, a code of good market practices consists of certain rules of conduct, in particular ethical and professional standards of traders who have undertaken to abide by the code in respect of one or more commercial practices (Article 2(5)).

It should be added that the catalogue of market practices (misleading and aggressive) that are unfair in all circumstances as listed in Articles 7 and 9 is a closed catalogue. The Polish legislator assumed, in a similar fashion as done under Directive 2005/29/EC, that market practices considered unfair in all circumstances are not subject to scrutiny under the general provisions, i.e. Articles 4–6 and Article 8. This means that they are prohibited *ex lege*, and no further assessment is necessary.[488]

II. Unfair Market Practices used by Traders towards Consumers

1. Introductory Remarks

The legislative proposals presented in the draft Act have been adopted in the Act on Counteracting Unfair Market Practices as drafted, with some more substantial amendments made only to Article 4, to which paragraph 3 was added,[489] and to Article 10, from which paragraph 3 was deleted.[490] Other modifications[491] were only cosmetic and had no effect on the entirety of the solutions adopted.

---

[488] Explanatory memorandum to the draft Act on Counteracting Unfair Market Practices, Druk sejmowy V kadencji No 1682, p. 33.

[489] Paragraph 3 concerning the operation of a consortium system has been added. In the draft, this provision was in Article 4(2).

[490] Clause 3 of Article 10 of the Act on Counteracting Unfair Market Practices which regulates the conduct of business in the form of a consortium system, proposed in the draft Act, reading 'In the event of unfair market practices referred to in paragraphs 1 and 2, Article 4(1) shall not apply' has been repealed and moved to Article 4(3).

[491] See e.g., the amendments presented by the Senate in the Resolution of the Senate of the Republic of Poland of 11.7.2007 on the Act on Counteracting Unfair Market Practices, Sejm Paper No. 1981—art. 7 point 7, point 15, and point 22.

Subsequent amendments to the Act were also minor.[492] An important change affecting the way the provisions of the Act on Counteracting Unfair Market Practices are interpreted was the addition to Article 4(2), following the amendment of 30 May 2014,[493] of sentence 2 reading that 'These practices are not subject to assessment in the light of the conditions set out in 4(1)'.

Thus, when a market practice (misleading or aggressive) specified in Article 4(2) of the Act on Counteracting Unfair Market Practices occurs, it will not be assessed in the light of the general definition of an unfair market practice contained in Article 4(1) of that Act, and in consequence it is no longer necessary to demonstrate that a market practice as defined in Article 4(2) also meets the conditions of unfairness listed in Article 4(1) of the same Act.

The solutions adopted in the amendments were in line with the CJEU's interpretation of Directive 2005/29/EC, which is also reflected in the reasons for the amendment to the Consumer Rights Act of 17 January 2014,[494] resulting in the amendment to Article 4(2) of the Act on Counteracting Unfair Market Practices.

As a result of the amendment, it is now no longer necessary to prove that the premises of the existence of misleading market practices as defined in Articles 5–7 of the Act on Counteracting Unfair Market Practices, as well as aggressive market practices as defined in Articles 8–9 of the same Act, are contrary to good practice. Thus, in order to recognise that a misleading or aggressive market practice is unfair, it is no longer necessary that it fulfil the prerequisites of unfairness (a breach of good practice and a significant potential or actual distortion of consumers' decisions) set out in Article 4(1) of the Act on Counteracting Unfair Market Practices.[495] In this way, the scope of the general clause in Article 4(1) has been limited to the assessment of unnamed unfair market practices, and it no longer serves the purpose of

---

492 See amendments—the Consumer Rights Act; the Act of 5.8.2015 on the handling of complaints by financial market entities and the Financial Ombudsman Dz.U. of 2018, item 2038, as amended); the Act of 23.9.2016 on out-of-court resolution of consumer disputes (Dz.U. of 2016, item 1823).

493 Article 4(2) added by consumer law, which came into force on 25.12.2014

494 See Government proposal for a law on consumer rights of 17.1.2014 (Druk sejmowy VI kadencji No 2076) with justification <http://www.sejm.gov.pl/sejm7.nsf/PrzebiegProc.xsp?nr=2076> (accessed on 1.2.2026).

495 *R. Stefanicki*, Ustawa o przeciwdziałaniu nieuczciwym praktykom rynkowym, p. 89, Nb 15.

assessing named market practices in terms of whether they meet the premises of unfairness. As a matter of fact, the mere use of such practices is, in itself, unfair.[496]

2. The Concept of an Unfair Market Practice

Pursuant to Article 1 of the Act on Counteracting Unfair Market Practices, the Act refers only to market practices that are unfair and violate the interests of consumers and the public interest. In this regard, as set out in Article 2(4), a market practice should be understood as 'an act or omission by an entrepreneur, a course of conduct, a statement or commercial information, in particular advertising and marketing, directly related to the promotion or acquisition of a product by a consumer'. This concept of a market practice is an adoption of the definition of a commercial practice stipulated in Directive 2005/29/EC.

The adopted definition of a market practice is broad; nevertheless not every behaviour of a trader can be qualified as a market practice. Firstly, one has to agree with the view expressed in the literature that a single act or omission by an entrepreneur should not be treated as an unfair practice under the Act on Counteracting Unfair Market Practices. Only when it takes the form of a method of action towards consumers, then we may talk about a practice within the meaning of the Act. An incidental conduct directed against one consumer when the entrepreneur acts differently towards other consumers cannot be deemed a practice. The above also follows from the dictionary understanding of the term 'practice', which means 'a conscious, deliberate action performed on a regular basis'.[497] Secondly, the market practice must be directly related to the promotion or purchase of the product by the consumer. This means that the practice must be of a commercial, economic nature. Its purpose is to display certain products provided by the trader to the consumer or to induce the consumer to purchase them. Recital 7 of Directive 2005/29/EC refers to practices 'directly related to influencing consumers' transactional decisions in relation to products. It does not apply to commercial practices carried out primarily for other purposes, including, for example, commercial

---

[496] Judgement of the Court of Appeal in Warszawa of 5.5.2017, VI ACa 200/16, Legalis.
[497] PWN Dictionary <https://sjp.pwn.pl/sjp/praktyka;2507839.html> (accessed on: 1.2.2025).

communications aimed at investors, including annual reports and corporate promotional material'. The same will also be true for other traders' practices directed against another trader, e.g. providing false information to counterparties ('entrepreneurs') about the competitor (see Article 14) or taking over the entrepreneur's employees (see Article 12). Such practices should be examined under the Act on Combatting Unfair Competition and not under the Act on Counteracting Unfair Market Practices.

Article 3 of the Act on Counteracting Unfair Market Practices provides for a general prohibition of unfair market practices. Subsequent provisions of the Act (Articles 4–11) define the types of unfair market practices, which are as follows:

1. unnamed (non-standardised) practices contrary to good practice that distort or are likely to distort the market behaviour of the average consumer (Article 4(1));
2. misleading practices (Articles 4(2), 5–7);
3. aggressive practices (Articles 4(2), 8–9);
4. the consortium system (Art. 4(3), Art. 10);
5. use of an illegal code of good practice (Art. 4(2), Art. 11);
6. creation of a code of good market practice, the provisions of which are contrary to the law (Article 11(2)).

The Supreme Court was right to state[498] that in every analysis conducted to determine whether a given practice is of an unfair nature, the following stages of procedure must be applied:

1. Stage 1—it is necessary to examine whether the practice is on the so-called black list of misleading and aggressive practices. The list mirrors Annex I to Directive 2005/29/EC, except that in the Act on Counteracting Unfair Market Practices, the list was split into 2 smaller lists. One refers to unfair, misleading market practices, and the other one lists aggressive market practices. If the practice under examination is on one of these lists, there is no need to undertake further analysis, as the practice under examination is unfair in all circumstances.

[498] Judgement of the Supreme Court of 16.4.2015, III SK 24/14, OSNP 2017, No 5, item 64.

They are not subject to any assessment under Articles 4–6 and 8 and their use is prohibited *ex lege*;
2. Stage 2—if the practice under investigation is not listed among the practices on the 'black list', it is necessary to examine whether the behaviour in question (action or omission) falls within the general definitions of a market practice that is misleading by action (Article) or omission (Article) or an aggressive practice (Article), whether it is the conduct of business in the form of a consortium system (Article 10) or the application of a code of good practices whose provisions are contrary to the law (Article 11). If the practice falls within any of the above definitions or is an action as defined in Articles 10 or 11, the practice under investigation should be deemed to be an unfair market practice within the meaning of the Act;
3. Stage 3—only if, having passed stages 1 and 2, there is no positive answer, the entrepreneur's conduct (act or omission) should be assessed in the light of the general clause contained in Article 4(1) defining an unfair market practice. Pursuant to Article 4(2) and (3), practices at Stage 1 and Stage 2 are not assessed in light of the prerequisites of Article 4(1).[499]

According to the Explanatory memorandum to the draft Act, the Act introduces the prohibition of unfair market practices, and this prohibition is based on a general clause (Article 4(1)). As explained, the essential purpose of the general clause boils down to the coverage by the Act of the type of behaviour that cannot be qualified as a named act (Articles 5–11).[500] The general clause sets out two conditions whose cumulative fulfilment allows a practice to be classified as unfair. One relates to the conflict with good practice, and the other consists in the fact that the particular practice must distort or be likely to materially distort the market behaviour of the average consumer.

Article 4(1) implements Article 5(2) of Directive 2005/29/EC, according to which 'a commercial practice is unfair if it (i) is contrary to the requirements of professional diligence and (ii) materially distorts or is likely to materially

[499] Judgement of the Supreme Court of 16.4.2015, III SK 24/14, Legalis.
[500] Explanatory memorandum to the draft Act on Counteracting Unfair Market Practices, Druk sejmowy V kadencji No 1682, pp. 22–23.

distort the economic behaviour with regard to the product of the average consumer whom it reaches or to whom it is addressed, or of the average member of the group of consumers when a commercial practice is directed to a particular group of consumers'. Professional diligence under Directive 2005/29/EC is to be understood as 'the standard of special skill and care which a trader may reasonably be expected to exercise towards consumers, commensurate with honest market practice and/or the general principle of good faith in the trader's field of activity' (Article 2(h) of Directive 2005/29/EC).

3. Good Practice vs Professional Diligence

As explained in the memorandum, the use of the term 'good practice' in Article 4(1) of the Act on Counteracting Unfair Market Practices, despite the fact that Directive 2005/29/EC refers to 'professional diligence', was intentional since under the good practice clause 'there is both: special skill, professional diligence, integrity of action and good faith. Maintaining the principle of good practice constitutes a simplification for the Polish legislator, as it meant remaining consistently within the terminology in force today. With the proviso that the term should be assessed in the light of the consumer-trader relationship'.[501] Thus, the reference to the good practice clause will make it possible to subordinate the market practices of Polish entrepreneurs to the clause, which is well-known in the literature as well as in case law and has been discussed many times.

It was also argued in the Explanatory memorandum to the draft Act, citing in full the view of *J. Szwaja*,[502] that an economic-functional approach should be adopted when interpreting good practice. As explained, 'the essence of the economic-functional approach is that importance is attached not to the observance of good practice "in general", but to the conduct of entrepreneurs in the sphere of economic activity. Hence, good practice means the moral and customary norms followed in business activities'.[503] In this respect, therefore, the considerations relating to Article 3(1) set out in Chapter II of the Act on Combatting Unfair Competition remain valid.

---

501 *Ibidem*, pp. 24–25.

502 See *J. Szwaja*, in: *J. Szwaja* (ed.), Ustawa o zwalczaniu nieuczciwej konkurencji, 2006, Comments to Art. 3, p. 157, Nb 58.

503 Explanatory memorandum to the draft Act on Counteracting Unfair Market Practices, Druk sejmowy V kadencji No 1682, p. 24.

Despite such rationale for the solutions adopted by the Polish legislator, doubts emerged in the literature as to whether the adoption of the good practice clause constituted a proper implementation of the 'professional diligence' clause provided for in Directive 2005/29/EC. Doubts also arose as to whether the 'good practice' clause in the Act on Counteracting Unfair Market Practices meant the same as the 'good practice' clause in Article 3(1) of the Act on Combatting Unfair Competition.[504]

The need to remove inconsistencies relating to general clauses is expressed in Recital 13 of Directive 2005/29/EC, according to which 'in order to attain the objectives of the Community by removing barriers to the internal market, it is necessary to replace existing disparate general clauses and legal principles in the Member States'. The explanatory memorandum to the draft of Directive 2005/29/EC also explains that the concept of 'professional diligence' is analogous to the concept of good business conduct, which can be found in most Member States' legal systems. Professional diligence is a measure of the care and skill exercised by a good businessman in accordance with generally recognised standards of business practice in a particular sector of activity. This concept is necessary to ensure that normal customary business practices, such as advertising based on brand recognition or product placement, do not fall within the scope of Directive 2005/29/EC, even though they are capable of influencing the economic behaviour of the consumer. The EU legislator reminded that the conditions for a general prohibition must be met cumulatively. Thus, even if a practice is found to be contrary to professional diligence, it will only be unfair if the other conditions of the general prohibition are also met.[505]

In the Explanatory memorandum to the Proposal of the Directive 2005/29, it is further explained that 'professional diligence' encompasses" principles that were already well-established in Member States' legislation before the adoption of the Unfair Commercial Practices Directive, such as 'fair market practice', 'good faith', and 'good market practice'. These principles emphasise the normative values that apply in a given field of economic activity. In the

504 See *P. Podrecki*, Dyrektywa o nieuczciwych praktykach handlowych, pp. 378–384.

505 Proposal for a Directive of the European Parliament and of the Council concerning unfair business-to-consumer commercial practices in the Internal Market and amending directives 84/450/EEC, 97/7/EC and 98/27/EC (the Unfair Commercial Practices Directive) of 18.6.2003, COM (2003) 356 final, 2003/0134 (COD), p. 12, Nb 53.

Guidance, the decision of the Polish Office of Competition and Consumer Protection was cited as an example.[506] It concerned the practice applied by the entrepreneur Cyfrowy Polsat SA, which consisted of 'extending automatically contracts for the provision of satellite television access services concluded for a definite period of time, into contracts for another definite period of time, in the absence of an active action on the part of the consumer'.[507]

According to the President of the Polish Office of Competition and Consumer Protection, such a practice could constitute an unfair market practice within the meaning of Article 4(1) of the Act on Counteracting Unfair Market Practices. However, it was incorrectly stated in the Guidance that the President's decision was based on the 'lack of professional diligence on the side of the entrepreneur', whereas, in the justification of the decision, a reference was made to the good practice clause and the views expressed in the Polish literature that, with respect to relationships with consumers, good practice should 'manifest itself in providing adequate information about one's rights, refraining from using the position of a professional and treating contractual partners fairly. In such relations, of particular importance is the assessment of the behaviour of entities in the light of good practice, which refers to such values as respect towards the partner, honesty, sincerity, trust, loyalty, reliability and professionalism'.[508] It was further argued with regard to the practice under review, that good practice should be 'the right to terminate the legal relationship between the parties concerned upon the expiry of the time for which the contract for a specified period was concluded or to terminate a contract concluded for an indefinite period, without the consumer having to perform additional obligations imposed unilaterally by the stronger party to the legal relationship (the entrepreneur) aimed at preventing the automatic extension of the contract concluded for a specified period by a further specified period, the content of which at the stage of conclusion of the contract could not be questioned by the weaker party to the legal relationship (the consumer)'.[509]

---

506 The Guidance (pl), p. 62.

507 See decision No DDK 6/2014 of 23.12.2014, <https://decyzje.uokik.gov.pl/bp/dec_prez.nsf/1/ACD071BE06447B6CC1257EC6007BA844?editDocument&act=Decyzja> (accessed on: 1.2.2025).

508 Decision No DDK 6/2014, p. 16.

509 *Ibidem*, pp. 16–17.

According to the Guidance, the adoption of the professional diligence clause is intended to provide a safety net to ensure that any unfair market practice that cannot be qualified as unfair under the other provisions of Directive 2005/29/EC may still be penalised, which, in turn, will make it possible to extend the scope of the Directive also to unfair practices that might emerge in the future.[510]

It should be added that the premise of professional diligence is not an additional condition that must be cumulatively met in order for the practice under consideration to be deemed unfair. If a practice satisfies all the conditions provided for in Articles 6–9 of, or is listed in Annex I to Directive 2005/29/EC, it is not necessary to examine its compatibility with the requirements of professional diligence provided for in Article 5(2)(a) of that Directive.[511] Article 4(1) of the Act on Counteracting Unfair Market Practices should be interpreted in a similar manner.

There is a basically unanimous view in the Polish literature that the adoption in the Act on Counteracting Unfair Market Practices of the 'good practice' clause instead of the 'professional diligence' clause formulated in Directive 2005/29/EC is not a correct implementation of that Directive.[512]

J. Szwaja believes that such a legislative approach will disable achieving the objectives of Directive 2005/29/EC 'because good practice will not be understood in the sense that the Directive confers on professional diligence'.[513] *E. Nowińska* and *M. du Vall* argue that although the Polish definition of an unfair market practice does not correspond to the content of the EU

---

510 The Guidance (pl), p. 61, The Notice, p. 37.

511 Judgement of the CJEU of 19.9.2013, C-435/11, *CHS Tour Services*, ECLI:EU:C:2013:574, and of 16.4.2015, C-388/13, *Nemzeti Fogyasztóvédelmi Hatóság, przy udziale UPC Magyarország Kft.*, Official Gazette 198 of 2015, p. 4, in which the CJEU confirmed that 'Directive 2005/29/EC must be interpreted as meaning that, where a commercial practice meets all the criteria laid down in Article 6(1) of that Directive in order to be classified as misleading to the consumer, it is not necessary to determine whether such a practice is also contrary to the requirements of professional diligence within the meaning of Article 5(2)(a) of that Directive in order for it to be considered unfair and therefore prohibited under Article 5(1) of that Directive'.

512 *R. Skubisz* considers that this is an 'implementation defect' which should be remedied by the legislator; See: *R. Skubisz*, Cele i zakres zastosowania ustawy, p. 575.

513 *J. Szwaja*, *K. Jasińska*, in: *J. Szwaja*, *J. Kępiński* (eds.), Ustawa o zwalczaniu nieuczciwej konkurencji, 2024, Comments to Art. 3, p. 148, Nb 133.

regulation, it must be interpreted in a manner consistent with the regulation (Directive). Thus, a market practice consistent with good practice should be understood as a market practice that is consistent with professional diligence. The authors expect, however, that due to the well-established meaning of the good practice clause in Polish literature and case law, it will be interpreted differently under Article 3(1) of the Act on Combatting Unfair Competition than what is required by the EU legislator. It may also happen, in their view, that the interpretation of the professional diligence clause will affect the assessment of Article 3(1) of the same Act.[514]

Doubts are also raised by R. Stefanicki, who notes that Article 4(1) of the Act on Counteracting Unfair Market Practices does not reflect the construction of Article 5(2) of Directive 2005/29/EC, in which the focus was placed on the premise of professional diligence, which was omitted in the Polish Act.

Interpretation problems arising from the differences between the concept of 'good practices' in the Act on Combatting Unfair Competition and in the Act on Counteracting Unfair Market Practices are also noted on the grounds of Article 24(2) of the Act on Competition and Consumer Protection. In the Act on Competition and Consumer Protection, the concept of 'good practices' is an element of the definition of practices violating the collective interests of consumers. Commentators are of the opinion that 'good practice' should be interpreted in accordance with the rules applicable to the Act on Counteracting Unfair Market Practices and their interpretation in the light of EU law.[515]

Incorrect implementation shall not, however, prejudice the interpretation of national provisions in accordance with the purpose and principles set out in Directive 2005/29/EC.[516] In this respect, it will also be necessary to refer to the rulings of the CJEU. Thus, it may be concluded that although the

---

514 *E. Nowińska, M. du Vall*, Ustawa o zwalczaniu nieuczciwej konkurencji, Comments to Art. 3, p. 66, Nb 14; also *E. Nowińska*, in: *E. Nowińska, K. Szczepankowska-Kozłowska*, Ustawa o zwalczaniu, Comments to Art. 3, p. 95, Nb 15; and in: Zakaz nieuczciwych praktyk rynkowych (art. 3 u.p.n.p.r.) i klauzula generalna nieuczciwych praktyk rynkowych (art. 4 u.p.n.p.r.), in: *E. Nowińska, D. Kasprzycki* (eds), Nieuczciwe praktyki rynkowe. Ocena regulacji, Kraków 2012, pp. 153–154.

515 *A. Wędrychowska-Karpińska, A. Wiercińska-Krużewska*, in: *A. Stawicki, E. Stawicki* (eds), Ustawa o ochronie konkurencji i konsumentów, 2016, Comments to Art. 24, point 2.4, p. 638.

516 *M. Namysłowska*, Nowa ustawa o przeciwdziałaniu nieuczciwym praktykom, p. 1288.

aim of the Polish legislator who adopted the good practices clause in the Act on Counteracting Unfair Market Practices was to facilitate the application of these provisions, the adopted solution created unnecessary doubts. This is because the relation of the professional diligence clause to the good practice clause is not clear. These doubts are also reflected in the rulings of Polish courts. The Supreme Court emphasised that 'when implementing the Directive, the Polish legislator decided to depart from the literal wording of its Article 5(1), replacing the professional diligence premise with the good practice clause. These concepts are not the same. (...) Even if the Polish Act does not directly use the term "professional diligence", the interpretation of the concept of "good practices" under the Act on Counteracting Unfair Market Practices must be carried out taking into account the 'spirit' of the EU regulation, having regard to the criterion of "professional diligence" referred to in Directive 2005/29/EC'.[517] Undoubtedly, therefore, the use of the term 'good practice' in the Act on Counteracting Unfair Market Practices does not exempt the courts from the obligation to take into account the CJEU case law or the views expressed in the literature in the context of Directive 2005/29/EC.

Both Article 3(1) of the Act on Combatting Unfair Market Practices and Article 4(1) of the Act on Counteracting Unfair Market Practices refer to the 'good practice' clause. A further challenge is, therefore, to determine whether the concept of 'good practice' is identical under both Acts and, consequently, whether the extensive case law and literature 'developed' on the basis of Article 3(1) of one Act may be referred to when interpreting Article 4(1) of the other Act.

Two different positions emerge in the literature in this regard. According to one, the 'good practice' clauses in both Acts should be treated differently.[518] According to the other view, there is no reason not to refer to Article 3(1) of the Act on Combatting Unfair Market Practices when interpreting the 'good practice' clause in the Act on Combatting Unfair Market Practices. This is

---

[517] Judgement of the Supreme Court of 16.4.2015, III SK 24/14, OSNAPiUS 2017, No 5, item 64, p. 672.

[518] *J. Szwaja*, *K. Jasińska*, in: *J. Szwaja*, *J. Kępiński* (eds), Ustawa o zwalczaniu nieuczciwej konkurencji, 2024, Comments to Art. 3, p. 148, Nb 133; *P. Podrecki*, Dyrektywa o nieuczciwych praktykach handlowych, pp. 378–380.

because, according to the proponents of this position, there are no grounds for differentiating the concept of 'good practice' in these two Acts.[519]

Supporters of the first position note that the concept of good practice may be understood differently in B2B and B2C relationships (B2C).[520] Indeed, professional trading differs from trading with consumers. Therefore, when interpreting the concept of good practice, it is necessary to take into account the possible differences and, in particular, the legislator's intention to separate the protection of consumer interests in the Act on Counteracting Unfair Market Practices from the protection of entrepreneurs' interests regulated by the Act on Combatting Unfair Competition.[521] This objective of the legislative work found its expression in the deletion of the term 'consumers' from Article 1 of the Act on Combatting Unfair Competition. As a result of this, no equation between the two concepts of good practice provided for in the two Acts can be made. Having said that, it must also be said that reaching to the interpretation of the concept of good practice adopted under one of the Acts when interpreting this concept under the other Act cannot be excluded. This, however, cannot be done automatically, as it requires taking into account the existing differences between these Acts.[522] Other scholars argue that the concept of 'good practice' in the Act on Counteracting Unfair Market Practices should be interpreted in line with the concept of 'professional diligence' adopted in Directive 2005/29/EC.[523] In accepting such an assumption, it seems fair to take the view that actions contrary to the principle of professional diligence will also be contrary to good practice.[524] According to other views, the good

---

519 *J. Szwaja, K. Jasińska*, in: *J. Szwaja* (ed.), Ustawa o zwalczaniu nieuczciwej konkurencji, 2016, Comments to Art. 3, p. 148, Nb 133. Also: *Ł. Wściubiak*, Dobre obyczaje w ustawie o przeciwdziałaniu nieuczciwym praktykom rynkowym, PPH 2007, No 11, p. 42.

520 See *R. Skubisz*, Cele i zakres zastosowania ustawy, p. 575.

521 See *J. Szwaja, K. Jasińska*, in: *J. Szwaja, J. Kępiński* (eds), Ustawa o zwalczaniu nieuczciwej konkurencji, 2024, Comments to Art. 3, p. 149, Nb 134.

522 *P. Podrecki*, Dyrektywa o nieuczciwych praktykach handlowych, p. 382.

523 *J. Szwaja, K. Jasińska*, in: *J. Szwaja, J. Kępiński* (eds), Ustawa o zwalczaniu nieuczciwej konkurencji, 2024, Comments to Art. 3, p. 147, Nb 132; and also Judgment of the Supreme Court of 16.4.2015, III SK 24/14, Legalis.

524 *E. Nowińska, M. du Vall*, Ustawa o zwalczaniu nieuczciwej konkurencji, Comments to Art. 3., p. 66, Nb 14; and also *E. Nowińska*, in: *E. Nowińska, K. Szczepanowska-Kozłowska*, Ustawa o zwalczaniu, Comments to Art. 3, p. 97, Nb 15.

practice clause in the Act on Counteracting Unfair Market Practices requires an interpretation in the 'economic' spirit of Directive 2005/29/EC.[525]

The supporters of the other view are of the opinion that the intention of the legislator, voiced explicitly in the explanatory memorandum to the draft Act on Counteracting Unfair Market Practices, was to adopt the good practice clause in its Article 4(1), precisely in order to enable reference to the body of doctrine and case law under Article 3(1) of the Act on Combatting Unfair Competition. The above assumption is not invalidated by the fact that both Acts aim, as a rule, at protecting other interests—those of entrepreneurs (the Act on Combatting Unfair Competition) or consumers (the Act on Counteracting Unfair Market Practices). Indeed, it is argued that until the enactment of the Act on Counteracting Unfair Market Practices, the purpose of the Act on Combatting Unfair Competition had been also to protect the interests of consumers as participants in economic turnover. Thus, the concept of good practice in the Act on Combatting Unfair Competition was also interpreted from the perspective of consumer protection.[526] The supporters of this position, similarly to the supporters of the first view, believe that the concept of good practice referred to in the Act on Counteracting Unfair Market Practices should be assessed in light of the entrepreneur–consumer relationship and in the Act on Combatting Unfair Competition in the entrepreneur–entrepreneur relationship. Therefore, an entrepreneur's act or omission, although contrary to good practice, will not always automatically be deemed an act of unfair competition or an unfair market practice. Thus, the distinction in the application of the good practice clause in the Act on Combatting Unfair Competition and the Act on Counteracting Unfair Market Practices would be made at the stage of assessing the effects of a breach of good practice and not at the stage of interpreting the concept of 'good practice'.[527]

Summarising the above considerations, it will be to say that as seen in the literature, in a situation of the application of general clauses of the Act

---

[525] Presumably, the author means to refer to functional-economic assessments rather than moral-ethical assessments when assessing the concept of good practice. See: *T. Targosz*, Ustawa o przeciwdziałaniu nieuczciwym praktykom rynkowym, pp. 34–35.

[526] *J. Szwaja*, *K. Jasińska*, in: *J. Szwaja*, *J. Kępiński* (eds), Ustawa o zwalczaniu nieuczciwej konkurencji, 2024, Comments to Art. 3, p. 148, Nb 133.

[527] *Ibidem*, p. 148–149, Nb 133.

on Combatting Unfair Competition and the Act on Counteracting Unfair Market Practices, the provisions of both Acts should be taken into account with respect to good practices. On the other hand, such reference is excluded when the entrepreneur's conduct violates only the interests of another entrepreneur or only the consumer's interest.[528] However, given the close interrelation of the interests of one and the other market participant, in many situations it will be necessary to refer to the good practice clauses of both Acts.

However, an analysis of court decisions shows that Polish courts have problems in assessing the understanding of the concept of good practice under the Act on Counteracting Unfair Market Practices. Some courts, when interpreting good practice, refer to the concept of professional diligence as defined in Directive 2005/29/EC.

When defining the concept of good practice, courts refer to various assessments, including ethical and moral assessments. The Court of Appeal in Warsaw, in its ruling of 9 May 2017, adjudicating that the contractual templates used by an entrepreneur may be deemed unfair market practices, reasoned that 'good practices' are rules of conduct that are not contrary to ethics, morality and socially approved customs. Whereas actions aiming at misinforming, confusing, misleading, or taking advantage of the consumer's ignorance or naivety, i.e. actions commonly referred to as unfair, dishonest, or deviating from the accepted standards of behaviour, may be deemed contrary to good practice."[529] Similarly, the Court of Appeal in Warsaw in its ruling of 17 January 2013 referred not only to moral norms but also adopted the term 'good merchant customs', a concept that had been well established in the Act on Combating Unfair Competition. The Court of Appeal reasoned that 'good merchant customs are uncodified norms of conduct to be followed by an entrepreneur in his or her business, shaped by human attitudes, conditioned, *inter alia*, by professed moral values, economic purpose, and practice of business life. The principle of respecting them requires the observance of moral and ethical norms functioning at a specific level of economic activity, as they result from the ethical and moral standards in force in a given environment'.[530]

528 *R. Skubisz*, Klauzule generalne, pp. 87–88.
529 Judgement of the Court of Appeal in Warszawa of 9.5.2017, VI ACa 1788/14, Legalis.
530 Judgement of the Court of Appeal in Warszawa of 17.1.2013, VI ACa 1069/12, Legalis.

On the other hand, the Court of Appeal in Katowice, in its judgement of 24 June 2016, referred to the 'concept of professional diligence' when interpreting Article 4(1) of the Act on Counteracting Unfair Market Practices and held that 'reading (...) the concept of good morals must be done in the context of Article 2 letter h of the Directive on Unfair Commercial Practices (this provision provides a definition of professional diligence, which means the standard of special knowledge and care which a trader may reasonably be expected to exercise in relations with consumers, consistent with fair market practices and/or the general principle of good faith in the trader's field of activity)'.[531]

The above ruling of Katowice judges was based on an earlier judgement delivered by the Supreme Court on 16 April 2013,[532] in which it made extensive comments on the doubts signalled in the literature. First, the Supreme Court noted that the Polish legislator departed from the literal wording of Article 5(1) of Directive 2005/29/EC and replaced the premise of professional diligence with a good conduct clause. In the opinion of the Court, these are not identical concepts. The concept of professional diligence 'contains the clear contours of an objectively defined model of a trader. It follows from this regulation that equitable measures such as good faith or good practice are to perform a subsidiary, supplementary function in filling this concept of the Directive, which is central to the entire regulation, with concrete content. The content of the concept of professional diligence consists primarily of fairly well-defined intra-legal criteria, i.e. specific requirements regarding knowledge and the manner in which this knowledge is conveyed to consumers, which derive from the Directive and other secondary legislation transposed into national law. On the other hand, good practices, as provided for in Article 4(1) of the Act on Counteracting Unfair Market Practices, should be regarded as moral and customary norms to be followed by traders in their business activity. In relations with consumers, a breach of good conduct occurs as a result of dishonest or unfair behaviour by traders,

[531] Judgement of the Court of Appeal in Katowice of 24.6.2016, V ACa 562/15, OSAKat 2017, No 1, item 8. The Court of Appeal held that the investigated practice of the trader making the acceptance of a complaint about a defective phone conditional on the use of a guarantee constituted a practice contrary to Article 4(1) of the Act on Counteracting Unfair Market Practices.

[532] Judgement of the Supreme Court of 16.4.2015, III SK 24/14, Legalis.

and it deviates from generally accepted principles. The average consumer may expect the trader to act professionally, in accordance with the law and commonly applied standards. Good practice dictates that in its relationship with consumers a trader should, *inter alia*, treat consumers fairly, not make it difficult for them to enforce their rights or benefits against traders, and perform its obligations towards consumers properly'. Thus, the Supreme Court concluded that the concept of 'good practice' should be interpreted on the grounds of Article 4(1) of the Act on Counteracting Unfair Market Practices, taking into account the 'spirit' of Directive 2005/29/EC and the criterion of professional diligence defined in it.[533]

It follows from the analysis of selected case law that courts adjudicating in such matters are guided by both moral-ethical and functional-economic assessments when interpreting the concept of good practice in the Act on Counteracting Unfair Market Practices. Thus, a strict separation of one assessment from the other is not possible. Courts should be guided by different assessments and look first and foremost at the purpose of the legal solutions adopted, as well as at the protection of the interests of individual participants in economic trading, i.e. consumers, entrepreneurs, or the public interest. Undoubtedly, however, when interpreting the good practice clause in the light of Article 4(1) of the Act on Counteracting Unfair Market Practices, courts must take into account the differences between this provision and the provision of Article 3(1) of the Act on Combatting Unfair Competition. It is not possible to automatically adopt the *acquis* and case law relating to Article 3(1). It will also be necessary to refer to the criterion of professional diligence as a defined and expected pattern of behaviour of an entrepreneur in relations with consumers. The level of professional diligence may be different in relations with consumers as compared to that in relations with other entrepreneurs and may also be different depending on the products offered or services provided (e.g. banking services). As a rule, in relations with consumers, the level of professional diligence of the entrepreneur should be higher than in relations with other entrepreneurs.

533 *Ibidem*.

4. Contradiction with the Law

Unlike Article 3(1) of the Act on Combatting Unfair Competition, Article 4(1) of the Act on Counteracting Unfair Market Practices ignores the premise of contradiction with the law. In the opinion of A. Michalak, this is an obvious oversight of the legislator, and the contradiction of a practice with the law should lead to the recognition of a given behaviour of an entrepreneur as an unfair commercial practice. The author argues that an act contrary to the law will also contradict the premise of professional diligence and claims that if a practice has been found to be unlawful, it will not be necessary to demonstrate that it is contrary to accepted principles of good practice. In short, Michalak's point is that a commercial practice will be unfair both when it is contrary to the law and to good practice. He further believes that a commercial practice may also be unfair if it is legal (lawful) but contrary to good practice.[534]

The assumption that the Polish legislator 'overlooked' the premise of the contradiction with the law cannot be confirmed. It is clear from the explanatory memorandum to the draft Act on Counteracting Unfair Market Practices that the legislator accepted with full responsibility the premise of good practice and not the premise of the contradiction with the law. The good practice clause in the Act on Counteracting Unfair Market Practices is broad to include extra-legal norms, e.g. those contained in codes of professional ethics. Hence, the application of the good practice clause was also intended to cover special skills, professional diligence, integrity of actions, and good faith.[535]

The solution adopted by the Polish legislator should be interpreted in such a way that not every violation of the law by an entrepreneur will constitute grounds for claims under the Act on Counteracting Unfair Market Practices. Hence, a breach of law must amount to a breach of the good practice clause. In most situations, however, a breach of law will also constitute a breach of good practice. However, one may imagine (rare) situations in which an entrepreneur acted contrary to the law, although the behaviour complied

---

[534] *A. Michalak*, Przeciwdziałanie nieuczciwym praktykom rynkowym, p. 71. A different view on the absence of this premis holds *K. Kopaczyńska-Pieczniak*, Czyn nieuczciwej konkurencji a nieuczciwa praktyka rynkowa, MoPH 2012, No 3, p. 26.

[535] Explanatory memorandum to the draft Act on Counteracting Unfair Market Practices, Druk sejmowy V kadencji No 1682, p. 24.

with the principles of good practice. Thus, it is not justified to consider 'automatically' that every action contrary to the law is also contrary to good practice.[536] At the same time, it should be borne in mind that the construction of the Act on Counteracting Unfair Market Practices is different from that of the Act on Combatting Unfair Competition. The role of the general clause of Article 4(1) in the Act on Counteracting Unfair Market Practices is limited. In particular, its corrective function is 'pruned' when compared to the Act on Combatting Unfair Competition and will only apply when a practice is not on the 'black list'.

5. Material Distortion of the Average Consumer's Market Behaviour

The second prerequisite for the application of the general clause of Article 4(1) is the determination that the applied practice materially distorts or is likely to distort the market behaviour of the average consumer.

For guidance on the interpretation of this premise, the legislator refers to Directive 2005/29/EC in the explanatory memorandum to the draft Act on Counteracting Unfair Market Practices and explains that the premise has the nature of a general clause and its content should be shaped and fulfilled by the court rulings delivered, having taken account of EU law.[537] According to Article 2(e) of Directive 2005/29/EC, a 'significant distortion of consumers' economic behaviour' should be understood as meaning the use of a commercial practice to appreciably impair the consumer's ability to make an informed decision and thereby induce the consumer to take a transactional decision that would not have been taken otherwise. It seems to follow from the Guidance that the determining factor in assessing whether or not a commercial practice materially distorts consumer behaviour is whether or not the consumer would have taken a transactional decision in the absence of the practice in question.[538] One has to agree with the view expressed in the literature that distortion may take various forms, such as duress, misrepresentation by omission (disinformation, lack of information), or action (provision of false information).[539]

---

[536] Judgement of the Court of Appeal in Katowice of 24.6.2016, V ACa 562/15, Legalis.
[537] Explanatory memorandum to the draft Act on Counteracting Unfair Market Practices, Druk sejmowy V kadencji No 1682, p. 26.
[538] The Guidance (pl), p. 45, The Notice, p. 32.
[539] *A. Michalak*, Przeciwdziałanie nieuczciwym praktykom rynkowym, p. 73.

At the same time, it is irrelevant whether a particular decision has been made or not. It is sufficient that the practice in question is likely to influence the consumer's decision.[540] Hence, it will also be a practice that influences a consumer's decision regarding, for example, entering a shop, taking the time to make an online reservation, and refraining from moving to another service provider or purchasing another product, which will fall under that category.[541] It is therefore necessary to examine a particular commercial practice in relation to a specific factual situation (*in concreto* examination) and its likely impact on possible consumer decisions (*in abstracto* examination).

As an example, the Commission cited an advertisement in which the advertiser presented his car as 'the safest car in the world'. In deciding the dispute that arose, the Swedish court held that in order to assess whether such an advertising message was likely to influence a consumer's reasoned decision, it was sufficient that it was likely to arouse the average consumer's interest and cause him to take further action, such as going to a shop or visiting the advertiser's website. However, it is not clear from the example provided by the Commission whether, in the Court's view, such an advertising message materially distorted the consumer's decision. Indeed, not every distortion of a consumer's decision will justify considering a practice as unfair. A commercial practice must have a substantial effect on the decision the consumer makes. Even if there has been a distortion or there is a likelihood of distortion, but it concerns insignificant elements, one cannot argue that such a practice is unfair.[542] A material distortion would be, for example, a decision to conclude a contract where the trader concealed information about high shipping costs for the ordered goods. On the other hand, it would be a non-material distortion if a decision to purchase goods had been made as a result of a trader's advertising in a situation where the purchased goods differed slightly in shade from the colour of the goods presented in the advertisement.

---

540 *M. Sieradzka*, Ustawa o przeciwdziałaniu nieuczciwym praktykom rynkowym, p. 83.

541 The Guidance (pl), p. 45, The Notice, p. 32.

542 Such an assumption is aimed at eliminating trivial infringements. See: *A. Michalak*, Przeciwdziałanie nieuczciwym praktykom rynkowym, p. 73.

Both the Act on Counteracting Unfair Market Practices and Directive 2005/29/EC stipulate that the distortion must relate to the consumer's market behaviour (the Directive uses the term 'economic behaviour'. Economic behaviour is to be understood as behaviour undertaken in connection with participation in business transactions and relating to consumers' interests of an economic nature. It should be added that Directive 2005/29/EC does not cover provisions relating to non-economic interests. As provided for in recital 7 of the Preamble of Directive 2005/29/EC, it 'does not address legal requirements related to taste and decency which vary widely among the Member States. Commercial practices such as, for example, commercial solicitation in the streets, may be undesirable in Member States for cultural reasons. Member States should accordingly be able to continue to ban commercial practices in their territory, in conformity with Community law, for reasons of taste and decency even where such practices do not limit consumers' freedom of choice. Full account should be taken of the context of the individual case concerned in applying this Directive, in particular the general clauses thereof'.

It follows from the above that the premise of distortion (or its likelihood) of consumer market behaviour must be understood broadly. It will, however, be for the courts to examine whether the distortion was material and whether it affected consumers' market interests.

When assessing whether the distortion was material, reference should be made to the model of the average consumer. In addition, Article 5(1) of Directive 2005/29/EC clarifies that when assessing commercial practices that are likely to materially distort the economic behaviour of only a clearly identifiable group of consumers who are particularly vulnerable to the practice or the underlying product because of their mental or physical infirmity, age, or credulity in a way that the trader could reasonably be expected to foresee, they shall be assessed from the perspective of the average member of that group. This is without prejudice to the common and legitimate advertising practice of making exaggerated statements or statements that are not meant to be taken literally.

For example, in the case law of the Polish courts, the market behaviour of the average consumer is considered to be materially distorted by commercial practices consisting of:

1. making the acceptance of a defective phone complaint conditional on the use of a guarantee

2. in such a situation, the distortion of the consumer's market behaviour will already have occurred after the conclusion of the contract[543];
3. communicating the information about an amendment to the contract in a form that was hardly noticeable, in a manner inadequate to the importance of this information to subscribers. The court found that if the information about the amendment to the contract had been communicated to subscribers in such a way that it could not have gone unnoticed, the actual behaviour of consumers might have been different[544];
4. misrepresenting that online and telephone transfers are free of charge. The court reasoned that 'if a practice in any way influences a consumer's contractual decision-making behaviour, it is material'[545];
5. including a provision in the contract imposing an obligation on the consumer to return the performance made by the bank to a third party as a condition precedent to the effectiveness of the declaration on withdrawal from the contract. Such a contractual provision could, in the court's view, have influenced the average consumer's decision to waive the right to withdraw from the contract[546];
6. providing consumers with information about the change of standard contract terms on the last pages of a magazine published by the trader. It follows from the rationale of the verdict that the manner of providing information about the change in the contract templates was likely to mislead the consumer both as to the mere fact of the change in the template and as to the possibility of exercising the right of withdrawal.[547]

6. Misleading Practices by Action or Omission

When implementing Directive 2005/29/EC, the Polish legislator stipulated that a misleading practice may take the form of an action[548] or an omission

[543] Judgement of the Court of Appeal in Katowice of 24.6.2016, V ACa 562/15, Legalis.
[544] Judgement of the Court of Appeal in Warszawa of 29.11.2016, VI ACa 1067/15, Legalis.
[545] Judgement of the Court of Appeal in Warszawa of 30.11.2015, VI ACa 1685/14, Legalis.
[546] Judgement of the Court of Appeal in Warszawa of 14.1.2015, VI ACa 467/14, Legalis.
[547] Judgement of the Court of Appeal in Warszawa of 7.11.2014, VI ACa 161/14, Legalis.
[548] See Article 6 of Directive 2005/29/EC.

to act.[549] This division is reflected in the systematics adopted in the Act on Counteracting Unfair Market Practices. In its Article 5, the misleading practices by action[550] and in Article 6, misleading commercial practices by omission have been defined.[551] Article 7 in turn contains a blacklist of unfair commercial practices misleading in all circumstances.[552]

And so, under the Act, a misleading practice by the entrepreneur's action occurs, when it 'in any way causes or is likely to cause the average consumer to take a decision regarding the contract, which he or she would not have taken otherwise'. The most common forms of such practices include, among other things, (i) disseminating false information, (ii) disseminating true information but in a manner likely to mislead, (iii) marketing products which, through the use of packaging or trademarks, etc., may be misleading, (iv) and announcing that a trader follows the statutory code of good practice when in fact he fails to do so. As emphasised in the explanatory memorandum to the draft Act, the recognition of an action consisting of non-compliance with a code of good practices as an unfair market practice was a novelty in the Polish legal system. It was expected that the adoption of that solution would cause the existing, although malfunctioning, self-regulatory system, which had only been used for advertising purposes, to increase in importance.[553] Whether that goal was achieved is difficult to ascertain, as there is no case law on the matter. However, it must be emphasised that this type of practice is included in the list of practices that are unfair in all circumstances (Article 7(1).

Article 5(3) sets out, by way of example, the aspects to which misrepresentation may relate. The list extends to the existence of the product (type or availability), its characteristics, the entrepreneur's obligations in relation

---

549 See Article 7 of Directive 2005/29/EC.

550 Article 6 was amended on 1.12.2022 (Dz. U of 2022, item 2581). As a result of the amendment, the black list of unfair commercial practices misleading by action was expanded [see: Art. 5 (2)(5)].

551 Article 6 was amended on 1.12.2022 (Dz. U of 2022, item 2581). As a result of the amendment, the black list of unfair commercial practices misleading by omission was expanded [see: Art. 6 (4) (6–8)].

552 Article 7 was amended on 1.12.2022 (Dz. U of 2022, item 2581). As a result of the amendment, the black list of unfair commercial practices misleading in all circumstances was expanded [see: Art. 7 (11a) and 7 (24–26)].

553 Explanatory memorandum to the draft Act on Counteracting Unfair Market Practices, Druk sejmowy V kadencji No 1682, pp. 27–28.

to the product (service, advertising, delivery, etc.), the consumer's rights, the price (its calculation or price advantage), the type of sale, the reasons for the practice, or signs and statements relating to the entrepreneur (e.g. permits, status, affiliations, etc.). In turn, Article 5(4) provides that any assessment of whether a practice is misleading or likely to mislead must be carried out on a case-by-case basis, taking into account all the elements of the practice, the circumstances of the placing of the good on the market, and the manner in which it is presented. The above does not apply to misleading practices contained in the so-called blacklist of misleading practices contained in Article 7.

The same Article 7 implements partially Annex I of Directive 2005/29/EC, which contains a closed catalogue of commercial practices considered unfair in all circumstances. In my view, it was an unfortunate move on the part of the Polish legislator to adopt in Article 7 a list of unfair commercial practices misleading in all circumstances (the so-called black list of misleading practices), both for practices consisting of acts and omissions to act. It would have been more appropriate to separate the practices of action from those of omission and create two lists and place them directly in the general provisions relating to the specific type of misleading practices. At present, Article 5 contains provisions on practices misleading by action, then Article 6 deals with practices misleading by omission, followed by Article 7 once again referring to examples of both types of practices.

The solution of separately regulating practices by omission or by action would, under the Act, be more consistent with its design. However, the problem arises as to whether a precise separation of these practices is at all possible. After all, this is not done by the EU legislator, either. For the most part, however, the blacklist in Annex I of Directive 2005/29/EC concerns practices that are misleading by action. Indeed, the use of the phrases 'claiming', 'using', 'asserting', 'presenting', and 'advertising' suggests an action rather than an omission. However, it is possible that an action may be linked to an omission by the trader. Indeed, when offering a product, one may be silent on a certain entitlement the consumer has, e.g. with regard to the possibility to repair the product. On the other hand, an example of a practice that will be connected with an omission by a trader could amount to so-called surreptitious, or crypto, advertising [Article 7(11)]. This is because the trader ignores the fact that the message in question is intended to promote a product and is not merely neutral information.

If, on the other hand, we assume that a precise distinction between misleading practices by action and misleading practices by omission is not possible and expedient, it would be more appropriate to attach, as the EU legislator has done, an annex to the Act containing a so-called black list of misleading practices.[554]

Below there are several rulings in which courts, basing on the provisions of Article 5, established that the following were unfair market practices misleading by action:

1. a press advertisement of a loan describing it as the lowest-cost loan, when in fact it was not the cheapest on the market. Signs were also used suggesting that the activities carried out by the operator were subject to state supervision, whereas there was no such supervision[555];
2. information to policyholders that the premium and sum insured were indexed by the same percentage, when in fact the sum insured was indexed by a lower rate if the maximum sum insured was exceeded[556];
3. the use of the following provisions in the regulations of the online shop: 'Before putting the photo mural on the wall, check whether it is not defective, because once it has been put on the wall, the complaint will not be accepted'[557];
4. an internet advertising campaign suggesting that the consumer would pay nothing for online and telephone transfers, when in fact there were charges for European and foreign currency transfers made by electronic means[558];
5. the inclusion in the general conditions of insurance of a definition of myocardial infarction giving the impression that it was scientific and

[554] *M. Namysłowska*, Nowa ustawa o przeciwdziałaniu nieuczciwym praktykom, p. 1292, notes that 'although the literal incorporation of the "blacklist" into Polish law increases the harmonising effect intended by the European Commission, it was not a necessary measure'. Of a different opinion is *R. Stefanicki*, in: Ustawa o przeciwdziałaniu nieuczciwym praktykom rynkowym, p. 363, who believes that the list had to be introduced, but each Member State could choose how to introduce it.

[555] Judgement of the Court of Appeal of 23.3.2017, VI ACa 1812/15, Legalis.

[556] Judgement of the Court of Appeal in Warszawa of 15.3.2017, VI ACa 1864/15, Legalis.

[557] Judgement of the Court of competition and consumer protection (SOKiK) of 30.8.2016, XVII AmA 16/15, Legalis.

[558] Judgement of the Court of Appeal in Warszawa of 30.11.2015, VI ACa 1685/14, Legalis.

complete, which led the contracting party to believe that the insurance covered all myocardial infarctions and not just some, as was in fact the case[559];

6. provision of information during an advertising campaign concerning promotional offers for mobile Internet access services that the trader's offer includes 'The fastest Internet in a mobile phone. Unlimited. For PLN 5'. In reality, the limit in the offers in question was 50 MB per billing cycle, and the service subscription of PLN 5 per month was only valid during the first three billing cycles.[560]

According to the Explanatory memorandum to the draft Act on Counteracting Unfair Market Practices, a misleading practice consists in depriving the consumer of the opportunity to make an informed choice regarding the conclusion of a contract by depriving him of the opportunity to be given information of material significance.[561]

Under Article 6(1), a practice is considered misleading by omission when it 'ignores material information necessary for the average consumer to take a contractual decision and thereby causes or is likely to cause the average consumer to take a contractual decision that he or she would not have taken otherwise'. However, the explanatory memorandum to the draft Act clarifies that Article 6(1) does not impose positive obligations on the entrepreneur,[562] who is only obliged not to omit material information.

Material information is 'information which an entrepreneur who engages in a market practice is obliged to provide to consumers pursuant to separate regulations'. This applies to mandatory information obligations that arise from a number of legislative acts. A catalogue of those acts[563] was provided in the explanatory memorandum to the draft Act, but it did not mean that the information obligation is limited exclusively to those legislative acts quoted,

[559] Decision of the Supreme Court of 15.5.2014, III SK 75/13, Legalis.
[560] Judgement of the Supreme Court of 4.3.2014, III SK 34/13, Legalis.
[561] Explanatory memorandum to the draft Act on Counteracting Unfair Market Practices, Druk sejmowy V kadencji No 1682, p. 28.
[562] See *ibidem*, p. 30.
[563] See *ibidem*, p. 29.

being the implementation of the directives listed in Directive 2005/29/EC, which is anyway quite extensive.[564]

If the scope of the information obligations is not specified in any separate legal provisions, the entrepreneurs must determine the scope of the material (relevant) information themselves. As follows from Article 6(4), in the situation of an offer to purchase a product, the material or relevant information includes essential characteristics of the product, identification of the entrepreneur, specification of the price or the method of its calculation, method of payment, method of the delivery and manufacture of the product, procedures for handling complaints, and information on withdrawal from the contract or termination of the contract. It was emphasised in the explanatory memorandum to the draft Act on Counteracting Unfair Market Practices that such a regulation is relevant when there are no specific provisions imposing information obligations on the entrepreneur. Currently, the provisions relating to products offered to consumers are so extensive that one can hardly imagine that there would be any laws or legislative acts that would not specify information obligations imposed on entrepreneurs. On the other hand, it may be considered that the solution adopted in Article 6(4) imposes a certain minimum information obligation on the entrepreneur in a situation of an offer to purchase a product. However, in the ruling of 30 November 2015, the Court of Appeal in Warsaw took a different view, stating that 'internet advertising has its own specificity consisting in presenting the main, most attractive features of the offered product, in a short accessible form, which cannot however, be expected to contain all the information considered material within the meaning of paragraph Article 6(4)'.[565] This kind of position raises objections. Every type of advertising aims to highlight the best features of an offer. This, however, does not exempt entrepreneurs from certain information obligations. One must agree with the reasoning of the court of first instance, which argued that 'the plaintiff's behaviour could not be justified by the form of the advertising message adopted, which

[564] On the information obligations under various legal provisions in light of Article 10 of the Act on Combatting Unfair Competition, see. *M. Kępiński, J. Kępiński* in: *J. Szwaja, J. Kępiński* (eds), Ustawa o zwalczaniu nieuczciwej konkurencji, 2024, Comments to Art. 10, pp. 305–337, Nb. 22–109. These considerations remain valid also on the ground of the Act on Counteracting Unfair Market Practices.

[565] Judgement of the Court of Appeal in Warszawa of 30.11.2015, VI ACa 1685/14, Legalis.

limited the possibility of providing information about the fee for the card. The adopted formula undoubtedly required making necessary abridgements and limiting the presentation to the features of the product relevant to the target group in question, but the message could not be limited to highlighting the advantages of the product here—the free-of-charge nature of the account, with total disregard for the costs involved in concluding the agreement'. Such an argument is much more convincing under the Act on Counteracting Unfair Market Practices.

By way of example, the legislator specified that an entrepreneur's omission may be, in particular, (i) concealing or failing to communicate in a clear, unambiguous, or timely manner material information concerning the product or (ii) failing to disclose the commercial purpose of the practice if it is not clear from the circumstances and if it causes or is likely to cause the average consumer to take a decision concerning the contract that he or she would not have taken otherwise.

As in the case of practices misleading by action, each practice must be examined *ad casum*, taking into account all its elements and the circumstances of the product introduction or presentation. In addition, however, the legislator requires taking into account the spatial and temporal constraints that may arise from the specifics of communication with consumers and the measures that the entrepreneur undertook to make the information available as a result of the said constraints.

For example, it follows from the decisions of the courts that the following are considered to be misleading practices by omission:

1. failure to disclose to the consumer in the standard contract all the data necessary for the consumer to calculate independently the final amount of the agent's commission for the sale of the property[566];
2. failure to provide the consumer with the final price of the goods and services, i.e. the price inclusive of all taxes[567];
3. failure to supply the electricity consumer at the pre-contractual stage with essential information on the characteristics of the service, i.e. the

[566] Judgement of the Court of Appeal in Warszawa of 9.5.2017, VI ACa 1788/14, Legalis.
[567] Judgement of the SOKiK of 6.9.2016, XVII AmA 35/16, Legalis.

terms and conditions for the supply of electricity, which could have influenced that consumer's decision to conclude a contract[568];
4. failure to include explanatory information in the content of the complaint form provided to consumers that the use of the method of their choice of complaint handling does not deprive them of further claims[569];
5. failure to provide in the published rules of procedure the entrepreneur's name and address.[570]

While the courts held that it was not an unfair or misleading practice by omission:

1. to disseminate advertising leaflets advertising life and endowment insurance with an investment fund, without providing certain information. The Court of Appeal in Warsaw, which disagreed with the court of first instance as to the adopted model of the average consumer, held that 'a cautious and prudent average consumer, having read the entire content of the advertising materials and critically analysed them, should have come to the conclusion that the claimant offered services that were not bank deposits, which did not guarantee the protection of the entire funds deposited, nor did they guarantee the earning of a profit'.[571]
2. not to provide information in the advertisement presented on the Internet about a fee for using a payment card, at the same time omitting to include this service in the enumerated services for 0.00 PLN. In the opinion of the Court of Appeal, an average consumer who is well acquainted with the internet banking market should be aware that this service may be subject to a fee.[572]

---

568 Judgement of the Court of Appeal in Warszawa of 30.6.2015, VI ACa 1181/14, Legalis.
569 Judgement of the Supreme Court of 8.5.2014, III SK 45/13, OSNAPiUS 2015, No 9, item 130, p. 1218.
570 Decision of the Supreme Court of 15.10.2014, III SK 4/14, Legalis.
571 Judgement of the Court of Appeal in Warszawa of 20.4.2017, VI ACa 67/16, Legalis.
572 Judgement of the Court of Appeal in Warszawa of 30.11.2015, VI ACa 1685/14, Legalis.

Article 7 contains a catalogue of unfair market practices that are misleading in all circumstances, but no distinction is made between whether the practice is the result of an action or an omission.[573]

7. Aggressive Practices

Unfair commercial practices are also those defined in Article 8(1) of the Act on Counteracting Unfair Market Practices as aggressive practices. As the Guidance shows, Directive 2005/29/EC introduced a uniform definition of aggressive commercial practices, which extends to commercial practices that, by means of harassment, coercion, physical force, or undue influence, restrict the consumer's freedom of choice at the stage of advertising a product (marketing) or during or after the conclusion of a contract.[574] As emphasised in the Guidance, Directive 2005/29/EC establishes an additional level of protection that may be provided through public enforcement measures, without the need for resorting to criminal or civil proceedings. Aggressive commercial practices may also be sanctioned under other provisions of national law, whether criminal or civil.[575]

When a trader exercises unacceptable pressure that restricts or is likely to restrict the average consumer's freedom of choice or conduct with regard to the product, this is an aggressive practice that causes or is likely to cause a consumer to take a contractual decision that consumer would not otherwise have taken. It has been emphasised in the literature that Article 8(1) of the Act on Counteracting Unfair Market Practices may be regarded as a 'small' general clause relevant for the qualification of certain commercial practices as aggressive practices.[576] Articles 8(2) and 8(3) also specify general principles relating to the assessment of aggressive commercial practices and contain a definition of 'unacceptable pressure'. As explained in the explanatory

---

[573] Unfair practices have been described in detail by *M. Namysłowska*, Czarna lista nieuczciwych praktyk handlowych, pp. 322–482. Some of the unfair practices have been added by the Law of 1.12.2022 (Dz. U. of 2022, item 2581), which entered into force on 1.01.2023.

[574] See the Guidance (pl) p. 93, The Notice, p. 59.

[575] See the Guidance (pl), p. 94, The Notice, p. 60.

[576] On aggressive market practices see *D. Kasprzycki*, Agresywne praktyki rynkowe, in: *E. Nowińska*, *D. Kasprzycki* (eds), Nieuczciwe praktyki rynkowe. Ocena regulacji, Kraków 2012, p. 230.

memorandum to the Act on Counteracting Unfair Market Practices, the term 'unacceptable pressure' was not known in Polish law, and its definition had to be provided. And so 'unacceptable pressure' means any type of use of an advantage in relation to the consumer, in particular the use or a threat of use of physical or mental coercion in a way that significantly limits the average consumer's ability to make an informed decision regarding the contract. It is also explained that the differences between the definition of 'undue influence', a term used in Directive 2005/29/EC, and the definition of 'unacceptable pressure' in the Act on Counteracting Unfair Market Practices are merely linguistic. The latter term, as a concept that has already been known in Polish law, is also used in the Act without the need to modify the scope of the definition. As is further explained, as regards aggressive practices, both types of persuasive coercion (physical and psychological) and harassment by which the consumer's vulnerability is exploited in order to limit his or her freedom to make a decision in relation to the product are involved.[577] Directive 2005/29/EC distinguishes 3 forms of influence on the consumer: harassment, coercion, and undue influence. The Act on Counteracting Unfair Market Practices does not distinguish between these individual forms and subsumes them under one collective concept of 'unacceptable pressure'. This concept is autonomous and appears only in this Act, yet it should be interpreted in accordance with well-known institutions in Polish law, including in particular in the context of defects in a declaration of intent.[578]

Although it has been noted in the literature that there is a difference between the definition of 'undue influence' in Directive 2005/29/EC and the definition of 'unacceptable pressure' used in the Act on Counteracting Unfair Market Practices, the authors ultimately conclude that, despite the differences, the Polish legislator has ensured that the objectives of Directive 2005/29/EC are met.[579]

---

577 Explanatory memorandum to the draft Act on Counteracting Unfair Market Practices, Druk sejmowy V kadencji No 1682, p. 32.

578 *A. Michalak*, Przeciwdziałanie nieuczciwym praktykom rynkowym, p. 109.

579 *D. Kasprzycki*, Agresywne praktyki rynkowe, p. 234.

The Polish courts have held that such an example of unacceptable pressure may also be 'pressure exerted on debtors by disinforming and creating fears',[580] and not only 'pressure of a physical nature, but also the abuse of emotional elements leading to irrational actions',[581] or 'any kind of persuasive coercion that exploits the weakness of the other party',[582] but 'an action mechanism based on suggestion, creating a false image of the situation and exploiting consumers' emotions'.[583] An aggressive commercial practice, unlike an unfair misleading practice, must involve some active action on the part of the trader involving the use of specific means of influence. Pursuant to the Act on Counteracting Unfair Market Practices, each practice should be assessed *ad casum*, taking into account all its features and the circumstances in which the product was marketed. In particular, under scrutiny should be circumstances such as:

1. time, venue, type, or nuisance of practice;
2. exploitation by the entrepreneur of the consumer's involuntary position or of other circumstances that impair the consumer's ability to make an informed decision;
3. the use by the entrepreneur of onerous or disproportionate non-contractual barriers to prevent the consumer from exercising contractual rights (right of withdrawal, notice of termination, or cancellation);
4. threats of illegal action, use of abusive language.

Article 9 includes a catalogue of 8 examples of aggressive market practices that are unfair in all circumstances.[584] They are solutions that are an almost literal implementation of the provisions of Articles 8 and 9 and Annex I of Directive 2005/29/EC.

These practices consist of:

---

[580] Judgement of the SOKiK of 13.9.2013, XVII AmA 18/11, Legalis.

[581] Judgement of the Court of Appeal in Warszawa of 30.11.2012, VI ACa 574/12, Legalis.

[582] Judgement of the Court of Appeal in Warszawa of 20.1.2015, VI ACa 457/14, Lex No 1771064.

[583] Judgement of the Court of Appeal in Warszawa of 10.4.2013, I ACa 1220/12, Legalis.

[584] The practices placed on the black list have been analysed by *M. Namysłowska*, Czarna lista nieuczciwych praktyk handlowych, pp. 482–545, and *D. Kasprzycki*, Agresywne praktyki rynkowe, pp. 235–252.

1. creating an impression that the consumer cannot leave the entrepreneur's premises without concluding a contract;
2. paying visits to the consumer's home even if it is only where the consumer is not permanently resident and ignoring the consumer's request to leave or to cease such visits except in circumstances involving the enforcement of a contractual obligation, to the extent permitted by applicable law;
3. soliciting the purchase of products by telephone, fax, e-mail, or other means of distance communication, except in cases of enforcement of contractual obligations, to the extent permitted by the applicable legislation;
4. requiring that the consumer making a claim under an insurance contract produce documents that cannot reasonably be considered relevant to establishing the validity of the claim, or failing to respond to the relevant correspondence in order to make the consumer abstain from exercising the rights arising from the insurance contract;
5. including in an advertisement a direct appeal to children to buy advertised products or to persuade their parents or other adults to buy advertised products for them;
6. requesting immediate or deferred payment for the products or the return or safekeeping of products supplied by the trader but not solicited by the consumer;
7. informing the consumer that if the product is not purchased, the trader risks losing the job or the means of livelihood;
8. creating an impression that the consumer has already won, will win unconditionally, or will receive on completion of a particular act a prize or other equivalent benefit, when in fact there is no prize or other equivalent benefit, or obtaining the prize or other equivalent benefit is subject to the consumer paying money or incurring other expenses.

In the case law of Polish courts, cases relating to aggressive commercial practices mainly concern proceedings initiated by the President of the Office of Competition and Consumer Protection under Article 24(2) of the Act on Consumer and Competition Protection in relation to the violation of collective consumer interests.[585] Only a few relate to consumer claims against entrepreneurs engaging in unfair market practices.[586]

The ruling of the Court of Appeal in Warsaw of 30 November 2012, which only indirectly referred to aggressive commercial practices, provides us with valuable considerations on those practices. It mainly concerned the recognition of provisions of template agreements as prohibited. The court argued that in order to speak of an aggressive market practice, the pressure exerted on the consumer by the entrepreneur must be sufficiently strong to restrict the consumer's decision-making process in a significant manner due to the use of coercion. It is debatable, however, as raised by the court, whether an aggressive commercial practice must be characterised by persistence. On the other hand, in the court's view, a one-off action may also amount to an aggressive commercial practice.[587] However, in the ruling of 10 April 2013, the same court emphasised that for a commercial practice to be considered aggressive, it was important that it was not sporadic in nature.[588]

In a judgement of 20 January 2015, the Court of Appeal rightly noted that it was wrong for the Regional Court to assume that 'the necessary condition for considering an aggressive commercial practice as an unfair market practice is an additional finding that it is unlawful or contrary to good practice'. Indeed, the market practice in question was included in the catalogue of so-called black market practices. In such a situation, a finding that 'the entrepreneur applies an aggressive commercial practice must lead to the recognition that the practice is also an unfair practice'.[589] This type of practice is prohibited by the law itself and does not need to be analysed for unfairness under Article 4 of the Act on Counteracting Unfair Market Practices.[590]

---

585 Decision of the Supreme Court of 10.12.2014, III SK 35/14, Legalis; Judgement of the SOKiK of 27.10.2014, XVII AmA 134/14, Legalis; Judgement of the SOKiK of 13.9.2013, XVII AmA 18/11, Legalis; Judgement of the SOKiK of 11.9.2015, XVII AmA 3/14, Legalis; Judgement of the SOKiK of 11.9.2015, XVII AmA 7/14, Legalis; Judgement of the SOKiK of 29.10.2013, XVII AmA 41/12, Legalis.

586 Judgement of the Court of Appeal in Warszawa of 20.1.2015, VI ACa 457/14, Lex No 1771064; and of 10.4.2013, I ACa 1220/12, Legalis.

587 Judgement of the Court of Appeal in Warszawa of 30.11.2012, VI ACa 574/12, Legalis.

588 Judgement of the Court of Appeal in Warszawa of 10.4.2013, I ACa 1220/12, Legalis.

589 Judgement of the Court of Appeal in Warszawa of 20.1.2015, VI ACa 457/14, Lex No 1771064.

590 Judgement of the SOKiK of 29.10.2013, XVII AmA 41/12, Legalis.

The Court of Competition and Consumer Protection, in connection with proceedings initiated by the President of the Polish Office of Competition and Consumer Protection, found that the following were aggressive commercial practices:

1. inserting in the body of a letter notifying of direct debt collection information to the effect that the operational steps taken by inspectors involve direct visits to the debtor's premises between 7 a.m. and 9 p.m. with the aim of enforcing the payment[591];
2. sending letters to consumers requesting their personal appearance without specifying the factual or legal basis for the request and referring in the letters to the pre-litigation procedure and to Articles 498 to 502 of the Code of Civil Procedure)[592];
3. using by the bank in the contract with the client, the phrase 'the primary borrower resigns from the insurance knowing the consequences of such resignation'.[593]
4. organising an audio-text lottery, consisting of the formulation of short text messages suggesting the certainty of winning, addressed to consumers[594];
5. wording of text messages to consumers in the context of an audio-text lottery in a way that suggests the certainty of winning.[595]

In consumer lawsuits, on the other hand, the courts have found aggressive practices to be:

1. playing voice messages that read: 'your account balance is .... (remaining prepaid balance); to make further calls, top up your account once you have used up your balance', or 'your balance is.... (the amount of remaining prepaid credit); in order to make further calls, once this amount has been used up, top up your account', or similar messages

591 Judgement of the SOKiK of 13.9.2013, XVII AmA 18/11, Legalis.
592 Judgement of the SOKiK of 13.9.2013, XVII AmA 18/11, Legalis.
593 Judgement of the Court of Appeal in Warszawa of 30.11.2012, VI ACa 574/12, Legalis.
594 Judgement of the SOKiK of 29.10.2013, XVII AmA 41/12, Legalis.
595 Decision of the Supreme Court of 10.12.2014, III SK 35/14, Legalis. The court refused to accept the cassation complaint for review.

before each call, irrespective of the balance of the claimant's tariff units.[596]

2. organising audio-text lotteries along with sending information suggesting winning a prize and being the winner of the lottery without duly informing consumers of the rules of such a lottery.[597]

8. The Blacklist of Misleading and Aggressive Practices

The blacklist of misleading and aggressive practices constitutes Annex I to Directive 2005/29/EC, 'Commercial practices regarded as unfair in all circumstances', and covers both misleading practices (23 types) and aggressive practices (8 types). The Polish legislator, following the solutions proposed in Directive 2005/29/EC, has adopted that blacklist in the Act on Counteracting Unfair Market Practices, *almost verbatim*[598] but not in the form of an Annex but rather in the text of the Act. The blacklist was divided into two parts, i.e. into a catalogue of misleading practices in all circumstances (Article 7) and into a catalogue of aggressive practices in all circumstances (Article 9). The adoption of such a precise catalogue of practices qualifying certain commercial practices as unfair in all circumstances was a solution hitherto unknown to Polish law on unfair competition.

The purpose of creating a blacklist of commercial practices in Directive 2005/29/EC was to ensure greater legal certainty. According to recital 17 of Directive 2005/29/EC, the practices in Annex I 'are the only commercial practices which can be deemed to be unfair without a case-by-case assessment against the provisions of Articles 5 to 9. The list may only be modified by revision of the Directive'.

Thus, if a trader's practice is included in this list, there is no way to consider that it is not an unfair practice. The commercial practices listed must be considered unfair without the need for a case-by-case assessment in light of the

---

596 Judgement of the Court of Appeal in Warszawa of 20.1.2015., VI ACa 457/14, Lex No 1771064.

597 Judgement of the Court of Appeal in Warszawa of 10.4.2013, I ACa 1220/12, Legalis. However, despite acknowledging that the trader's practice was aggressive in nature, the claimant's claim (the surrender of the award or its equivalent) did not merit consideration.

598 It met with criticism in Polish literature, see *J. Szwaja*, *A. Tischner*, Implementacja dyrektywy 2005/29/WE, p. 1120.

provisions of Articles 5–9 of Directive 2005/29/EC (as well as Articles 4, 5 to 6, and 8 of the Act on Counteracting Unfair Market Practices). Furthermore, Member States may not interfere with the catalogue or, in particular expand it on their own initiative. It may only be modified by reviewing and amending Directive 2005/29/EC.[599]

The intention of the EU legislator was that the blacklist would ensure greater legal certainty. When a trader can be proved to have engaged in a blacklisted practice, the relevant authorities of the Member States may take action to impose certain consequences on such a trader without the need for a case-by-case assessment (i.e. assessing the likely impact of the practice on the economic behaviour of the average consumer).

With regard to one of the commercial practices listed in Annex I,[600] the CJEU also took a stance and presented its view on the practice described in point 31, which refers to the practice of, *inter alia*, creating a false impression that a consumer will obtain or has already obtained a prize or other comparable benefit after performing a certain act, when in fact the prize or other comparable benefit does not exist. The CJEU, in a dispute between the Purely Creative (along with other traders) and the Office of Fair Trading, found that the commercial practice used by a group of traders in their dealings with consumers was an aggressive market practice.[601] The defendants, who were a company that as part of its commercial practices (advertisements in the form of targeted letters, coupons, or newspaper and magazine inserts) addressed to consumers, gave the customers a false impression that they had won a prize. The prizes included, for example, a Swiss watch or a Mediterranean cruise. However, the consumer had to take additional steps in order to collect the prize. The additional steps involved finding out about the nature of the prize

---

[599] See also *M. Namysłowska*, Czarna lista nieuczciwych praktyk handlowych, pp. 164–165 and p. 571.

[600] Judgement of the CJEU (sixth chamber) of 18.10.2012, C-428/11, *Purely Creative Ltd, Strike Lucky Games Ltd, Winners Club Ltd, McIntyre & Dood Marketing Ltd, Dodd Marketing, Adrian Williams, Wendu Ruck, Catherine Cummings, Peter Henry v. Office of Fair Trading*, ECLI:EU:C:2012:651 (hereinafter referred to as *Purely Creative*). Also see *M. Namysłowska*, Kiedy przyznanie nagrody jest nieuczciwą praktyką handlową? – glosa do wyroku TS z 18.10.2012 r. w sprawie C-428/11 Purely Creative and others. EPS 2013, No1, pp. 42–48.

[601] For a detailed description of the commercial practice, see paragraphs 14–16 in the judgement.

or the manner in which it could be received and required the consumer to pay a certain amount of money or bear other additional costs. For example, in order for a consumer to receive a watch 'presented as Swiss but made in Japan, the consumer had to spend £18 (£8.95 for the phone call cost, £8.50 for insurance and postage, and the cost of two envelopes and two stamps). If the postal route was chosen, the consumer spent GBP 9.50. If the telephone was used, the company earned a total of £15.71 (£7.21 for the telephone call and £8.50 for insurance and postage), while its cost amounted to £9.36'. The Court considered that this type of practice was an aggressive commercial practice included in the 'blacklist' (see the second indent of point 31 of Annex I of Directive 2005/29/EC).

As the CJEU held, it is irrelevant whether the cost imposed on the consumer (e.g. the cost of a postage stamp) is insignificant in relation to the value of the prize and that it does not generate any income for the trader. It is irrelevant in the Court's view that the consumer has a choice of several ways of receiving the prize, at least one of which is free of charge, if at least one or more of the ways proposed to the consumer requires the consumer to incur additional costs.

According to the CJEU ruling, the principle should be that when a prize is awarded to a consumer, the receipt of the prize must not require the consumer to pay or incur other costs. However, traders have argued that proper information provided to the consumer regarding the nature of the prize as well as the terms and conditions of receiving it should make it possible to conclude that the practice in place is not unfair.[602] The CJEU stated that it is for the national courts to examine whether the information provided to consumers by traders was clear and comprehensible. In doing so, the courts should follow the guidelines set out in recitals 18 and 19 of Directive 2005/29/EC.[603] The CJEU has made it clear that 'a court, when applying national law, is required to interpret it as far as possible in the light of the wording and objectives of the directive, aiming to achieve the result sought by it, in accordance with Article 288(3), TFEU'.[604]

---

602 See points 51 and 52 of the CJEU's judgement in *Purely Creative*.

603 See *ibidem*, point 55.

604 See *ibidem*, point 41.

9. Business Conducted in the Form of a Consortium System (Article 10 of the Act on Counteracting Unfair Market Practices)

Article 10 of the Act on Counteracting Unfair Market Practices provides that it is an unfair commercial practice to conduct business in the form of the Argentine consortium system (paragraph 1), or to organise a group with the participation of consumers for the purpose of financing a purchase in a consortium system (paragraph 2). According to the statutory Glossary (Article 2(10)) a 'consortium system' is to be understood as 'the conduct of a business activity consisting in the management of property pooled within a group with consumer participation, formed to finance the purchase of a product for the benefit of group participants'.

This type of practice is not regulated by Directive 2005/29/EC, which regulates misleading and aggressive practices, but following an autonomous decision of the Polish legislator, it is subject to regulation under provisions contained in Article 17e of the Polish Act on Combatting Unfair Competition,[605] regulating this type of unfair competition act, which in its entirety has been transposed to the Act on Counteracting Unfair Market Practices.

In the legislator's opinion, business conducted in the form of the Argentine consortium system posed a particular threat to consumers and should therefore be included in the Act on Counteracting Unfair Market Practices, as the purpose of that Act was to ensure consumer protection. Another argument in favour of the adopted move was that it gave consumers the right to file claims, which, under the Act on Combatting Unfair Competition, was not possible.

The need to introduce a prohibition of the consortium system into the Polish system of combatting unfair competition was explained in the reasons for the 2004 amendment to the Act on Combatting Unfair Competition,[606]

---

605 Article 17e of the Act on Combatting Unfair Competition: '(1) It shall be an act of unfair competition to carry out a business activity consisting in the management of property accumulated within a consumer group formed for the purpose of financing the purchase of rights, movable property, immovable property or services for the benefit of group members (consortium system). (2) It shall also be an act of unfair competition to organise a group with the participation of consumers for the purpose of financing purchases in a consortium system as referred to in clause 1'.

606 See Druk sejmowy IV kadencji No 2162 of 16.9.2003, Komisyjny projekt ustawy o zmianie ustawy o zwalczaniu nieuczciwej konkurencji oraz ustawy o kredycie konsumenckim, <http://orka.sejm.gov.pl/proc4.nsf/opisy/2162.htm> (accessed on: 1.2.2025).

in which that prohibition was established.[607] They read that the purpose of the amendment was 'implementation of the constitutional principle of consumer protection contained in Article 76 of the Constitution of the Republic of Poland. The Act aims at delegalising activities that are contrary to the provisions of the Polish legal system (...). The condition for delegalising the activity of managers and organisers of consortium schemes is the recognition of their activity as an act of unfair competition (...)'.[608] Undoubtedly, the primary objective of the introduced regulation was to protect consumers—participants of consortium schemes, who, according to the drafters, suffered all the consequences of irregularities and abuses by entrepreneurs arising from the organisation of consortium schemes. The adopted ban was a reaction to numerous consumer complaints, which were submitted to the Office of Competition and Consumer Protection, to consumer advocates, and to consumer organisations, as well as to the Police, the Public Prosecutor's Office, and the Ombudsman. Consumers alleged that, despite signing the contract and paying the initial fee, they never saw the allocation of the subject of the contract. Consumers alleged also that in the majority of cases (80%) they were misled about the substance of the contract they had signed and had problems with the final settlement when they resigned or were excluded from the programme. Pursuing subsequent claims was difficult, and the entrepreneurs could not be traced, so criminal proceedings were discontinued, and civil proceedings were very ineffective and took years. Proceedings before the Polish Office of Competition and Consumer Protection were also unsuccessful due to numerous formal requirements and lengthy procedures.[609] In view of the above, it was decided to take up the necessary legal work.[610]

At the beginning of the 21st century, it was indeed quite a common practice in Poland that entrepreneurs organised and managed consortium schemes with the participation of consumers. However, there were numbers

---

[607] Act of 17.6.2004 on the amendment of the Act on Combatting Unfair Competition and the Act on Consumer Credit (Dz.U. No 162, item 1693).

[608] Druk sejmowy IV kadencji No 2162, p. 8.

[609] Druk sejmowy IV kadencji No 2162, pp. 4–6.

[610] The Government considered the initiative justified; however, it made a number of critical comments on the draft amendment. See the Government's position on the commission's draft act amending the Act on Combating Unfair Competition and the Act on Consumer Credit (Druk Sejmowy IV kadencji No 2162) of 19.2.2004.

of customers (participants in the consortium) who were misled and made to believe that a loan or a good would be provided to them at an imminent, unspecified time. This practice was therefore considered to be capable of being qualified as a misleading practice, and the legislator saw a need to address it, proposing solutions aimed at its regulation.[611] There were a number of reasons the practice amounted to a misleading practice:

1. despite the entrepreneur's assurances, the consumer would not always receive a loan or a product;
2. the consumer was convinced that the product or a loan would be provided within a specified period (1–3 months)[612];
3. the consumer was misinformed about the possibility of withdrawing from the contract[613];
4. where loans were made, the consumer was contracting with an entrepreneur who should have held a licence or permit for conducting this type of activity (which was not always the case).[614]

Each of the circumstances led to the conviction that this type of scheme could qualify as a misleading unfair commercial practice. What is more, it is quite plausible that it was a practice that could qualify as aggressive, particularly if it entailed taking advantage of the forced position of a consumer in a difficult life situation seeking to obtain a loan or subsequently restricting the consumer's ability to withdraw from the contract.

The explanatory memorandum to the amended Act contained a relatively detailed list of requirements for a consortium system to qualify as a prohibited system: first and foremost, it must be a self-financing scheme, as its members should *de facto* self-finance the cash loans or products they receive. To become a member of the consortium, the consumer has to sign a contract and pay a certain amount, which partly serves to cover the entrepreneur's administrative costs for operating the scheme and realising a profit. The remaining amount is used to provide a loan to members of the scheme or to provide a product. Upon joining the scheme, the participant is obliged to pay a monthly

---

611 Druk sejmowy IV kadencji No 2162, p. 6.
612 *Ibidem*.
613 *Ibidem*.
614 *Ibidem*, p. 5.

instalment equal to the loan instalment, even though the loan has not yet been received. The way in which a loan or a product is allocated can be done in three ways: according to a scoring system, a system of declarations of the participation or a system of a random draw.[615] What must be noted, though, is that it may also happen that regardless of the instalment payment made, a loan will never be granted to a participant or a product will never be received due to their shortage. What was also pointed out was that entrepreneurs who offer cash loans violate the provisions of banking law. Under Article 171[616] of banking law, unauthorised activities such as pooling funds from other natural persons, legal persons, or unincorporated organisational entities with the aim of granting credits, money loans, or otherwise placing these funds at risk are penalised.

The consortium system should be distinguished from the pyramid promotional system (Article 7(14) of the Act on Counteracting Unfair Market Practices) and avalanche contracts (Article 17c of the Act on Combatting Unfair Competition).[617]

The wording of Article 7(14) is an almost *verbatim* implementation of the provision of point 14 of Annex I of Directive 2005/29/EC, which makes it an unfair commercial practice in all circumstances to 'Establish, operate or promote a pyramid promotional scheme whereby the consumer gives a performance in return for the opportunity to receive remuneration which is conditional primarily on the introduction of other consumers into the scheme rather than on the sale or consumption of products'. This prohibition applies only to B2C relationships.

On 3 April 2014, in response to a question for a preliminary ruling referred to it by a Lithuanian court regarding the prohibition of pyramid-type promotional schemes, the CJEU held[618] that 'point 14 of Annex I to Directive

---

615 *Ibidem*, p. 5.

616 Act of 29.8.1997 – Banking Law (Dz.U. of 2024 item 1646 as amended).

617 See *M. Kępiński, J. Kępiński*, in: *J. Szwaja, J. Kępiński* (eds), Ustawa o zwalczaniu nieuczciwej konkurencji, 2024, Comments to Art 17c, pp. 673–674, Nb 24–26, and *J. Kępiński, M. Kępiński*, Umowy lawinowe i umowy do nich podobne, in: *J. Barta, J. Chwalba, R. Markiewicz, P. Wasilewski* (eds), Qui bene dubitat, bene sciet. Księga jubileuszowa dedykowana Profesor Ewie Nowińskiej, Warszawa 2018, pp. 241–257.

618 Judgement of the CJEU of 3.4.2014, C-515/12, *"4finance" UAB v. Valstybinė vartotojų teisių apsaugos tarnyba i Valstybinė mokesčių inspekcija prie Lietuvos Respublikos finansų ministerijos*, EU:C:2014:211; also see: *M. Namysłowska*, Glosa do wyroku TS z 3.4.2014,

2005/29/EC (...) must be interpreted as meaning that a pyramid promotional scheme constitutes a commercial practice which may be regarded as unfair in all circumstances only where such a scheme requires the consumer to make a financial contribution, however small, in return for the possibility of receiving remuneration which is dependent primarily on the introduction of other consumers into the scheme and not on the sale or consumption of products'. The Court emphasised that the recognition of a scheme as a 'pyramid promotional scheme' requires the existence of a link between the benefits paid by newly joining members and the reward (compensation) received by existing members (point 27 of the judgement).

Avalanche contracts, on the other hand, are regulated by Article 17c, according to which 'it is an act of unfair competition to organise an avalanche sales scheme consisting in offering to purchase goods or services by promising the purchasers of those goods or services a material benefit in exchange for inducing other persons to carry out the same transactions, who would obtain similar material benefits by inducing further persons to participate in the scheme'. Article 17c (2), in turn, describes circumstances in which organising a sales system in the manner regulated in paragraph 1 does not constitute an act of unfair competition.[619]

A consortium system differs from avalanche contracts in that a participant makes a payment in order to enter the system, and only then, depending on the agreement with the organiser of the system, may be granted a loan or a product, allocated in order in a specific way (a scoring system, declaration of participation, or draw of lots). The participant is obliged to pay certain

---

C-515/12, EPS 2014, No 11, pp. 47–51 oraz *M. Sieradzka*, Glosa do wyroku TS z 3.4.2014, C-515/12, LEX/el. 2014.

619 Pursuant to Article 17c(2) of the Act on Combatting Unfair Competition, organising a sales scheme referred to in paragraph 1 does not constitute an act of unfair competition if the following conditions are met: (1) the material benefits obtained from participation in the sales system come from funds obtained from the purchase or sale of goods and services at a price the value of which may not grossly exceed the actual market value of such goods and services; (2) the person resigning from participation in the sales system has the right to resell to the organiser of the system for at least 90% of the purchase price of all saleable goods, information and instructional materials, samples of goods or presentation kits purchased from the organiser within 6 months preceding the date of submission of resignation to the organiser of the sales system (Articles 17c para 2 point 1 and 2).

stipulated amounts. In a consortium system, unlike in avalanche and pyramid contracts, there is no requirement to bring in a new participant, which conditions the receipt of a bonus, while in an avalanche contract, the participant purchases the product specified in the contract but may expect a bonus for introducing new participants to the system. A pyramid promotional scheme, on the other hand, differs from avalanche contracts in that the payment into the scheme is a payment for participation only, which opens up a later opportunity for the scheme participant to obtain a reward. There must be a link between the benefits paid by newly joining members (participants) of the scheme and the rewards obtained by existing members. A common element of avalanche and pyramid contracts is the obligation to attract new people to the scheme, and coupled with this obligation is the possibility of obtaining a certain financial benefit. However, an avalanche contract appears to be less harmful to the consumer than a pyramid contract, because entry into the scheme in the avalanche contract is by payment for a good or service and not for mere participation in the scheme, as is the case with pyramid contracts. However, the similarity of avalanche contracts to pyramid contracts makes it necessary, in the light of Directive 2005/29/EC, also to examine carefully avalanche contracts with consumers to check whether they fulfil the general criteria laid down in Article 5 of Directive 2005/29/EC. Some avalanche sales schemes may amount to aggressive economic practices regulated by Articles 8 and 9 of Directive 2005/29/EC.

Under Article 10 of the Act on Counteracting Unfair Market Practices, participation of consumers in a consortium system is necessary to classify the system as prohibited. However, entrepreneurs may also participate in such a system. If this is the case, this type of practice will not fall under the prohibition of Article 10 but will be capable of being considered as an act contrary to Article 3(1) of the Act on Combatting Unfair Competition, and once Article 17e has been repealed, in relation to entities that are not consumers, a consortium system should, in principle, be subject to the provisions of the above-mentioned Article 3(1) of the Act.

10. Application of a Code of Good Practice Contrary to the Law (Article 11 of the Act on Counteracting Unfair Market Practices)

The literature explains that codes of commercial practice are part of the broader concept of corporate social responsibility. This concept implies that the management of a company takes into account not only the interests of the company and the business itself but also respects the interests of the environment, including consumers.[620] Voluntary codes of good practice are an expression of self-regulation and self-control as a system of market practice. This involves 'on the one hand, the voluntary adoption of certain rules of conduct (self-regulation), and on the other hand, the construction of an appropriate system to ensure their observance (self-control)'.[621] However, this system cannot replace the legal system but only complement it. This is also the assumption underlying Directive 2005/29/EC.

Recital 20 of Directive 2005/29/EC explains that the aim of the proposed measures was to give due weight to codes of practice, and it states further that in some Member States there is a tradition of using codes of conduct that define norms and standards of business conduct not otherwise enshrined in law. The purpose of such codes may be, for example, to present how certain statutory solutions are applied (explained in a consumer-friendly manner) or to explain which solutions not regulated by law have been adopted (e.g. after-sales support).[622]

Codes of good practice may be relevant to the consumer when choosing the services or goods of a trader who adheres to certain codes of conduct. The consumer, guided by such codes, may trust that the trader will behave in the manner set out in the code.

Directive 2005/29/EC was designed to create legal remedies to prevent traders from taking undue advantage of the trust that consumers may place in codes of conduct, which are considered to be self-regulatory instruments adopted voluntarily by traders.[623]

---

[620] *A. Mokrysz-Olszyńska*, Rola kodeksów dobrych praktyk w ochronie konsumenta, in: *C. Banasiński* (ed.), Ochrona konkurencji i konsumentów w Polsce i Unii Europejskiej (studia prawno-ekonomiczne), Warszawa 2005, p. 272.

[621] *Ibidem*, pp. 263–264.

[622] *Proposal for a Directive of the European Parliament and of the Council concerning unfair business-to-consumer commercial practices in the Internal Market and amending directives 84/450/EEC, 97/7/EC and 98/27/EC* (the Unfair Commercial Practices Directive) of 18.6.2003, COM (2003) 356 final, 2003/0134 (COD), p. 15, Nb 72.

[623] The Guidance (pl), p. 74, The Notice, p. 44.

Article 11 of the Act on Counteracting Unfair Market Practices[624] implements the provisions of the Codes of Conduct referred to in Directive 2005/29/EC. In the Polish Act, these Codes have been termed 'codes of good market practices'.[625] This term denotes 'a set of rules of conduct, and in particular ethical and professional standards of entrepreneurs who have undertaken to observe them in relation to one or more market practices'. The unfair commercial practices referred to in the Code of Good Market Practice comprise four types of practices and include:

1. use of a code of good market practice whose provisions are contrary to the law (Article 11(1));
2. creation of codes of good market practice that are contrary to the law (Article 11(2)
3. misrepresentation consisting of ensuring compliance with a code of good practice where this is not the case (Article 7(1)). This is an unfair commercial practice included in the blacklist of unfair commercial practices that is misleading in all circumstances;
4. failure to comply with a code of good practice to which the trader has voluntarily subscribed despite the assurance of the commitment to the provisions of the code of good practice (Article 5(2)(4)). Such a practice is a misleading practice.

The use of a code of good market practice contrary to the law is not subject to assessment against the provisions of Article 4(1). Regarding the creation of codes of good market practice contrary to the law, they must be assessed through the prism of the general clause. It should be noted that Article 4(2) was amended in 2014 in this regard.[626] However, before this amendment, for

---

[624] Regulations relating to codes of good practice are also to be found in Articles 4(2), 5(3)(4) and 7(1) of the Act on Counteracting Unfair Market Practices.

[625] Doubts about conceptual differences are voiced by *R. Stefanicki*. See *R. Stefanicki*, Ustawa o przeciwdziałaniu nieuczciwym praktykom rynkowym, p. 462. While according to *M. Wyrwiński* the differences in terminology are not particularly significant and the content of the Directive has been properly implemented. *M. Wyrwiński*, Kodeksy dobrych praktyk, in: *E. Nowińska, D. Kasprzycki* (eds), Nieuczciwe praktyki rynkowe. Ocena regulacji, Kraków 2012, p. 270.

[626] Article 4 clause 2 was added in the reading of the Act of 30.5.2014 (Dz.U. of 2014 item 827) which entered into force on 25.12.2014.

a use of a code of practice contrary to the law to be found an unfair practice, the practice in question also had to satisfy the premises specified in Article 4(1) of the Act on Counteracting Unfair Market Practices. The Supreme Court explained that prior to the entry into force of the amendment, 'it was an unfair commercial practice to apply an unlawful code of good practice if its application was also contrary to good practice and materially distorted or was likely to distort the market behaviour of the average consumer before, during or after the conclusion of a product contract'.[627]

After the enactment of the amendment, there is no need to assess such a practice under the general clause. However, such an assumption was criticised by the Supreme Court, which held that 'it does not follow from Article 11(1), fourth sentence (b) of Directive 2005/29/EC that Member States are entitled to expand the catalogue of unfair commercial practices prohibited in all circumstances to include a practice such as that regulated in Article 11 of the Act on Counteracting Unfair Market Practices. The provision of Article 11 of Directive 2005/29/EC only gives Member States the right to introduce the possibility of applying to the creators of codes of good practice measures provided for in national law to counter unfair commercial practices. By contrast, the Supreme Court held that it was clear from the wording of the provisions of the Act that the national legislator wished to include the creators of codes of good practice within the scope of application of the Act'. According to the Supreme Court, provisions of national law prohibiting *per se* practices other than those listed in Annex I to Directive 2005/29/EC are contrary to this Directive.[628] The position of the Supreme Court is not an isolated one. Similar criticisms have also been raised with regards to Article 10 of the Act.[629] However, it seems that the Supreme Court did not distinguish very precisely between the practice of applying codes of good practices that are contrary to the law and the creation of such codes. This distinction should have been emphasised, as the practice of creating codes of good market practice contrary to the law ought to be assessed with reference to Article 4(1) of the Act on Counteracting Unfair Market Practices. Its Article 4(2) only mentions the use of an unlawful code of good market practice. The application of Article

---

[627] Judgment of the Supreme Court of 9.4.2015, III SK 47/14, Legalis.
[628] *Ibidem*.
[629] See above point 10.

4(1) will therefore depend on what is to be assessed, whether it is the practice of applying an unlawful code or the practice of creating a code that is unlawful. In the first situation, there is no need to assess the practice in light of the general clause. In the second situation, however, in order to determine whether the author of the code has engaged in unfair commercial practices by creating the code, this activity must be assessed in terms of whether the premise of Article 4(1) has been fulfilled. As a matter of fact, this was also the interpretation of Article 11(2) before the amendment.

The market practice of an entrepreneur who claims to have undertaken to comply with a code of good practice does not have to be examined through the prism of Article 4(1) either, if this is untrue. Placing such a practice on the blacklist (Article 7(1)) means that this practice is unfair in all circumstances, and therefore, its assessment under Article 4(1) is unnecessary.[630]

Even though the practice of non-compliance with a code of good practice to which the entrepreneur has voluntarily subscribed has not been blacklisted, it will be unnecessary to assess the practice under Article 4(1) if the prerequisites of Article 5(1) have been fulfilled.[631] Pursuant to Article 13 of the Act, the burden of proof that a particular market practice does not constitute an unfair commercial practice is on the entrepreneur being alleged of using an unfair market practice. In the case of an allegation of a practice specified in Article 5(1), it will be difficult for the entrepreneur to prove that the communication of compliance with the code of good market practice did not or could not have caused a contractual decision that otherwise the consumer would not have taken.

As stated in the explanatory memorandum to the draft Act on Counteracting Unfair Market Practices, the Polish legislator decided to apply the same measures and procedures that apply to entrepreneurs applying conflicting codes of good market practices also with respect to code owners.[632] For the avoidance of possible doubts of interpretation, an addition was made in Article 11(3) of the Act, stating that the author of a code of good practice should be considered to be ‘any entity, in particular an entrepreneur or an association

630 *M. Namysłowska*, Czarna lista nieuczciwych praktyk handlowych, pp. 276–277.

631 Judgement of the CJEU of 19.9.2013, C-435/11, *CHS Tour Services*, ECLI:EU:C:2013:574.

632 This possibility is provided for in Article 11 of Directive 2005/29/EC, and was also provided for in Article 5(2) of Directive 2006/114/EC of the European Parliament and of the Council of 12.12.2006 concerning misleading and comparative advertising.

of entrepreneurs, responsible for the preparation and implementation or supervision of compliance with a code of good practice'.[633] This definition is modelled on the definition adopted in Article 2(g) of Directive 2005/29/EC.[634]

The translation into Polish of the English term code owners as 'creators of the code' may raise some doubts. However, such a translation already appeared earlier in Directive 2006/114/EC concerning misleading and comparative advertising. Indeed, the use of the term creator may suggest that what is meant here is a creator within the meaning of Article 8 of the Act on Copyright and Related Rights.[635] This is probably not the case, as the author of a code may also be an entity that has not made any creative contribution to the creation of the code, and it would be difficult to speak of co-creators. Moreover, the codes of good practice themselves can hardly be qualified as works. Undoubtedly, therefore, the term 'creators of codes of good practice' should be used autonomously for the purposes of the Act on Counteracting Unfair Market Practices. Moreover, the term creator will most often denote not a single entity but a specific collective body.[636] Also the view that an act described in Article 11(2) may be committed only by an entrepreneur also seems correct. A non-entrepreneur, for example a consumer organisation participating in the drafting (or creating) of a code, will not be held liable.[637]

The drafters of Directive 2005/29/EC were concerned with codes of conduct that the trader undertakes to observe voluntarily. This follows from the definition of the 'code of conduct' referred to in Directive 2005/29/EC, according to which, a 'code of conduct' is 'an agreement or set of rules, not imposed by law, a regulation, or an administrative provision of a Member State, which defines the behaviour of traders who undertake to be bound by the code in relation to one or more particular commercial practices or business sectors' (Article 2(f) of Directive 2005/29/EC). What is missing in

---

633 Similarly, Article 2(g) of Directive 2005/29/EC, as well as Article 2(e) of Directive 2006/114/EC.

634 Article 2(g) defines a code developer as 'any entity, including a trader or group of traders, responsible for drafting the code of conduct, amending it and/or supervising its observance by all those who have undertaken to comply with it'.

635 Act of 4.2.1994 on copyright and related rights (Dz.U. of 2025 item 24 as amended).

636 *R. Stefanicki*, Ustawa o przeciwdziałaniu nieuczciwym praktykom rynkowym, p. 462; *A. Mokrysz-Olszyńska*, Rola kodeksów dobrych praktyk w ochronie konsumenta, p. 276

637 *Ibidem*.

the Act on Counteracting Unfair Market Practices is an emphasis on this element of voluntariness. However, the omission of the element of 'voluntariness' by the Polish legislator does not mean that the Polish provisions refer to mandatory codes of conduct. The Directive is unambiguous in this respect,[638] as it is about an entrepreneur's submission to so-called self-regulation.[639] Adopting a different interpretation would be inconsistent with Directive 2005/29/EC. A code of good market practices in the meaning of the Act on Counteracting Unfair Market Practices should also be understood as regulations which the entrepreneur voluntarily undertakes to comply with and which are communicated in commercial communications.

Article 10 of Directive 2005/29/EC provides for the possibility for code owners to control unfair commercial practices and for the possibility for persons or organisations referred to in Article 11 of the Directive to have recourse to bodies that bring together owners of codes of good market practices. As A. Mokrysz-Olszańska rightly points out, the development of a code does not end the process of its creation because for self-regulation to function smoothly, a code of good practice should be supervised by 'an independent third party who is in a position to judge its effectiveness, initiate extensions to it, its updating and propose legislative solutions when the code does not meet expectations'.[640] It is also proposed that the codes of good practice should be controlled by a designated public administration body, as it is likely that codes will be created that will not comply with current legislation.[641]

---

638 See *M. Wyrwiński*, Kodeksy dobrych praktyk, p. 272. Also see: *Proposal for a Directive of the European Parliament and of the Council concerning unfair business-to-consumer commercial practices in the Internal Market and amending directives 84/450/EEC, 97/7/EC and 98/27/EC* (the Unfair Commercial Practices Directive) of 18.6.2003, COM (2003) 356 final, 2003/0134 (COD), p. 15.

639 According to the Guidance Note, point 1.5, p. 34, it should be recognised that 'when the principles contained in self-regulatory codes are rigorous and strictly adhered to by those applying the code, these principles may indeed contribute to reducing the need to initiate administrative or judicial proceedings to enforce the provisions of the Unfair Commercial Practices Directive. Moreover, when standards are high and sectoral operators largely adhere to them, such rules can provide a useful benchmark for national authorities and courts when assessing whether a commercial practice is unfair'.

640 *A. Mokrysz-Olszańska*, Rola kodeksów dobrych praktyk w ochronie konsumenta, p. 279.

641 *Ibidem*, p. 282.

Such a measure (recital 20 of Directive 2005/29/EC), based on control performed by code owners at the national and the Community's levels, was intended to lead to the elimination of unfair commercial practices, which in turn would eliminate the need for recourse to administrative or judicial procedures. This solution would not, however, replace the possibility of seeking redress in judicial or administrative proceedings but would only be complementary to those proceedings.

Furthermore, recital 20 proposed that consumer organisations be informed and invited to participate in the development of codes of conduct. Such a solution could ensure a high level of consumer protection.

The Polish legislator chose not to introduce any specific solutions in this respect. Possible claims should therefore be formulated under Article 12 of the Act on Counteracting Unfair Market Practices.

Despite the growing role of codes of good practice, there are few rulings on practices described in Article 11 of the Act on Counteracting Unfair Market Practices. The rulings that have been published concern the assessment of the same code of good practice, or in fact a supplement to the code called 'Catalogue of the Principles underlying the Developer Contract'. The proceedings were initiated by the President of the Office of Competition and Consumer Protection in a case for recognition of this practice of developing the Catalogue in question as violating the collective interests of consumers. The President of the Polish Office of Competition and Consumer Protection deemed the use of the supplement to be such a practice and decided that the catalogue created by the developer contained unlawful provisions, including the possibility of withdrawing from the contract in the event of an amendment to it resulting from a change in the area of the premises by 2% during its construction. After a long judicial proceeding, however, that decision was cancelled.[642] In its rulings, the Court of Appeal in Warsaw, following the guidelines of the Supreme Court, held that 'the grounds indicated in the Decision of the President of the Office of Competition and Consumer Protection for declaring the provisions of the Code as unlawful within the

642 Judgement of the Court of Appeal in Warsaw of 22.1.2014, VI ACa 761/13, Legalis. A cassation appeal was filed. The Supreme Court overturned the judgement of the Court of Appeal and referred the case for reconsideration. The final decision of the Court of Appeal in Warszawa may be found in the judgement of 8.7.2015, VI ACa 831/15, Legalis.

meaning of Article 11 of the Act on Counteracting Unfair Market Practices, as well as the premises cited in the reasons to determine the Code as being contrary to the law provided in the rationale of the judgment of the court of first instance, could not constitute a legitimate basis for such a claim'. The Court of Appeal argued that the fact that a code of good practice contains prohibited clauses entered in the list of prohibited clauses cannot be the basis for declaring it unlawful. This is because the list does not contain legal norms. It contains only clauses whose abusiveness was established by a court decision and the conflict of these clauses with good practice had been confirmed. Following the guidelines of the Supreme Court, the Court of Appeal held that this premise, as well as the contradiction with the principles of social co-existence, was insufficient to recognise a conflict with the law within the meaning of Article 11(1) of the Act on Counteracting Unfair Market Practices.[643]

§ 5. Procedural Issues (Active and Passive Legal Standing, Prescription of Claims)

I. Active Standing

Pursuant to Article 12(1) of the Act on Counteracting Unfair Market Practices, first and foremost, individual claims against the entrepreneur as defined in the Act may be brought by a consumer whose interest has been violated or has been threatened. The following may be demanded:

1. to discontinue the use of the practice[644];
2. to remove the effects of the practice;
3. to make one or more statements of appropriate content and form[645];
4. price reduction[646];
5. to make good the damage done according to the general rules;
6. to award an appropriate sum of money for a specific social purpose.

---

[643] Judgement of the Court of Appeal of 8.7.2015, VI ACa 831/15, Legalis.
[644] See Article 11(1) of Directive 2005/29/EC.
[645] See Article 11(2) of Directive 2005/29/EC.
[646] Article 12(1)(3a) added by the Act of 1.12.2022 (Dz. U. of 2022, item 2581), which entered into force on 1.01.2023.

As the analysis of the published rulings shows, despite the fact that consumers are granted active standing, they relatively rarely take legal action against entrepreneurs.

However, claims may also be brought on their behalf by the Ombudsman, the Financial Ombudsman, or a national or regional organisation whose statutory objective is to protect consumers, as well as by the county (municipal) consumer ombudsman. The catalogue of their claims is nevertheless limited to demanding that a specific practice be discontinued, making a statement, or awarding an appropriate sum for a specific social purpose.

Claims under the Act on Counteracting Unfair Market Practices may not be brought by an entrepreneur nor a competitor of the entrepreneur who uses unfair commercial practices. It is worth noting that Directive 2005/29/EC left Member States free to exercise this choice. In the second sentence of Article 11(1) of Directive 2005/29/EC, there is a list of competitors entitled to initiate legal proceedings regarding unfair commercial practices or challenge unfair commercial practices before an administrative authority. There are opinions expressed in the literature that the mention of competitors of other entrepreneurs expresses the view, also reflected in recital 6 of the preamble to Directive 2005/29/EC, that unfair commercial practices that directly harm the economic interests of consumers also harm, indirectly, the economic interests of legitimate competitors. These views contradict, and this should be emphasised, other opinions sometimes also voiced that Directive 2005/29/EC disregards completely B2B relations. Indeed, the intention of the EU legislator was—by directly protecting the economic interests of consumers – to ensure indirectly the protection of legitimate traders from competitors who do not comply with the rules set out in the Directive.[647] Such an approach had much in common with Scandinavian legislation relating to market practices but was unknown in the German legal tradition of combatting unfair competition.[648] As *U. Bernitz* pointed out, some of the commercial practices contained in Directive 2005/29/EC have a particularly strong connection with the interests of competitors and may thus be considered as an example

---

[647] See Recital 8 of the Preamble of Directive 2005/29/EC.

[648] *U. Bernitz*, The Unfair Commercial Practices Directive: Its Scope, Ambitions and Relation to the Law of Unfair Competition, in: *S. Weatherill*, *U. Bernitz* (eds), The Regulation of Unfair Commercial Practices under EC Directive 2005/29. New Rules and New Techniques, Oxford–Portland–Oregon 2007, p. 41.

of the inclusion of a protection against unfair practices in B2B relations in the Directive. Among the practices that are considered unfair from the point of view of both consumers and competitors, the author listed:

1. use of a company name, trademark, or packaging that misleads the average consumer and leads to the purchase of the product under the influence of erroneous perceptions (Articles 6(2)(a) and 6(1)(b));
2. practices that give the wrong impression about the geographical origin (Article 6(1)(b));
3. misleading practices that imply possession of certain characteristics (Article 6(1)(b)).

What is not covered by the scope of the Directive are B2B relations, as they do not concern consumers.[649] Despite the possibility provided for in the Directive, the Polish legislator did not confer active standing on entrepreneurs who cannot seek redress under the Act on Counteracting Unfair Market Practices. Instead, where an unfair commercial practice also fulfils the criteria of a delict of unfair competition, entrepreneurs may take action against other entrepreneurs under the Act on Combatting Unfair Competition.

II. Passive Standing

Passive standing is enjoyed by the entrepreneur or entrepreneurs of whom it is alleged that they have used an unfair commercial practice. These may also be entrepreneurs who jointly apply unfair commercial practices. However, the relationship between entrepreneurs will not always determine their liability.

The judgement of the Supreme Court of 27 August 2014 contains important considerations on the passive standing (legitimation) of entrepreneurs operating in the distribution system of telecommunications services offered to consumers.[650] The court held that, despite the close relationship between entrepreneurs, the main beneficiary of a distribution system cannot be held liable for the practices of entrepreneurs connected to its distribution network. The judgement of the Supreme Court concerned a situation in which entrepreneurs acted within the distribution network of telecommunications

---

[649] *Ibidem*, pp. 42–43.

[650] See the Judgement of 27.8.2014, III SK 80/13, Legalis.

services. Polkomtel SA offered its services to consumers through a distribution network that consisted of outlets (showrooms) it was running independently and outlets in its distribution network run by independent traders. As the facts showed, consumers treated Polkomtel (later claimant) and its distribution network as a whole. The sales network operated under Polkomtel's trademark, according to uniform standards defined by it, from interior design to customer service principles. Polkomtel also derived substantial benefits from the operations of the distribution network and was liable to consumers for non-performance or improper performance of telecommunications service contracts. The President of the Office of Competition and Consumer Protection alleged that Polkomtel SA applied unfair commercial practices by 'acting to impede the exercise by consumers of their right to terminate a contract for the provision of telecommunications services in connection with the introduction of new terms and conditions for the provision of telecommunications services and telecommunications services to consumers'.

As a result of Polkomtel's litigation efforts, the case finally reached the Supreme Court, which found that, on the one hand, the claimant's argumentation that 'the principle of individualisation of repressive liability for the breach of the prohibition of practices violating the collective interests of consumers excludes the possibility of holding the claimant liable for the behaviour of the distribution network acting in its name and on its behalf' was incorrect. According to the Supreme Court, 'negating the possibility of attributing liability to the claimant for the anti-consumer behaviour of the members of such a distribution network would be unfair, as it would absolve the main beneficiary of such behaviour from liability and would lead to the transfer of the entire risk of liability for a breach of Article 24 of the Act on Competition and Consumer Protection to entities that benefit to a negligible extent from any infringement of consumer rights'.

On the other hand, however, the Supreme Court argued that unfair market practices were prohibited, and therefore the prohibition applied to the one who used the practice, i.e. behaved in a manner described in Article 2(4) of the Act on Counteracting Unfair Market Practices, and that behaviour fulfilled the prerequisites of Article 4(1) of the same Act. By defining the concept of unfair market practice, Article 4(1) also provides for the use of a market practice by entrepreneurs towards consumers. Contrary to the literal wording of the provision, in order for a market practice to be considered unfair, it is not necessary for it to be used by at least two entrepreneurs. However, 'the provision of Article 4(1) allows (...) the use of a single practice to be attributed to several entrepreneurs if they "jointly" engage in an unlawful conduct or if their conduct viewed as a whole can be qualified as a practice." By contrast, it does not follow from Article 4(1) that entrepreneur A may be held liable for the conduct of entrepreneur B where that conduct of entrepreneur B exhausts the characteristics of an unfair market practice'.

Eventually, the Supreme Court held that 'under Article 24 of the Act on Competition and Consumer Protection, in conjunction with Articles 4 and 5 of the Act on Counteracting Unfair Market Practices, the claimant may not be held liable for the misleading information about the possibility and manner of exercising the right to terminate the contract conduct provided by the entrepreneur's employees who constituted the claimant's distribution network'. While the Supreme Court found that the claimant was responsible for some of the obstructions, those did not justify attributing to it the practice of misleading consumers alleged by the President of the Office of Competition and Consumer Protection.

III. Prescription of Claims

The prescription period for all claims, except for the claim for damages, is 3 years and starts separately with regard to each violation (Article 14 of the Act on Counteracting Unfair Market Practices). The legislator explained that the 3-year time limit promotes effective consumer protection while not being unduly burdensome for entrepreneurs.[651] The legislator clarified that the 3-year prescription period referred only to claims that 'are specific to the (...) Act, are of a different nature and to which it would be difficult to apply the general provisions, which would in consequence lead to non-uniformity of these time limits'.[652] It was further clarified that there was no such need in relation to claims for damages to which the general time limits relating to limitation, its commencement, and running should be applied. In such a situation, a claim for damages should be time-barred in the same way as

[651] Explanatory memorandum to the draft Act on Counteracting Unfair Market Practices, Druk sejmowy V kadencji No 1682, p. 38.

[652] See *ibidem*.

in any situation where damage has been caused by the non-performance or improper performance of a contract or as a result of a delict.

As regards misleading practices, Article 13 of the Act on Counteracting Unfair Market Practices shifted the burden of proof that a practice in question is not an unfair market practice to the entrepreneur alleged of having applied a misleading practice. Such a solution is aimed at protecting weaker market participants and making it easier for them to assert their rights.[653] It was also argued that doing so only in relation to misleading practices was justified; otherwise, it would be very difficult for consumers to prove that the information provided by the trader was true. This would entail high costs for research and expert opinions.[654] Shifting the burden of proof to the entrepreneur in the event of unfair commercial practice makes it easier for consumers to enforce their rights. It is sufficient to indicate that in the consumer's opinion the practice applied by the entrepreneur is misleading, and the latter must prove that such practice has misled or is not likely to mislead the average consumer. Although correct, this solution has raised a number of controversies in the literature.[655]

It is worth emphasising that the conviction underlying the drafting of the Act on Counteracting Unfair Market Practices was that issues concerning liability for the use of unfair practices were to be based on the solutions set out in the Act on Combatting Unfair Competition, which appeared to be in line with the requirements of Directive 2005/29/EC.[656] Thus, the provisions of Articles 12–14 of the Act on Counteracting Unfair Market Practices are structurally similar to Articles 18–22 of the Act on Combatting Unfair Competition, having accounted for the differences underlying each law. This applies primarily to the granting of standing to consumers (Act on Counteracting Unfair Market Practices) or entrepreneurs (Act on Combatting

---

653 See *ibidem*, p. 37.

654 See *ibidem*, pp. 37–38.

655 The introduction of such a requirement was assessed by some as correct (see *R. Stefanicki*, Ustawa o przeciwdziałaniu nieuczciwym praktykom rynkowym, p. 506, and also *M. Sieradzka*, in: *M. Zdyb*, *M. Sieradzka* (eds), Ustawa, kom. do art. 13, s. 264), others considered it not right (see *T. Targosz*, Odpowiedzialność cywilna – roszczenie o wydanie korzyści, odszkodowanie, ciężar dowodu, in: *E. Nowińska*, *D. Kasprzycki* (eds), Nieuczciwe praktyki rynkowe, p. 299).

656 Explanatory memorandum to the draft Act on Counteracting Unfair Market Practices, Druk sejmowy V kadencji No 1682, p. 36.

Unfair Competition). Similarities also concern the catalogue of claims and their prescription, as well as the reversal of the burden of proof in the situation of market practices and acts of unfair competition that are misleading. The differences concern the claims for damages. In the Act on Counteracting Unfair Market Practices, the legislator stipulated that it is also possible to claim, as damages, the cancellation of a contract with the obligation of mutual restitution of services and reimbursement by the entrepreneur of the costs related to the purchase of the product. There is no such provision in the Act on Combatting Unfair Competition. On the other hand, under the Act on Combatting Unfair Competition, an award of an appropriate sum of money for a specific social purpose associated with supporting Polish culture or protecting national heritage is conditional on the existence of fault on the part of the entrepreneur. There is no such requirement in the Act on Counteracting Unfair Market Practices. In addition, the Act on Combatting Unfair Competition provides for a claim for a return of unduly obtained benefits, and this option is not listed in the Act on Counteracting Unfair Market Practices.[657]

Despite the existing similarities, there is a reason to agree with the position expressed in the literature that the literal and structural convergence of provisions located in different legislative acts does not prejudge the fact that they cannot be interpreted differently.[658]

§ 6. Conclusions

The implementation of Directive 2005/29/EC in the Polish legal system was done in the form of a new Act on Counteracting Unfair Market Practices, which contains and covers all the adopted solutions in their entirety. As a result, the issues of unfair commercial practices are now contained in a single legislative act, which, together with the earlier Act on Combatting Unfair Competition, constitutes the foundation of the Polish system of combatting unfair competition. Such a legislative procedure was intended to ensure

---

[657] See also *T. Targosz*, Odpowiedzialność cywilna, p. 294.

[658] *M. Wyrwiński*, Odpowiedzialność cywilna—roszczenia o: zaniechanie, usunięcie skutków, złożenie oświadczenia, zasądzenie sumy pieniężnej na cel społeczny, in: *E. Nowińska*, *D. Kasprzycki* (eds), Nieuczciwe praktyki rynkowe, pp. 277–278.

transparency and clarity of legal regulations. However, the consequence of such a solution is that there are now two Acts on unfair competition,[659] and their scope and subject matter are impossible to separate in a very precise manner.

Yet, enacting the Act of 23 August 2007 on Counteracting Unfair Market Practices, the Polish legislator wished to make a clear separation between the two Acts. The attempt to separate the scope of the two Acts can be seen, *inter alia*, in the amendment of Article 1(1) of the Act on Combatting Unfair Competition, pursuant to which the phrase 'and in particular consumers' was deleted. The purpose of such a move was to emphasise that the Act on Combatting Unfair Competition aims to protect against unfair competition in business activities in the public interest and in the interest of entrepreneurs and customers, and not consumers. However, as has already been shown, this procedure was only of a purely technical nature, and the Act on Combatting Unfair Competition also protects (albeit indirectly) the interests of consumers.

Another attempt to separate the scope of the two Acts was the repeal, in connection with the entry into force of the Act on Counteracting Unfair Market Practices, of Article 17e of the Act on Combatting Unfair Competition on conducting and organising activities in a consortium system, and transferring it to the Act on Counteracting Unfair Market Practices. As explained in the draft to this Act, the transfer of this provision to the Act on Counteracting Unfair Market Practices was a consequence of the intention to create a new regulation that would envisage sanctions for unfair market practices in trade with consumers. However, this procedure not only failed to separate the scope of the two legislative Acts but also raised doubts as to its compliance with Directive 2005/29/EC.

Indeed, the Polish legislator assumed that conducting and organising activities in a consortium system is an unfair market practice in all circumstances, and consequently, pursuant to Article 4(3) of the Act on Counteracting Unfair Market Practices, it is not subject to assessment in light of the general prerequisites of the general clause contained in its Article 4(1). This solution was modelled on the blacklists contained in Articles 7 and 9, and in this way, in fact, the Polish catalogue of unfair market practices in all circumstances has

---

659 See *M. Namysłowska*, Nowa ustawa o przeciwdziałaniu nieuczciwym praktykom, p. 1287.

been expanded to include an additional practice—conducting business in the form of a consortium system. This solution met with a variety of assessments in the literature. Some believe that it is a correct solution,[660] others argue that it violates the 'principle of a closed nature of the prohibitions *ex lege*, on which Directive 2005/29EC is based'.[661] Such an adoption of the regulation in light of the maximum harmonisation of Directive 2005/29/EC seems to be incorrect. The Directive imposed a strictly defined catalogue of unfair commercial practices in all circumstances. It is clear from its recital 17 that Annex I contains the full list of practices that are unfair in all circumstances. These are the only commercial practices that can be considered unfair without a case-by-case assessment in the of Articles 5–9 of Directive 2005/29/EC, and Member States cannot expand this catalogue on their own. Thus, the solution adopted in the Act on Counteracting Unfair Market Practices may be regarded as contrary to Directive 2005/29/EC. Therefore, the unlawfulness of the consortium scheme should be subject to the criteria of dishonesty considered in the light of Article 4(1) of the Act on Counteracting Unfair Market Practices rather than an absolute prohibition modelled on the blacklist. It does not matter whether an absolute prohibition of a consortium scheme were to be found in the Act on Combatting Unfair Competition or the Act on Counteracting Unfair Market Practices. This is because the scope of the adopted regulation falls within the scope of Directive 2005/29/EC and thus must be examined for its compliance with the Directive regardless of the Act in which it was adopted.

In Polish law on combatting unfair competition, an attempt to carry out a strict separation of the subject and object scope of both Acts is not easy, or even possible, as the interests protected under both Acts coincide. The Act on Counteracting Unfair Market Practices protects the interests of consumers as the weaker party participating in market trading, but the beneficiary of the Act is also the entire community (collectivity), including honest entrepreneurs. The Act also protects the public interest and therefore, albeit indirectly, the entrepreneurs. The interests of consumers, traders, and the collective

660 *A. Michalak*, Przeciwdziałanie nieuczciwym praktykom rynkowym, p. 118. Also see *K. Włodarska-Dziurzyńska*, Problematyka systemów konsorcyjnych (tzw. systemów argentyńskich), in: *E. Nowińska*, *D. Kasprzycki* (eds), Nieuczciwe praktyki rynkowe, pp. 264–265.

661 *R. Stefanicki*, Ustawa o przeciwdziałaniu nieuczciwym praktykom rynkowym, p. 460.

interest are closely intertwined. Despite this assumption, claims under the Act on Counteracting Unfair Market Practices may not be brought by an entrepreneur nor a competitor of an entrepreneur who uses unfair market practices. An analysis of the case law under the Act on Counteracting Unfair Market Practices shows that generally consumers do not bring claims under its provisions, either. The available examples of such proceedings are very few. The Act primarily provides the grounds for the President of the Polish Office of Competition and Consumer Protection and the courts upon which they may assess the unfair market practices that violate the collective interests of consumers. Unfair market practices belong, in fact, to the category of such practices, and their assessment must be made against the concepts defined in the Act on Counteracting Unfair Market Practices.

Apart from the attempt to separate the scopes of the two Acts, another attempt was made to ensure consistency in the use of certain terms in both Acts. An example is the concept of a 'consumer'. Under the Act on Counteracting Unfair Market Practices, the term consumer is to be understood as defined in Article 22(1) of the Civil Code. That reference in the Act to the definition of a consumer contained in the Civil Code is justified, and now the concept of a consumer under both Acts must be interpreted in the same manner.[662] Adopting an autonomous definition of a consumer in the Act on Counteracting Unfair Market Practices might have led to doubts as to the mutual relation of the adopted definition with other definitions of a consumer in the Polish legal system. Common courts as well as the President of the Polish Office of Competition and Consumer Protection have dealt with the fact that the definition of a consumer in the Act on Counteracting Unfair Market Practices must be interpreted in accordance with the purpose and scope of application of the Act and have indeed correctly reconstructed who the consumer was. Surely, such a solution ensures the consistency of the solutions adopted.

However, the solution adopted by the Polish legislator to the effect that there exist two similar but different definitions of an entrepreneur, one in the Act on Combatting Unfair Competition and the other in the Act on Counteracting Unfair Market Practices, raises objections. The subject matter

[662] *J. Szwaja*, *A. Kubiak-Cyrul*, in: *J. Szwaja*, *J. Kępiński* (eds), Ustawa o zwalczaniu nieuczciwej konkurencji, 2024, p. 82, Nb 42.

and scope of these Acts overlap, and it would definitely be much better if these terms were interpreted identically. By way of example, it may be mentioned that the German legislator, when implementing Directive 2005/29/EC into the UWG, adopted, instead of referring to the concept of entrepreneur in the BGB, a uniform definition of an entrepreneur in the law on combatting unfair competition.[663] Such a legislative intervention would have been fully justified and desirable also in Polish law. Currently, doubts may arise when interpreting the concept of entrepreneur under both Acts. When interpreting these concepts, the existing differences need to be borne in mind.

The reference in Article 4 of the Act on Counteracting Unfair Market Practices to the good practice clause is also wrong. A better solution would be to adopt the professional diligence clause because the reference to a good practice clause is inconsistent with Directive 2005/29/EC, which imposes the adoption of a 'professional diligence' clause (Article 5(2)(a) of the Directive). In the explanatory memorandum to the draft Act on Counteracting Unfair Market Practices, it was explained that the reference to the good practices clause was the most appropriate, as it allowed market practices to be subordinated to the existing and well-established clause of 'good practices' used in doctrine and case law, and therefore allowed the existing terminology to be maintained.[664] It may be argued that although the conceptual scope of these two general clauses does not overlap, they do not contradict each other, either. The concept of professional diligence, as explained by the Polish legislator, falls within the concept of good practice. On the other hand, such a broad approach to the good practice clause may carry the danger of assessing a given practice outside the EU professional diligence clause.[665] P. Podrecki is right in his view that in the interpretation of the term 'professional diligence', the entrepreneur–consumer relationship should be taken into account. It is because this is the relationship that sets the standards of the entrepreneur's behaviour. The purpose of the adopted regulations, namely that 'setting a high level of consumer protection in the relationship between entrepreneur and consumers obliges the entrepreneur to observe specific rules of conduct

---

663 See: § 2 (5)UWG.

664 Explanatory memorandum to the draft Act, Druk sejmowy V kadencji No 1682, pp. 23–25. Also see *M. Strzelecki*, Klauzula generalna nieuczciwej praktyki rynkowej, PPH 2008, No 11, pp. 39–44.

665 *E. Nowińska*, Zakaz nieuczciwych praktyk rynkowych, p. 151.

referred to as "professional diligence". Consequently, the entrepreneur should be honest and act in line with good practice'.[666]

The implementation of Directive 2005/29/EC in Poland has been criticised. The voices in the literature agree that the implementation of this Directive should have taken into account the system of law on combatting unfair competition as a whole. Since this was not done at the time when the Directive was being implemented, it is now necessary to carry out a thorough reform of the law relating to the fairness of market behaviour and, consequently, to the integration of the Act on Combatting Unfair Competition and the Act on Counteracting Unfair Market Practices. However, there is no consensus on how this integration should be executed.

---

666 *P. Podrecki*, Dyrektywa o nieuczciwych praktykach handlowych, pp. 379–380.

Chapter IV

Bonus Sales under Polish Law against Unfair Competition

§ 1. Bonus Sales before the 2002 Amendment

Before the amendment of 5 July 2002,[667] as a result of which Article 17a was added to the Act on Combatting Unfair Competition, bonus sales were generally allowed under Polish law. However, even before the amendment, it had been argued that bonus sales as a means of sales promotion could be considered as acts of unfair competition and their use by an entrepreneur could be considered as being contrary to good practice, because in a situation in which gifts (bonuses) of significant value were given away, the recipient might feel obliged to make a purchase.[668]

E. Łętowska was particularly critical of all types of consumer transactions related to the offering of gifts, bonuses, or participation in lotteries and competitions. In her opinion, such activities, although allowed in principle, were subject to many immoral, even perverse, practices. She noted that such practices were a new phenomenon in Poland in the 1990s and consequently posed problems with their correct legal qualification.

---

667 The amendment entered into force 3 months after its announcement, on 10.11.2002 (Article 2). Act of 5.7.2002 on amending the Act on Combatting Unfair Competition (Dz.U. No. 126, item 1071), see Art. 1 item 4 of the Act.

668 See *A. Surdacka*, Reklama wartościowa, PPH 1996, No 12, p. 28. Also *R. Skubisz*, *J. Dudzik*, in: *J. Szwaja* (ed.), Ustawa o zwalczaniu nieuczciwej konkurencji, 2013, p. 672, Nb 39.

She also argued that certain practices could be 'categorised according to many different criteria: from the point of view of the type of promotional activity (unfair advertising), from the point of view of the nature of the contract or contracts occurring singly or in a specific combination, or in the scope of financial law, where the classification of games and bets is also carried out for the purposes of rationing and burdens provided for in this branch of law'.[669]

This problem turned out to be big enough to prompt the Polish legislator to limit the admissibility of bonus sales. In 2002, the legal situation in this respect in the EU Member States was not uniform, either. As can be seen from the explanatory memorandum to the draft of the amendment, the Polish amendment was modelled on the solution adopted in the French Consumer Code[670] (*Code de la consommation*), which in Articles 121–135 put a ban on the use of certain forms of bonus (awards),[671] as a result of which it was prohibited to sell or offer to sell goods or services that entitled the consumer to receive free of charge, either immediately or after a set period of time, a bonus in the form of products, goods, or services, unless they were identical to the products or services being sold or provided. There were exceptions to this prohibition, and they related to small items, services of low value, or samples.[672]

---

[669] *E. Łętowska*, Prawo umów konsumenckich, Warszawa 1999, pp. 431–434.

[670] *Code de la consommation*, version of 1.2.2025, <https://www.legifrance.gouv.fr/codes/texte_lc/LEGITEXT000006069565/> (accessed on: 1.2.2025).

[671] See Explanatory Memorandum to the draft Act on Combatting Unfair Competition put forward by the government. Druk sejmowy IV kadencji No 375 of 10.4.2002, p. 4, <http://orka.sejm.gov.pl/proc4.nsf/opisy/375.htm> (accessed on 1.2.2019).

[672] Articles 121–35 as read in 2002: *Est interdite toute vente ou offre de vente de produits ou de biens ou toute prestation ou offre de prestation de services faite aux consommateurs et donnant droit, à titre gratuit, immédiatement ou à terme, à une prime consistant en produits, biens ou services sauf s'ils sont identiques à ceux qui font l'objet de la vente ou de la prestation. Cette disposition ne s'applique pas aux menus objets ou services de faible valeur ni aux échantillons.* (...).

§ 2. Prohibition of Bonus Sales in the Act on Combatting Unfair Competition

I. The Adopted Solutions

Article 17a, added to the Act on Combatting Unfair Competition in November 2002, prohibits the sale of goods or services to consumers when it is combined with the granting of a free bonus. The literature refers to such sales as bonus sales or sales with a bonus.[673] These terms can be used interchangeably.

Article 17a (1) reads that an act of unfair competition constitutes a sale of goods or services combined with an offer of a free-of-charge bonus made to all or some of the purchasers of the goods or services, and the bonuses offered are different than the object of the original sale. An act of unfair competition will be committed when all the conditions indicated below are met cumulatively:

1. the entrepreneur had awarded a bonus;
2. the bonus was granted to the consumer;
3. the bonus was granted free of charge;
4. the bonus was granted in connection with the conclusion of a sales contract with the consumer;
5. the bonus comprised goods and services different from those constituting the object of the sale.

There are some exceptions to this rule. Offering a bonus, which is:

1. of low value, or it is a sample of goods, or
2. a prize won in a promotional lottery organised according to the provisions on gambling[674] or contests in which the result is not accidental,

will not be considered as an act of unfair competition. According to Article 17a (1), a bonus may also consist of goods that are identical to the goods or services that were the subject of the contract of sale. Thus, all promotions

---

[673] The term 'sale with a bonus' is used for example by *J. Szwaja*, See: *J. Szwaja*, Ostatnie nowelizacje ustawy, part. I. Both terms may be used interchangeably.

[674] Within the meaning of the provisions of the Act of 19.11.2009—Gambling Law (Dz. U. of 2023, item 227 as amended).

that take the form of offering multiple products for the price of one, e.g. two products for the price of one, or giving a certain quantity of a product for free, e.g. 100 g free, 10% free, etc., are allowed.

II. Rationale

The wording of Article 17a added to the Act on Combatting Unfair Competition in 2002 had not undergone any significant changes until 2009, when it was slightly amended in connection with the entry into force of the new Gambling Act. This amendment, however, was strictly technical and had no impact on the interpretation of the provision.[675]

One of the objectives of the 2002 amendments was to define and include new acts (delicts) of unfair competition. The drafters proposed to introduce (1) a ban on sales at an abnormally low price, (2) a ban on bonus sales, (3) a ban on promotional lotteries, and (4) a ban on 'avalanche sales'.[676] It was believed that 'the entry into force of the Act will contribute to a better functioning of market mechanisms and the formation of integrity in trading'. The new provisions were to ensure a more effective protection for small and medium-sized companies facing competition. The proposed amendments were pro-consumer in nature and had taken into account, first and foremost, the need for broader consumer protection, ensuring their positive socio-economic impact."[677]

The introduction of a new Act of unfair competition that prohibited bonus sales was intended to 'counteract economic disproportions that distort

---

[675] Also *J. Szwaja*, *A. Kubiak-Cyrul*, in: *J. Szwaja*, *J. Kępiński* (eds), Ustawa o zwalczaniu nieuczciwej konkurencji, 2024, p. 654, Nb 1, while *A. Zientara*, in Ostatnie zmiany ustawy o zwalczaniu nieuczciwej konkurencji, MoP 2011, No 6, clarifies that the new Gambling Law defines the concept of a 'promotional lottery' in the same way as the repealed earlier Act of 23.7.1992 on games and mutual wagering (Dz.U. of 2004. No. 4, item 27 as amended.)

[676] The amendment also concerned the amendment of Article 11 of the Act on Combatting Unfair Competition in connection with the accession of Poland to TRIPS (Agreement on Trade-Related Aspects of Intellectual Property Rights), competence and procedural provisions (Article 1, point 5 of the draft amendment) and penal provisions (Article 1, points 6–8 of the draft amendment).

[677] See Explanatory Memorandum, Druk sejmowy IV kadencji No 375, p. 8, <http://orka.sejm.gov.pl/proc4.nsf/opisy/375.htm> (accessed on: 1.2.2025).

competition in the free market and to level up the playing field for all enterprises'. As explained, bonus sales that are on the Polish market take the form of free-of-charge goods or services, which, as a rule, have no functional relation to the item sold and considerably worsen the situation of small and medium-sized enterprises because it is usually the large retail chains and economically strong entrepreneurs that can afford such bonuses.[678]

The primary objective of the introduction of Article 17a was clearly to protect small and medium-sized entrepreneurs who could not afford to attach any additional awards or bonuses of significant value to the goods sold or services provided[679]; thus, it was not really protecting consumers, although their protection was nevertheless derivative and, in a way, an indirect consequence of the introduced Article 17a.[680] It is important for further considerations and, in particular, the legitimacy of leaving this regulation in the Act on Combatting Unfair Competition, to determine the main beneficiary of the amendment made.

---

678 The explanatory memorandum to the draft (p. 3) clearly states the purpose of the amendment: 'The phenomenon of bonus sales with free prizes in the form of goods or services is becoming more and more widespread on the domestic market. As a rule, prizes have no functional relationship with the item sold. Instead, they are very attractive to consumers because of their value (e.g. a trip abroad as a bonus for buying a certain amount of goods). These types of bonuses are used by large retail chains or economically strong manufacturers, which makes it easier for them to sell. As a rule, small and medium-sized enterprises cannot afford to fund valuable bonuses for consumers and, as a result, their market position deteriorates. In order to counteract the above-mentioned economic disproportions distorting competition on the free market and to level the playing field for entrepreneurs, a new Article 17a is proposed to be added to the Act on Combatting Unfair Competition, prohibiting the use of certain forms of rewards (of significant value, different from the object of sale). This amendment is introduced by Article 1(4) of the draft. It should be mentioned that a similar solution is contained in the French Consumption Code in Article L. 121–35'.

679 However, as some have argued, 'the difficulty of grasping the interests of small and medium-sized entreprises which are to be protected under Article 17a of the Act on Combatting Unfair Competition entitles one to conclude that the unfairness of awarding bonuses of excessive value (...) should be assessed first and foremost from the point of view of endangering the consumer'. See *Z. Okoń*, Czyny nieuczciwej konkurencji w działalności promocyjnej, in: E. Traple (ed.) Prawo reklamy i promocji, Warszawa 2007, p. 740.

680 Also *P. Podrecki*, in: *M. Kępiński* (ed.), System Prawa Prywatnego, vol. 15, Prawo konkurencji, chapter XII, p. 551, Nb 2.

III. Criticism of the Amendment

From the beginning, Article 17a had been met with critical opinions.[681] It was argued, *inter alia*, that by limiting the various possible forms of sales promotion, the amendment went against the current trends observed in Community law.[682] The Office of Competition and Consumer Protection (UOKiK) pointed out that certain problems may arise in interpreting the concepts of 'dissimilarity of the goods or services from those being the object of the sale' and 'low value'.[683] In the literature, Z. Okoń rightly noted that the solution contained in the added Article did not correspond to the goals for which it was introduced, i.e. protection of the interests of small and medium-sized entrepreneurs. The new Article was intended to equalise the opportunities of economically weaker entrepreneurs who, unlike the large entrepreneurs, could not afford to include free gifts in their sales offers. Under Article 15(1)(1) of the Act on Combatting Unfair Competition, bonus sales would be categorised as an act of unfair competition (dumping sales), and consequently, there was no need to introduce a new delict in the amended Act. Other comments eventually led to a conclusion that bonus sales, being one of the most popular means of sales promotion, had been unnecessarily restricted under Polish law.[684]

On the other hand, there was an opinion prepared by the Committee on European Integration in which it was argued that although bonus sales were not prohibited by Community law, the controversial nature of the regulation related to this group of commercial practices justified the introduction of the proposed amendments, which were compatible with Community law.[685] E.

---

681 More in: *J. Szwaja, A. Kubiak-Cyrul*, in: *J. Szwaja, J. Kępiński* (eds), Ustawa o zwalczaniu nieuczciwej konkurencji, 2024, p. 654, Nb 3, the authors point out that this regulation has been criticised in particular by the Polish Confederation of Private Employers, according to which this type of sale is an essential tool for marketing.

682 Also *K. Korus*, Zwalczanie nieuczciwej konkurencji. Komentarz do zmian wprowadzonych ustawą z dnia 5 lipca 2002 r. o zmianie ustawy o zmianie nieuczciwej konkurencji, LEX/el. 2002, kom. do art. 17a. Also see *J. Szwaja*, Ostatnie nowelizacje ustawy, part I, and *P. Podrecki*, Ustawa o zwalczaniu nieuczciwej konkurencji, pp. 550–551.

683 Interpretation of the provisions of the amendment to the Act on Combatting Unfair Competition of 16.4.1993 (Dz.Urz. UOKiK of 2003, No 1, item 240).

684 *Z. Okoń*, Czyny nieuczciwej, pp. 739–740.

685 See Opinion on the compatibility of the draft Law on the Amendment to the Law on Combatting Unfair Competition of 8.4.2002 Druk sejmowy IV kadencji No 375,

Łętowska argued that the extras (advantages) posed a threat to the consumer, as they obscured the clarity of choice (comparison of price and quality), had the effect of pushing up prices (the trader has to compensate in some way for the cost of the extras), and became a source of confusion for the consumers as to their legal position.[686] The importance of the amendment was also emphasised by *R. Stefanicki*, who noted that pathological phenomena occurred in the case of competitions and promotional lotteries, and the amendment in the adopted scope was demanded by consumer organisations.[687]

IV. Entry into Force of the Act on Counteracting Unfair Market Practices

As it happened, Article 17a of the Act on Combatting Unfair Competition had not been amended[688] because, in 2007, an Act on Counteracting Unfair Market Practices came into force as an implementation of Directive 2005/29/EC. Neither Directive 2005/29/EC (in particular Annex I of the Directive) nor the Act (Article 7) listed bonus sales among the unfair market practices. Accordingly, bonus sales in relations with consumers were to be permitted. Potentially, bonus sales could be considered to constitute an unfair market practice if the prerequisites set out in Article 4 of the Counteracting Unfair Market Practices have been met. According to J. Szwaja and A. Kubiak-Cyrul, 'it seems controversial (...) to restrictively recognise bonus sales as an act of unfair competition in B2B relations. Leaving Article 17a of the Act on Combatting Unfair Competition can only be justified by the protection of economically weaker entrepreneurs who cannot afford to offer costly

---

pp. 16–19, <http://orka.sejm.gov.pl/proc4.nsf/opisy/375.htm> (accessed on: 13.1.2019).

686 *E. Łętowska*, Prawo umów konsumenckich, 2002, pp. 534–535. O zagrożeniach dla funkcjonowania uczciwych reguł gry rynkowej i prawa konsumenta w związku z nagradzaniem zakupów upominkiem czy reklamowym prezentem. Also see *R. Stefanicki*, Prawne granice swobody przedsiębiorcy, p. 45.

687 *R. Stefanicki*, Prawo reklamy w świetle przepisów ustawy o zwalczaniu nieuczciwej konkurencji na tle prawnoporównawczym, Poznań 2003, p. 166. The author also cites exemplary judgements of Polish courts.

688 However, the Act on Combatting Unfair Competition has to some extent been amended. Articles 1 and 25(2) have been modified, and Articles 17b, 17e and 19(1)(3), 24b and 27(1a) have been repealed. More on the amendments see. *J. Szwaja*, Kolejne nowelizacje ustawy, and *A. Zientara*, Ostatnie zmiany ustawy.

bonuses to consumers for purchasing their goods'.[689] P. Podrecki, on the other hand, questions the need for provisions governing bonus sales in the Act on Combatting Unfair Competition in the context of the existing provisions of the Act on Counteracting Unfair Market Practices.

§ 3. Definitions

I. Absence of Definitions in the Act on Combatting Unfair Competition

There is no definition of the concept of 'bonus sales' in the Act on Combatting Unfair Competition. The other concepts used in its Article 17a, in particular the concepts of 'different goods and services', 'bonus', or 'sample of goods', have not been defined either. Their precise definition is, however, crucial when interpreting this provision. Thus, it is necessary to refer to the regulations concerning lotteries and contests as exceptions to the prohibition of bonus sales.

II. Bonus Sales

1. Bonus Sale vs Combined Sale

It is assumed in the literature that a bonus sale, including a sale agreement with an element of randomness ('participation in a prize draw'), is a form of sale agreement. J. Rajski is of the opinion that this form of sale does not require special rationing, as is the case for contracts of games of chance and betting. At the same time, he notes that although in a bonus sale with the element of randomness the obligations of the seller are of a random nature, such a sale cannot be qualified as a game contract. Bonus sales are different from them in terms of their legal nature, content, and objectives, and they perform different social and economic functions. Neither is there a need to

---

689 *J. Szwaja*, *A. Kubiak-Cyrul*, in: *J. Szwaja* (ed.), Ustawa o zwalczaniu nieuczciwej konkurencji, 2013, p. 807, Nb 1.

create special regulations for bonus sales, as is the case for contracts of games of chance and betting.[690]

W.J. Katner agrees with the above view and qualifies sales contracts involving the addition of a bonus or a draw as a special type of sale falling outside the provisions of the Civil Code. He considers them to be consumer sales contracts. However, he also points out that doubts may arise in relation to the legal assessment of the contract 'when prizes, bonuses, participation in draws, contests, etc. incentives to buy things are provided for. In certain situations, such a sale will still be a sale and the additional bonus will be considered to be included in the price with the buyer's consent. The provisions, e.g. on warranty, will then apply as for the primary item. In other situations, especially in the event of winning a lottery, contest, etc., the item will be acquired by way of donation with our consent. There will then be two contracts: the sale of the thing proper and the donation, as the term suggests – a gift'.[691] Another feature of a bonus sale is 'that any buyer who satisfies the announced conditions is entitled to a prize (bonus). The issuance of the prize must not entail any additional performance by the buyer'.[692]

W. Kocot argues that bonus sales should not be confused with combined sales. In the case of a bonus sale, the seller 'undertakes to provide an incidental, consequential performance in the form of delivering a designated prize to the buyer in exchange for the purchase of a designated good', while the essence of a combined sale is 'the provision by the seller of at least two different products', and the reward in a bonus sale may be a tangible benefit of different kinds. And yet, apart from bonuses such as discounts, rebates or reductions, there are other types of sales promotion measures,[693] the purpose

690 See *J. Rajski*, Szczególne rodzaje sprzedaży premiowanej nagrodami a umowy gry, PPH 1995, No 1, pp. 28–30.

691 *W. Kocot* considers that a bonus sale is not of the nature of a gratuitous act. The reward (bonus) is of the nature of a discount obtained with the purchase of goods or services. See *W. Kocot*, Pozakodeksowe umowy sprzedaży (szczególne umowy sprzedaży), in: *W.J. Katner* (ed.), System Prawa Prywatnego,Prawo zobowiązań – umowy nienazwane, ed. 4., Warszawa 2018, Nb. 49–57, p. 87–93.

692 *W.J. Katner*, Szczególne rodzaje sprzedaży poza przepisami Kodeksu cywilnego, in: *J. Rajski* (ed.), System Prawa Prywatnego, vol. 7, Prawo zobowiązań – część szczegółowa, ed. 4, Warszawa 2018, p. 34, Nb 84.

693 A bonus may take the form of cash as well as in-kind, a small gift, the right to buy again at a lower price, an extra copy, quantity or packaging of a purchased product, or

of which is not to provide an additional benefit for the buyer but to reduce the price of a product or service.[694] W. Kocot distinguishes between a bonus sale and a sale that is subject to prize draws. This separation is not easy to make, and even he himself qualifies a sale that is subject to a prize draw as a type of bonus sale contract. However, it seems that both types of sale should be qualified as non-named bonus sales contracts. Whether the trader will award a prize to a person who has satisfied certain conditions or a winner of a prize draw will have no effect on the qualification of the sales contract in question. Both are aimed at sales promotion and are examples of a bonus sales agreement.

Also, in the literature relating to the Act on Combatting Unfair Competition, it has been emphasised that bonus sales should be clearly distinguished from combined sales, as in the case of a combined sale in which 'the subject of the agreement and the entrepreneur's performance are two (or more) different products or a product and a service (...) for one price paid, the buyer receives two different performances. It is irrelevant to the buyer how the trader has calculated the sale price, whether as the sum of two (or more) prices or otherwise'.[695] The proponents of such a distinction refer to the interpretation of the concept of 'coupled sale' (*Koppelungsangebote*) developed under German law and conclude that under Polish law combined sales, unlike bonus sales, are not prohibited.[696]

A different view is represented by P. Podrecki, who argues that a bonus sale should be classified as a particular form of combined sale because this type of obligation involves more than one performance of the trader, and there may be different performances, products, or services. In German literature

---

even identity cards entitling the holder to receive certain benefits (goods or services).

694 *W. Kocot*, Pozakodeksowe umowy sprzedaży, in: *W.J. Katner* (ed.), System Prawa Prywatnego, vol. 9, Prawo zobowiązań – umowy nienazwane, pp. 87–92, Nb 49–55.

695 See *J. Szwaja*, *A. Kubiak-Cyrul*, in: *J. Szwaja*, *J. Kępiński* (eds), Ustawa o zwalczaniu nieuczciwej konkurencji, 2024, p. 663, Nb 30. It can also be pointed out that the concept of tying appears in competition law, see also *I. Małobęcki*, Sprzedaż wiązana i pakietowa jako potencjalne naruszenie europejskiego prawa konkurencji – ekonomiczna i prawna analiza problemu, Warszawa 2013, p. 9, www.uokik.gov.pl/download.php?plik=14380 (accessed on: 1.2.2025).

696 See *J. Szwaja*, *A. Kubiak-Cyrul*, in: *J. Szwaja*, *J. Kępiński* (eds), Ustawa o zwalczaniu nieuczciwej konkurencji, 2024, p. 663, Nb 30. Such a distinction is also favoured by *Z. Okoń*, Czyny nieuczciwej konkurencji, pp. 741–742.

these are referred to as combined or coupled sales. A comparison of contracts for combined sales with bonus sales in civil law terms is also regarded as justified. Another question is the classification of a given conduct as an act of unfair competition. Recognising a given conduct as an act of unfair competition has further consequences. For instance, the recognition that a contract has been entered into in breach of Article 17a of the Act on Combatting Unfair Competition may result in the nullity of the former (Article 58 of the Civil Code).[697] Regarding the Act on Combatting Unfair Competition, other authors make no distinction at all between bonus sales and combined sales.[698]

According to Article 101(1)(e) TFEU, 'the following shall be incompatible with the internal market and shall be prohibited: all agreements between undertakings, all decisions by associations of undertakings and all concerted practices which may affect trade between Member States and which have as their object or effect the prevention, restriction or distortion of competition within the internal market, and in particular those which consist in: (e) making the conclusion of contracts subject to acceptance by the parties of supplementary obligations which, by their nature or according to commercial usage, have no connection with the subject-matter of those contracts'.

In turn, Article 9(1) and (2)(4) of the Act on Competition and Consumer Protection provides that 'the abuse of a dominant position in the respective market by one or more entrepreneurs is prohibited. The abuse of a dominant position consists in particular in making the conclusion of a contract dependent on the acceptance or performance by the other party of a service that is not substantially or customarily related to the subject matter of the contract'.

In competition law, tying is thus understood as a situation in which the sale of one good (the so-called tying good) is made conditional on the purchase

697 See *P. Podrecki*, Sprzedaż premiowa, in: *M. Kępiński* (ed.), System Prawa Prywatnego, vol. 15, Prawo konkurencji, p. 555, Nb 12.

698 See *M. Sieradzka*, Ustawa o przeciwdziałaniu nieuczciwym praktykom rynkowym, p. 719, Nb 11. No distinction either is made by *E. Nowińska*, *M. du Vall*, in Ustawa o zwalczaniu nieuczciwej konkurencji, pp. 399–403, or *E. Nowińska*, in: *E. Nowińska*, *K. Szczepanowska-Kozłowska*, Ustawa o zwalczaniu, Warszawa 2022, Comments to Art. 17a, pp. 545–550 Also see: *M. Sieradzka*, Oferta wiązana jako rodzaj praktyki handlowej – glosa do wyroku TS of 23.4.2009 in joint cases: C-261/07and C-299/07 VTB-VAB NW v. Total Belgium NV and Galatea BVBA v. Sanoma Magazines Belgium NV, EPS 2010, No 8, pp. 52–57. The author interchangeably uses the terms premium sales and tied-in sales.

of another good (the so-called good), which is traded as a separate good. As noted in the literature, in tying sales there are two types of products: 'tied-in products, which are also sold separately, and tying products, offered only with tied-in products. The seller of the tied-in product may be either the same entity that sells the tying product, as well as the entity appointed by it'.[699]

Tying, more commonly referred to as combining (hence 'combined offers' or 'combined sales'), may affect competition in two ways. Firstly, 'combined transactions may force the dominant enterprise's customers to take actions that are disadvantageous to them and that they would not take under competitive conditions (as customers might prefer to purchase each product separately and from a different producer). As regards the second aspect, the practice followed by the dominant enterprise may seriously impede the development of competition in the combined product market. This is because the dominant enterprise's customers are forced to behave in a certain way (i.e. to purchase the tied-in product from the dominant enterprise), which limits their ability to make such purchases from other entities. Therefore, there arises a barrier to entry or a serious impediment to the development of competition in the market for the combined product'.[700]

Table 1. Comparison of combined sales with bonus sales

Combined sale	**Bonus sale**
In principle allowed (unless misleading)	Not allowed (with certain exceptions specified in Article 17a of the Act on Combatting Unfair Competition).
Means of sales promotion	Means of sales promotion.
May be classified as a commercial (market) practice under Directive 2005/29/EC and the Act on Counteracting Unfair Market Practices	May be classified as a commercial (market) practice under Directive 2005/29/EC and the Act on Counteracting Unfair Market Practices.

[699] See *I. Małobęcki*, Sprzedaż wiązana i pakietowa, p. 9; *A. Stawicki*, in: *A. Stawicki*, *E. Stawicki* (ed.), Ustawa o ochronie konkurencji i konsumentów, 2016, p. 373, where a products id defined as a basic product or a related product.

[700] See *A. Stawicki*, in: *A. Stawicki*, *E. Stawicki* (eds), Ustawa o ochronie konkurencji i konsumentów, 2016, p. 374.

Table 1. Continued

Combined sale	**Bonus sale**
Aims at an offer made up of two or more products or services to be sold together for one price	The bonus is not the essential part of the sales contract but is nevertheless an integral part of it and has an economic purpose—to promote a product or a service.
The common feature extends to two or more products or services. The price is one for all. There is no need to single out individual elements of the offer.	The free of charge prize (bonus) in the form of low-price products or samples, following the main purchase. It may also be a prize won in a lottery.
May only be addressed to selected customers	Every customer who satisfies the conditions announced is eligible to get the bonus.
	Releasing the bonus may not be dependent on any other performance by the customer.
	The legal status of the customer's right to a bonus is similar to a public promise.
Is allowed in B2C and B2B relations	Is allowed in B2C and B2B relations. In principle, with a few exceptions, not allowed in B2C relations (Article 17a of the Act on Combatting Unfair Competition).

2. 'Combined Offers' (*Kopplungsangebote*) Under German Law—Definition and Acceptability

Advocate General *V. Trstenjak* referred in her opinions (with regard to two cases *Plus*[701] and *Total*[702]) to the concept of combined offers adopted in German law. The reference to German law is significant, as since 2001 there has been

[701] Judgement of the ECJ of 14.1.2010 in C-304/08 *Zentrale zur Bekämpfung unlauteren Wettbewerbs eV v. Plus Warenhandelsgesellschaft mbH*, Legalis; opinion of 3.9.2009, ECLI:EU:C:2009:511.

[702] Judgement of the ECJ of 23.4.2009, C-261/07, *VTB-VAB NV v. Total Belgium NV*, Legalis; opinion of 21.10.2008, ECLI:EU:C:2008:581.

a gradual liberalisation of the rules relating to combined offers. The liberal approach of the German legislature to the admissibility of combined offers was also reflected in the case law of the CJEU. Indirectly, therefore, the amendments to German law had an impact, through the CJEU case law, on the national legislation of other Member States.

In German literature, combined offers have been included in the broader category of sales promotion measures (*Verkaufsförderungsmaßnahmen*). They are considered to be one form of advertising, referred to as advertising with value, or worth advertising (*Wertreklame*).[703] In this type of advertising, the 'value' is the good or service that the customer receives cheaply or free of charge in connection with the conclusion of a transaction for another good or service. Thus, in value advertising, the entrepreneur advertises goods or services not with words (as in the case of so-called verbal advertising (*Wortrwerbung*) or with images (as in so-called image advertising, *Bildwerbung*), but with certain material values (*Vergünstigung*) that are given away as presents (*schenkweise*). Characteristically, this type of advertising does not advertise, or only advertises to a limited extent, the characteristics of the goods offered (quality, price), but persuades customers to purchase the offered goods or services by emphasising the financial benefits of various kinds that the customer. These benefits usually have nothing to do with the goods or services offered. The purpose of such advertising is therefore to promote the sale or purchase of services against payment (*entgeltliche Leistungen*). If this element is missing,

---

703 Briefly on the development of these concepts in German law *D. Travers*, Kopplungsangebote, Eine Studie zum Vertrags- und Lauterkeitsrecht, Frankfurt am Main 2015, pp. 70–78. Value advertising should be distinguished from traditional forms of advertising, e.g. verbal advertising (*Wortreklame*), or pictorial advertising (*Bildreklame*). Fore more see: Zugaben und Rabatte als Erscheinungsformen der Wertreklame, in *M. Eppe*, Zugaben und Rabatte in Anwendungsbereich des UWG, Köln 2003, p. 181. The concept of 'valuable advertising' is also used in Polish literature (although the correctness of the translation of the term itself needs to be considered) e.g. in relation to medicinal products—see *K. Grzybczyk*, Advertising of medicinal products, in: *M. Kępiński, J. Kępiński, K. Klafkowska-Waśniowska, R. Sikorski* (eds), Rynek farmaceutyczny a prawo własności intelektualnej, Warsaw 2013, p. 117; *R. Stefanicki*, Prawne granice swobody przedsiębiorcy, p. 45 and *G. Rączka*, Wprowadzenie do terminologii prawa reklamy, in: *M. Namysłowska* (ed.), Reklama. Aspekty prawne, Warszawa 2012, p. 36.

according to the case law of the German courts, such an action cannot be assessed from the point of view of value advertising.[704]

Examples of value advertising include not only combined offers but also: (i) gifts and other kinds of giveaways (*Zuwendungen*) (e.g. advertising gifts, coupons added at the time of purchase, free addition of newspapers and other products, free transport for customers, free sightseeing tours); (ii) discounts (e.g. special offers, cash coupons); (iii) loyalty systems aimed at binding the customer (*Kundenbindung*) (e.g. pay-back system, loyalty systems); (iv) aleatoric activities, i.e. connected with the randomness of winning (*Veranstaltungen aleatorischer* Art) (e.g. competitions, gambling games, lotteries, draws, auctions, bidding); (v) powershopping (community-shopping); (vi) progressive winning of customers, e.g. pyramid system.[705]

Within the category of combined offers, certain specific forms are distinguished based on the case law of the German courts, and these may include add-ons (*Zugabe*), samples of goods (*Warenproben*), financial transactions (*Finanzierungsgeschäfte)*, editorial support of the advertiser (*Redaktionelle Unterstützung*), guarantees (*Garantine*), reimbursement of travel expenses (*Fahrkostenerstattungen*), and free transportation of customers (*Kundenbeförderungen*), including any advertising and sales trips, as well as participation in sightseeing tours.[706]

3. Bonus Sales vs Premium Sales

It is noteworthy that in some other Polish legislative acts there also appear concepts semantically similar to the notion of a 'bonus sale'. For example, in the Act on Personal Income Tax,[707] a term 'premium sale' is used (See Art. 21 (2) point 68 and Art. 30 (1) point 2). Article 21 (2) point 68 of the Income Tax Act introduces an exception to the general rule of income tax liability for all benefits received by a taxpayer from an entity engaged in business activity and states that 'the value of prizes won in contests and games organised and broadcast (announced) by mass media (press, radio and television) and

704 See: *O. Sosnitza*, § 4a Aggressive geschäftliche Handlungen, in *A. Ohly*, *O. Sosnitza* (ed.), Gesetz gegen den unlauteren Wettbewerb mit Preisangabeverordnung, Kommentar, München 2023, Rn 46.

705 *O. Sosnitza*, § 4a, Rn. 46–54.

706 *O. Sosnitza*, § 4a Rn. 81–91.

707 Dz.U. of 2024, item 226 as amended.

contests in the field of science, culture, art, journalism and sport, as well as prizes related to the bonus sale of goods or services – if the one-off value of such prizes or awards does not exceed PLN 2,000 – shall be exempt from income tax; 'the tax exemption for prizes related to the premium sale of goods or services does not apply to prizes received by a taxpayer in connection with a non-agricultural business activity and constituting income from such activity'. On the other hand, Article 30 (1) point 2 sets the amount of the flat-rate tax on prizes related to bonus sales at 10%.

However, in the absence of the definition of the term 'premium sale' in Act on Personal Income Tax, this concept has been attempted to be defined by courts. For example, the Supreme Administrative Court in its ruling of 29 October 2015[708] confirmed the already well-established position that the term 'premium sale' should be interpreted in the common (colloquial) sense.[709] When stating the reasons for its ruling, the Supreme Administrative Court argued that 'since the expression "premium sale" was taken from colloquial language, its meaning for the purposes of interpreting Articles 21 and 30 of

[708] Judgement of the Supreme Administrative Court of 29.10.2015, II FSK 3345/14, OSG 2016, No. 4, item 32, p. 19. The ruling was a consequence of a request for an individual interpretation. The applicant for the interpretation explained in the application 'that in the course of its business it issues debit and credit cards. In turn, in order to increase the satisfaction and loyalty of its customers, it introduces bonus programmes and promotional campaigns, as part of which it enables customers – users of debit and credit cards – to receive bonuses for undertaking actions specified in the regulations of the promotional campaigns. Card users, when making purchases with certain partners with which the applicant organises promotional actions, receive bonuses of an amount representing a percentage of the value of purchases made with dedicated debit and credit cards. The amount of the bonus is determined in accordance with the regulations of the relevant campaign. The applicant credits the amount of the bonus to the bank (card) accounts of customers who have fulfilled the conditions set out in the regulations. The granting of the bonus is not of a competitive nature. Nor is it the result of chance. All customers who have fulfilled the conditions receive the bonus in the form of a direct cashback on their account). The accrual of the bonus can take place either in billing periods (monthly or quarterly) or a one-off at the end of a given promotional action. The amount of the bonus in a given settlement period shall not exceed PLN 760'.

[709] In the rationale for the judgement, the Supreme Administrative Court refers to its Judgement of 27.3.2015, II FSK 2758/14, Przeg. Pod. 2015, No. 7, p. 54; its judgement of 18.6.2015, II FSK 1540/13, Legalis; its judgement of 17.7.2015, II FSK 1452/13, Legalis and its judgement of 3.9.2015, II FSK 1666/13, Legalis.

the Act should also be taken in the colloquial sense. Since sale in the colloquial meaning (...) means both the sale of goods and services, premium sale should be understood as the sale of goods and services connected with the receipt of a prize by the purchaser. This understanding of the expression premium sale is also supported by a purposive interpretation. A flat-rate tax is levied on prizes from premium sales (Article 30)'. Further, since premium sales constitute a specific type of sale and the term is not defined in the legal language, it cannot be defined by means of an external systemic interpretation, including the Civil Code, either.[710] Following the position of the Supreme Administrative Court, it may be concluded that, in the colloquial sense, the notion of a premium sale may be understood similarly to the notion of a 'bonus sale' under the Act on Combatting Unfair Competition. However, the concept of a bonus sale regulated under Article 17a is in fact narrower than the concept of a premium sale. In a premium sale, there are no restrictions as to the subject of the prize (bonus), while in a bonus sale, the bonus may be only goods that are not different from the subject of the sale. To conclude, to a certain extent, although these concepts overlap, they cannot be regarded as identical.

III. Goods (Products) and Services

1. Introductory Remarks

It follows from Article 17a that a bonus may be added to the main object of sale as long as it is identical with that object.[711]

It is rightly assumed in the literature that the concept of 'goods' and 'services' is to be understood broadly, and Article 17a of the Act on Combatting Unfair Competition does not introduce any restrictions with respect to bonus sales allowed with regard to certain goods or services. However, certain restrictions may arise from other laws that introduce further restrictions on bonus sales in respect of certain goods or services (cf. § 6 below). It is rightly assumed in the literature that the concept of 'goods' and 'services' is to be

---

[710] Judgement of the Supreme Administrative Court of 3.9.2015, II FSK 1666/13, Legalis.

[711] See *E. Nowińska*, *M. du Vall*, Ustawa o zwalczaniu nieuczciwej konkurencji, Nb 3, p. 401; *E. Nowińska*, in: *E. Nowińska*, *K. Szczepanowska-Kozłowska*, Ustawa o zwalczaniu, 2022, Nb 4, p. 547.

understood broadly. There are no restrictions in this respect in Article 17a, but restrictions may arise from other laws that introduce restrictions on bonus sales with respect to certain goods or services (§ 6 below).

2. Dissimilarity of Goods and Services

The concept of 'dissimilarity of goods and services', although crucial for the interpretation of this provision, has not been defined by the legislator, nor has it been defined by judges who delivered verdicts in line with the provisions of the Act on Combatting Unfair Competition. Hence, doubts as to when a good or service is dissimilar and when it is identical to the subject matter of the contract.

The Office of Consumer and Competition Protection favours the application of a broader criterion, i.e. the criterion of functionality rather than only the criterion of identity, when making an assessment. In the case of the identity criterion, only bonuses in the form of goods and services identical to the main object of the sales contract would be allowed. If, on the other hand, the functionality criterion is applied, not only would the same goods and services be allowed but also, for example, 'ancillary' goods or services, i.e. goods or services that increase the functionality or improve the functioning of the object of the contract. An example is the commercial practice of mobile phone operators of attaching a charger to a mobile phone. Such an accessory does not have the character of a bonus, and its addition does not constitute a breach of the prohibition of bonus sales.[712] The same treatment would apply to such other accessories added to the phone, like keypads, cases, etc., as they are useful when added to the phone and remain in a factual relationship with it.

On the other hand, goods and services that 'do not remain in a factual (economic) and legal relationship with the object of sale' should be treated as dissimilar, or different, goods and services. An example would be a T-shirt or backpack attached to a telephone.[713]

---

[712] Interpretation of the provisions on the Act on Combatting Unfair Competition of 16.4.1993 (Dz.Urz. UOKiK of 2003 No 1, item 240).

[713] See *A. Sobczak*, Ochrona przed nieuczciwą konkurencją, chapter V <http://archiwum.rp.pl/artykul/399426-Ochrona-przed-nieuczciwa-konkurencja--poradnik-dla-przedsiebiorcow-i-konsumentow.html> (accessed on: 13.1.2019).

J. Szwaja and A. Kubiak-Cyrul[714] are also in favour of such a liberal interpretation of the concept of dissimilarity of goods and services. However, in their view, in certain cases this might allow offering bonuses even of significant value, e.g. winter tyres and insurance for a car, because under a liberal interpretation of the concept of 'dissimilarity', these would be related goods and services. Indeed, in such a case, the low-value requirement, which applies only in the case of a bonus in the form of goods or services distinct from the object of sale, will not be applicable. It will also be acceptable to add a year's supply of washing powder to a washing machine or to offer in-home installation with the purchase of a refrigerator. However, adding a radio to the purchase of a TV set, a bicycle to the purchase of a car, or a high-value mascot to the purchase of chocolate would be questionable. These are different goods that do not have any functional relationship with the object of the contract of sale.

K. Korus is of a similar opinion, although he stresses the need for a rather strict interpretation of this prohibition. In his view, the goods or services that constitute a bonus need not be exactly the same as the goods or services that are the object of the contract of sale. Rather, they should 'belong to the same product line in which the goods and services are usually produced in modern industry or remain in the usual functional relationship. This way of thinking is further supported by the fact that even less affluent entrepreneurs can afford to give bonuses in the form of goods and services they produce themselves, as opposed to buying commercially attractive goods and services from external parties'.[715]

There is also nothing to prevent the bonus from taking the form of a good or a service, regardless of whether the contract concerns a good or a service. When concluding a contract for the sale of goods, the consumer may receive a bonus in the form of an identical good (e.g. when purchasing a bottle of engine oil, a second bottle of engine oil is added free of charge) or a service in relation to the object of sale (e.g. when purchasing engine oil, a free replacement service is offered), whereas, by entering into a service contract, he could receive a bonus in the form of an identical service (e.g. by ordering

---

714 *J. Szwaja, A. Kubiak-Cyrul*, in: *J. Szwaja, J. Kępiński* (eds), Ustawa o zwalczaniu nieuczciwej konkurencji, 2024, p. 656–657, Nb 9–11.

715 *K. Korus*, Zwalczanie nieuczciwej konkurencji, kom. do art. 17a.

a shirt laundry, another shirt laundry is free of charge) or a service-related good (e.g. with a car wash service, fragrance would be added to the car).

IV. Bonus

1. The Concept of a Bonus

The concept of a 'bonus' may involve similar problems with its interpretation as the above-discussed 'dissimilarity of goods and services', also appearing in other legislative acts,[716] which, like the Act on Combatting Unfair Competition, do not contain its legal definition. The dictionary definition of a 'bonus' denotes a 'free addition' or a 'reward which is intended to encourage the person rewarded to do something'.[717] *E. Nowińska* and *M. du Vall* are right to stress that a bonus entails 'an increase in the basic value'.[718] Undoubtedly, in the situation of receiving a bonus, its beneficiary receives some additional value.

2. Bonus Not to be for Pay

The prohibition of bonus sales as described in Article 17a of the Act on Combatting Unfair Competition applies to situations where the bonus is free of charge. Thus, if the consumer has to pay for the bonus, it will no longer be a bonus sale within the meaning of this provision. In the case of a bonus free of charge, its beneficiary (the consumer) does not incur any additional costs in connection with its receipt. The receipt of the bonus

---

716 By way of example, one can point to Article 615 of the Civil Code, which refers to a 'monetary bonus' and a 'bonus in kind' in a contracting agreement.

717 According to the dictionary definition 'premia' (<https://sjp.pwn.pl/szukaj/premia.html>, accessed on 1.2.2024), a bonus may be understood as '1. a salary supplement granted to an employee depending on his/her work performance; 2. a reward for something, often intended to encourage the rewarded person to do something; 3. a free allowance for subscribers of a magazine, publication, etc.; 4. in a cycling competition: a place on the race course where the first riders to pass can earn extra points; also: points so earned'.

718 *E. Nowińska, M. du Vall*, Ustawa o zwalczaniu nieuczciwej konkurencji, p. 400, Nb 2, also *E. Nowińska*, in: *E. Nowińska, K. Szczepanowska-Kozłowska*, Ustawa o zwalczaniu, 2022, p. 545–546, Nb 2.

must not involve any additional cost or price that the consumer would have to pay to the entrepreneur.[719]

Thus, a justified doubt arises as to what happens if the entrepreneur, in order to circumvent the prohibition on bonus sales, slightly increases the original price of the goods or services because of the addition of the bonus. In such a situation, the consumer will not receive the good or service (bonus) free of charge but will have to pay an additional benefit to the entrepreneur. It must be concluded that such an action to circumvent the prohibition cannot be regarded as acceptable. Even if it does not violate the prohibition in Article 17a of the Act on Combatting Unfair Competition, it can be qualified as contrary to Article 3(1).[720]

However, the above provision does not prohibit an entrepreneur from charging a higher price for the combined products or services (as a result of combining the main product or service with an ancillary product or service). Such a practice cannot be classified as a bonus sale. It will be a combined sale which does not fall within the substantive scope of the prohibition of Article 17a of the Act on Combatting Unfair Competition. Nevertheless, there will undoubtedly be other obligations on the entrepreneur in such a situation, for example, a need to clearly demonstrate that the price of the combined products or services is higher as a result of the added bonus. The consumer should be aware that the added product is not free and that he is paying for it. The literature suggests that giving the impression that the bonus is free, when in fact the consumer has to pay for it, is also an unfair commercial practice under Directive 2005/29/EC. Under the Act on Counteracting Unfair Market Practices, presenting a product as 'free' or 'at no cost' when the consumer has to pay even a very small amount is considered an unfair market practice. An exception to the cost to the consumer is direct expenses for the receipt or delivery of the product and the like.

---

719 *J. Szwaja, A. Kubiak-Cyrul*, in: *J. Szwaja, J. Kępiński* (eds), Ustawa o zwalczaniu nieuczciwej konkurencji, 2024, p. 662, Nb 28.

720 *E. Nowińska, M. du Vall*, Ustawa o zwalczaniu nieuczciwej konkurencji, p. 400, Nb 2; and *E. Nowińska* in: *E. Nowińska, K. Szczepanowska-Kozłowska*, Ustawa o zwalczaniu, 2022, p. 546, Nb. 3.

3. A Low Value of the Bonus

Article 17a(2) of the Act on Combatting Unfair Competition puts a ban on a bonus sale unless it is of low value. The notion of 'low value' raises justified interpretative doubts.[721] The first attempts to clarify this concept envisaged a provision specifying that the term 'low value' referred to 'goods and services of a low value, not exceeding the unit price of the good or service included in the bonus sale'. This provision, however, was omitted during the legislative process.[722] It was pointed out in the literature that the proposed definition of 'low value' was criticised for its lack of precision and that there could be a problem in determining what constituted the unit price in the case of the purchase of many units of a given good (e.g. several tens of litres of fuel) or goods or items of different value. It was also argued that such wording would make it impossible to run long-term loyalty programmes where the rewards may be of high value, provided they are accompanied by multiple transactions of significant value.[723]

From the beginning of the legislative work, it was stressed that it was not clear whether the value of the good or service should be objectively low or whether the bonus should be of low value in relation to the value of the good or service sold. Both interpretations were possible and justified and would have to be assessed on a case-by-case basis.[724]

J. Szwaja and A. Kubiak-Cyrul outlined at least four ways of understanding the concept of low value. First, it may refer to the low value of the bonus in relation to the goods or services that are the subject of the sales contract. The reference for assessing the value of the bonus would then be the value of the main good or service. Secondly, the criterion could be the low cost to the trader of producing or acquiring the additional good or service compared to the cost of the main good or service sold. Thirdly, it could be the objectively low market value of the good or service constituting the bonus. Fourthly, since the provision referred to consumer sales, the low value would have to be assessed from the point of view of the consumer receiving the good or

---

721 *R. Stefanicki*, Prawo reklamy, p. 160; and *R. Stefanicki*, Prawne granice swobody przedsiębiorcy, p. 46

722 See Explanatory Memorandum, Druk sejmowy IV kadencji No 375, p. 3.

723 *Z. Okoń*, Czyny nieuczciwej, p. 744.

724 See: Interpretation of the provisions of the Act on Combatting Unfair Competition of 16 April 1993 (Dz.Urz. UOKiK of 2003 No 1 item 241), Lex.

service as a bonus. However, they, the authors, not specify which of the above concepts they considered to be the most appropriate but simply concluded that each case had to be assessed on its own merits, with all the circumstances being taken into account in the light of good practice in consumer sales.[725]

On the other hand, according to K. Korus, it would be most appropriate to assess the concept of 'low value' through the prism of the costs of the entrepreneur offering the bonus. Korus referred to the provision contained in Article 17a of the Act on Combatting Unfair Competition and its purpose of protecting economically weaker entrepreneurs. Consequently, such an interpretation would allow the benefits of scale to be taken into account.[726]

J. Szwaja and A. Kubiak-Cyrul did not share this view and argued that such an interpretation would favour large entrepreneurs who could afford large orders or a high volume production of items to be given away as bonuses. Moreover, it would be contrary to the purpose of Article 17a.[727] Another view expressed was that in order to create equal promotion opportunities for all entities, regardless of the value of the goods they sell, the 'low value' of the added gift should be relativised to the value of the goods sold.[728]

E. Nowińska and M. du Vall argued that 'the assessment of the value of the added good should be made separately, i.e. in relation to that particular good and therefore separately from the price at which the trader purchased it and (...) from the price of the main good sold'. In such a case, the scale of values that takes into account the feelings of the average market participant will be appropriate. Z. Okoń has a similar opinion and refers to Article 17a, asserting that since its purpose is primarily to protect consumers, a bonus of a higher value is a bonus that 'leads to a significant distortion of the economic behaviour' of consumers.[729]

---

[725] *J. Szwaja, A. Kubiak-Cyrul*, in: *J. Szwaja, J. Kępiński* (eds), Ustawa o zwalczaniu nieuczciwej konkurencji, 2024, pp. 658–659, Nb 12–20.

[726] *K. Korus*, Zwalczanie nieuczciwej konkurencji, Comments to Art. 17a.

[727] *J. Szwaja, A. Kubiak-Cyrul*, in: *J. Szwaja, J. Kępiński* (eds), Ustawa o zwalczaniu nieuczciwej konkurencji, 2024, p. 659, Nb 17.

[728] See *K. Szczepanowska-Kozłowska*, Co przepis to wątpliwość. Rzeczpospolita of 17.10.2002. The main theses of the publication are available in the Lex legal information service.

[729] *Z. Okoń*, Czyny nieuczciwej, p. 745.

Yet in another opinion it was argued that making the assessment solely from the perspective of the purchaser-consumer who assesses the value of the bonus is not sufficient. It should be remembered that the Act on Combatting Unfair Competition applies to B2B relations, and therefore the cost of the bonus should be considered when determining the scope of the term 'low value'.[730] As can be seen from the above, the issue of the low value of a bonus is highly controversial. Unfortunately, none of the Polish courts has yet defined this premise. In fact, it is not really possible to adopt a single criterion for assessing the low value of the bonus, as it is necessary to take into account the purpose of the provision (primarily the protection of small and medium-sized businesses, but also the protection of consumer interests), to whom the bonus sale is directed (definition of the model of the average consumer), and the value of the main product or service. Only by looking at this premise in this way, one determine whether the bonus is of little value. Indeed, it appears that a bonus in the form of a washing machine or a package holiday will not always be a prohibited bonus, even if the value of the bonus is objectively significant. This may be the case, for example, where a consumer buys an apartment and the trader adds, for example, a washing machine or a weekend trip to a spa as part of a promotional campaign. After all, the cost of a washing machine or a holiday seems relatively small to both the trader and the consumer when buying an apartment. The same would apply to a bonus in the form of a bicycle when buying a luxury car. It would also seem acceptable to include a CD or DVD with a newspaper, although in such a case, when assessing the value of the bonus, account should be taken not only of the cost of producing the CD (which is relatively small) but also of other costs, in particular the cost of the licence, which can be significant. It therefore appears that the bonus for a bicycle may sometimes be lower in relation to the total contract than the bonus for a CD included in a newspaper.

It can therefore be postulated that several criteria should be assessed when determining the low value:

1. whether a bonus in a certain form could be offered by small or medium-sized businesses on an equal footing with large businesses;

---

[730] *M. Sieradzka*, in: *M. Zdyb*, *M. Sieradzka* (eds), Ustawa, p. 970, Nb 5.

2. whether, from the point of view of the consumer with whom the contract is concluded, the bonus is significant and could determine the choice the consumer has made;
3. whether the value of the bonus is, in relation to the value of the whole contract, significant or a tiny fraction of it.

Setting a single criterion for all cases is not possible or justified. It is necessary to examine, as postulated in the literature, different situations in each case, guided by different criteria and circumstances.

As an example, reference can also be made to the Act on Goods and Services of 2004 (Value Added Tax),[731] which defines the concept of a 'gift of a low value'. According to Article 7(4) of the Act, gifts of a low value are '(...)) are goods given by a taxpayer to a person: 1) the total value of which does not exceed PLN 100 in a tax year, provided that the taxpayer keeps records enabling the identification of such person; 2) if their transfer has not been entered in the records referred to in point 1, if the unit purchase price of the goods (excluding tax) and, if there is no purchase price, the unit production cost determined at the time of the transfer of the goods does not exceed PLN 20'. However, the Act does not set a limit on the value of samples.

According to Article 21(1) point 68 of the Act on personal income tax, prizes related to bonus sales of goods or services are exempt from income tax if the one-off value of such prizes or awards does not exceed PLN 2,000.

Although the values specified in the VAT Act are not binding for the interpretation of Article 17a of the Act on Combatting Unfair Competition, they may provide a certain point of reference. The adoption of an objective and verifiable criterion of purchase or production costs would certainly facilitate the interpretation of the term 'low-value bonus'. The lack of case law in this area does not allow for a clear definition of binding criteria for such an assessment.

However, it is reasonable to suggest that, when assessing the low value of a good or service, the real market value and not the promotional value of

[731] Dz.U. of 2024 item 361 as amended

the good or service, which is often much lower than the market value of this product, should be taken into account.[732]

V. Sample

Another exception to the general prohibition of bonus sales is the possibility to include a sample of goods as a bonus (Article 17a(2)(1) of the Act on Unfair Competition). This exception does not cause much controversy in the literature. According to the dictionary definition of the term, a 'sample' is 'a small amount of some commodity, usually a cosmetic product, given free of charge to the customer for testing'.[733] It seems that the 'sample of goods' referred to in the Act should be understood in the same way.[734]

A definition of the term 'sample' can also be found in Article 7 (7) of the Act on Goods and Services of 2004, pursuant to which a sample is understood 'to mean a specimen of a good or a small amount of a good, identifiable as a sample, which allows an assessment of the characteristics and properties of the good in its final form, whereby its delivery by the taxpayer (i) is intended to promote that good, and (ii) does not essentially serve to satisfy the needs of the final recipient of the good, unless satisfying the needs of that recipient is inherent in the promotion of that good and is intended to induce that recipient to purchase the promoted good'.[735]

---

[732] *A. Sobczak*, Ochrona przed nieuczciwą konkurencją, chapter V, <http://archiwum.rp.pl/artykul/399426-Ochrona-przed-nieuczciwa-konkurencja--poradnik-dla-przedsiebiorcow-i-konsumentow.html> (accessed on: 1.2.2025), the author recalls as an example the value of a mobile phone, which is added at a promotional price when a contract for the provision of telecommunications services is concluded.

[733] See: Słownik języka polskiego PWN, <http://sjp.pwn.pl/> (accessed on: 1.2.2025).

[734] See e.g.: *J. Szwaja, A. Kubiak-Cyrul*, in: *J. Szwaja, J. Kępiński* (eds), Ustawa o zwalczaniu nieuczciwej konkurencji, 2024, p. 660, Nb 21.

[735] The exclusion of VAT from the taxation of a gratuitous transfer of samples follows from Article 16(2) of Directive 2006/112/EC (of 28.11.2006 on the common system of value added tax, OJ L 347 of 2006, p. 1 as amended). Pursuant to Article 16 of that Directive, in its judgement of 30.9.2010, C-581/08, *EMI Group v. The Commissioners for Her Majesty's Revenue and Custom* (judgement of 2010, p. I-08607) the CJEU attempted to define the term 'sample'. According to the Court's ruling, a 'sample is a specimen of a product intended to promote its sale and to allow an assessment of its characteristics and qualities without an end use other than that inherent in such promotional activities'. The Court also concluded that goods provided as samples may be the same as

Pursuant to Article 17a of the Act on Combatting Unfair Competition, it will therefore be permissible to add, free of charge, when concluding a contract for the sale of goods or services with a consumer, a small amount of a good different from the object of the contract. This is because, pursuant to Article 17a (2) of the same Act, it is permissible to add samples of

the same goods as the main object of sale. An exception applies to samples of dissimilar goods. What remains relevant here is the problem indicated above as to whether the criterion of identity or the criterion of functionality should be applied in assessing the dissimilarity of goods. So under the Act on Combatting Unfair Competition, it is permissible to add without limitation samples of identical goods, e.g. a sample of washing powder when buying washing powder, as well as dissimilar goods to the extent permissible under the Act on Combatting Unfair Competition, e.g. a sample of mouthwash when buying toothpaste.

At the same time, it seems that in the case of a sample of goods, there is no need to assess that through the prism of the criterion of 'low value' since the very nature of a sample implies that its value is rather low and that the purpose of adding it is to enable testing a product and its promotion. It is therefore more appropriate here to adopt a quantitative criterion, i.e. a small amount of a good.[736]

However, even this criterion is vague and may cause controversy. And yet, these interpretations concern predominantly samples of goods supplied to other traders with the purpose of checking their quality or suitability, e.g. a sample of material weighing up to 1,250 kg because the machine used by the contractor needs a certain sample to check the suitability of the good.[737] Such samples of goods could not be treated as samples of goods within the meaning of the Act on Combatting Unfair Competition.

For example, in one case the Director of the Tax Office decided that a sample of goods may be: (1) cartons of products containing the same goods (5–20 pieces); (2) cartons of products containing different goods, being a mix

---

the final product intended to be placed on the market (see points 26–28 of the reasons for the judgment).

736 *P. Podrecki*, in: *M. Kępiński* (ed.), System Prawa Prywatnego, vol. 15, chapter XII, p. 557, Nb 18.

737 See Interpretation of the Director of the Tax Chamber in Warsaw of 15.4.2015, IPPB5/4510-15/15-4/AM.

of goods (5–20 pieces).[738] He justified his decision by saying that in assessing the concept of a 'small amount', he took into account the fact that the amount or value of the samples provided did not indicate their commercial nature. However, it should be clarified that the described sample of goods was addressed to traders (potential buyers) and not consumers. Where a manufacturer offers a sample of products to another trader (a potential customer), the intention is to give the trader an opportunity to check the products (their properties, suitability, etc.) and possibly order them in the future.

Undoubtedly, the provision of Article 17a of the Act on Combatting Unfair Competition does not cover such samples because it refers to consumer sales. For the same reason, a sample of goods in the form described above, due to its size, would not be an admissible sample if addressed directly to a consumer.

Article 17a envisages an addition of a small packet of washing powder when the consumer buys a dishwasher, a sachet of powder or cosmetics to a newspaper being bought, or a soap bar when buying a perfume. It could also be proposed, for the avoidance of any doubt, that samples of goods added to the main product should be labelled as a 'sample', 'sample not for sale', or 'free of charge'. This would also be in line with the requirements of the Act on Goods and Services, in which it is clearly specified that a 'sample' must be 'identifiable as a sample' and should therefore be properly labelled. The recipient of a sample should have no doubt that the product received has the nature of a sample.[739]

VI. Promotional Lottery and a Contest

1. Promotional Lottery

Another exception to the general prohibition of bonus sales is an option to add a bonus in the form of goods or services if it constitutes winnings in promotional lotteries organised pursuant to the provisions on gambling games or contests whose outcome does not depend on chance. Interestingly,

---

738 See Individual interpretation of the Director of the Tax Chamber in Łódź of 26.2.2016, 1061-IPTPP1.4512.1.2016.2.AK, Lex.

739 *A. Surdacka*, Reklama wartościowa, p. 28; also *R. Stefanicki*, Prawne granice swobody przedsiębiorcy, p. 47.

many scholars consider promotional lotteries to be one of the most effective forms of promotion of goods and services.[740]

Article 17a refers to the regulation on promotional lotteries in the Act of 2009—Gambling Law[741] and consequently, the award of a bonus in a promotional lottery will have to comply with its provisions.[742]

The Gambling Law provides that a promotional lottery is a form of a game of chance and defines it as a lottery in which participation in the game means purchasing goods, services, or other evidence of participation, by which joining in the lottery is free of charge, and the organiser (promoter) of the lottery offers winnings in cash or in kind.

The purpose of a promotional lottery is to promote goods and services, so there is no doubt that a promotional lottery in which the opportunity to participate is linked to the purchase of goods or services will have such a character. However, the purchase of goods or services will not always be necessary to participate in a lottery. Sometimes it may be sufficient to present another proof of participation in the game, which may be 'anything that the organiser in its regulations deems to confirm it, irrespective even of whether the acquisition of such proof was connected with the intention to buy it and participate in the contest',[743] or in a lottery.

Of key importance is that the lottery is organised to promote goods or services.[744] There is no requirement that a specific profit be achieved; it will be sufficient to merely demonstrate the intention of the organisers to promote

---

740 *M. Świerczyński*, in: *E. Traple* (ed.), Prawo reklamy i promocji, Warszawa 2007, p. 501.

741 On the subject of the promotional lottery on the grounds of the old Act of 29.7.1992 on games and mutual wagering (Dz.U. of 2004 No. 4, item 27 as amended) see: M. Świerczyński, Loterie promocyjne, in: *E. Traple* (ed.), Prawo reklamy i promocji, pp. 501–552. To a large extent the analysed issues have remained applicable up-to-date on the grounds of that Act – Gambling Law.

742 See *P. Podrecki*, in: *M. Kępiński* (ed.), System Prawa Prywatnego, vol. 15, Chapter XII, p. 557, Nb 18, p. 558, Nb 21; also *J. Szwaja, A. Kubiak-Cyrul*, in: *J. Szwaja, J. Kępiński* (eds), Ustawa o zwalczaniu nieuczciwej konkurencji, 2024, p. 660, Nb 22.

743 Judgement of the Supreme Administrative Court of 5.1.2000, II SA 1201/99, Legalis

744 Judgement of the Supreme Administrative Court of 6.12.1999, II SA 1513/99, Legalis

sales.[745] While the absence of the promotional element means that the lottery cannot be qualified as a promotional lottery.[746]

In the case of a promotional lottery, which is a form of a game of chance, its outcome depends on chance (randomness), and it is this element of randomness that is decisive when classifying a game as a game of chance.[747] This is also how the term 'lottery' is defined in dictionaries. According to them, a lottery is 'a game in which participants purchase tickets and the winning is decided by drawing lots', or it is 'a risky and uncertain situation or action, the outcome of which depends only on chance'.[748] It is therefore rightly argued in the literature that in the case of a lottery, fate (chance) must be decisive. If the participant's knowledge or certain skills are decisive, or at least have a significant influence on the outcome of the game, then such a game cannot be qualified as a lottery, i.e. a game of chance.[749] In games of chance, randomness is a constitutive, immanent feature of such a game.[750]

As the concept of a game of chance was defined in the Act of 19.11.2009 on games of chance, when interpreting it, one should refer to the case law of the courts developed on the grounds of this Act. This is because the administrative courts, in quite a number of rulings, have clarified in detail the nature of the analysed element of randomness (chance).

In one of the rulings, the Supreme Administrative Court clarified and upheld the previous interpretation on the grounds of the previous Act on Games and Mutual Wagering,[751] that randomness is to be understood as a situation where 'the outcome of any stage of a game defined as a competition

---

[745] Judgement of the Supreme Administrative Court of 5.1.2000 II SA 1201/99, Legalis and a reference in it to the judgement of the Supreme Court – III K 1450/96.

[746] *M. Świerczyński*, in: *E. Traple* (ed.), Prawo reklamy i promocji, p. 524.

[747] *J. Szwaja, A. Kubiak-Cyrul*, in: *J. Szwaja, J. Kępiński* (eds), Ustawa o zwalczaniu nieuczciwej konkurencji, 2024, p. 660–661, Nb 24; also *A. Bartosiewicz*, Konkurs promocyjny a loteria promocyjna – czyli jak uniknąć ewentualnej odpowiedzialności karnej skarbowej, MoPd 2011, No 10, p. 25.

[748] Słownik języka polskiego PWN, <http://sjp.pwn.pl/> (accessed on: 1.2.20245).

[749] *A. Bartosiewicz*, Konkurs promocyjny, p. 25.

[750] *M. Świerczyński*, in: *E. Traple* (ed.), Prawo reklamy i promocji, pp. 509–510.

[751] Act of 29.7.1992 on Games and Mutual Wagering (Dz.U. of 2004, No. 4, item 27 as amended). It has been emphasised in the literature that the understanding of games of chance developed by the case law on the grounds of the earlier Act has remained valid on the grounds of the Act – Gambling Law.

is incidental and therefore independent of the will (knowledge, skill) of the participant in the game'. The Supreme Administrative Court stated also that 'the introduction of an additional element of knowledge into a competition at a stage where a prize in cash or in kind is already assigned to each participant after the result of the first stage of the competition only creates the appearance of a lack of randomness and cannot change the assessment that we are dealing with a game of chance'.[752] It was a well-established position under the earlier Act that 'the introduction of additional elements into games of chance in the form of an "element of knowledge" or "dexterity" intended to create the appearance of a lack of randomness, and they do not significantly affect the conditions for entitlement to the prize does not deprive the statutory characteristics of a game of chance (i.e. the dependence of the outcome of the game on chance)'.[753]

Thus, even the fact that an element of knowledge was introduced into the competition at one of its stages (guessing how many leaves there are on the tree) could not be decisive in depriving the game of its characteristic of a game of chance, because its final outcome was not determined by the participant's possession of a certain type of knowledge (or the level of knowledge), which is subject to objective assessment and verification, thereby determining the outcome of the competition, but depended on chance, that is to say, on a factor over which the participant has no influence.[754]

The Supreme Administrative Court also held that the following amounted to a promotional lottery:

---

752 Judgement of the Supreme Administrative Court of 11.6.2013., II GSK 849/11, Legalis.

753 Judgement of the Supreme Administrative Court of 6.12.1999, II SA 1513/99, Legalis; Judgement of the Supreme Administrative Court of 11.6.2013, II GSK 849/11, Legalis. This line of jurisprudence has been maintained also at present, see e.g. the judgement of 5.7.2007, II GSK 87/07, Legalis, where the Supreme Administrative Court held that: 'the introduction of an additional requirement to answer a question does not automatically determine that the game does not have the character of a game of chance. What needs to be considered in such a situation is whether the introduction of the element of knowledge is not aimed only at creating the appearance of the absence of randomness'.

754 Judgement of the Supreme Administrative Court of 30.9.2014, II GSK 1852/13, Legalis.

1. a competition for purchasers of discount cards, in which prizes were awarded to holders selected by computer following an answer to a simple question concerning the regulations,[755]
2. a competition for subscribers in which winners were selected by drawing, and one of the conditions for participation in the competition was the submission of a coupon with the correct answers.[756]

According to the definition of a promotional lottery provided for in the Gambling Act, an entity organising a promotional lottery must offer winnings in cash and in kind.[757] The concept of cash and in-kind winnings, however, is not defined in the Act.

Winnings in cash are to be considered as monetary winnings. It is irrelevant how this prize will be handed over to the lottery winner. It may be given in the form of a cheque, transfer to a bank account, payment in cash, etc.[758]

The other type of winnings is winnings in kind. These can take various forms. First of all, it may be a property or a movable item. Most often the winnings will be related to the acquisition of ownership of the thing. The Supreme Court ruled that pursuant to the existing regulations[759] 'a winning in kind (...) is not only gaining ownership of a thing, but also acquiring the right to use the thing pursuant to another legal title. This may be, for example, the right to use it (Article 710 of the Civil Code) or the usufruct (Article 252). This ruling, despite the subsequent amendment to the law, has retained its validity and has been repeatedly cited in subsequent court decisions. In the literature, prizes in the form of various types of services

---

755 Judgement of the Supreme Administrative Court of 6.12.1999, II SA 1513/99, Legalis.

756 The Supreme Administrative Court reasoned that 'it does not in any way change the nature of the game of chance (promotional lottery) that subscribers entering the competition were required to answer the competition questions correctly'. Judgement of the Supreme Administrative Court of 5.5.2003, II SA 2145/01, Legalis.

757 Article 2(1) of the Gambling Law defines cash lotteries (point 2), in which exclusive cash winnings are offered, and prize draws (point 9), in which only winnings in kind are won.

758 *M. Świerczyński*, in: *E. Traple* (ed.), Prawo reklamy i promocji, p. 514. The author believes that a cash win would also be a debit card with a certain amount of money to be spent.

759 The Act of 1992 on games and mutual wagering.

are also considered to be winnings in kind.[760] On the other hand, qualifying as winning in kind—the mere possibility of continuing to play—raises doubts.[761]

Sometimes it may be difficult to identify a particular project as a game of chance or a contest. The literature points out that 'the appearance of chance as one of the preliminary elements, or as one of the elements preceding a contest, does not make a project a game of chance'.[762] Thus, the mere selection of participants in a competition by drawing lots should not yet lead to the qualification of a competition as a game of chance. It is also submitted that various considerations should be taken into account when assessing a given project, such as (1) whether the project is a two-stage project in which the first stage consists of selecting, by lot, participants in a competition from among all persons who have purchased a good or service, and in the second stage the drawn participants have to demonstrate knowledge or skills; (2) and whether the drawn participants who have purchased a good or service have, if they agree, the opportunity to take part in a competition in which certain knowledge or skills have to be demonstrated.[763]

It seems that in the first case, such an undertaking would qualify as a game of chance. However, this may also depend on the difficulty of the questions or tasks in the second stage. After all, if the questions are trivial and the tasks are simple and everyone is able to answer or complete them, the element of knowledge or skill is not apparent, and the prize is *de facto* decided by a draw of lots.[764] The whole promotional event would therefore have to be qualified as a game of chance. In the other case, it would be a competition, as the element of randomness is not decisive for receiving the prize. It is also argued that an important circumstance for the appropriate qualification of a promotional event may also be the order of the individual

---

760 *M. Świerczyński*, in: *E. Traple* (ed.), Prawo reklamy i promocji, p. 517.

761 For more see: *M. Świerczyński*, in: *E. Traple* (ed.), Prawo reklamy i promocji, pp. 515–517 together with the literature and case law cited therein.

762 *A. Bartosiewicz*, Konkurs promocyjny, p. 26.

763 *Ibidem*, p. 27.

764 The Supreme Administrative Court points out that an assessment of the extent of knowledge necessary to give a correct answer is helpful in this respect, as is the way in which this knowledge is tested. See: Judgement of the Supreme Administrative Court of 5.7.2007, II GSK 87/07, Legalis.

stages of the event (first the drawing of lots and then answering the questions or performing the task, or vice versa)[765] or the goal and intention of the organiser.[766]

Thus, as can be seen from the above considerations, it will not always be easy to determine unequivocally whether the promotional event under examination can be qualified as a permissible exception under Article 17a(2) of the Act on Combatting Unfair Competition. Alternatively, it will have to be considered whether the activity in question qualifies as a competition that is not a game of chance, in which case it is not required that the conditions required for a game of chance be met when the competition is organised.

2. Contest

Another exception to the general prohibition of bonus sales is the admissibility of awarding a bonus if it is a prize in a contest, the outcome of which does not depend on chance, but the decisive factor in its determination is the participant's knowledge, dexterity, or another objectively verifiable skills.[767]

What is important in organising promotional lotteries is that a contest that is not a game of chance does not have to fulfil the statutory conditions (no permit or approval of the rules of the planned contest is required) referred to in the Act on Gambling when organising promotional lotteries. In consequence, in order to avoid the requirements imposed by the Act, entrepreneurs attempt to create the impression that a promotional lottery is a contest by introducing elements that involve specific knowledge or skills of potential participants. However, as can be seen from the case law, there

765 See: *A. Bartosiewicz*, Konkurs promocyjny, p. 28.

766 *Ibidem*.

767 *Ibidem*, pp. 23–28, The author emphasises that entrepreneurs organising various types of competitions and promotional actions must be aware that some of their promotional undertakings may be classified as promotional lotteries and, consequently, must meet all the requirements set out in the Act-Gambling Law. The author explains that the decisive factor for the classification of an activity as a promotional lottery will be the existence of chance (fate) as being material to the participant's winnings. If other circumstances (knowledge, skills, will of the participants) here have a decisive or significant influence on the outcome of the entire activity, then it is not a game of chance—a promotional lottery.

were numerous instances when, contrary to the organisers conviction that they had organised a contest, the courts or the competent minister found it to be a promotional lottery.[768] The fact that such a promotional event required, for example, the answering of a trivial question or the performance of some simple activity was not decisive.

There is a justified argument in the literature that a contest 'must represent an appropriate level of difficulty in order to avoid the suspicion of the circumvention of the rules'.[769] The case law of the Supreme Administrative Court defines quite precisely which circumstances allow a promotional event to be considered, for example, a contest of knowledge, precluding the random nature of such an event. Such circumstances included (1) the course of the contest was supervised by the competition committee, which verified the answers; (2) the questions were of a significant degree of difficulty, the answers were not prompted or suggested and could not be derived from the content of the questions; (3) the participant answered the questions 'live', independently, without consulting anyone, in the presence of the contest committee; (4) the contest committee was composed of persons of public trust; (5) and the result of the contest was determined by the knowledge of the participant, who gave the number of correct answers specified in the regulations.[770]

It is also argued that in the assessment of a contest, circumstances relating to the contest questions themselves, such as the number of correct answers or tasks performed by the participants, may also be relevant. The fewer correct answers and well-performed tasks, the more likely it is that

---

768 There are many examples in the case las of administrative courts. See: e.g. Judgement of the Supreme Administrative Court of 30.9.2014, II GSK 1852/13, Legalis (promotional lottery); Judgement of the Supreme Administrative Court of 11.6.2013, II GSK 849/11, Legalis (audio-text lottery); Judgement of the Supreme Administrative Court of 11.6.2013, II GSK 1010/11, Legalis (audio-text lottery); Judgement of the Supreme Administrative Court of 5.7.2007, II GSK 87/07, Legalis (internet game); Judgement of the Supreme Administrative Court of 5.5.2003, II SA 2145/01, Legalis (promotional lottery); Judgement of the Supreme Administrative Court of 6.12.1999, II SA 1513/99, Legalis (promotional lottery); Judgement of the Supreme Administrative Court of 10.2.1998, II SA 1260/97, Legalis (prize draw and cash raffle).

769 *K. Korus*, Zwalczanie nieuczciwej konkurencji, kom. do art. 17a.

770 Judgement of the Supreme Administrative Court of 4.12.2014, II GSK 1296/13, Legalis; and of 5.7.2007, II GSK 87/07, Legalis.

the contest was not an attempt to circumvent the rules. On the other hand, disclosing questions or tasks to participants before a contest may indicate that it was a sham.[771]

Contests are regulated in Article 921 of the Civil Code. Pursuant to it, a contest is one of the types of a public promise called a 'promise of a contest prize'. It differs from an ordinary promise (Articles 919–920), first of all, in that the conditions of the promised prize are defined differently.[772] In the case of an ordinary promise, the prize is awarded to the person who performs the action indicated by the promisor of the prize (Art. 919 of the Civil Code). However, in the situation of a promise of a contest prize, the mere performance of the work or activity is not sufficient to receive the prize, as the prize will be awarded only to the best performer of the contest work or action (Article 921(1)). It is up to the promisor to assess whether and which work or action deserves the prize, unless otherwise stipulated in the promise of the contest prize (see Article 921 § 2 KC). If so, the award of the prize may therefore be decided by, for example, the jury of the contest.

It is accepted in the literature that a public promise (ordinary and of a contest prize) is a declaration of will by the promisor. Thus, it requires the fulfilment of certain general prerequisites required for any declaration of will, as well as specific prerequisites required only for a public promise.[773] Such a specific requirement is the requirement that the promise be publicly announced· owing to which it may reach a greater undefined number of unnamed individuals.[774] Moreover, the promisor must designate the prize, as well as 'indicate who may compete for the prize, specify for what the prize is due and, and further, also specify the period within which the prize may be claimed'[775] and stipulate that the prize will be awarded for the best action

---

771 *A. Bartosiewicz*, Konkurs promocyjny, p. 28.

772 *K. Zawada*, in: *J. Panowicz-Lipska* (ed.), System Prawa Prywatnego. Prawo zobowiązań – część szczegółowa, vol. 8, Warszawa 2011, p. 894, Nb 2.

773 See: *ibidem*, p. 907, Nb 49.

774 See: *K. Zawada*, in: *J. Panowicz-Lipska* (ed.), System Prawa Prywatnego, vol. 8, p. 895, Nb 6.

775 See *ibidem*, p. 908, Nb 55.

or work.[776] The requirements relating to the action or the contest work must be designated by objective features. However, their assessment in the case of a promise of a contest prize belongs, as a rule, to the promisor, unless otherwise stipulated in the prize promise (see Article 921(2)).

The promisor may also, pursuant to Article 921(3), specify that he or she acquires ownership of the prize-winning work. In such a case, the acquisition of ownership takes place upon the payment of the prize. The promisor may also stipulate many other provisions, e.g. the option of changing the terms and conditions of the competition or the way in which information about the contest results will be provided.[777]

It is accepted[778] that a public promise (ordinary and contest prize) is a unilateral act binding the promisor to pay the prize if certain legal conditions are fulfilled.[779] Consequently, as soon as the activity or work in a contest has been performed and the conditions, if any, have been fulfilled, the performer of the activity or work acquires a claim against the promisor of the prize.[780]

A prize may take various forms. Most often it will be a monetary award, but it can also be a non-monetary award in the form of a diploma, medal, etc. There may also be a specified number of prizes, e.g. prizes of different degrees and different amounts.

It may be argued that a bonus being a prize won in a promotional lottery or in a contest may be of greater value. The condition of a small value of bonus contained in Article 17a of the Act on Combatting Unfair Competition does not seem to apply to winnings. Thus, winnings may also be goods or services different from the main object of the contract.[781]

---

776 It is pointed out that, in this respect, the promisor has a great deal of freedom and may specify the various characteristics to be taken into account in their assessment. See: *ibidem*, p. 908, Nb 58.

777 See: *ibidem*, p. 910, Nb 64.

778 *M. Mularski*, in: *M. Gutowski* (ed.), Kodeks cywilny, vol. 3, 2022, Comments to Art. 919, p. 1123–1124, Nb 1.

779 See: *K. Zawada*, in: *J. Panowicz-Lipska* (ed.), System Prawa Prywatnego, vol. 8, chapter XVI, p. 921, Nb 103. The author also stresses that the conclusion of a contract may also trigger a competition.

780 See: *ibidem*, p. 925, Nb 109.

781 *K. Korus*, Zwalczanie nieuczciwej konkurencji, kom. do art. 17a.

§ 4. Bonus Sales in Directive 2005/29/EC and the Act on Counteracting Unfair Market Practices

I. Sales Promotions in Directive 2005/29/EC

Directive 2005/29/EC regulates to a certain degree sales promotions,[782] which is a reflection of the results of work by the European Commission (presented in its Report in 2013[783]) undertaken after the work on the regulation of the European Parliament and the Council on sales promotion in the Internal Market[784] had failed. The Commission pointed out that the (unadopted) regulation envisaged a number of information requirements aimed at ensuring that commercial communication with regard to sales promotions was transparent and that its recipients received all relevant information. The consequence of the adoption of provisions on sales promotions in Directive 2005/29/EC, due to its complete nature, is that Member States must adopt the same solutions as those provided for in the Directive. At the same time, the solutions adopted in the laws of the Member States cannot be more restrictive or prescriptive than those of the Directive. The above presumption has an important bearing on the CJEU's answers to the preliminary questions

782 *H.-W. Micklitz* notes, however, that it was not clear at the outset whether the Directive was intended to address sales promotion issues at all. However, its broad scope meant that it would have been difficult to take sales promotion measures out from under its scope, *H.-W. Micklitz*, Full Harmonisation, p. 372. See also *G. Anagnostaras*, The Unfair Commercial Practices, p. 154, who emphasises that the concept of commercial practices in the Directive is understood broadly and that the Directive takes a liberal approach in assessing commercial practices regulated by the Member States.

783 See: Report of the Commission to the European Parliament, the Council and the Economic-Social Committee of 14 March 2013, *First Report on the application of Directive 2005/29/EC of the European Parliament and of the Council of 11 May 2005 concerning unfair business-to-consumer commercial practices in the internal market and amending Council Directive 84/450/EEC, Directives 97/7/*EC, *98/27/EC and 2002/65/EC of the European Parliament and of the Council and Regulation (EC) No 2006/2004 of the European Parliament and of the Council ('Unfair Commercial Practices Directive')*, COM(2013) 139 final, p. 11, <http://eur-lex.europa.eu/legal-content/pl/ALL/?uri=OJ%3AC%3A2013%3A327%3ATOC> (accessed on 1.2.2025).

784 Draft presented by the Commission on 4.10.2001, Proposal to the European Parliament and the Council on sales promotion in the internal market, COM(2001) 546 final – 2001/0227(COD).

of the national courts concerning the interpretation of national provisions relating to sales promotions in light of the Directive.[785]

When analysing the issue of sales promotions, it is important to bear in mind that Directive 2005/29/EC only covers commercial practices concerning sales promotions that harm the economic interests of consumers. Sales promotion practices that harm the interests of traders but do not affect the interests of consumers are outside its scope, and Member States are free to introduce rules applying to B2B relationships that are more restrictive and prescriptive than those provided for in the Directive. In such a situation, the provisions adopted in individual Member States will have to be assessed under the laws against unfair competition in force in each respective Member State.[786] Consequently, the laws of the Member States may also differ with regard to sales promotion practices. However, as the CJEU's rulings show, it will not always be effective to argue that a provision has been introduced in national law to protect competition and competitors rather than consumers.[787]

---

785 Judgement of the ECJ of 23.4.2009, C- 261/07, *VTB-VAB NV v. Total Belgium NV* in C-299/07, *Galatea BVBA v. Sanoma Magazines Belgium NV*, ECLI:EU:C:2009:244. The judgement was preceded by the opinion of the Ombudsman General V. Trstenjak of 21.10.2008, ECLI:EU:C:2008:581; Judgment of the ECJ of 14.1.2010, C-304/08, *Zentrale zur Bekämpfung unlauteren Wettbewerbs eV v. Plus Warenhandelsgesellschaft mbH.*, See verdict 2010, p. I-00217, ECLI:EU:C:2010:12. The judgement was preceded by the opinion of the Ombudsman General V. Trstenjak presented on 3 September 2009, ECLI:EU:C:2009:511; Judgement of the ECJ of 11 March 2010, C-522/08, *Telekomunikacja Polska SA w Warszawie v. Prezes Urzędu Komunikacji Elektronicznej*, See verdict 2010, p. I-02079, ECLI:EU:C:2010:135; Judgement of the ECJ of 9 November 2010, C-540/08, *Mediaprint Zeitungs- und Zeitschriftenverlag GmbH & Co. KG v. Österreich-Zeitungsverlag GmbH*, See verdict 2010, p. I-10909, ECLI:EU:C:2010:660. The judgement was preceded by the opinion of the Ombudsman General V. Trstenjak presented on 24 March 2010., ECLI:EU:C:2010:161; Judgement of the ECJ of 18 July C-265/12, *Citroën Belux NV v. Federatie voorVerzekerings- en Financiële Tussenpersonen (FvF)*, ECLI:EU:C:2013:498.

786 See: *G. Anagnostaras*, The Unfair Commercial Practices, p. 152.

787 For example, the Judgement of the ECJ of of 14.1.2010, C-304/08, *Zentrale zur Bekämpfung unlauteren Wettbewerbs eV v. Plus Warenhandelsgesellschaft mbH*, See verdict 2010 I-00217, ECLI:EU:C:2010:12. The Court did not accept the argument that the main purpose of the provisions of the German UWG, unlike those of Directive 2005/29/EC, is not to protect consumers but to protect competitors against unfair commercial practices by certain operators and that, therefore, such provisions do not fall within the scope of that Directive.

The concept of 'sales promotion' was not defined in Directive 2005/29/EC itself. The definition was contained in Article 2b of the proposal for a regulation on sales promotions. As provided in that draft, sales promotions can take various forms, namely discounts, premium offers, free gifts, promotional contests, and games.[788] I believe that, also under Directive 2005/29/EC, the concept of 'sales promotion' should be understood broadly, in the way adopted in the proposal for the aforementioned regulation. Indeed, the work on these pieces of legislation (directive and regulation) went on simultaneously and overlapped. Although the regulation was never adopted, an analysis of the legislative work allows us to understand the basis and assumptions of the ongoing deliberations. The European Commission is of the opinion that Article 6(1)(d) of Directive 2005/29/EC contains provisions regulating promotional sales, stating that 'a commercial practice shall be regarded as misleading if it contains false information and is therefore untruthful or in any way, including overall presentation, deceives or is likely to deceive the average consumer, even if the information is factually correct, in relation to one or more of the following elements, and in either case causes or is likely to cause him to take a transactional decision that he would not have taken otherwise: (...) (d) the price, the manner in which the price is calculated or the existence of a specific price advantage'.

The Commission also explained that Annex I of Directive 2005/29/EC also identifies practices that can be qualified as relating to sales promotion. Consequently, under all conditions, commercial practices such as:

(1) 'bait advertising', which is an invitation to purchase products at a particular price without disclosing that the trader has reasonable grounds to believe that he will not be able to offer for supply or to procure from another trader a supply of those or equivalent products at such price for that period and in such quantities that are reasonable, taking into account the product, the scale of advertising of the product, and the price offered (point 5 of the Annex);
(2) false claims concerning the availability of a product for a certain period of time, which suggest that the product will only be available

[788] Commission Communication on Sales Promotion in the Internal Market 52001DC0546, p. 3. <https://eur-lex.europa.eu/legal-content/EN/TXT/HTML/?uri=COM:2001:546:FIN> (accessed 1.2.2025)

for a limited period of time or that it will be available under certain conditions for a limited period of time. These claims are designed to induce consumers to make an immediate decision and deprive them of the opportunity to make an informed choice or of the time needed to make it (point 7 of the Annex);

3) a competition or price promotion that does not result in the award of the promised prize (point 19 of the Annex);
4) use of the phrase 'free of charge' when in fact the product is not free of charge. This practice applies to any representation of a product as 'gratis', 'free', 'free of charge', or any other similar manner where the consumer has to pay anything other than the unavoidable cost of responding to the commercial practice or picking up or delivering the product (point 20 of the Annex);
(5) claiming a prize when in fact there is no prize. In this type of practice, the trader gives the false impression that the consumer has already obtained, will obtain, or, having performed a particular act, will obtain a prize or other comparable benefit, when in fact the prize or other comparable benefit does not exist or the opportunity to perform a particular act in relation to obtaining the prize or other comparable benefit is subject to the consumer paying money or incurring a cost (point 31 of the Annex).

It is not clear why the Commission in its 2013 Report classified only these commercial practices as relating to sales promotion. Perhaps, in the Commission's view, these were the most common examples of unfair commercial practices relating to sales promotion. However, it seems that the catalogue of practices relating to sales promotion presented in the Report is not a closed catalogue. Undoubtedly, other commercial practices listed in the Directive could also be characterised as related to sales promotion. These would be, above all, all forms of advertising (e.g. point 11 of the Annex—surreptitious advertising, point 13—advertising suggesting the origin of the product from another producer, point 28—advertising targeting children) and forms of conducting sales (point 14 – pyramid scheme), etc.

There are also further insights from the Report. Some Member States have raised that in consequence of the implementation of the Directive, they will have to repeal certain national provisions that had been aimed at a higher level of consumer protection than that provided for in the Directive. Those countries claimed that the repeal of such laws might significantly worsen consumer protection against misleading sales promotion practices and make it more difficult to enforce these provisions.[789] The Report also showed that some Member States had reported the need for legislative changes with regard to sales promotion, while other Member States rejected the possibility of further regulation in this area or indicated that they would welcome further guidance on the application of the Directive. In the Commission's view, most of the concerns raised by Member States regarding sales promotions should be addressed through measures aimed at increasing legal certainty and uniform application of the Directive.[790]

II. Unfair Commercial Practices Relating to Sales Promotions

1. Introductory Remarks

The catalogue of sales promotion practices adopted in the 2013 Report coincides with the catalogue set out primarily in point 1.3 of the Guidance.[791]

It follows from them that:

1) the Directive aims at full harmonisation of the laws of the Member States falling within the scope of the Directive. Thus, Member States may not adopt more restrictive/prescriptive measures than those provided for in the Directive;

---

789 According to the Report from the Commission to the European Parliament, the Council and the Economic and Social Committee of 14.3.2013, there are more restrictive measures than those provided for in the Directive in most Member States, p. 11.

790 See: Commission Report to the European Parliament, the Council and the Economic and Social Committee of 14.3.2013, p. 12.

791 The Guidance (pl), point. 1.3.1, p. 13. It is clear from the Guidance that the Directive covers commercial practices 'such as combined or combined offers, rebates, price reductions, promotional sales, trade lotteries, contests and coupons'. The Directive also contains a number of provisions regulating promotional practices. The practices listed are those described in Article 6(1)(d) of the Directive and in points 5, 7, 19, 20, and 31 of Annex I to the Directive.

2) the Directive does not allow Member States to adopt a general (blanket) ban on combined offers[792];
3) national regulations require entrepreneurs to present reduced prices in a certain way, and the justification for the reduction is not compatible with the Directive[793];
4) The Directive does not contain a provision imposing an obligation on entrepreneurs to present prices in a certain way and justify price reductions. It is therefore not justified for national legislation to provide for stricter rules on the presentation and reduction of prices;
5) more restrictive rules than those provided for in the Directive may be introduced for financial services and immovable property (Article 3(9) of the Directive).

A number of examples of commercial practices that had been addressed by Member States' national bodies were presented together with the Commission's guidance in the detailed section of the Guidance. Among the examples provided, the Commission also referred to some of the practices that were qualified by the Commission in the 2013 Report as relating to sales promotions. The commercial practice of describing a product as 'gratis' or 'free of charge' (Annex I—point 20 of the Directive) and the commercial practice whereby a trader gives the impression that the consumer will obtain or has obtained a prize when, in fact, there is no prize or the obtaining of the prize is subject to the payment of a sum of money (Annex I—point 31 of the Directive) were discussed in detail.[794]

2. Implementation of the Act on Counteracting Unfair Commercial Practices

The examples of commercial practices relating to sales promotions referred to in the Commission Report were implemented in the Act on Unfair Market Practices in:

---

[792] This view arises from the judgement of the ECJ of 23 April 2009, C- 261/07, *VTB-VAB NV v. Total Belgium NV* and C-299/07, *Galatea BVBA v. Sanoma Magazines Belgium NV*, ECLI:EU:C:2009:244.

[793] Guidance(pl) point 1.3.1, p. 14. See: judgement of the ECJ of 10.7.2014, C-421/12, *European Commission v. Kingdom of Belgium*, ECLI:EU:C:2014:2064.

[794] Guidance (pl), point 4.4, pp. 104–108 and point 4.5, pp. 113–115.

1. Article 7(5) and (6) (the provision corresponds to points 5 and 6 of Annex I of Directive 2005/29/EC), concerning 'bait advertising';
2. Article 7(7) (the provision corresponds to point 7 of Annex I of Directive 2005/29/EC), which concerns making false claims about the availability of a product;
3. Article 7(19) (the provision corresponds to point 19 of Annex I to Directive 2005/29/EC), which relates to claims of organising competitions or promotions with prizes and then failing to award prizes or their equivalent;
4. Article 7(20) (the provision corresponds to point 20 of Annex I to Directive 2005/29/EC; only the wording 'any costs' in the Directive has been changed to 'direct costs'), which refers to the presentation of a product 'gratis' or 'free of charge' if the consumer has to pay something as a result;
5. Article 9(8) (corresponding to point 31 of Annex I of Directive 2005/29/EC). This practice consists of 'creating the impression that the consumer has already obtained, will obtain unconditionally, or upon the performance of a particular act, a prize or other comparable benefit, when in fact the prize or other comparable benefit does not exist or the obtaining of the prize or other comparable benefit is subject to the consumer paying a sum of money or incurring other costs'.

The above-mentioned provisions, despite the fact that the Act has been in force for more than 15 years, have not been the subject of wider academic interest, nor have they been extensively analysed by Polish courts. The considerations are thus limited to the Guidance, a few judgements, and the views presented in the literature.

3. Bait Advertising (Articles 7(5) and 7(6) of the Act on Counteracting Unfair Market Practices)

Articles 7(5) and 7(6) of the Act on Counteracting Unfair Market Practices provide for two cases of unfair practices referred to as bait advertising.

The common element of both cases is that a trader makes an offer to a consumer and promises to sell a product and then fails to perform as promised. In the first situation, the trader may not supply the advertised product at a certain price, while in the other situation, the trader may not supply the advertised product, but instead he will present another in the hope that, enticed by the advertisement, the consumer will purchase that other product.

The prohibition of both types of commercial practices is designed to protect consumer confidence in a commercial proposal made by the trader, which gives the consumer a reasonable expectation of the product offered or of the benefit expected to be derived from the conclusion of the contract,[795] whereas in reality these expectations cannot be met. It is argued in the literature that it is a matter of protecting the consumer's economic interests in the pre-contractual sphere and that the issue of the availability of the goods is counted among the essential elements concerning the product.[796] It is essential that consumers have clarity about the availability of products, as well as trust traders involved in the trade, and both types of practices significantly reduce consumer confidence in the proposals they make.

One such practice is bait advertising, which, like any advertising, aims to encourage the consumer to take an interest in the product offered by the trader, but the reprehensibility of this practice lies in the fact that the trader may not be able to deliver the advertised product. According to Article 7(5), it is an unfair market practice to 'bait advertising by offering to buy a product at a particular price without disclosing that the entrepreneur may have reasonable grounds for believing that he will not be able to supply or procure another trader to supply those or equivalent products at that price, for such period and in such quantities as are reasonable having regard to the product, the extent of advertising of the product and the price offered'. An offer to purchase a product should be understood as a 'commercial communication setting out the characteristics of the product and its price, in a way appropriate to the means of communication used to communicate with consumers, which directly influences or is likely to influence the consumer's contractual decision' (Article 2(6)).

Bait advertising, however, differs from ordinary advertising in that the trader does not disclose to consumers that he or she may have (objectively) legitimate grounds[797] to believe that the products will not be supplied or will

---

795 *R. Stefanicki*, Nieuczciwe praktyki handlowe w świetle prawodawstwa Unii Europejskiej – dyrektywa 2005/29/WE, Warszawa 2007, p. 212.

796 *Ibidem*, pp. 211–212.

797 For more on 'legitimate grounds', see: *M. Namysłowska*, Czarna lista nieuczciwych praktyk handlowych, p. 356.

not be capable of being ordered from another supplier. However, dishonesty on the part of the trader can only be claimed if the trader has failed to disclose that he had reasonable grounds, based on certain objective considerations, to believe that an offer would be impossible to fulfil. At the same time, the provision does not explain how the trader should disseminate such information. It seems that such information should be disseminated in the same way as the advertisement of the product, and the message should be clear and legible to the consumer. The mere information that the 'offer is valid while the stock lasts' will not be sufficient."[798] Thus, a common practice consisting of a widely publicised advertising campaign for certain products with the proviso that the offer is valid only until stocks run out, which are then available in shops in very small quantities (a few copies), could qualify as such a practice. Indeed, the trader's main objective is to lure the consumer with a very attractive offer that is in fact unavailable.

An example of this type of practice is provided by the judgement of the Court of Appeal in Warsaw.[799] In the case in question, the trader advertised the sale of flats in the press and said in the advertisements, 'We sell cheaper than you think. Prices from as little as PLN 9,000 per square metre' attaching photographs of residential buildings. However, it was beyond any dispute that not a single flat was offered at such a price. Under these facts, the President of the Office of Competition and Consumer Protection found that by doing so, the trader infringed the collective interests of consumers.[800] The trader appealed but the Court of Appeal held that the advertisement constituted a 'bait advertisement' within the meaning of Article 7(5) of the Act on Counteracting Unfair Market Practices which states that 'if a trader

---

798 *R. Stefanicki*, Ustawa o przeciwdziałaniu nieuczciwym praktykom rynkowym, p. 378.

799 Judgement of the Court of Appeal in Warsaw of 27.9.2013, VI ACa 279/13, Legalis. An earlier decision of the President of the Office of Competition and Consumer Protection was cited in Commission's Guidance, Decision No. RWA-25/2010, President of the Office of Competition and Consumer Protection, Delegation in Warsaw of 28.12.2010 in the case of Eko-Park S.A., p. 87.

800 According to point I.C of the decision of the President of the Office for Competition and Consumer Protection, it was found 'as a practice infringing the collective interests of consumers referred to in Article 24(2)(3) in connection with Article 24(1) of the Act on Competition and Consumer Protection, the practice of the complainant of using advertisements with the wording: (...), while at the time of publication of the advertisements, the Complainant's offer did not include flats at that price (...)'.

directs an invitation to consumers to induce them to purchase goods without disclosing that he or she has reasonable grounds to believe that their delivery will be impossible (or the order of delivery of those or equivalent goods from another trader will not be possible), it may be concluded that we are dealing with a deliberate action of the trader who, when addressing an invitation to consumers to make a purchase, knew that the products would not be available or that the offer would be very limited. When the trader makes a favourable offer to consumers, particularly in terms of price, the trader should have anticipated that interest in the offer may exceed the supply of the product'. In the court's view, in the case under review, the consumer who was lured by the unfair content of the advertisement was deceived because there was no opportunity to make use of the offer. Moreover, there was an additional risk that, as a result of the use of bait advertising, the consumer would be persuaded, while already in the real estate sales office, to purchase another, more expensive flat, which would not have interested him or her earlier had it not been for the action of the offeror of the flats.

The other case of a prohibited market practice is so-called bait and switch advertising. It consists of 'offering a product at a certain price and then refusing to show it to consumers, or refusing to take orders for the product or deliver it within a reasonable time, or demonstrating a defective sample of the product, with the intention of promoting another product'.

One has to agree with the view expressed in the literature that it was not necessary to distinguish between as many as two unfair market practices relating to bait advertising. Indeed, their essential and recurring element was attracting the consumer unfairly by means of unfair advertising.[801] The circumstance of whether—and if so—what—the trader offers to a customer seems to be of a secondary consideration. What is really reprehensible is for a trader to act in a manner that undermines the consumer's confidence in the truthfulness of the commercial information he disseminates. In the case of switch bait advertising, the trader advertises a fictitious product in order to actually offer a different product that is intentionally inferior or more expensive.[802] On the other hand, one may wonder whether, if a trader offered a better product at the same price as the advertised product, in the

---

[801] *R. Stefanicki*, Nieuczciwe praktyki handlowe, p. 213.
[802] *A. Michalak*, Przeciwdziałanie nieuczciwym praktykom rynkowym, p. 100.

absence of the advertised product, such an action could be considered an unfair market practice. As already highlighted, the purpose of introducing this type of practice in the regulation is to protect the consumer from false, fictitious offers by traders. Taking this criterion as decisive, such an offer could also be considered misleading. As a general rule, the consumer should be sure that he or she will receive the advertised product and not another product, even a better one.

Following bait advertising, a trader may:

1. refuse to show the advertised product;
2. refuse to accept the order;
3. refuse to deliver the product within a reasonable time;
4. demonstrate a defective sample of the product, i.e. one that does not correspond to the advertised product. Had a non-defective sample been provided, the consumer could have made a different decision.

Such practices were, prior to the entry into force of the Act on Counteracting Unfair Market Practices, considered unacceptable by the President of the Office of Competition and Consumer Protection and by the courts and were qualified as delicts of unfair competition pursuant to Article 16(1)(2) of the Act on Combatting Unfair Competition (being misleading advertising). In one of the cases, the court examined whether an advertisement in which an entrepreneur advertised loans and credits was acceptable. In fact, the advertised product was not a loan or credit but participation in an organised financial scheme. The funds for the operation of the scheme came from timely payments by participants.[803] The Regional Court held that the entrepreneur's action was unlawful because, among other things, the entrepreneur advertised a product that was not in his offer. The court reasoned that the advertisement disseminated by the entrepreneur indicated in its content that the consumer could obtain a loan or credit. At the same time, the advertisement gave the impression that the credit or loan would be granted without the applicant having to fulfil specific conditions required by banks and, in addition, that it would be done within a short period of time. This created an environment in which the addressees of the advertisement were misled as to the content of

[803] Judgement of the UOKiK of 23 June 2004, XVII Ama 66/03, Legalis.

the advertised product. It was only in the course of the preparatory activities for signing the contract that the consumer, who had already decided to take advantage of the advertised offer in the mistaken belief that it concerned a loan or credit found out about the actual rules of participation in the organised financial scheme. The advertisement for a loan and credit turned out in fact to be an advertisement for a different product, i.e. a financial scheme, the funds for which came from the contributions of its participants.

4. Making False Claims about the Availability of a Product (Article 7(7) of the Act on Counteracting Unfair Market Practices

It is also an unfair and misleading market practice if a trader claims that a product will only be available for a very limited time, or that it will be available on certain terms for a very limited time, for the purpose of inducing the consumer to make an immediate contractual decision and depriving him of the opportunity to make an informed choice about the product if the received information turns out to be untrue. What is reprehensible in this type of action by a trader is that the consumer is deprived of the opportunity to make an informed, considered decision when choosing a product. The purpose of the trader's action is to give the consumer a misleading impression that, if he or she does not immediately decide to accept the offer, the goods will not be available any longer or the conditions under which the product will be available later will be less favourable. In reality, however, the product will be available later on the same terms and conditions, and the trader does not really intend to offer the product only for a limited period of time or on particularly favourable terms. Disseminating such untrue information constitutes an unfair market practice.

It is argued in the literature that an example of such a practice would be information on the liquidation of the trader's business, which is in fact fictitious.[804] In reality, no liquidation is

taking place, and the consumer is 'lured' by such a false claim, expecting a particularly favourable offer because of the closure of business ('everything

[804] *A. Michalak*, Przeciwdziałanie nieuczciwym praktykom rynkowym, p. 101. The literature also includes among the same type of practices those listed in Article 7 points 15 and 18 of the Act on Counteracting Unfair Market Practices. See: *R. Stefanicki*, Nieuczciwe praktyki handlowe, 214.

must go'). The same could be said of a practice where a trader indicates that certain products are on sale and therefore better priced, when in fact their price is the regular price and the specific product is not on special offer.

On the other hand, it is an acceptable practice to claim that a particular product offer will last for a certain period of time, like, for example, a summer sale period, or that the sale will go on until the trader goes out of business. When such claims are true and accurate, they can qualify as legitimate market practices.[805] It will be unacceptable to disseminate a false claim that may influence the consumer's decision-making in relation to the product offered.

A false claim may also refer to information about the service provided, e.g. free delivery of goods. A judgement of the Court of Competition and Consumer Protection in Warsaw provided such an example.[806] The trader running an online shop informed on his website that the offer of free delivery of goods was only available for a limited period of time, i.e. 'only until Friday'. This information was untrue, as the offer on identical terms was repeated at the beginning of each following week. The President of the Office of Competition and Consumer Protection found that such practice constituted an unfair market practice (Article 7 point 7) of the Act on Counteracting Unfair Market Practices and infringed collective consumer interests. The entrepreneur appealed against the decision of the President of UOKiK to the court. The court dismissed the entrepreneur's appeal and upheld the decision of its President, finding that the information provided by the entrepreneur was objectively untrue and could be misleading. In the opinion of the UOKiK, the entrepreneur's action was contrary to good practice, as it led to confusion and caused misconception among consumers. The trader's action was aimed at giving consumers the impression that a favourable offer would not be repeated. The court reasoned that 'an immediate decision by the consumer means (...) depriving the consumer of the right to make an informed choice. When making a purchase via online shops, the consumer usually first selects the goods he is interested in and only secondly, in order to make the most advantageous purchase, compares the prices of the chosen product in the

---

805 *R. Stefanicki*, Nieuczciwe praktyki handlowe, p. 213.

806 Judgement of the SOKiK of 27 March 2015, XVII AmA 144/13, Legalis. See also Judgement of the Court of Appeal in Warsaw, VI Aca 652/18, Legalis.

various online shops. From this point of view, the delivery costs of the goods are often the most significant element differentiating the total prices of the goods in the individual online shops, and therefore the information about free delivery is crucial and will usually result in the selection of the online shop with such a promotional offer. Particularly since the delivery costs of many of the products offered by the Company (e.g. fridges, washing machines, televisions) can be significant. Reliable information that the promotion on the same terms and conditions will be renewed the following week could have influenced the consumer to make a different decision on the purchase of the product and the associated free delivery service'.

5. Organisation of Prize Contests (Article 7(19) of the Act on Counteracting Unfair Market Practices)

It is also an unfair and misleading market practice to inform that 'a contest or promotion with prizes is organised and subsequently fail to award the prizes or their respective equivalent as promised'. Although this provision refers literally only to contests and promotions with prizes, it should be assumed that it also covers with its scope the organisation of promotional lotteries.[807] A promotional lottery also involves a prize, but its outcome, unlike a competition, depends on chance and not, for example, on the knowledge or skills of the participants. In practice, however, doubts may arise as to whether we are dealing with a contest or a promotional lottery. The concept of promotion with prizes should be understood broadly. It includes all kinds of practices relating to the promotion of products or services involving the granting of various prizes in the form of products, money, vouchers, additional services, discounts, etc. Certainly, a promotion with prizes will also include a promotional lottery.

Prior to the entry into force of the Act on Counteracting Unfair Market Practices, attempts were made to regulate certain actions of entrepreneurs relating to promotional lotteries in the Act on Combatting Unfair Competition. Pursuant to Article 17b of this Act, which was repealed on the date of entry into force of the Act on Counteracting Unfair Market Practices, it is 'an act of unfair competition with respect to promotional lotteries to

---

[807] *M. Sieradzka*, Ustawa o przeciwdziałaniu nieuczciwym praktykom rynkowym, pp. 194–195.

formulate offers in such a way that the consumer, regardless of the outcome of the draw or his or her knowledge, is certain to win, provided she or he places an order for the goods or services covered by the promotion or pays some amount in advance to the offeror. The act referred to in paragraph 1 includes, in particular, offers made in the form of a document issued in the consumer's name that has the characteristics of an official document (paragraph 2)'. The introduction of this provision was intended to protect consumers against such practices.[808]

The reason for the inclusion of this type of practice in Annex I of Directive 2005/29/EC was to ensure that a consumer who, driven by the desire to win a prize, makes a certain market decision has a real chance (conditioned on fulfilling certain requirements) of receiving it. Indeed, unless misled about the possibility of obtaining a prize, the consumer would not (even potentially) make a particular decision. It is pointed out in the literature that such promotional measures linked to the expectation of receiving a prize significantly obscure the clarity of consumers' choices. The desire to obtain a prize may, in fact, be one of the decisive factors that induces the consumer to make certain decisions.[809] The entrepreneur's action in this respect should therefore be transparent and fair. If the entrepreneur decides to use this type of sales promotion measure, a contest, promotional lottery, or promotion should be organised, and the rules for awarding the prizes should be made available. The terms and conditions for awarding prizes should be clearly set out in the rules of the contest, promotional lottery, or promotion, and the promised prizes paid, while their equivalents should be given only in certain circumstances (e.g. force majeure).[810]

It is also emphasised that there is a similarity between this type of practice and an aggressive marketing practice described in Article 9(8) of the Act on Unfair Market Practices, which consists in 'creating the impression that the consumer has already obtained, will obtain unconditionally, or after performing a certain action, a prize or another comparable benefit, when in fact the prize or other comparable benefit does not exist or the obtaining

---

[808] See Government proposal to amend the Act on Combatting Unfair Competition of 11.4.2002 (Druk sejmowy IV kadencji No. 375 <http://orka.sejm.gov.pl/proc4.nsf/opisy/375.htm> accessed on 13 January 2019.

[809] See: *E. Łętowska*, Prawo umów konsumenckich, Warszawa 2002, pp. 534–538.

[810] *A. Michalak*, Przeciwdziałanie nieuczciwym praktykom rynkowym, p. 106.

of the prize or other comparable benefit is subject to the consumer paying a certain amount of money or incurring other costs'.

6. Describing the Product as 'gratis', 'free', or 'free of charge' (Article 7(20) of the Act on Counteracting Unfair Market Practices)

According to Article 7(20) of the Act on Counteracting Unfair Market Practices, it is an unfair market practice in all circumstances to present a product as 'gratis', 'free', or 'free of charge', or in a similar manner if the consumer has to pay any amount for it, except for the direct costs connected with the response to the market practice, collection, or delivery of the product.

The practice of adding various types of free bonuses (so-called 'freebies') is a popular form of sales promotion. It is emphasised in the literature that, as a general rule, the permitted rewarding of purchases with a gift or a free bonus is often subject to degeneration.[811] The main criterion for assessing this type of practice will be the question of payment associated with the product received. Thus, if the consumer has to pay even a small amount, it will not be a free, complimentary product. For example, a newspaper supplement for which the consumer has to pay an additional price, even if it is at a much better price than the same product offered at retail price, is not free. Likewise, it is unacceptable to present as a 'free supplement' a bidon added to an isotonic drink even if the combined product is only 1 euro more expensive than an isotonic drink alone. The view that may sometimes be found in the literature is that 'the Directive does not prescribe 'freebies' to be completely free 'freebies, because consumers expect certain cost attached to products marked as complimentary'[812] is erroneous. Such a liberal approach may cause traders to abuse this practice. When a trader presents a product as 'free of charge', the consumer must not incur any additional, even small, costs in connection with its purchase.

This does not exclude the possibility of imposing on the consumer additional chargeable costs directly related to responding to the practice or collecting or delivering the goods. According to the Commission' Guidance, the use of the phrase 'free of charge' or 'free' is only allowed if consumers

[811] *E. Łętowska*, Prawo umów konsumenckich, 1999, p. 432.

[812] *M. Namysłowska*, Czarna lista nieuczciwych praktyk handlowych, p. 456. The author refers to the position expressed in German literature.

actually receive the product without any additional charge.[813] However, there are situations where consumers will have to cover certain costs, but even then, those costs must be limited:

1. to the minimum and unavoidable costs associated with responding to a commercial practice (the official postage cost, the cost of a standard telephone call, or the simple cost of sending a text message);[814]
2. to the actual costs of transport or delivery;
3. to the costs associated with any travel to collect the subject of the offer;
4. to the non-recurring costs needed to purchase or install the equipment (e.g. access to free-to-air TV channels requires the appropriate equipment).

Traders must always inform consumers of such upfront costs. The costs of packaging, handling, or maintenance associated with the free product are no longer justified costs.

As indicated in the Guidance, problems may arise with 'combined offers' that involve more than one product. Here, certain principles have been proposed to be taken into account when assessing the legality of a particular commercial practice. Firstly, the addition of a free product must not result in a deterioration in the quality, a change in the composition, or an increase in the price of the product to which the free product is added. Secondly, the use of the term 'free' is not allowed in relation to one of the elements of a total package if the cost of that element is included in the price of the package. Thus, if the price of a package has increased, the standard of the package has decreased as a result of the addition of an element; the new element cannot be described as 'free'.

And yet, the term 'free of charge' may continue to be used in so-called conditional purchase promotions (such as 'buy one, get one free' offers), where consumers have to buy other products in order to receive a free product, if:

1. it is made clear to consumers that they have to pay all costs;

---

813 The Guidance (pl), point 4.4, p. 104, The Notice, point 3.4, p. 66.

814 The Notice, point 3.4, p. 66. Also in *M. Sieradzka*, Ustawa o przeciwdziałaniu nieuczciwym praktykom rynkowym, p. 200.

2. the quality or composition of the paid-for items has not been reduced; and
3. the price of the paid-for items has not been inflated to recover the cost of supplying the free item.[815]

It should be emphasised that in the case of such offers, the product described as free of charge must be separate from and additional to the paid products. When assessing the practice in question, in order for it to be considered acceptable, the trader would have to show that:

1. the free item is genuinely additional to the item(s) usually sold for that price, or the free item is genuinely separable from the paid-for item(s);
2. they only supply the 'free' item with the paid-for item(s) if the consumer complies with the terms of the promotion;
3. consumers are aware of the stand-alone price of the item(s) they are paying for and that that price remains the same with or without the free item.[816]

The comments made in the Guidance (and in the Notice) relating to online sector services are also interesting. These are situations where traders offer free services (products); however, obtaining them is conditional on providing personal data. It is argued in the Guidance document that describing such services or products as free of charge without informing consumers how their data will be used may, under certain circumstances, be considered a misleading practice[817] because the provision of data entails a specific benefit for the trader, and the service or product offered does not necessarily have to be free of charge.

An example of this type of practice is provided by the judgement of the Court of Competition and Consumer Protection of 30 May 2014.[818] In the con-

---

[815] See: The Guidance (pl), p. 105, The Notice, p. 67.

[816] See: *ibidem*, p. 106, The Notice, p. 67.

[817] See *ibidem*, p. 108. As an example, the Commission cites the Italian AGCM (*Autorità Garante della Concorrenza e del Mercato*) Decision of 2000 (Decision PI2671), according to which an Italian ISP was prohibited from disseminating claims in advertising about its free services, since the use of these services involved agreeing to accept onerous conditions.

[818] Judgement of the SOKiG of 30.05.2014, XVII AmA 95/12, Legalis.

text of the proceedings initiated by the President of the Office for Competition and Consumer Protection for collective infringement of consumers' interests, the court found that the entrepreneur's practice constituted an unfair market practice that was misleading. The practice consisted of 'including in SMS/MMS messages addressed to consumers information suggesting the possibility of free use of an interactive game dedicated to mobile phones (...) with the content': 'CONGRATULATIONS: you can get a game for FREE! (...) is waiting for you at m.(...). pl/(...)', when the only thing that is free is ordering the game application and using it in a certain mode, which constitutes an unfair market practice." The court found that the consumer was misled in relation to the price. In its reasoning, the Court stated that 'the average consumer's attention is focused on the word FREE! From the explanations (...) given to consumers, it appeared that the provision of the game was free, whereas the download of the application was already subject to a charge for the Internet connection, calculated according to the price list of the network operator (...). Even if the language of the advertisement is peculiar, the form of the message cannot exempt the provider from the obligation to provide fair information'. The court, referring to the content of Article 7(20), considered that the cost of the Internet connection was not a direct cost of reception, since it was paid to a third party and was incurred in order to play the game provided by the operator. In support of its position, the Regional Court referred to the CJEU ruling in Purely Creative.[819]

7. Creating a False Impression of an Award or Prize (Article 9(8) of the Act on Counteracting Unfair Market Practices)

Article 9(8) defines as an aggressive market practice in all circumstances a practice of creating an impression that the consumer has obtained a prize or will obtain it unconditionally or after performing a particular act or other comparable benefit when in fact the prize or another comparable benefit does not exist or the obtaining of the prize or other comparable benefit is subject to the consumer paying a certain amount of money or incurring other costs. In the literature, this type of practice receives a particularly negative assessment, and the examples quoted include a situation where

[819] Judgement of the ECJ of 18.10.2012, C-428/11, *Purely Creative Ltd and others v. Office of Fair Trading*, ECLI:EU:C:2012:651.

'the consumer is offered an attractive prize, allegedly already awarded to him, on condition that he buys some goods from a catalogue presented by the contracting party for a certain amount. The consumer believes that the main performance is the prize he has already obtained; while in fact, the intention is to induce the consumer to make a purchase (...). Despite to what he thinks, he has not yet won the prize, as was suggested to him when he was entering in a transaction, but merely has been given an opportunity to participate in a draw at a later time- if he makes a purchase and sends back the voucher'.[820] This practice, compared to other sales promotion practices, has been examined relatively frequently by the ordinary courts. The courts found that this type of practice was:

1. organising an audiotext lottery consisting of the formulation of the content of short text messages, with content suggesting the certainty of winning, addressed to consumers[821];
2. formulating the content of text messages addressed to consumers as part of an audiotext lottery in a way that suggests the certainty of winning[822];
3. sending text messages to consumers informing them that the documents to collect the car were ready and in their names and that in order to receive the car all they had to do was send a text message, while in reality, despite text messages sent, they never received the prize[823];

[820] *E. Łętowska*, Prawo umów konsumenckich, 1999, p. 432.

[821] Judgment of the SOKiK of 29.10.2013, XVII AmA 41/12, Legalis. The court found that it was also a practice that misled consumers by informing them that they had already won a prize. See also *M. Namysłowska*, Czarna lista nieuczciwych praktyk handlowych, pp.534–545.

[822] Decision of the Supreme Court of 10 December 2014, III SK 35/14, Legalis. The Supreme Court refused to accept the cassation appeal for examination, however, the reasons for the decision of the Court of Appeal in Warsaw were presented in the reasons.

[823] See judgement of the Court of Appeal in Warsaw of 10.4.2013, I ACa 1220/12, Legalis. The District Court found that the entrepreneur's action was an unfair market practice. Nonetheless, it held that the claimant-consumer had not, as a result of not being granted a car, suffered damage. The court reasoned that 'it cannot be said that the plaintiff suffered damage in the form of loss of the equivalent value of the car he had expected to win. There is no causal link between the damage so indicated and the unlawful action of the defendant company'.

4. informing consumers participating in demonstrations of the goods offered by the trader that they are taking part in medical research covered by the reimbursement and that they have the possibility of benefiting from a subsidy for the purchase of the products offered, when in fact the benefit of the reimbursement and the subsidy does not exist.[824]

This practice is also discussed in detail in the Guidance and the Notice.[825] The Commission highlighted that two situations could be considered under this practice. In the first, no prizes were provided at all, and in the second, the award of the prize was made conditional on the consumer taking an additional action to receive the prize or other benefit (e.g. calling a special premium rate number and purchasing an additional product or service).

The Commission referred to the ruling of the CJEU in case C-428/11 of 18.10.2012. (case *Purely Creative*).[826] The dispute concerned a practice that British traders were using. They disseminated advertisements that took a variety of forms. The common feature of those advertisements was their message, which implied that the consumer had won a prize of a certain value. The consumer could find out what prize he or she had received/won by contacting the trader in various ways (by calling a premium rate number, by a paid text message, or by sending a letter by mail). In 99% of cases, the value of the prize corresponded to the costs incurred by the consumer trying to obtain information about the prize, as well as delivery and insurance costs. The Court, when assessing this type of practice, stated that according to point 31 of sentence 2 of Annex 1 of Directive 2005/29/EC, the trader may

---

824 See: SOKiK judgement of 25.4.2017, XVII AmA 144/14, Legalis. It was apparent from the facts that the trader did not inform about the source of the reimbursement, indicating, however, that this benefit resulted from participation in the presentation. Consumers invited to the examinations were asked to bring with them an identity document and an insurance card proving that they had social security. Consumers were under the impression that the refund was due to the fact that they were covered by social security. The consultants informed consumers that refunds for participation in the survey were possible once a year and that the consumer would be charged PLN 470 for subsequent participation in the survey.

825 The Guidance (pl), pp. 113–115, The Notice, pp. 71–72.

826 The Guidance (pl), p. 115, The Notice, p. 72. Judgement of the ECJ of 18 October 2012, C-428/11, *Purely Creative Ltd and in. v. Office of Fair Trading*, p. 18.

not impose any additional costs on the consumer for winning the prize. According to the CJEU ruling, 'it is irrelevant that the cost imposed on the consumer, for example the cost of a postage stamp, is insignificant in relation to the value of the prize and that it does not generate any income for the trader. It is also irrelevant that the act of receiving the prize can be done in several ways suggested to the consumer by the trader, at least one of which is free of charge, if one or more of the ways suggested to the consumer requires the consumer to incur costs in order to obtain information about the nature of the prize or the possibilities of obtaining it'.

Undoubtedly, therefore, the trader is obliged to award prizes if, as a result of his practices, the consumer is entitled to assume that prizes will be awarded. Furthermore, the award of the prize must not be made conditional on the consumer incurring any costs, even the smallest ones. Thus, in the case of commercial practices where prizes are promised, the main objective is to ensure that the consumer is confident that a prize will be awarded if he performs a certain action and does not have to incur any additional costs as a result.

One has to agree with the position expressed in the literature that there is a strong similarity with the misleading practice described in Article 7(20) of the Act on Counteracting Unfair Market Practices.[827]

§ 5. Restriction of Bonus Sales in Other Laws

I. Preliminary Remarks

In addition to the provisions of the Act on Combatting Unfair Competition and the Act on Counteracting Unfair Market Practices, there are also regulations in other acts that affect the interpretation of the provisions on bonus sales. Specific provisions provide for a number of restrictions on the promotion of goods and services in the broad sense, including, above all, their advertising. This applies primarily to so-called sensitive[828] products, i.e. medicinal products, tobacco products, and alcoholic beverages.

---

827 *M. Sieradzka*, Ustawa o przeciwdziałaniu nieuczciwym praktykom rynkowym, p. 227.

828 See *E. Nowińska*, *M. du Vall*, Ustawa o zwalczaniu nieuczciwej konkurencji. Komentarz, kom. do art. 16, pp. 307–334. The authors analyse the problem of advertising contrary to the law. They consider alcohol, tobacco, as well as drugs and other medical devices

II. Medicinal products

The Act of 6 September 2001—the pharmaceutical law[829] regulates the issues concerning advertising the medicinal products (Article 1, clause 1, point 3).[830] The detailed regulations can be found in Chapter 4, Articles 52–64 of the Act[831]. The Act on pharmaceutical law defines advertising of a medicinal product as an 'activity consisting in informing or encouraging the use of a medicinal product with the aim of increasing: the number of prescriptions, the supply, sale or consumption of medicinal products'. Among the forms of such advertising is listed the 'provision of samples of medicinal products. In contrast to the solutions adopted in Article 17a of the Act on Combatting Unfair Competition, the provision of samples of this type of product is very limited, and the possibility of providing free samples requires the fulfilment of the conditions set out in Article 54 of the Act on Pharmaceutical Law.

Most importantly, advertising that involves the provision of free samples cannot be initiated and can only be addressed to persons authorised to issue prescriptions (doctors). And it is the doctor who must address the sales or medical representative in writing, requesting free samples. The person supplying the sample must keep a record of the samples supplied. No sample supplied may be larger than the smallest package of a medicinal product authorised for marketing on the territory of the Republic of Poland. The sample must be labelled 'free sample – not for sale' and must be accompanied by either the Summary of Product Characteristics of Medicinal Products or the Summary of Product Characteristics of Veterinary Medicinal Products. The legislator has also introduced a quantitative limitation, as the number of samples of the same medicinal product supplied to the same person may not exceed five packs per year. What is important, though, is that samples of medicinal products containing narcotic drugs or psychotropic substances are prohibited from this kind of advertising (Article 54(5)). Doctors who

---

to be sensitive products. See also: *E. Nowińska*, in *E. Nowińska*, *K. Szczepanowska-Kozłowska*, Ustawa o zwalczaniu, 2022, pp. 430–441, Nb. 9–15.

829 Dz.U. of 2024 item 686 as amended.

830 For more on advertising medicinal products see: *J. Adamczyk*, *M. Świerczyński*, in: *E. Traple* (ed.), Prawo reklamy i promocji, Warszawa 2007, pp. 61–102.

831 See: *K. Grzybczyk*, Reklama produktów leczniczych, in: *M. Kępiński*, *J. Kępiński*, *K. Klafkowska-Waśniowska*, *R. Sikorski* (eds), Rynek farmaceutyczny a prawo własności intelektualnej, Warszawa 2013, p. 117.

received free samples of medicinal products may give them to patients, and it is understood that such provision of free samples does not constitute advertising of a medicinal product.

III. Subsidised Medicines, Foodstuffs for Particular Nutritional Uses, and Medicinal Products

Even more restrictive than for medicinal products are the provisions of the Act of 12 May 2011 on subsidised medicines, foodstuffs for special nutritional purposes, and medical products.[832] Its Article 49 clause 3 prohibits: (1) an entrepreneur engaged in the manufacture or marketing of subsidised medicines, foodstuffs for special nutritional purposes, and medical products; and (2) a pharmacy operator, a pharmacy manager or a person dispensing subsidised medicines, foodstuffs for special nutritional purposes and medical products in connection with the realisation of prescriptions for subsidised medicines, foodstuffs for special nutritional purposes and medical devices to carry out conditional sales, or offer discounts, rebates, bonuses, packages and loyalty programmes, donations, prizes, trips, games of chance, bets, all forms of lending, combined transactions, all types of vouchers and coupons, or to grant other unspecified material or personal benefits to recipients and beneficiaries.

This list is merely exemplary. It should be assumed that, in principle, the Act prohibits the granting of all pecuniary and personal benefits; however, it does not define them anywhere. As follows from the explanatory memorandum to the draft act,[833] the purpose of introducing such restrictions was numerous 'pathological phenomena'. Such negative phenomena included 'medically unjustified increases in medicine subsidies or refinancing, purchasing of medicines for one *grosz* (one penny), rewarding patients for supplying a prescription for a subsidised medicine, a situation in which patients search in multiple pharmacies for a product with the lowest patient co-payment or a bonus, competition, reward (so-called "reimbursement tourism"),

---

[832] Dz.U. of 2024 item 930 as amended.

[833] Draft of the Act on subsidising pharmaceuticals, foodstuffs for special nutritional purposes and medicinal products proposed by the government on 18 October 2010, Explanatory memorandum, VI kadencji No 3491, <http://orka.sejm.gov.pl/Druki6ka.nsf/wgdruku/3491> (accessed on: 1.2.2025).

non-uniform wholesale margins applied to pharmacies, pseudo-gift schemes, pseudo-donations, and so on'.[834]

Initially, Article 49(3) used the wording that 'any form of inducement is prohibited'. However, this wording raised numerous questions of interpretation.[835] It was argued in the literature that the use of the phrase 'inducement' made traders fear that 'any action related in any way to subsidised products could be considered as an inducement'. In this way, each form of support to healthcare providers through various educational campaigns and training, as well as donations to hospitals, was prohibited. For this reason, at the beginning of 2012, entrepreneurs withdrew from various support programmes for fear that they would be qualified as a violation of Article 49(3)."[836] Subsequently the term 'any form of inducement' was changed into 'pecuniary and personal benefits'[837] which was, in the literature, considered to be a limitation of that prohibition.[838]

The scope of this prohibition is limited to relations between the entities that have been expressly mentioned in Article 49(3). These are entrepreneurs involved in the manufacture or marketing of such products or operators of a pharmacy, managers of a pharmacy, or persons dispensing such products on the one hand, and recipients or entitled persons on the other hand. However, there is no prohibition for such actions taking place between other parties, e.g. entrepreneurs (in a B2B relationship). It is thus understood that this provision does not introduce a general prohibition on the overall granting of benefits.[839]

---

834 *Ibidem*, p. 11.

835 See the announcements issued by the Ministry of Health on the issue of blood glucose meters or the donation of equipment purchased through the GOCC. Cited in: *M. Mądry*, in *R. Stankiewicz, M. Pieklak* (eds), Ustawa o refundacji leków, środków spożywczych specjalnego przeznaczenia żywieniowego oraz wyrobów medycznych. Komentarz, Warszawa 2014, Legalis, Comments to Art. 49, Nb 24.

836 See: *M. Mądry*, in: *R. Stankiewicz, M. Pieklak* (ed.), Ustawa o refundacji leków, Comments to Art. 49, Nb 22.

837 There was a change in the result of an amendment of 14 June 2012 (Dz.U. of 2012 item 742), which entered into force on 30 June 2012.

838 *M. Mądry*, in: *R. Stankiewicz, M. Pieklak* (eds), Ustawa o refundacji leków, kom. do art. 49, Nb 30.

839 Permissible forms of cooperation including marketing actions are listed, as examples, by *M. Mądry*, in: *R. Stankiewicz, M. Pieklak* (eds), Ustawa o refundacji leków, kom. do art. 49, Nb 30.

The sanction for failing to comply with the prohibition listed in Article 49(3), which may be offering pecuniary or personal benefit to the recipient or entitled persons, is a financial penalty. (Article 50 of the pharmaceutical law).

IV. Tobacco Products

Regulations in force in Member States relating to tobacco products, including their advertising and promotion, have been influenced by EU legislation.

Of particular relevance to tobacco advertising and promotion is Directive 2003/33/EC of the European Parliament and of the Council of 26 May 2003 on the approximation of the laws, regulations, and administrative provisions of the Member States relating to the advertising and sponsorship of tobacco products.[840] It follows from recital 3 of the preamble to that Directive that 'the approximation of the laws of the Member States is intended to protect public health by regulating the promotion of tobacco as an addictive product causing more than half a million deaths in the Community every year; thereby eliminating the early initiation of smoking among young people as a result of advertising and leading to addiction'. As highlighted in the literature, the conduct of tobacco promotion is not regulated by Directive 2003/33/EC, and it is therefore up to the discretion of Member States to introduce restrictions in this area.[841]

Under Polish law, the Directive was implemented in the Act of 9 November 1995 on health protection against the consequences of the use of tobacco and tobacco products (the Tobacco Act).[842] Pursuant to Article 8 of the Tobacco Act, the advertising and promotion of tobacco products, electronic cigarettes, spare containers or tobacco props, and their imitations is prohibited. Article 8 not only prohibits advertising and promotion of such products but also specifies the places and ways in which there is a prohibition on advertising and promotion of such products.[843] Furthermore, it is prohibited to use wrappers and packages that may suggest economic benefits in the form of

---

840 O.J. EU L 152 of 2003, pp. 16–19.

841 *Z. Okoń*, in: *E. Traple* (ed.), Prawo reklamy i promocji, p. 48.

842 Dz.U. of 2024 iktem 1162 as amended.

843 This includes: television, radio, cinema, healthcare providers, schools, and educational establishments, children's and youth press, sports and leisure facilities, and other public places, posters, including large-format posters, and IT services.

accompanying printed coupons or offers of products at a reduced price or free of charge, such as two-for-one or other similar offers (Article 8, clause 5).

Article 2, clause 23, of the Tobacco Act defines promotion of tobacco products, which may take the form of:

1. distributing tobacco products, electronic cigarettes, spare containers, or tobacco props to the public;
2. organising tastings of tobacco products, electronic cigarettes or spare containers;
3. organising premium sales of tobacco products, electronic cigarettes, spare containers or tobacco props, or competitions based on their purchase and other forms of public inducement to purchase or use them, irrespective of the form in which they are addressed;
4. offering tobacco products to consumers at a reduced price in relation to the price printed on the unit packet.

The solutions adopted in this way significantly restrict various forms of tobacco promotion. It is clear from them that any form of bonus sale is prohibited, although it is not defined in the Tobacco Act. In my view, this provision should be interpreted to mean that any form of sale that involves the granting of any bonus within the meaning of Article 17a of the Act on Combatting Unfair Competition is prohibited. At the same time, the exemption contained in Article 17a(2) of the same Act does not seem to apply in this regard in connection with Article 8(5) of the Tobacco Act. Thus, bonuses in the form of vouchers, gifts of small value, or the promise of winning a lottery or a competition will not be allowed. Given the nature of the product, it is not permissible to add a lighter, a box of matches, or even other small extras to a packet of cigarettes. Public promotion of such products should, in principle, be prohibited. At the same time, it seems possible to carry out promotional actions of a private nature (and not of a public nature) aimed at entrepreneurs involved in the production, distribution, and sale of this type of product.[844] Indeed, the forms of promotion indicated in the Tobacco Act refer to public forms of encouraging the purchase of tobacco products.

[844] *Z. Okoń*, in: *E. Traple* (ed.), Prawo reklamy i promocji, p. 48.

The judgement of the Supreme Administrative Court of 2001 provides some guidance.[845] The court held that the decision of the Minister of Finance to refuse permission to organise a promotional lottery aimed at promoting cigarettes was justified. The Minister found that the form of promotion was a lottery and that the entrepreneur intended to promote tobacco products in, inter alia, a periodical that should be classified as a youth press. The entrepreneur complained that the Minister, when issuing the decision, inaccurately explained the facts and, in particular, ignored the fact that the participation in the lottery was to be non-public (private correspondence) and unjustifiably classified the periodical in the category of youth press. The court dismissed the entrepreneur's complaint. The court justified its decision by arguing that the forms of prohibited advertising and promotion listed in the Tobacco Act are only exemplary. Furthermore, it held that 'all promotion and advertising is of a public nature since it is addressed to a large number of people who are intended to be induced to buy tobacco products. Advertising may be homogeneous and one-part, but it may also consist of two or more parts or phases. The fact that some of these phases involve direct contact with a larger number of people who are encouraged to buy the products does not change the assessment that each of the parts of the advertising and promotion interpreted is of a public nature'. Although Article 8 of the Tobacco Act[846] has been amended since then, the judgement still appears to be valid in principle, even though lotteries are not currently listed in Article 8.

V. Alcoholic Beverages

Extensive sales promotion regulations also apply to alcoholic beverages. The Act of 26 October 1982 on Upbringing in Sobriety and Counteracting Alcoholism (the Sobriety Act)[847] separates the promotion of alcoholic

---

[845] Judgement of the Supreme Administrative Court of 4 April 2001, II SA 1016/00, Legalis.

[846] At the time of the judgement, Article 8 read 'It shall be prohibited to advertise and promote tobacco products, tobacco props and products imitating tobacco products or props, and symbols associated with tobacco use, and in particular: 1) on television, radio, cinemas, health care facilities, schools and educational institutions, in the children's and youth press, on the premises of sports and recreational facilities and in other public places, 3) on posters, including large-format posters'.

[847] Dz.U. of 2023 item 2151 as amended.

beverages from their advertising,[848] additionally regulates the issue of sponsoring alcoholic beverages.[849] The list of forms of alcoholic beverages (art. 2^1 clause 2) includes the public tasting of alcoholic beverages, the distribution of props related to alcoholic beverages, and the organisation of premium sales of alcoholic beverages, as well as other forms of public encouragement to purchase alcoholic beverages.[850]

Despite the distinction between advertising and promotion, the regulations are largely the same. At the same time, it is argued in the literature that the regulations on the restrictions on advertising of alcoholic beverages are among the most extensive, which is the consequence of the differentiation of the rules on advertising, promotion, and sponsorship depending on the alcohol content of alcoholic beverages (beer and other spirits).[851] Pursuant to Article 13^1 of the Sobriety Act, advertising and promotion of alcoholic beverages is generally prohibited. An exception to this rule is the permissibility of advertising and promotion of beer. Its advertising and promotion is permitted; however, it must comply with the conditions set out in the Act (see Article $13,^1$ clause 1). The Act prohibits:

1. the promotion of products and services the name, trademark, graphic design, or packaging of which bears a resemblance to or is identical with the designation of an alcoholic beverage or any other symbol objectively referring to an alcoholic beverage (Article $13,^1$ clause 3);

---

848 The term 'advertising of alcoholic beverages' is defined in Article $2,^1$ clause 1, point 3, of the Sobriety Act. It is 'the public dissemination of the trademarks of alcoholic beverages or graphic symbols associated with them, as well as the names and graphic symbols of entrepreneurs producing alcoholic beverages, not different from the names and graphic symbols of alcoholic beverages, with the aim of popularising the trademarks of alcoholic beverages; information used for commercial purposes between entrepreneurs involved in the production, wholesale and trade of alcoholic beverages shall not be considered as advertising'.

849 The concept of 'sponsoring' has been defined in Article 2^1 clause 1 point 4 of the Sobriety Act.

850 Initially, 'competitions based on the purchase of alcoholic beverages' were excluded from the scope of promotion. See Dz.U. of 2001, No. 60, item 610, however, as a result of the amendment of 28 March 2003 (Dz.U. No. 80, item 719), this provision was deleted.

851 See: *Z. Okoń*, in: *E. Traple* (ed.), Prawo reklamy i promocji, p. 142.

2. entrepreneurs and other entities to use in their advertising image a name, trademark, graphic design, or packaging relating to an alcoholic beverage, its producer, or its distributor (Article 13,[1] clause 4).

What is worth stressing is that pursuant to Article 13,[1] clause 9, of the Sobriety Act, the prohibitions laid down in paragraphs 1–8 do not extend to the advertising and promotion of alcoholic beverages carried out on the premises of wholesale outlets, separate stands or outlets exclusively selling alcoholic beverages, and on the premises of outlets selling alcoholic beverages for consumption at the point of sale. This provision therefore allows for non-public advertising and promotion. At the same time, the Supreme Administrative Court emphasised that the legislator deliberately used the word 'inside', the use of which 'suggests a certain spatial limitation, and when interpreting it in connection with the subsequent premises for the admissibility of the place of advertising and promotion, one should also take into account the visual limitations that come to mind. Article 13,[1] clause 9, of the Act, contains references to allowing advertising and promotion inside wholesalers' premises, which are, after all, associated with wholesale trade, which is in principle professional, and, as far as retail/consumer trade is concerned, only inside separate stands or outlets selling exclusively alcoholic beverages'.[852] Thus, it would be permissible to conduct a non-public promotion, i.e. one that would not be open to the general public but only to invited entrepreneurs or individually identified consumers. Promotion at the point of sale would also be allowed, but only at points specified in the law. No promotion of alcoholic beverages, other than beer, will be allowed in grocery shops outside of dedicated stands. Thus, it is argued in the literature that 'there is no impediment to carrying out promotional actions in the places listed in Article 13[1] clause 9 of the Sobriety Act, the continuation of which is carried out through individual communication. This may consist, for example, in the

[852] See judgement of the Supreme Administrative Court of 13. July 2017, II GSK 982/17, Legalis. The judgement concerned the revocation of a concession to sell alcoholic beverages, due to a violation of the provisions of the Sobriety Act through the presentation in a shop's window of high-alcoholic beverages with trademarks visible from the outside of the shop.

distribution of coupons entitling the holder to participate in a competition or promotional lottery'.[853]

Neither in the Act of 26 October 1982 on Upbringing in Sobriety and Counteracting Alcoholism (the Alcohol Act) nor in other acts, including the Act of 9 November 1995 on Protection of Health against the Consequences of the Consumption of Tobacco and Tobacco Products (the Tobacco Act), is there a definition of premium sales. It seems that a premium sale should be understood in the manner adopted in Article 17a of the Act on Combatting Unfair Competition. It is relatively common for alcoholic beverages to be promoted on the market by offering them with various types of premiums, most often with glasses to go with a bottle of whisky, a glass to go with vodka, or a distinctive drink used to make drinks with an alcoholic beverage (apple juice to go with Żubrówka, Pepsi to go with whisky, etc.). In principle, if such bonuses are goods of little value, they may be permitted under Article 17a(2) of the Act of Combatting Unfair Competition. Lotteries or contests are also permitted. Indeed, the Sobriety Act does not provide for such restrictions as, for example, those contained in Article 8(5) of the Tobacco Act (see point IV above).

§ 6. Conclusions

Bonus selling is a form of sales contract aimed at promoting goods or services. By adding a free bonus (in the form of various goods or services), the trader arouses the interest of consumers in his goods or services and induces them to make a purchase or use the services. Through this form of sales promotion, the trader can attract new customers or increase the value of the purchases they make.[854] Market observations show that this form of promotion is frequently used in consumer trade and is very popular.

In Poland, since 2002, there has been a (relatively liberal) ban on bonus sales (Article 17a of the Act on Combatting Unfair Competition) in force. The purpose of introducing this ban was to protect small and medium-sized entrepreneurs who could not compete with economically stronger entrepreneurs offering free bonuses. It was the intention of the

---

853 See: *Z. Okoń*, in: *E. Traple* (ed.), Prawo reklamy i promocji, p. 168.
854 *M. Świerczyński*, in: *E. Traple* (ed.), Prawo reklamy i promocji, p. 496.

Polish legislator that the adopted ban would apply to B2B relationships. The protection of consumers' interests was not the purpose of the ban imposed and is only an indirect effect of it. Despite this initial assumption, it has been argued in the literature that bonus sales not only pose risks for small and medium-sized entrepreneurs but are also a threat to the consumer.

The prohibition of bonus sales in Article 17a raises questions of interpretation caused by the fact that the concepts such as the differentiation of goods and services, a premium, or a small value, which are of significant importance for the proper application of the ban, have not been defined. In my view, these concepts should be, if only possible, interpreted liberally so that bonus sales are not unduly restricted. Indeed, the sale of goods and services with the addition of a free bonus constitutes an important means of shaping competition. If a liberal interpretation is adopted, then the award of bonuses in the form of goods or services that are functionally related and not merely identical to the main object of the contract may be permitted. What is more, such bonuses do not have to be completely devoid of value. As explained above, various criteria must be taken into account when interpreting the circumstance of low value. However, I believe that even if a liberal approach to the prohibition of bonus sales is adopted, a free bonus must not entail any additional, even minor, costs on the part of the consumer. Therefore, the common practice of slightly increasing the price of a product when a product free of charge is added cannot be accepted. Such a practice should be qualified not only as contrary to Article 17a of the Act of Combatting Unfair Competition but also as an unfair, misleading market practice (Article 7(20) or Article 9(8) Counteracting Unfair Market Practices).

When interpreting this prohibition, reference must also be made to the provisions of other laws. This applies in particular to sensitive goods, the bonus sales of which may be even more restricted than provided for in Article 17a. Under Polish law, the concept of a 'bonus sale' should be distinguished from the concept of a combined sale and the concept of a 'tied offer'. I agree with the position that in the case of a bundle sale, the subject of the agreement and the trader's performance are two (or more) different goods or a good and a service, and for one price paid the buyer receives two different performances. It is, however, irrelevant how the trader has calculated the sale price, whether as the sum of two (or more) prices or otherwise.[855] There is no need to indicate the prices of the individual elements of the offer. In a bonus sale, on the other hand, the permitted bonus does not constitute the essence of the sales contract but is an integral part of it. A bonus is an incidental, consequential performance following the purchase of goods or services. The granting of a bonus has an economic justification, i.e. the promotion of goods or services. I therefore consider that, in Polish law, combined sales are not subject to the prohibition in Article 17a of the Act of Combatting Unfair Competition, as they do not fall within its scope.

However, despite the need to distinguish bonus sales from combined sales, in many situations it may be difficult to strictly separate them from each other. The practice of adding a free-of-charge mug to a package of coffee (functionally related goods) could be regarded as a permitted bonus sale, assuming, however, that the value of the mug itself in relation to the value of the coffee offered is small. It would also be acceptable to add a sample of tea or biscuits to a pack of coffee. The bonus in either situation must be free of charge. Adding a mug to a packet of coffee for which the consumer would have to pay extra would already constitute tying.

Particular attention should be paid to offers in which one of the products is not offered free of charge but for a symbolic, very small amount (e.g. 1 grosz or 1 zloty). Such action by entrepreneurs would allow them to circumvent the prohibition in Article 17a. In my opinion, under the Act on Combatting Unfair Competition, such offers, although beneficial to consumers, should be treated as a form of bonus sales. They would therefore be subject to the restrictions arising from Article 17a in question. On the other hand, the prevalence of such practices calls into question the necessity to restrict them. However, it should be borne in mind that the purpose of the prohibition in Article 17a was to protect small and medium-sized entrepreneurs. If we look at this restriction from this perspective, and not from the perspective of consumer benefit, then the ban on this type of promotion is justified. Awarding products for a symbolic amount would have the same effect as awarding them free of charge. Regrettably, despite the 22 years of Article 17a of the Act of Combatting Unfair Competition, there are no rulings

---

855 See: *J. Szwaja*, *A. Kubiak-Cyrul*, in: *J. Szwaja*, *J. Kępiński* (eds), Ustawa o zwalczaniu nieuczciwej konkurencji, 2016, p. 663, Nb 30.

addressing this regulation that would be helpful in defining precise criteria for the application of this prohibition.

The distinction between the concept of a bonus sale and the concept of a combined offer is also important in relation to the case law of the CJEU, which has examined the compatibility of national legislation on combined offers with Directive 2005/29/EC. It follows from the rulings of the CJEU that it regards as a combined offer an offer by which a trader makes an offer to a consumer to purchase a good or to provide a service if its purchase, or acceptance of which, is linked to the consumer receiving an additional (free of charge or for a payment[856]) good or service in one total price. The added goods or services do not have to be functionally related to the good offered or service provided,[857] but they may be received subject to the purchase of the goods offered or acceptance of the service provided. The price of the individual elements of a combined offer need not, in principle, be indicated.[858] Their direct purpose is to promote and increase sales.[859]

In a similar manner to that of the CJEU, a 'combined offer' is defined in German literature on the law against unfair competition. It is an offer in which the same, similar, or different goods or services are offered at a single price. Neither is it necessary to distinguish the price of the individual goods or services, and the decisive factor for tying is that the goods or services are only available for purchase in one combined price offer. Under German law, such offers are, in principle, admissible and are assessed from the point of view of the principles of fair competition. The decisive factor in such

---

[856] Generally, it is the free receipt of goods or services; however, it follows from the CJEU ruling that the second service does not have to be free of charge (CJEU ruling of 11. March 2010, C-522/08, *Telekomunikacja Polska SA w Warszawie v. Prezes Urzędu Komunikacji Elektronicznej*, ECLI:EU:C:2010:135).

[857] There is no functional link between, for example, a discount on underwear upon the purchase of a periodical, or participation in a competition in connection with the purchase of goods. In contrast, there will be a link between the purchase of a car and the service of its insurance.

[858] See: point 51 of the reasons for the judgement of the CJEU of 7 September 2016, C-310/15, *Vincent Deroo-Blanquart v. Sony Europe Limited, the legal successor of Sony France SA*, ECLI:EU:C:2016:633.

[859] See: point 28 of the reasons for the judgement of the CJEU of 7 September, C-310/15, *Vincent Deroo-Blanquart v. Sony Europe Limited, the legal successor of Sony France SA*, ECLI:EU:C:2016:633.

an assessment is whether the offer may have caused the rationality of the decision-making of a prudent, average consumer to become of secondary importance, or whether his freedom of decision-making has been severely restricted by harassment or unacceptable influence. However, such cases should be considered exceptional and narrowly limited. As stressed by the BGH in the *Gesamtpreisangebot* judgement, which is, so to speak, the starting point for a liberal approach to the interpretation of combined offers, the combination of different goods or services by a trader in a single offer is an expression of freedom of competition, and possible restrictions on combined offers could only be taken to prevent unfair competition or in situations of abuse of market forces.[860]

The institution of bonus sales in question could, under German law, be classified as one of the forms of sales promotion, referred to in German law as advertising with value (*Wertreklame*). Thus, the opinion that the concept of a 'bonus sale' in the Act on Combatting Unfair Competition is different from the concept of a 'combined offer' adopted in CJEU case law and German law is justified. The concept of a 'combined offer' is an overriding concept in relation to the concept of a 'bonus sale' and covers not only the cases described in Article 17a of the Act on Combatting Unfair Competition but also other forms of sales promotion in which several goods and services are combined in a single price offer.

In my view, combined offers are in principle permitted under Polish law, and no general prohibition of combined offers may be reconstructed from Article 17a of this Act. On the other hand, distinguishing whether an addition to the object of the sales contract is an element of a combined offer or whether it constitutes a bonus may, in certain cases, pose difficulties. The assessment of such a situation will depend on all the factual circumstances.

---

[860] See the judgement in BGH of 27 February 2003, I ZR 253/00, *Gesamtpreisangebot*, GRUR 2003, p. 538.

Chapter V

The Impact of the CJEU's Case Law on the Interpretation of the Prohibition on Bonus Sales under Polish Law

§ 1. The Obligation to Interpret National Laws in Conformity with EU Law

The adoption of Directive 2005/29/EC on Unfair Commercial Practices imposed a number of obligations on Member States. The main one was to transpose the Directive into respective national legal systems. As a general rule, Member States are allowed to choose the form and means of the implementation of the Directive, but they are nevertheless bound by the result to be achieved.[861] It must be borne in mind that Directive 2005/29/EC is a 'maximum' Directive. This means that Member States could not adopt any stricter provisions than those laid down in it, even if they aimed to increase the level of consumer protection.[862] The scope of Directive 2005/29/EC is

[861] Article 288 TFUE. See: *F. Henning-Bodewig*, Der Schutzzweck, p. 238.

[862] However, see: Article 3(5) of Directive 2005/29/EC, which allowed regulations more restrictive or prescriptive than those in the Directive to remain in place, but only for 6 years starting on as of 12 June 2007. This means that it is currently not possible to adopt regulations in national legislation that are more restrictive than those in the Directive.

also limited to unfair B2C commercial practices of traders applied before, during, and after a commercial transaction and does not directly regulate the relations between traders operating in the market. Thus, individual legislations in Member States may differ with respect to the level of regulation of trader-to-trader relations and may extend to also cover the relations between traders and consumers. Another consequence of the implementation of the Directive is the obligation to interpret the national provisions falling within the scope of the Directive through the prism of the solutions adopted in it.[863]

Thus, the provision of Article 17a of the Act on Combatting Unfair Competition regarding bonus sales should be assessed through the prism of the solutions adopted in Directive 2005/29/EC. When interpreting the provisions of the Directive, it is also necessary to take into account the extensive case law of the Court of Justice of the European Union, which should also be taken into account when interpreting national provisions.[864] The case law of the CJEU related to bonus sales may be divided into rulings issued before and after the enactment of Directive 2005/29/EC. This is because after the adoption of the Directive, the line of judicial reasoning changed dramatically. The rulings are presented chronologically within the most important issues examined by the CJEU.

---

[863] This follows from the so-called doctrine of indirect effect. According to this doctrine, provisions of European Union law, even if not directly effective, must be taken into account by national courts when interpreting national law. This doctrine applies primarily to directives that cannot directly impose obligations on individuals. See: *T.C. Hartley*, The Foundations of European Community Law, New York 2003, pp. 219–220.

[864] The rulings have been summarised by the Commission in its Guidance on the implementation/application of Directive 2005/29 on unfair commercial practices of 25.5.2016, SWD 2016, 163 final (The Guidance (pl)) and then in the Commission Notice—Guidance on the interpretation and application of Directive 2005/29/EC of the European Parliament and of the Council concerning unfair business-to-consumer commercial practices in the internal market, of 29.12.2021, 2021/C 526/01, OJ C 526, 29.12.2021, p. 1–129 (The Notice)

§ 2. The Case Law of the Court of Justice of the European Union

I. CJEU Case Law on Bonus Sales Prior to the Enactment of Directive 2005/29/EC

In justifying the introduction of Article 17a to the Act on Combatting Unfair Competition, the Polish legislator referred[865] to the CJEU's ruling of 15 December 1982, C-286/81, regarding the Dutch company *Oosthoek Uitgeversmaatschappij BV* (*Oosthoek*)[866] and the ruling of 26 June 2007, C-368/95, regarding the Austrian case *Vereinigte Familiapress Zeitungsverlag v. Henrich Bauer Verlag* (*Familiapress*).[867] Both highlight the controversial nature of the regulations on bonus sales and justify the subsequent ban on bonus sales introduced into Polish law against unfair competition.

The first case concerned a preliminary question relating to the interpretation of Articles 30, 34, and 36 of the Treaty establishing the European Economic Community (EEC Treaty)[868] related to the restrictions under Dutch law on offering gifts in bonus sales. Indeed, there was a general rule in Dutch law that prohibited sales promotion involving added gifts. However, there were some exceptions to this rule. It was permitted to include gifts if their use was linked to the product sold or service offered. Such gifts had to be

---

[865] Explanatory memorandum, Druk sejmowy IV kadencji No 375 and contained in it 'Opinia o zgodności projektu ustawy o zmianie ustawy o zwalczaniu nieuczciwej konkurencji' of 8.4.2002 pp. 16–19, <http://orka.sejm.gov.pl/proc4.nsf/opisy/375.htm> (accessed on: 1.2.2025).

[866] Judgement of the CJEU of 15.12.1982, 61981J0286, ECR 1982, p. 4575, <http://eur-lex.europa.eu/legal-content/EN/TXT/?uri=CELEX:61981CJ0286> (accessed on: 1.2.2025).

[867] Judgement of the CJEU of 26.6.1997, *Vereinigte Familiapress Zeitungsverlags- und vertriebs GmbH v. Heinrich Bauer Verlag* together with the opinion prepered by Advocate General Tesauro, ECLI:EU:C:1997:325, <http://curia.europa.eu/juris/liste.jsf?language=en&-jur=C,T,F&num=368/95&td=ALL> (accessed on: 13.1.2019).

[868] Treaty of 25 March 1957 establishing *the European Economic Community*), CELEX 11957E/TXT, Article 30 Quantitative restrictions on importation and all measures with equivalent effect shall, without prejudice to the following provisions, hereby be prohibited between Member States, Article 34 1. Quantitative restrictions on exportation and any measures with equivalent effect shall hereby be prohibited as between Member States. 2. Member States shall abolish, not later than at the end of the first stage, all quantitative restrictions on exportation and any measures with equivalent effect in existence at the date of the entry into force of this Treaty.

clearly marked in a permanent (non-abrasive) manner that they were a gift, and their value could not exceed 4% of the sale price of the product.

Under this legal situation, Oosthoek sold encyclopaedias written in the Dutch language in territories where Flemish is spoken (the Netherlands, parts of Belgium, and a small part of France). Some of the encyclopaedias on offer were folded and printed in the Netherlands, while others were printed in Belgium.[869] In order to promote the sale of the encyclopaedias, the company advertised that those who subscribed to the encyclopaedias would receive a free gift in the form of a dictionary, atlas, or small encyclopaedia, depending on the value of the subscription. This system of promoting the sale of the product by Oosthoek was found to be contrary to Dutch law (under Article 2 of the Wet Beperking Cadeaustelsel 1977), and the Public Prosecutor initiated proceedings against Oosthoek.

In the national proceedings, the national court of second instance (following an appeal by Oosthoek) referred a question to the European Court of Justice for a preliminary ruling on the compatibility of Dutch law with Community law, in particular with regard to the abolition of quantitative restrictions between Member States under Articles 30 and 34 of the EC Treaty.

In reply to the question referred, the Court of Justice held that Articles 30 and 34 of the Treaty did not preclude such prohibitions as those provided for by the Netherlands legislation.[870] The Court noted that while the regulations under consideration might have had an impact on the number of imported products, certain restrictions, e.g. prohibiting the addition of free gifts, could be justified from the point of view of consumer protection and fair trade. The Court considered the examined prohibition in the Dutch law to be such a justified solution. The Court emphasised that the addition of free gifts could mislead the consumer as to the actual price of the product purchased and distort competition.[871] In this case, the national provisions implementing this prohibition were found to be compatible with Community law.

The second of the judgements concerned the assessment of the compatibility with Article 30 of the Treaty establishing the European Community

---

[869] It must be added that there were also some restrictions under Belgian law. See point 2 of the reasons stated in *Oosthoek*, p. 4580.

[870] See *ibidem*, points 1–21, pp. 4584–4590.

[871] See *ibidem*, points 15–18, pp. 4587–4588.

of the provisions of Austrian law prohibiting offering anyone free gifts in connection with the sale of products or the provision of services.[872] The facts of the case were as follows. The publishing house Heinrich Bauer offered its readers, primarily German but also Austrian citizens, a weekly magazine called 'Laura', which contained crossword puzzles. Readers who sent the correct solution to the crossword puzzle participated in a game of chance for a cash prize. According to Familiapress, the action of the Bauer publishing house was contrary to Austrian legislation (under Article 9a (1)(1) of the Gesetz über unlauteren Wettbewerb 1992). Article 9a (1)(1) of the Austrian UWG[873] which contained a ban on offering free gifts in conjunction with the sale of goods or services. Initially, there was an exception to this rule in Article 9a (2)(8) of the Austrian UWG, which excluded this prohibition for small prize competitions and games of chance. In the meantime, that provision was repealed.

Thus, at the time, the dispute arose, under Austrian law, magazine publishers could not offer readers who were purchasers of the magazine the opportunity of participating in games of chance. German law, on the other hand, did not provide for such restrictions. In this state of affairs, the Austrian court referred the question to the Court for a preliminary ruling in order to clarify whether Austrian legislation complied with Article 30 of the Treaty establishing the European Community concerning the prohibition of quantitative restrictions and measures having similar effects.

The Court ruled that Article 30 of the Treaty did not, in principle, preclude national legislation that would otherwise have prohibited the distribution on the territory of that country by an operator from another country of a magazine containing puzzles, crosswords, and competitions with a chance to win a prize, even if such puzzles, crosswords and competitions are permitted under the law of the State in which the magazine is published. The Court emphasised that national courts would have to decide whether the ban was proportionate to maintain the diversity of the press and whether there was

---

872 *Treaty Establishing the European Community, Consolidated version 2002*, OJ EU C 324, of 2002, pp. 33–184, OJ EU C 340, 1997, p. 173, CELEX 12002E/TXT. Chapter 2 (Articles 28–38) of this Treaty dealt with the prohibition of quantitative restrictions between member states.

873 The Austrian Anti-Unfair Competition Act 1984 (BGBl. I, 448/1984), as amended by the BGBI. I, 136/2001.

no possibility of introducing less restrictive measures.[874] The national courts will also have to assess whether a magazine offering the opportunity to win a prize is in a competitive relationship with those magazines that do not have the capacity to offer such prizes. In addition, national courts must determine whether the chance to win a prize may constitute an incentive that is likely to alter demand.[875] The Court also added that the prohibition cannot constitute an obstacle to the advertising of a magazine containing competitions with prizes even if readers from the country where the prohibition applies do not have the opportunity to win the prize.

Taking into account the above-cited rulings of the Court, the Polish legislator had grounds to introduce in 2002, based on the position of the CJEU, a ban on bonus sales in the wording adopted as in Article 17a of the Act on Combatting Unfair Competition. In the opinion of the Bureau of Sejm Analyses, the submitted proposal of the ban on bonus sales was a very liberal one, as it allowed, for example, the sale of two identical goods at the price of one.[876]

It is noteworthy that the solutions then existing in the laws of the EU Member States relating to bonus sales were not uniform.

Polish courts have had no chance or case to analyse the interpretation of this ban since the enactment of Article 17a in 2002. However, the compatibility of the introduced ban with EU law should be assessed through the prism of CJEU rulings issued after the implementation of Directive 2005/29/EC.

II. CJEU Case Law on Combined Sales and Bonus Sales after the Implementation of Directive 2005/29/EC

The above-mentioned line of CJEU rulings in the Oosthoek and Familiapress cases concerning national regulations prohibiting bonus sales changed after the entry into force of Directive 2005/29/EC. Indeed, the Court prohibited in principle the introduction of unconditional restrictions on combined sales

---

874 See points 25–27 of the reasons for judgment in *Familiapress*, p. 3717.

875 See *ibidem*, point 28, p. 3717.

876 See *Z. Monkiewicz* (Bureau of Seym Analyses), Opinia prawna w sprawie rządowego projektu ustawy o zmianie ustawy o zwalczaniu nieuczciwej konkurencji (Druk sejmowy No 375), p. 3, <http://orka.sejm.gov.pl/proc4.nsf/opisy/375.htm> (accessed on: 13.1.2019).

in national regulations. It would thus appear that, although these rulings concerned combined sales and not strictly bonus sales (cf. Chapter IV, § 4), Article 17a of the Unfair Competition Act should also be interpreted in their light. The first case, C-261/07 and C-299/07 of 23 April 2009 (*Total*),[877] concerned two joined cases, *VTB-VAB NV v. Total Belgium NV* and *Galatea BVBA v. Sanoma Magazines Belgium NV.*

In the first of the disputes, Total, which mainly distributes fuel at petrol stations, offered Total Club card owners free roadside assistance for 3 weeks every time they filled up a car with at least 25 litres or a moped with at least 10 litres. In this state of affairs, VTB-VAB, a roadside assistance service provider, filed for an injunction to stop such a commercial practice, which it believed constituted a combined offer, which was prohibited under Article 54 of the Belgian law 1 on commercial practices and consumer information and protection.[878]

In the other dispute, the Belgian company Galatea, which operates a lingerie shop in Belgium, alleged that Sanoma, a publisher of numerous magazines, had breached the prohibition of Article 54 by attaching a supplement to the magazine, which entitled customers to a discount of between 15% and 25% of the value of the underwear sold in certain shops located in the Flemish region, while combined sales were prohibited in Belgium.

In both disputes, the Belgian courts referred to the CJEU for an interpretation of the compatibility of Article 54 of Belgian law with Directive 2005/29/EC.[879]

The CJEU held that an interpretation of the Directive 'prevents the adoption of national provisions ... which, subject to certain exceptions, and without taking account of the specific circumstances of the individual case, prohibit any combined offer (Kopplungsangebote) made by a vendor to a consumer'. The Court then explained that combined sales were a commercial practice within the meaning of Article 2(d) of Directive 2005/29/EC and that the

---

877 Judgement of the CJEU of 23.4.2009, C-261/07, *VTB-VAB NV v. Total Belgium NV* and C-299/07, *Galatea BVBA v. Sanoma Magazines Belgium NV*, ECLI:EU:C:2009:244. The ruling was preceded by the Opinion of Advocate General Trstenjak of 21.10.2008, ECLI:EU:C:2008:581. See also *M. Sieradzka:* Oferta wiązana jako rodzaj praktyki handlowej, p. 52–57.

878 See point 14 of the reasons for the judgement in *Total*.

879 See points 22 and 26 of the reasons for the judgement in *Total*.

Directive exhaustively listed prohibited commercial practices. Thus, the provision of Belgian law had to be considered as contrary to the Directive, as it established a ban on general and preventive combined offers, regardless of any verification of their unfairness under the criteria set out in Articles 5–9 of Directive 2005/29/EC.[880] The introduction of certain derogations, exceptions to the general prohibition, did not give grounds to consider that Article 54 of the Belgian law was compatible with Directive 2005/29/EC.[881]

The next CJEU ruling in C-304/08 of 14 January 2010 (*Plus*)[882] involved an assessment of the activity of a German company, Plus Warenhandelsgesellschaft mbH (Plus), by *Zentrale zur Bekämpfung unlauteren Wettbewerbs eV*[883] (*Zentrale*). Plus, they ran an advertising campaign entitled 'Your chance of a million'. Customers of Plus shops collected points and, once they had reached a sufficient number, could enter a prize draw free of charge. Zentrale considered this practice to be unfair within the meaning of Section 3 in conjunction with Section 4(6) UWG[884] due to the fact that it made consumers' participation in the lottery conditional on the purchase of goods and sought an injunction requiring Plus to cease that practice. The national courts of first and second instance found that Plus' actions were incompatible with the UWG. Following a review, the case went to the BGH, which referred to the

---

880 See *ibidem*, point 62.

881 See *ibidem*, points 64 and 65.

882 Judgement of the CJEU of 14.1.2010, C-304/08, *Zentrale zur Bekämpfung unlauteren Wettbewerbs eV v. Plus Warenhandelsgesellschaft mbH.*, ECLI:EU:C:2010:12The ruling was preceded by an opinion of Advocate General *Verica Trstenjak* presented on 3.9.2009, ECLI:EU:C:2009:511. See also *H. Köhler*, Kopplungsangebote neu bewertet. Zugleich Besprechung der 'Plus Warenhandelsgesellschaft' – Entscheidung des EuGH, GRUR 2010, pp. 177–183.

883 *Zentrale zur Bekämpfung unlauteren Wettbewerbs eV* is a union that controls implementation of provisions n fair competition. For more on the union see: <https://www.wettbewerbszentrale.de/> (accessed on: 13.1.2019).

884 § Section 3 UWG states that: 'Acts which constitute unfair competition and which are likely to distort competition in more than a negligible way to the detriment of competitors, consumers or other market participants shall be unlawful'. In turn, § 4(6) UWG states: 'An unfair act within the meaning of § 3 is committed by anyone who: point 6. makes the participation of consumers in a prize competition or lottery conditional on the purchase of a good or service, unless the competition or lottery is immanently linked to the good or service'.

CJEU with a question about the compatibility of the UWG provisions at issue with Directive 2005/29/EC.

The CJEU held that Directive 2005/29/EC 'must be interpreted as precluding national legislation prohibiting, in principle, commercial practices which make the participation of consumers in a prize competition or lottery conditional on the purchase of goods or services, regardless of the specific circumstances of the case in question'. As in the earlier judgement in Total's case, the Court held that Directive 2005/29/EC defined the concept of commercial practice in a broad manner and the promotional campaign of Plus was, within the meaning of that Directive, a commercial practice.[885] The Court did not find merit in the arguments put forward by the Czech and Austrian governments that the main purpose of the provisions of the German UWG, unlike those of Directive 2005/29/EC, was not to protect consumers but to protect competitors (traders) against unfair commercial practices adopted by certain entities (other traders). Thus, their national provisions analysed by the CJEU did not fall within the scope of Directive 2005/29/EC. The Court noted that Directive 2005/29/EC had a wide scope and covered 'all commercial practices having a direct relationship with the promotion, sale or supply of a product to consumers'. Excluded from its scope was only 'national legislation on unfair commercial practices harming "solely" the economic interests of competitors or relating to transactions between traders'.[886] Further in its reasoning, the Court repeated the arguments presented in the Total judgement.

Another CJEU ruling in case C-522/08 of 11 November 2010 referred to a dispute between Telekomunikacja Polska SA and the President of the Office of Electronic Communications (TP).[887] TP SA made the conclusion of an agreement for the provision of Internet access services with an end-user conditional on the conclusion of an additional telephone service agreement by the end-user. The President of the Office of Electronic Communications issued a decision prohibiting such a practice, arguing that TP's action is incompatible

885 See points 36–37 of the reasons for judgement in *Plus*.

886 See point 39 of the reasons for judgement in *Plus*.

887 Judgement of the CJEU of 11 March 2010, C-522/08, *Telekomunikacja Polska SA w Warszawie v. Prezes Urzędu Komunikacji Elektronicznej*, ECLI:EU:C:2010:135. See also *M. Sieradzka*, Glosa do wyroku TS of 11.3.2010, C-522/08, LEX/el. 2010, as well as *M. Namysłowska*, Glosa do wyroku TS z 11.3.2010, C-522 /08, LEX/el. 2010.

with Article 57 (1) (1) of the Telecommunications Act.[888] TP challenged the decision at the Supreme Administrative Court, which asked the CJEU whether Community law allowed Member States to prohibit all companies providing telecommunications services from combining or tying in a service agreement with the purchase of another service ('combined sale' or 'tied-in sale'). As a matter of fact, the preliminary question did not concern the interpretation of the provisions of the Act on Combatting Unfair Competition but the compatibility of the Telecommunications Act with Directives 2002/21/EC and 2002/22/EC[889] governing telecommunication services. However, in its reasoning, the Court also referred to Directive 2005/29/EC. Thus, this ruling is relevant for the consideration of the prohibition of combined offers.

First, the Court held that Directive 2002/21/EC and Directive 2002/22/EC did not preclude national legislation that prohibits making the conclusion of a service contract subject to the conclusion of a contract for the provision of other services by the end-user. Secondly, however, the Court (and this is the most relevant for our considerations here) held that Directive 2005/29/EC precluded national legislation that, apart from certain exceptions and without taking account of the specific circumstances of the case in question, prohibits any combined offer made by a vendor to a consumer. In its reasoning for the judgement, the Court referred to the ruling in the Total case and emphasised that the interpretation adopted in it concerned provisions designed to protect consumers. The Court considered that Article 57(1)(1) of the Telecommunications Act was also such a provision. Indeed, the aim of this provision was to strengthen the protection of consumers in their relations with operators of telecommunications services.[890]

---

888 The basis for the ban was Article 57(1)(1) of the Telecommunications Act (Dz.U. of 2024, item 34, as amended). The Act is no longer in force.

889 The question referred for a preliminary ruling concerned the interpretation of Directive 2002/21/EC of the European Parliament and of the Council of 7 March 2002 on a common regulatory framework for electronic communications networks and services (Framework Directive) (OJ 2002 L 108, p. 33, as amended) and Directive 2002/22/EC of the European Parliament and of the Council of 7 March 2002 on universal service and users' rights relating to electronic communications networks and services (OJ 2002 L 108, p. 51, as amended.)

890 See the position of the President of the Office of Electronic Communications and the Polish Government in point 29 of the reasons for judgement in the TP case.

Another case, C-540/08 (*Mediaprint*),[891] concerned the dispute between the press companies Mediaprint Zeitungs- und Zeitschriftenverlag GmbH & Co. KG and Österreich-Zeitungsverlag GmbH. The Österreich publishing house organised a competition to choose the footballer of the year and invited readers to participate in it *via* the Internet or by means of a voting coupon included in the daily newspaper. Participation in the competition offered the chance to win a dinner with the selected footballer. Mediaprint argued that making the possibility of winning conditional on the purchase of a newspaper constituted a prohibited add-on within the meaning of Section 9a(1)(1) of the Austrian Unfair Competition Act (hereinafter Austrian UWG)[892] and referred the case to the national court.

The Austrian Supreme Court (Oberster Gerichtshof) referred preliminary questions to the Court of Justice on the compatibility of the national legislation under review with the provisions of Directive 2005/29/EC. It enquired whether Directive 2005/29/EC allowed for the introduction of a prohibition in national law under which the announcing, offering, or granting of free add-ons to periodicals, as well as the addition of free add-ons to other goods or services, subject to certain exceptions, is prohibited. At the same time, it argued that the adopted prohibition served not only consumer protection but also other purposes. Those other purposes, such as maintaining media pluralism or protecting weaker competitors, do not fall within the substantive scope of the Directive.[893]

---

891 Judgement of the CJEU of 9.11.2010, C-540/08, *Mediaprint Zeitungs- und Zeitschriftenverlag GmbH & Co. KG v. Österreich-Zeitungsverlag* GmbH, See Judgement of 2010, I-10909, ECLI:EU:C:2010:660 together with the opinion of Advocate General V. Trstenjak of 24.3.2010, ECLI:EU:C:2010:161.

892 § Section 9a (1) (1) of the Austrian UWG, as derived from BGBl. I, 136/2001, read as follows: '1. Whoever, in commercial dealings for competitive purposes: (1) announces in public notices or other communications to a larger circle of people that he will grant free allowances (bonuses) to consumers in addition to goods and services, or offers, announces or grants free allowances (bonuses) to consumers in addition to periodical prints, or (2) offers, announces or grants free allowances (bonuses) to entrepreneurs in addition to goods or services, may be sued for failure to act and for damages. This also applies if the free of charge allowance is camouflaged by the general price of the goods and services, the apparent price of the allowance or otherwise'.

893 See point 13, points 23–25 of the reasons for judgement in *Mediaprint*.

The Court held that Directive 2005/29/EC must be interpreted 'as precluding national legislation which provides for a general prohibition of sales with ad-ons and which seeks not only to protect consumers but also pursues other objectives', and pointed out that since such a practice was not included among the 31 practices listed in Annex I to Directive 2005/29/EC, it could not be prohibited in all circumstances. In order to determine that a practice not listed in Annex I was an unfair commercial practice, each practice in question must be analysed individually. Also, the opportunity to take part in a competition does not constitute an unfair commercial practice within the meaning of Article 5(2) of Directive 2005/29/EC merely because, for at least some of the consumers concerned, the opportunity to take part in the game constitutes a decisive reason inducing them to buy that newspaper.

The CJEU's ruling in case C-428/11 concerning the dispute between Purely Creative and others and the Office of Fair Trading may be helpful.[894] The dispute concerned a practice employed by British traders who distributed advertisements that took a variety of forms, including letters addressed to specific individuals, coupons, and other inserts in newspapers and magazines. A common feature of these advertisements was their message, which implied that the consumer had won a prize of a certain value. The consumer could find out about the prize by contacting the trader in various ways (by calling a premium rate number, by paid text message, or by postal delivery). There was no information provided about the cost of the call to the trader, and what was more, there were (in some cases) additional costs for delivery and insurance of the prize. In 99% of the cases, the value of the prize corresponded to the sum of the costs incurred by the consumer to obtain the prize information, delivery, and insurance costs.[895]

The High Court of Justice, England & Wales classified such practices as unfair commercial practices, and the traders appealed. The Court of Appeal decided that first it was necessary to interpret paragraph 31 of Annex I to Directive 2005/29/EC correctly and referred extensive questions to the Court

---

894 Judgment of the CJEU of 18.10.2012, C-428/11, *Purely Creative Ltd, Strike Lucky Games Ltd, Winners Club Ltd, McIntyre & Dood Marketing Ltd, Dodd Marketing, Adrian Williams, Wendu Ruck, Catherine Cummings, Peter Henry v. Office of Fair Trading*, ECLI:EU:C:2012:651 (hereinafter: *Purely Creative*), <http://curia.europa.eu/juris/liste.jsf?num=C-428/11&language=ENG> (accessed on: 1.2.2025).

895 See points 14–16 of the reasons for judgement in *Purely Creative*.

for a preliminary ruling.[896] The questions concerned the interpretation of paragraph 31 of Annex I to Directive 2005/29/EC and in particular the costs customers had to suffer in connection with obtaining a prize and the interpretation of the concept of 'false impression'.[897]

The CJEU explained that paragraph 31 of Annex I to the Directive must be interpreted as 'prohibiting aggressive commercial practices by which traders create a false impression that the consumer has won a prize, where the performance of acts in relation to claiming the prize, such as enquiring about the nature of the prize or taking possession of it, involves the consumer in paying a sum of money or incurring any expense'. A false impression is created when one of the facts described in paragraph 31 occurs, i.e. when the prize does not exist or when certain actions are required in order to obtain it, which involve the payment of a certain amount of money.[898] It was further explained that paragraph 31 should be interpreted with reference to paragraph 20 of Annex I to the Directive.[899] Therefore, the consumer should not be charged with any costs associated with winning the prize (not even a postage stamp or a telephone call). Whether such cost is high or low in relation to the value of the prize is irrelevant. Furthermore, the consumer should be provided with clear and adequate information allowing him to identify the prize and assess its value.[900]

Another ruling concerned case C-265/12 of 18 July 2013 regarding a dispute between a Belgian company, Citroën Belux NV, and Federatie voor Verzekerings- en Financiële Tussenpersonen (FvF) (*Citroën*).[901] Citroën ran an advertising campaign under the title 'I want everything'. Under the terms of the advertising campaign, the purchaser of a new passenger car and a commercial vehicle received 6 months' insurance free of charge on the newly purchased car. FvF considered that Citroën's offer constituted a combined

---

[896] See point 23 *ibidem*.

[897] See point 23 of the reasons for judgement in *Purely Creative*.

[898] See point 26 *ibidem*.

[899] Point 20 of Annex I to the Directive lists as a misleading commercial practice: 'Describing a product as "gratis", "free", "free of charge" or similar if the consumer has to pay anything other than the unavoidable cost of responding to the commercial practice, collecting or delivering the product'.

[900] See points 41 and 48 of the reasons for judgement in *Purely Creative*.

[901] Judgement of the CJEU of 18.6.2013 C-265/12, *Citroën Belux NV v. Federatie voorVerzekerings- en Financiële Tussenpersonen (FvF)*, ECLI:EU:C:2013:498 (hereinafter: *Citroën*).

offer prohibited under Belgian law (Article 72 § 1 of the Belgian Act of 6.4.2010 on market practices and consumer protection Citroën).[902] The national court (*Hof van Beroep te Brussel*) referred a preliminary question to the Court of Justice about the compatibility of the contested provision of Belgian law prohibiting cross-selling with Directive 2005/29/EC and, in particular, with Article 3(9) of the Directive, which is an exception to the principle of full harmonisation in relation to financial services, and Article 56 TFEU on the freedom to provide services.

In response to the question referred, the Court stated that Article 3(9) of the Directive and Article 56 TFEU must be interpreted as 'not precluding a provision of a Member State which provides for a general prohibition, subject to cases exhaustively listed by law, of tied-in offers in which one or more elements are financial services'.

It should be stressed that the decisive factor in this case was that the Court considered that the insurance service offered by Citroën in connection with the purchase of a new car was a financial service within the meaning of Directive 2005/29/EC.[903] Thus, the exception provided for in Article 3(9) of Directive 2005/29/EC, which allows Member States to impose stricter requirements than those provided for by Directive 2005/29/EC in the field of financial services, could be applied in the present case. The Court argued that 'financial services are, by nature, complex and entail specific risks with regard to which the consumer is not always sufficiently well informed. Secondly, a combined offer is, in itself, such as to generate on the part of the consumer the idea of a price advantage. It follows that a combined offer of which one component is a financial service is more likely to be lacking in transparency as regards the conditions, the price, and the exact content of that service. Accordingly, such an offer may well mislead consumers as to the true content and actual characteristics of the combination offered and, at the same time, deprive them of the opportunity of comparing the price and quality of that offer with other corresponding services from other economic operators'.[904]

---

[902] *Belgisch Staatsblad* of 12.4.2010, p. 20803. Article 72 § 1 read as follows: 'Any combined offer in which at least one component is a financial service and which is offered to the consumer by an undertaking or by different undertakings pursuing a common purpose shall be prohibited'.

[903] See points 21–23 of the reasons for judgement in *Citroën*.

[904] See point 39 *ibidem*.

Another CJEU ruling connected with combined offers was issued on 7 September 2016 in case C-310/15 (referred to as *Sony*[905]). The facts of the case show that a French consumer, Mr V. Deroo-Blanquarta, purchased a SONY portable computer together with pre-installed software (an operating system with applications). The computer and the software formed a single and indivisible package. The total price quoted by the trader included both elements of the offer. At the same time, it did not specify how much each of the pre-installed programmes cost. It was also not possible to buy the same computer model without the software. When the computer was first used, the consumer-buyer refused to sign the operating system licence agreement and subsequently asked Sony to refund part of the purchase price of the computer corresponding to the cost of the pre-installed software. Sony offered to refund the purchase price of the computer in exchange for the return of the purchased hardware. The buyer did not agree and took Sony to court, alleging, *inter alia*, unfair market practices. The national courts dismissed all of the consumer's claims. The case was referred to the Cour de Cassation (Court of Cassation) on appeal. The Cour de cassation referred the question to the CJEU for a preliminary ruling: does Sony's practice of selling a computer together with pre-installed software in a combined offer constitute an unfair commercial practice?

First, the ECJ referred to its previous rulings and confirmed that combined offers were commercial practices within the meaning of Directive 2005/29/EC. The Court therefore held that it was necessary to assess, first, whether Sony had failed to exercise due care in the circumstances and, second, whether its actions had significantly distorted or were likely to distort the economic behaviour of the average consumer. In its assessment of the facts, the Court found that Sony had not breached the requirements of professional diligence. In fact, consumers were duly informed of the pre-installation of software on the computers and of the features of the software. In addition, the consumer had the opportunity to enter into the licence agreement for the pre-installed software or to withdraw from the sales contract at the time of the first use of the computer. Further, the sale of computers with software met the expectations of a significant proportion of consumers who wanted to

[905] Judgement of the CJEU of 7.9.2016, C-310/15, *Vincent Deroo-Blanquartv. Sony Europe Limited*, the legal successor of *Sony France SA*, ECLI:EU:C:2016:633 (hereinafter: *Sony*).

buy ready-to-use hardware, i.e. with software.[906] The CJEU also stated, when assessing the second circumstance, that the national court must examine whether the consumer was duly informed and whether he knew that a particular model of computer was not sold without pre-installed software and whether he could have chosen a different model of computer, of a different brand with comparable characteristics, or whether he had limited capacity to make an informed decision.

The Court also ruled that the failure to indicate the price of each of the pre-installed programmes did not constitute a misleading commercial practice within the meaning of the Directive (Articles 4(a) and 7), as the consumer was able to take an informed decision and the information about the price of each of the pre-installed programmes did not constitute material information.[907]

What is noteworthy is that, in this ruling, the CJEU for the first time did not assess the compatibility of national rules prohibiting or restricting combined offers but addressed the commercial practice itself. First and foremost, it confirmed the admissibility of combined offers and set out the guidelines to be followed for such practices.

III. CJEU Case Law on the Interpretation of the Provisions of Directive 2005/29/EC Affecting the Ban on Bonus Sales under Polish Law

1. Introductory Remarks

When analysing the rulings of the CJEU issued after the enactment of Directive 2005/29/EC, one cannot overlook those which, although not directly related to bonus sales, have a direct impact on the interpretation of the provisions of Directive 2005/29/EC. The rulings of the CJEU have an impact not only on the national provisions implementing Directive 2005/29/EC but also on the provisions of other legal acts whose scope includes the issues regulated by Directive 2005/29/EC: the adoption of practices that are more restrictive than those provided for by Directive 2005/29/EC and the jurisdiction of national courts when assessing practices by traders.

---

906 See point 35 of the reasons for judgment in *Sony*.

907 See points 51 and 52 *ibidem*.

2. A Ban on Applying Practices more Restrictive than those Provided for in the Directive

In its judgements, the CJEU referred not only to the key concepts of Directive 2005/29/EC but also assessed the compatibility with it of the prohibitions existing in Member States' legislation. When examining the existing prohibitions, it is necessary to identify the purpose for which the prohibition was introduced. If it can be demonstrated that the purpose of the prohibition was, at least indirectly, to protect the interests of consumers, such a prohibition will have to be interpreted in the light of Directive 2005/29/EC and the CJEU case law to date.

Thus, according to the CJEU's case law governed by Article 4 of the Directive[908] as well as indirectly by Article 3(5) of the same Directive, it follows that Member States may not apply more restrictive and prescriptive measures than those provided for in the Directive. There are only certain exceptions to this rule.[909]

The Court found the following prohibitions in national legislation to be incompatible with the Directive:

1. Prohibition of combined sales (Article 54 of the Belgian Trade Practices and Consumer Information and Protection Act—Total Belgium case, Sections 3 and 4(6) of the German Act on Combatting Unfair Competition—Plus case, Article 57(1) of the Polish Telecommunications Act—TP case, Section 9(1)(1) of the Austrian Act on Combatting Unfair Competition—Mediaprint case);
2. Prohibition of price reductions in periods prior to sales (Article 53 of the Belgian Act on Trade Practices and Consumer Information and Protection—Wamo case[910] and Inno case[911]);

---

[908] Article 4 of Directive 2005/29/EC provides that 'Member States may not restrict the freedom to provide services or the free movement of goods for reasons falling within the field approximated by this Directive'.

[909] Article 3(9) of Directive 2005/29/EC with resoect to financial services.

[910] Decision of the CJEU of 30.6.2011, C-288/10, *Wamo BVBA v. JBC NV, Modemakers Fashion NV*, ECLI:EU:C:2011:443

[911] Decision of the CJEU of 15.12.2011, C-126/11, *INNO v. Unie van Zelfstandige Ondernemers et al.*, ECLI:EU:C:2011:851.

3. Prohibition of announcing sales without permission of the competent administrative authority (Section 33a(1) of the Austrian Unfair Competition Act—Köck case);
4. Prohibition of selling at a loss (Section 101(1) of the Belgian Market Practices and Consumer Protection Act – Euronics case[912]);
5. Prohibition of price reductions not based on a reference price when marking or quoting a price (Article L 113-3 of the French Consumer Code—Discout case[913]).

It follows from the Court's case law that Directive 2005/29/EC does not allow national legislators to impose general prohibitions if they are not in line with practices listed in Annex I to it. As a rule, prohibiting practices that are not listed in that Annex is not allowed. A prohibition may only be established after a specific analysis has been carried out to establish the unfair nature of the trader's practice.[914]

However, if the prohibitions introduced are not aimed at protecting consumers, such regulations do not fall within the scope of Directive 2005/29/EC. Thus, the CJEU considered that the ban on opening shops 7 days a week introduced in Belgium with an aim to protect workers' interests did not fall within the scope of Directive 2005/29/EC.[915]

3. The Role of National Courts

An analysis of the CJEU's rulings shows that national courts play a very important role when interpreting national laws transposing Directive 2005/29/EC. The Court emphasised that it is their task, and not that of the Court, to examine the national law of the respective Member States.[916] In

---

[912] Decision of the CJEU of 7.3.2013, C 343/12, *Euronics Belgium CVBA v. Kamera Express BV, Kamera Express Belgium BVBA*, ECLI:EU:C:2013:154.

[913] Decision of the CJEU of 8.9.2015, C-13/15, *Criminal proceedings against Cdiscount SA*, ECLI:EU:C:2015:560.

[914] See Decision of the CJEU of 30.6.2011, C-288/10, *Wamo BVBA v. JBC NV, Modemakers Fashion NV*, ECLI:EU:C:2011:443, and point 39 of the decision of 8.9.2015, C-13/15 *Cdiscount SA v. Ministère public*, ECLI:EU:C:2015:560.

[915] See decision of the CJEU of 4.10.2012, C-559/11, *Pelckmans Turnhout NV v. Walter Van Gastel Balen NV et al.*, ECLI:EU:C:2012:615.

[916] Decision of the CJEU of 8.9.2015, C-13/15, *Cdiscount SA*, ECLI:EU:C:2015:560, and also point 28 of the reasons in *Wamo*.

one of the cases analysed by the CJEU, a French court referred a question for a preliminary ruling as to whether 'a domestic ban on price reductions that have not been set against a reference price as provided for in the implementing provisions (the regulation on price reduction announcements to the consumer) is compatible with the Directive'. Admittedly, the CJEU held that Directive 2005/29/EC must be interpreted as precluding national legislation that 'provides for a general prohibition of announcements of price reductions which do not indicate a reference price when marking or quoting prices, without a case-by-case assessment enabling to establish the unfair nature of those announcements'. On the other hand, however, the CJEU emphasised 'that it is not for the Court to rule on the interpretation of national law in the context of a reference for a preliminary ruling. This is the exclusive role of the referring court. The Court must take account, under the division of jurisdiction between the Courts of the European Union and the national courts, of the factual and legislative context, as defined in the decision for reference, in which the questions put to it are set'.[917]

Thus, in accordance with the CJEU's recommendations, the tasks of the national courts will include:

1. firstly, to ascertain whether the national legislation actually pursues consumer protection objectives. This is necessary in order to determine whether the national legislation at issue falls within the scope of Directive 2005/29/EC;
2. secondly, if the Court finds that this is the case, to determine whether the prohibited conduct (e.g. the ban on the display of discount notices that do not indicate a reference price when indicating or quoting a price) constitutes a commercial practice within the meaning of Directive 2005/29/EC and is therefore covered by its provisions;
3. and thirdly, if the court finds that the prohibition relates to a commercial practice within the meaning of Directive 2005/29/EC, to assess whether Directive 2005/29/EC precludes the prohibitions under national law.[918]

---

917 See point 28 of the reasons in *Cdiscount*.

918 See points 29–38 of the reasons in *Cdiscount*.

Only by carrying out such an analysis will the national courts be able to assess the compatibility of national measures with Directive 2005/29/EC. It may be noted that pursuant to Article 258 TFEU, the Commission may take specific action against a Member State that has failed to fulfil its obligations under Directive.[919] An example of such an action by the Commission is the Court's ruling of 10 July 2014 in Case C-421/12 European Commission v. Belgium.[920] The Commission submitted that Belgium, despite having made legislative changes to its national law arising from the obligation to implement Directive 2005/29/EC, had failed to fulfil its obligations. Specific allegations were formulated.[921] The CJEU found that Belgium had failed to fulfil its obligations under Articles 2(b) and (d), 3, and 4 of Directive 2005/29/EC. In such a situation, according to Article 260(1) TFEU, if the CJEU finds that a Member State has failed to fulfil one of its obligations under the Treaties, the State is obliged to take measures to ensure compliance with the Court's judgement. Failure to comply with a judgement of the Court may result in the imposition of a lump sum or periodic penalty payment.[922]

Table 2 brings together the most CJEU rulings analysed above. They have been divided thematically—according to the legal issues raised in them, i.e.:

1. combined sales;
2. the interpretation of the concept of a prize;
3. the control of branches (failures) related to the implementation of the Directive.

[919] Article 258 TFEU provides that 'If the Commission considers that a Member State has failed to fulfil an obligation under the Treaties, it shall deliver a reasoned opinion on the matter after giving the State concerned the opportunity to submit its observations. If the State concerned does not comply with the opinion within the period laid down by the Commission, the latter may bring the matter before the Court of Justice of the European Union'.

[920] Judgment of the CJEU of 10.7.2014, C-421/12, *European Commission v. Kingdom of Belgium*, ECLI:EU:C:2014:2064.

[921] These concerned: (1) the exclusion of certain professional groups in the Belgian law implementing the Directive; (2) the obligation to indicate the prices of the reduction by reference to the lowest price applied during the month preceding the reduction; (3) the prohibition of door to door and fair sales above €250.

[922] See Article 260, clause 2, et seq. of the TEEU.

Table 2. The most important CJEU rulings affecting the interpretation of Directive 2005/29/EC and Member States' legislation

Combined sales issue			
	Case	**National legislation prohibiting combined sales**	**The CJEU's ruling**
1	***Total*** (C-261/07) and ***Galatea*** C-299/07) further *Total* (together with the opinion of Advocate General *V. Trstenjak*)	National legislation (Belgium): 1) Article 54 of the Law of 14.7.1991 on commercial practices and consumer information and protection 2) Prohibition of combined sales (with certain exceptions)	1) The combined offer is a commercial practice 2) The Belgian legislation is contrary to the Directive 3) Belgian law prohibits general and preventive combined offers, notwithstanding any verification of their unfairness on the basis of the criteria set out in Articles 5–9 of the Directive
2	***Plus*** (C-304/08) (together with the opinion of Advocate General *V. Trstenjak*)	National regulations (Germany): 1) § Sections 3 and 4 UWG (German Unfair Competition Act) 2. It is unfair to make the participation of consumers in a prize competition or lottery conditional on the purchase of goods or services	1) Broad definition of the term 'commercial practice' 2) A combined offer is a commercial practice 3) The national legislation is contrary to the Directive in that it prohibits, as a matter of principle, commercial practices that make the participation of consumers in a prize competition or lottery conditional on the purchase of goods or services, irrespective of the specific circumstances of each case
3	***TP*** (C-522/08)	National legislation (Poland) 1) Article 57 of the Telecommunications Act 2) prohibition of combined offers for telecommunications services	The directive precludes national legislation that, subject to certain exceptions and without taking account of the specific circumstances of the case in question, prohibits any combined offer by a vendor to a consumer

Table 2. Continued

Combined sales issue			
	Case	**National legislation prohibiting combined sales**	**The CJEU's ruling**
4	***Mediaprint*** (C-540/08) (together with the opinion of Advocate General *V. Trstenjak*)	National provisions (Austria) 1) § 9a Austrian UWG 2) Prohibition of combined offers with free add-ons or bonuses (sales with add-ons)	1) The Directive precludes national legislation that provides for a general prohibition of sales with add-ons and that not only seeks to protect consumers but also pursues other objectives 2) Furthermore, the possibility of participating in a competition does not constitute an unfair commercial practice within the meaning of Article 5(2) of the Directive merely because, for at least some of the consumers concerned, the opportunity to take part in the game constitutes a decisive reason inducing them to buy that newspaper
5	***Citroën*** (C-265/12)	National legislation (Belgium) (1) Article 72 of the Market Practices and Consumer Protection Act 2) Prohibition of combined offers where at least one component is a financial service	1) The directive (Article 3(9)) does not preclude a provision of a Member State that provides for a general prohibition, subject to cases that are exhaustively listed by law, on the making to the consumer of combined offers in which at least one element is a financial service. 2) There is a financial service (here: an insurance service)

Table 2. Continued

Combined sales issue			
	Case	**National legislation prohibiting combined sales**	**The CJEU's ruling**
6	***Sony*** (C-310/15)	National legislation (France) The commercial practice of selling a computer together with pre-installed software in a single joint offer, without distinguishing the price of the individual elements of the offer, was assessed	1) A commercial practice consisting of selling a computer equipped with pre-installed software while the consumer is unable to purchase a computer of the same model without the software pre-installed does not constitute, as such, an unfair commercial practice unless it is contrary to the requirements of professional diligence and materially distorts or is likely materially to distort the economic behaviour of the average consumer with regard to that product. 2) That is for the national court to determine, having regard to the specific circumstances of the case in the main proceedings 3) Selling a computer with pre-installed software without indicating the price of each of the pre-installed programmes does not constitute a mislead-ing commercial practice

Table 2. Continued

	Case	Commercial practice	The CJEU's ruling
Interpretation of the concept of a 'prize'			
7	***Purely Creative*** (C-428/11)	Domestic traders' practice of sending out advertisements stating that the consumer has won some prize of a certain value	1) Point 31, second indent, of Annex I to the Directive must be interpreted as prohibiting aggressive commercial practices whereby undertakings give the false impression that the consumer has won a prize, even though the act of winning the prize, such as enquiring about the nature of the prize or taking possession of it, involves the consumer in paying a sum of money or incurring a charge of any kind 2) The consumer should not be charged any costs in relation to winning the prize 3) The consumer should be provided with clear and adequate information allowing him to identify the prize and assess its value
Monitoring of failures in relation to the implementation of the Directive			
8	***European Commission v. Kingdom of Belgium*** (C-421/12)	Belgium introduced legislative changes to its national law to comply with the obligation to implement the Directive. However, it left certain national provisions in place and excluded certain professional groups from the scope of the law transposing the Directive	By adopting and maintaining certain provisions, Belgium failed to fulfil its obligations under Articles 2(b) and (d), 3, and 4 of the Directive

§ 3. Conclusions

When analysing the judgements of the CJEU (and in particular those relating to combined sales), it should be considered whether the Polish solution contained in Article 17a of the Act on Combatting Unfair Competition, which introduced a general blanket ban on bonus sales, is consistent with Directive 2005/29/EC. The answer to this question is important for the legitimacy of this prohibition in Polish law against unfair competition. If the answer to this question were to turn out negative, there would be grounds for calling for its repeal. There have been opinions raised in the literature (in the light of CJEU rulings) that the prohibition of Article 17a should be repealed when the Act is amended in the future.[923] Once this has been done, there will be no restrictions under the Act on Combatting Unfair Competition on bonus sales as a means of promoting goods and services. However, such restrictions would continue to be permissible under other laws and will apply to relations between entrepreneurs or in the case of practices that do not harm the economic interests of consumers.

In considering the legality of maintaining the existing prohibition regarding, in particular, tied-in offers, the guidance provided by the CJEU should be taken into account. However, it should be borne in mind that the concept of combined sales and that of bonus sales are not the same. The concept of combined sales is broad and covers not only the cases described in Article 17a but also other types of sales promotions that tie in the purchase of several goods and services in a single price offer.

According to Polish literature and the explanatory memorandum of the 2002 amendment to the Act on Combatting Unfair Competition, the main purpose of the adoption of Article 17a was to protect small and medium-sized entrepreneurs. It was the intention of the proponents of this amendment that the adopted provision should fulfil two functions. On the one hand, it was intended to ensure the protection of the competitors of large entrepreneurs, i.e. small and medium-sized entrepreneurs, who, for financial reasons, cannot afford to add free bonuses and thus compete with large entrepreneurs. On the other hand, it was also intended to protect consumers who should be able to make informed decisions that are not distorted by various free bonuses

---

923 *M. Sieradzka*, Oferta wiązana jako rodzaj praktyki handlowej, p. 57.

offered to them. However, the protection of consumers' interests had come second, like an offshoot of the protection of traders' interests.

However, in the light of the presented CJEU rulings, the attempt to argue that the aim of Article 17a was to protect the interests of entrepreneurs and was not aimed at protecting the interests of consumers and, consequently, this prohibition should not be assessed from the perspective of the solutions adopted in Directive 2005/29/EC is doomed to fail. Indeed, it should be assumed that the purpose of Article 17a, albeit indirect, is also to protect consumers. Thus, the Polish regulation should remain in line with Directive 2005/29/EC, and the courts should assess the adopted solutions in light of its provisions.

A similar argument was raised by the Polish government in the Plus case. The Polish side argued that the compatibility of the German ban on combined sales (§ 4(6) of the German UWG2004[924]) with the Directive must not be questioned because the reason behind its introduction was protection of competitors, not consumers.[925] A similar argument was made by the Austrian government, which took the view that 'the Directive (...) primarily serves the objectives of consumer-protection policy and is therefore not applicable to national measures which are designed to protect the interests of competitors and the latter are not affected'.[926] The Czech government also argued that the contested national legislation was aimed at protecting competition, not consumers.[927] Other Member States (Belgium, the Czech Republic, Finland, Germany, Italy, Portugal, and Spain) also raised numerous arguments in

---

[924] 'An unfair act within the meaning of § 3 is committed by one who: 6. makes the participation of consumers in a prize competition or lottery conditional on the purchase of goods or services, unless the competition or lottery is immanently linked to the goods or services'.

[925] See point 34 of the Opinion of Advocate General V. Trstenjak of 3.9.2009 in *Plus*. It reads: 'Relying primarily on recital 5 of the Directive, the Polish Government points out that the EU legislator wished to draw a clear distinction between, on the one hand, commercial practices harming consumers in business-to-consumer relations—which the Directive sought to regulate—and, on the other hand, commercial practices harming the economic interests of competitors in business-to-business relations—which in turn fall outside the scope of Directive 2005/29. Consequently, the compatibility with Directive 2005/29 of a national provision intended to protect competitors cannot be called into question'.

[926] See point 35 of the Advocate General's Opinion in *Plus*.

[927] See *ibidem*, point 23.

support of the view that the prohibition of combined sales under German law was compatible with the Directive and its objectives.

The Advocate General explained that the position of the Polish Government, which made the inclusion of the contested German law provision within the scope of the Directive conditional on whether it was intended to protect consumers, was correct. She emphasised that the Directive only regulated the area of B2C relations and further explained that the provision of German law at issue was also intended to protect consumers because:

1. the German law against unfair competition served not only to protect competitors and other market players but also to protect consumers from unfair competition;
2. the provision at issue, as can be seen from the explanatory memorandum to the German draft law introducing this provision, as well as from the literature, was intended to protect consumers. Consumers were to be protected against traders who might want to exploit their desire to play a game that would restrict their freedom of decision. The Advocate General cited the views presented in the German literature on the subject, from which it followed that 'at the heart of this provision is the recognition that by tying participation in games of chance and the sale of goods, the purchase decision of a reasonable ordinary consumer can also be influenced in such a special way that it no longer results from rational considerations but is driven by the desire for a stipulated prize'.

Thus, despite the numerous arguments raised by the Member States, the Advocate General concluded that the national provision at issue fell within the scope of Directive 2005/29/EC.[928] It would thus appear that if the compatibility of Article 17a with Directive 2005/29/EC were to be assessed, it would be ineffective to raise the argument that the purpose of Article 17a is to protect competitors, in particular small and medium-sized businesses. As has already been shown, Article 17a protects as well, albeit indirectly, the interests of other market players, above all the consumers.

---

[928] See *ibidem*, points 66–67.

Arguments that Article 17a had been in force before the date of entry into force of Directive 2005/29/EC and was not a provision introduced in order to implement it will also be ineffective. Indeed, it follows from the position of the CJEU expressed in the Total case that:

1. 'the scope of application of the Directive includes not only national provisions transposing the provisions of the Directive, but, as from its entry into force, also pre-existing national provisions which may have an effect on the conformity of national law with that Directive'[929];
2. 'during the period allowed for transposition of the Directive, Member States are required to refrain from adopting provisions whose nature seriously jeopardises attainment of the objective of the Directive'. The above presumption also applies to the interpretation of national law. Indeed, the Court argues that 'the courts of the Member States are required, to the extent possible, to refrain from interpreting national law in a manner which would seriously compromise, after the period prescribed for transposition of the directive has expired, the attainment of the result prescribed by the directive'.[930] Undoubtedly, such an obligation exists not only during the transposition period but also after that period.

Article 17a must be interpreted in such a way that it is compatible with the purpose and effect of the Directive. It must therefore first be examined whether the bonus sales regulated in Article 17a may be classified as a 'commercial practice' within the meaning of Article 2(d) of the Directive. As emphasised, the concept of 'commercial practice' is to be understood broadly, and it refers to all types of commercial activities that concern traders' commercial strategies to promote and facilitate sales. In Total, the Advocate General explained that a combined offer involves linking two or more different offers of goods and services and selling them as a single whole. In her view, from the point of view of business economics, such offers 'are a means of pricing and communication, the two most important strategies used in marketing. Since it is rather rare to find markets where there would be no competition

929 See point 35 of the reasons in *Total.*
930 See point 39 *ibidem*; point 29 of the reasons stated in *Plus.*

and advertisers must almost always go up against other sellers in order to differentiate themselves in a competitive environment, market participants are forced to create offers that are not only interesting but also strongly attract specific consumers. Combined offers, because of the unique combination of different goods or services in a single offer and the resulting combination of actually or seemingly favourable prices, should induce customers to buy. In other words, they serve to attract customers and increase the purchasing potential of the company'. The Advocate General thus pointed out that those offers should be defined as commercial activities or information, including advertising and marketing of operators, which are directly linked to sales promotion or sales. Consequently, bonus sales are also fully covered by the concept of commercial practices under the Directive.[931] Leaving aside whether the concept of bonus selling fully corresponds to the concept of tied-in, or combined offers,[932] it should be recognised that bonus sales are undoubtedly a form of marketing that primarily aims to increase the sales of a good or increase the sale of services provided by granting a free bonus. The granting of a free bonus upon the purchase of a good or service makes the sales offer more attractive to its recipients. Thus, following the position of the Advocate General, bonus sales may be categorised as a commercial strategy employed by entrepreneurs, aimed at promoting and facilitating sales.[933] Consequently, it should be assumed that bonus sales must be classified as a commercial practice within the meaning of Article 2(d) of the Directive and thus fall within the scope of the Directive.

Secondly, assuming that the practice described in Article 17a is a commercial practice within the meaning of the Directive, it should be assessed whether the prohibition established by the Polish legislator may be deemed compatible with the Directive. The first step is to examine Annex I of Directive 2005/20/EC. Indeed, if a general prohibition of certain commercial practices is established in national law, it must be reflected in this Annex.[934] Such commercial practices, as the CJEU explained, do not need to be assessed

---

931 See points 69 and 70 of the Opinion of Advocate General V. Trstenjak of 21.10.2008, joint cases C-261/07 and C-299/07 *VTB-VAB NV v. Total Belgium NV I and Galatea BVBA v. Sanoma Magazines Belgium NV*, ECLI:EU:C:2008:581.

932 In the view of the Advocate General, these concepts are not sufficiently differentiated

933 See point 50 of the reasons in *Total*.

934 Also in *M. Sieradzka*, Oferta wiązana jako rodzaj praktyki handlowej, p. 56.

on a case-by-case basis. Bonus sales, however, are not listed among the 31 commercial practices in Annex I of the Directive. The absence of a specific practice in Annex I means that such a practice cannot be prohibited in a general manner without taking into account the specific circumstances of the case. Thus, the prohibition of bonus sales at issue must be assessed on a case-by-case basis under Articles 5 to 9 of the Directive.[935]

Consequently, it must be assumed that the establishment of a general prohibition of bonus sales in Article 17a, even despite the indication in it of a few exceptions, is contrary to Directive 2005/20/EC. Indeed, that provision establishes, as a general and preventive measure, the prohibition of bonus sales, irrespective of any verification of their unfair nature based on the criteria set out in its Articles 5–9.[936] Such a solution, however, is contrary to Article 4 of the Directive, which must be interpreted as meaning that Member States may not maintain or adopt national legislation providing for more restrictive measures than those provided for in the Directive, even if they were intended to ensure better consumer protection.[937] The exceptions to that prohibition provided for in Article 17a(2) are not sufficient to render the prohibition compatible with the Directive. It is clear from the Court's reasoning that, although the exceptions 'may limit the scope of the prohibition of combined offers, the fact remains that where, as in the cases in the main proceedings, there is a practice which is not listed in Annex I to the Directive, they cannot by virtue of their limited and predetermined nature replace the assessment of whether a commercial practice is "unfair". This must necessarily be made on the basis of the relevant facts of the case in the light of the criteria set out in Articles 5 to 9 of the Directive'.[938]

In other words, it should be considered that Directive 2005/29/EC makes it impossible to establish or maintain a prohibition such as that laid down in Article 17a. The assessment of such commercial practices should always be carried out in the light of Articles 5–9 of the Directive. As the Commission argues, it may be that, provided the consumers are correctly informed, such a commercial practice satisfies the condition of fairness laid down in the

---

935 See points 56–58 of the reasons in *Total*; and point 34 in the reasons in *Mediaprint*.
936 See point 63 of the reasons in *Total*.
937 See point 52 *ibidem*; and point 41 of the reasons *Plus*.
938 See point 65 of the reasons in *Total*; point 53 in the reasons in *Plus* and point 40 in the reasons in *Mediaprint*.

Directive.[939] A commercial practice not listed in Annex I to the Directive may only be regarded as unfair if it has been subjected to a concrete analysis and assessed against the criteria listed in Articles 5–9 of the Directive.[940]

The CJEU explained that Article 5 of the Directive provided for the prohibition of unfair market practices and listed the criteria defining a commercial practice as unfair. In Article 5(4) of the Directive, a distinction is made between two types of unfair practices: misleading practices (Articles 6 and 7 of the Directive) and aggressive practices (Articles 8 and 9 of the Directive). It is for the national court to assess on a case-by-case basis whether a given trader's behaviour constitutes an unfair commercial practice. Thus, the Polish court, in the event of a dispute under Article 17a, should first determine whether to interpret the prohibition of bonus sales in the light of Directive 2005/29/EC and, if so, it should, accordingly, conclude that bonus sales are incompatible with its provisions. The above does not exempt the court from assessing the commercial practice in question in the light of Articles 5–9 of the Directive (implemented in Articles 3–6 of the Act on Counteracting Unfair Market Practices). Only a careful analysis of the facts will make it possible to assess the unfairness of a specific commercial practice by traders towards consumers.

To conclude, Article 17a serves to protect the interests of entrepreneurs, in addition to protecting the interests of consumers. It also concerns the sale of goods and services to consumers. Bonus sales constitute a commercial practice within the meaning of Directive 2005/29/EC. They are commercial in nature, which means that they involve a trader's action related to the promotion, sale, or supply of products to consumers. Thus, Article 17a falls within the scope of Directive 2005/29/EC. Finally, bonus sales are not listed in Annex I to Directive 2005/29/EC, and the exceptions provided for in Article 17a(2) do not constitute a legitimate reason for considering the prohibition to be in compliance with Directive.[941]

A ban on bonus sales outside the scope of Directive 2005/29/EC would therefore have to apply to B2B relations only. Currently, however, such an interpretation of this provision is impossible. Article 17a makes it clear that the ban refers to the 'sale of goods or services to consumers'.

---

939 See point 66 of the reasons in *Total*.

940 See point 43 of the reasons *Mediaprint*.

941 See points 64 and 65 of the reasons in *Total*.

It is worth recalling the opinion expressed by the Advocate General in the Plus case, who emphasised the importance of interpreting the national legislation. She reasoned that 'with regard to the question whether a provision of national law is contrary to Community law, it is necessary to take into account not only the wording of that provision, but also how it is interpreted by the national courts. In view of the fact that the case-law of a Member State reproduces the interpretation of the law which has binding effect for all persons, that national case-law is the essential criterion for judging whether the implementation and interpretation of national law are in compliance with Community law'.[942]

942 See point 82 of the Opinion of Advocate General *V. Trstenjak* of 3.9.2009 in *Plus*, ECLI:EU:C:2009:511.

Concluding Remarks

The law against unfair competition in Poland is built on a model of integrated protection against unfair competition. In this system, the protection of consumers' and entrepreneurs' interests and of the public interest is interrelated and interdependent.[943]

This assumption is expressed, *inter alia*, in Article 1 of the Act on Combatting Unfair Competition of 1993, which states that 'the Act regulates the prevention and suppression of unfair competition in economic activities, in particular industrial and agricultural production, construction, trade and services – in the interest of the public, of the entrepreneurs and of the customers'. The omission of consumers in this provision does not mean that their interests are not protected. It is accepted that a customer may also be a consumer and that the protected interests are equal. The position that the Act on Combatting Unfair Competition only protects the interests of entrepreneurs is unfounded. Its purpose is also to protect the interests of other participants in the economic turnover—customers, including consumers, as well as the public interest. Similarly, it cannot be argued that the Act on Counteracting Unfair Market Practices of 2007 'cuts itself off' from the protection of entrepreneurs' interests and protects only those of consumers. And although Article 1 does not explicitly mention the interests of entrepreneurs and states that 'the Act defines unfair market practices in economic and professional activities and rules to counteract these practices in the interest

[943] See *R. Skubisz*, Cele i zakres zastosowania ustawy, p. 576.

of consumers and in the public interest', it does mention the public interest. The emphasis on the protection of the public interest, which is not found in Directive 2005/29/EC, is an expression of the model of integrated protection. The public interest contains the interest of entrepreneurs as well. This is not incompatible with Directive 2005/29/EC, as the protection of entrepreneurs' interests is confirmed in the recitals of its preamble, which explains that while the Directive directly protects the economic interests of consumers, it indirectly protects legitimate traders from competitors who do not respect the rules of fair competition. It should therefore be assumed that although the subject matter of the Act on Counteracting Unfair Market Practices is limited to unfair market practices by entrepreneurs towards consumers, it affects the object of protection and not the scope of the protected interests. Under the Act, first of all, the interests of consumers and the public interest are protected, but indirectly, protection is also due to the interests of entrepreneurs. Given these conclusions, I am not in favour of basing EU legislation on a separation of B2C and B2B commercial practices. Indeed, there are commercial practices that affect both relationships. In an integrated model of protection, which would be more correct to adopt, not the criterion of the relationship to which the practices relate (B2C and B2B), but the criterion of whose interests these practices harm—those of consumers, of traders, of customers, or the public interest.[944]

One has to agree with the view presented by R. Skubisz that the two Acts cannot be treated as totally separate and independent and that their separation would negate the classic model of integrated protection. Although both Acts place different emphasis on securing the interests of certain participants in business dealings, as is primarily reflected in granting active legal standing only to certain entities, their overriding aim is to guarantee fair competition.

The separation of the two Acts is of great practical significance with regard to the granting of active legitimation. Under the Act on Combatting Unfair Competition, only entrepreneurs and a national or regional organisation whose statutory objective is to protect the interests of entrepreneurs are entitled to file claims. The Act on Counteracting Unfair Market Practices grants this right primarily to consumers, but action may also be taken by the Ombudsman, the Financial Ombudsman, a national or regional organisation

---

[944] *M. Namysłowska*, Nieuczciwe praktyki handlowe, p. 604.

whose statutory objective is to protect consumers, as well as a district (or municipal) consumer ombudsman. It is, therefore, the provisions defining active standing that mark the clearest separation between the two Acts.

It would seem that consumers will frequently use the rights granted to them to take action under the Act on Counteracting Unfair Market Practices, in particular when a practice of a trader has been found to be on the black-list of unfair market practices. As practice shows, however, this is not the case. There are few published judgements based on actions brought on the initiative of consumers. Most often, unfair market practices are addressed by the President of the Office of Competition and Consumer Protection in a situation where the collective interests of consumers are infringed by Article 24(2)(3) of the Act on Competition and Consumer Protection of 2007. When assessing them, references are made to their definition contained in the Act on Counteracting Unfair Market Practices.

The public interest is protected primarily by the entities specified in Article 19(1) of the Act on Combatting Unfair Competition and in Article 12(2) of the Act on Counteracting Unfair Market Practices) as well as by the President of the Office of Competition and Consumer Protection on the grounds of the Act on Competition and Consumer Protection.

It is worth emphasising that certain entrepreneurs' behaviours may be qualified both as an unfair market practice and an act of unfair competition.[945] In a situation where an unfair market practice is used, the basis for liability under the Act on Combatting Unfair Competition will most often be Article 3(1), unless some unfair practice has fulfilled the characteristics of one of the specific delicts of unfair competition. This could be the case, for example, if a product is wrongly labelled as 'gratis' or 'free of charge' when in fact the consumer has to pay for it. Such an action may be qualified as a misleading practice, which is unfair in all circumstances (Article 7(20) of the Act on Counteracting Unfair Market Practices), as well as an act of unfair competition consisting of marking goods in a way that misleads customers (Article 10 of the Act on Combatting Unfair Competition). In such a case, it will not be necessary to demonstrate the prerequisites of Article 3(1) of that

[945] *J. Dudzik* considers that there can be no cumulative application of the provisions of the two Acts. *J. Dudzik*, Legitymacja czynna, pp. 640–641.

Act, due to the assumption that the corrective function of Article 3(1) should only apply in a limited number of exceptional cases.

A special situation will arise when the entrepreneur's conduct is an unfair market practice that has been blacklisted (Articles 7 and 9 of the Act on Counteracting Unfair Market Practices). In such a case, to consider that the conduct does not constitute an unfair competition act under the Act on Combatting Unfair Competition would be in conflict with Directive 2005/29/EC, which defines such practices as unfair in all circumstances. However, in order to bring specific claims, the claimant ('entrepreneur') would have to show that the conduct of the other entrepreneur ('defendant') affected (threatened or infringed) that entrepreneur's interests.

In such a situation, the premise of the existence of a competition relationship as a basis for pursuing claims under the Act on Combatting Unfair Competition would be important. An entrepreneur wishing to bring a claim against another entrepreneur who has used an unfair market practice constituting at the same time a delict of unfair competition under the Act on Combatting Unfair Competition would have to demonstrate not only that the other entrepreneur used an unfair market practice that also constituted a delict of unfair competition, but he would as well have to show that he remained in a broadly understood competition relationship with the entrepreneur. The competition relationship will therefore not be a premise for the application of the Act on Combatting Unfair Competition, but it will justify the entrepreneur's active standing. The normative basis for the entrepreneur's demonstration of an infringement of or a threat to his interest will be Article 18 of the Act on Combatting Unfair Competition.

Article 17a of the Act on Combatting Unfair Competition, on the other hand, may serve as an example that in many situations separating the scope of the two Acts would pose a great difficulty. This provision prohibits the promotion of the sale of goods and services to consumers by granting them free bonuses in the form of products different from the object of sale. This prohibition was intended to ensure that economically weaker entrepreneurs—small and medium-sized businesses—could compete with large entrepreneurs who can afford to promote their products and services by granting free bonuses to consumers. This reasoning, as well as the inclusion of this provision in the Act on Combatting Unfair Competition, might indicate that the prohibition applies to B2B relations and is not covered by the scope of

Directive 2005/29/EC. However, such a claim would be unfounded. Firstly, Article 17a of the Act on Combatting Unfair Competition serves, in addition to the protection of business interests, the protection of the interests of consumers. Consequently, this provision falls within the scope of the Directive. Moreover, bonus sales may also qualify as a commercial practice aimed at increasing sales of goods or services to consumers, thus falling within the scope of the Directive.

All in all, if a practice is not on the blacklist (Annex I of Directive 2005/29/EC), it cannot be prohibited either in a general or preventive manner. Such a practice must be examined on a case-by-case basis, taking into account all the circumstances listed in Articles 5–9 of Directive 2005/29/EC (Articles 3–6 of the Act on Counteracting Unfair Market Practices), but the national legislator alone cannot amend the list of black practices.

An example of an erroneous extension of this list is provided by the Polish Act on Counteracting Unfair Market Practices, which added to the list the practice of conducting and organising activities in a consortium system (Article 10 in conjunction with Article 4(3) of the Act on Counteracting Unfair Market Practices). Such an extension is contrary to Directive 2005/29/EC, which imposed a strictly defined catalogue of unfair commercial practices in all circumstances. At the same time, the argumentation offered by the Polish legislator when the Act on Counteracting Unfair Market Practices was enacted—that the transfer of this practice (from Article 17e of the Act on Combatting Unfair Competition to Article 10 of the Act on Counteracting Unfair Market Practices) was a consequence of creating a new regulation that sanctioned unfair market practices in trade with consumers—will not be effective.

The Polish legislator faced a tricky task in 2007. With the benefit of hindsight, it appears today that the implementation of Directive 2005/29/EC has turned out to be flawed in many aspects. The proposed method of implementation, which is based on an attempt to separate the scopes of the two Acts (those covering B2B and B2C relations) in an integrated protection model, is not practically feasible. On the other hand, a complete separation would mean a break with concepts hitherto well-established in case law and judicature. Today, what is necessary is a comprehensive amendment to the Polish law against unfair competition, and the best solution would be to create a new piece of legislation that would combine the provisions of both Acts in a coherent, systematic, and well-thought-out manner. This may not be a simple task. It would require not only rethinking the entire implementation of Directive 2005/29/EC but also amending the Act on Combatting Unfair Competition. It would be necessary to redefine an act of unfair competition that would combine acts of unfair competition from the Act on Combatting Unfair Competition and prohibited market practices from the Act on Counteracting Unfair Market Practices.[946] It would be necessary to create, on the basis of Article 3(1) of the Act on Combatting Unfair Competition and Article 4(1) of the Act on Counteracting Unfair Market Practices, a single general clause that would take into account the differences between the good practice clause from the Act on Combatting Unfair Competition and the professional diligence clause from Directive 2005/29/EC. The stipulated catalogue of acts of unfair competition (Articles 5–17 f of the Act on Combatting Unfair Competition), including in particular Article 17a, would also need to be rethought. A fresh look would have to be taken at the way in which Annex I of Directive 2005/29/EC has been 'adopted' or transposed, although the EU legislator did not leave much freedom to the Member States in this respect.

The revision could be guided by the experience of the German legislator who had to resolve the same dilemmas. The German literature recommended two possible options for the reform: either maintaining an integrated system or creating two systems with coordinated rules, one for B2C relations and one for B2B relations.[947] The first option was eventually adopted, following the long tradition of German law against unfair competition. However, it raises a number of problems, which arise primarily from the principle of full harmonisation of the Directive.[948]

I agree with the view of Prof. Skubisz that the Act on Combatting Unfair Competition should not be repealed and that the provisions on the protection of entrepreneurs' interests against unfair competition should not be transferred to the Act on Counteracting Unfair Market Practices. This would mean breaking with the excellent Polish tradition of the law against unfair

946 *R. Skubisz*, Cele i zakres zastosowania ustawy, p. 578.
947 *F. Henning-Bodewig*, Der Schutzzweck, p. 245.
948 *B. Guthy*, Die Umsetzung der Richtlinie 2005/29/EG in Deutschland und Großbritannien – eine rechtsvergleichende Betrachtung, München 2011, p. 205.

competition, whose solutions have proved to be an effective guarantor of fairness in trade. Moreover, the Act on Combatting Unfair Competition, unlike the Act on Counteracting Unfair Market Practices, is frequently the basis for the substantiation of entrepreneurs' claims. Depending on the economic situation and the need to respond to certain competitors' behaviours, some of the provisions of the Act on Combatting Unfair Competition are more 'popular' than others. This does not mean that the remaining ones are not important for maintaining the coherence of the entire system.

It should be added that the amendment to the Polish law against unfair competition would require closer cooperation between the Polish legislator and legal scholars. An example of such fruitful cooperation was the 1993 draft Act on Combatting Unfair Competition prepared by a distinguished group of academics,[949] which provided the basis for the enactment of the modern Act on Combatting Unfair Competition, still in force today.

The example of Directive 2005/29/EC, which is a directive of a maximum nature, shows clearly that its implementation is a much more difficult task than when implementing directives of a minimum nature. Indeed, effective implementation would have required redefining the entire national system of law against unfair competition, which was not done.

While further reforms of the law against unfair competition in Poland should be undertaken sooner or later, the respective legislative work should be phased in over time. This will allow the work to take into account not only the EU provisions already in force, which must be correctly implemented, but also a comprehensive rethinking of the entire model of protection to be put in place.

[949] The following participated in the work on the draft: prof. *M. Kępiński*, prof. *R. Markiewicz*, prof. *M. Poźniak-Niedzielska*, prof. *T. Skoczny*, prof. *R. Skubisz*, prof. *S. Sołtysiński*, prof. *J. Sroczyński*, prof. *A. Szajowski*, prof. *J. Szwaja*, prof. *I. Wiszniewska*.

Bibliography

Adamczak A., Szewc A. (eds), Konwencja paryska o ochronie własności przemysłowej. Komentarz, Warszawa 2008

Adamczyk J., Świerczyński M., w: *E. Traple* (ed.), Prawo reklamy i promocji, Warszawa 2007

Anagnostaras G., The Unfair Commercial Practices Directive in context: From legal disparity to legal complexity, Common Market Law Review 2010, No 47 (1)

Antczak B., Nieuczciwa konkurencja pracownika – wybrane zagadnienia, MoPP 2016, No 11

Augenhofer S., European Union, w: *F. Henning-Bodewig* (ed.), International Handbook on Unfair Competition, Monachium 2013

Banasiński C. (ed.), Ochrona konkurencji i konsumentów w Polsce i Unii Europejskiej (studia prawno-ekonomiczne), Warszawa 2005

Banasiński C., w: Ochrona przed nieuczciwą konkurencją – poradnik dla przedsiębiorców i konsumentów, Vademecum Rzeczpospolitej z 28.8.2002 r.

Banasiński C. (ed.), Standardy wspólnotowe w polskim prawie ochrony konsumenta, Warszawa 2004

Banasiński C., Sobczak A., Wesołowska I., Wrona J., Ochrona przed nieuczciwą konkurencją – poradnik dla przedsiębiorców i konsumentów, Vademecum Rzeczpospolitej z 28.8.2002 r.

Barnard C., The Substantive Law of the EU. The Four Freedoms, New York 2010

Barta J., Chwalba J., Markiewicz R., Wasilewski P., Qui bene dubitat, bene sciet. Księga jubileuszowa dedykowana Profesor Ewie Nowińskiej, Warszawa 2018

Bartosiewicz A., Konkurs promocyjny a loteria promocyjna – czyli jak uniknąć ewentualnej odpowiedzialności karnej skarbowej, MoPd 2011, No 10

Beater A., Europäisches Recht gegen unlauteren Wettbewerb – Ansatzpunkte, Grundlagen, Entwicklung, Erforderlichkeit, ZEuP 2003, No 11

Bernitz U., The Unfair Commercial Practices Directive: Its Scope, Ambitions and Relation to the Law of Unfair Competition, w: *S. Weatherill, U. Bernitz* (eds), The Regulation of Unfair Commercial Practices under EC Directive 2005/29. New Rules and New Techniques, Oxford–Portland–Oregon 2007

Bodenhausen G.H.C., Guide d'application de la Convention de Paris pour la protection de la propriété indusrielle, Telle que revisée a Stockholm en 1967, Genewa 1968

Correra C.M., Trade Related Aspects of Intellectual Property Rights, A Commentary on the TRIPS Agreement, New York 2007

Czajkowska-Dąbrowska M., Przesłanki, zakres zastosowania i funkcje klauzuli generalnej (art. 3 ust. 1 ustawy o zwalczaniu nieuczciwej konkurencji) w świetle orzecznictwa Sądu Najwyższego, w: Studia i analizy Sądu Najwyższego, t. IV, Warszawa 2010

Dauman J., O "nieuczciwej konkurencji" de lege ferenda, Miesięcznik Prawa Handlowego i Wekslowego 1937, No 5–8

Dolata T., The Fight Against Unfair Competition in Poland in the Years 1918–1939, Wroclaw Review of Law, Administration & Economics 2012, t. 2, No 1

Dudzik J., Legitymacja czynna na podstawie przepisów ustawy o zwalczaniu nieuczciwej konkurencji – aktualne problemy, w: *T. Skoczny* (ed.), Prawo konkurencji 25 lat. Pierwszy Polski Kongres Prawa Konkurencji, Warszawa 2016

Dudzik J., Skubisz R., w: *J. Szwaja, J. Kępiński* (eds), Ustawa o zwalczaniu nieuczciwej konkurencji. Komentarz, Warszawa 2024

Eppe M., Zugaben und Rabatte in Anwendungsbereich des UWG, Köln 2003

Fezer K.-H., Büschler W., Obergfall E.I. (eds), Lauterkeitsrecht. Kommentar zum Gesetz gegen den unlauteren Wettbewerb (UWG), München 2016

Fuchs D., Szymański Ł., Kodeks dobrych praktyk na gruncie ustawy o przeciwdziałaniu nieuczciwym praktykom rynkowym z 23.8.2007 r. W kontekście ubezpieczeniowym, MoP 2015, No 5

Gersdorf M., Raczkowski M., Odpowiedzialność za pracowniczy czyn nieuczciwej konkurencji, PiZS 2005, No 1

Giesen B., O "stosunku konkurencji" w prawie o zwalczaniu nieuczciwej konkurencji, w: Wyzwania dla ochrony konkurencji i regulacji rynku. Księga jubileuszowa dedykowana profesorowi Tadeuszowi Skocznemu, Warszawa 2017

Giesen B., Pojęcie konkurencji, w: *M. Kępiński* (ed.), System Prawa Prywatnego. Prawo konkurencji, t. 15, Warszawa 2014
Giesen B., Przedmiot ochrony przewidzianej ustawą o zwalczaniu nieuczciwej konkurencji, MoP–dodatek 2014, No 6
Glöckner J., Richtlinievorschlag über unlautere Geschäftspraktiken, deutsches UWG oder die schwierige Umsetzung von europarechtlichen Generalklauseln, WRP 2004
Götting P.H., § 4a Aggressive geschäftliche Handlungen, w: *P.H. Götting, A. Nordemann* (eds), UWG, Handkommentar, Baden-Baden 2016
Götting P.H., Nordemann A. (eds), UWG, Handkommentar, Baden-Baden 2016
Guthy B., Die Umsetzung der Richtlinie 2005/29/EG in Deutschland und Großbritannien – eine rechtsvergleichende Betrachtung, München 2011
Gutowski M. (ed.), Kodeks cywilny. Komentarz, t. 1 i 2, Warszawa 2016
Gutowski M., w: *M. Gutowski* (ed.), Kodeks cywilny. Komentarz do art. 1–449^{11}, t. 1, Warszawa 2016
Harte-Bavendamm H., Henning-Bodewig F. (eds), Gesetz gegen den unlauteren Wettbewerb (UWG) mit Preisangabenverordnung. Kommentar, München 2016
Hartley T.C., The Foundations of European Community Law, New York 2003
Hauser R., Niewiadomski Z., Wróbel A. (eds), System Prawa Administracyjnego, t. 8a, Publiczne prawo gospodarcze, Warszawa 2018
Heermann P.W., Lauterkeitsrechtliche Informationspflichten bei Verkaufsförderungdmaßnahmen, WRP 2005
Henning-Bodewig F., w: *F. Henning-Bodewig* (ed.), International Handbook on Unfair Competition, Monachium 2013
Henning-Bodewig F., Der Schutzzweck des UWG und die Richtlinie über unlautere Geschäftspraktiken, GRUR 2013
Henning-Bodewig F., Die Bekämpfung unlauteren Wettbewerbs in den EU-Mitgliedstaaten: eine Bestandsaufnahme, GRUR Int 2010
Henning-Bodewig F., Die Richtlinie 2005/29/EG über unlautere Geschäftspraktiken, GRUR Int 2005
Henning-Bodewig F. (ed.), International Handbook on Unfair Competition, Monachium 2013

Henning-Bodewig F., International Protection Against Unfair Competition, w: *F. Henning-Bodewig* (ed.), International Handbook on Unfair Competition, Monachium 2013

Henning-Bodewig F., International Unfair Competition Law, w: *R.M. Hilty, F. Henning-Bodewig* (eds), Law Against Unfair Competition, Berlin–Heidelberg 2007

Henning-Bodewig F., Stellungnahme des Max-Planck-Insttuts zum Vorschlag einer Richtlinie über unlautere Geschäftsprktiken vom 18.6.2003 und einer Verordnung über die Zusammenarbeit im Verbraucherschutz vom 18.7.2003, GRUR Int 2003

Henning-Bodewig F., Unfair Competition Law, European Union and Member States, Haga 2006

Hilty R.M., Henning-Bodewig F. (eds), Law Against Unfair Competition, Berlin–Heidelberg 2007

Höpperger M., Senftleben M., Protection Against Unfair Competition at the International Level – The Paris Convention, the 1996 Model Provisions and the Current Work of the World Intellectual Property Organisation, w: *R.M. Hilty, F. Henning-Bodewig* (eds), Law Against Unfair Competition, Berlin–Heidelberg 2007

Jacyszyn J., Przedsiębiorca w regulacjach prawnych, part 1, EP 2015, No 4

Jacyszyn J., Przedsiębiorca w regulacjach prawnych, part 2, EP 2015, No 5

Kasprzycki D., Agresywne praktyki rynkowe, w: *E. Nowińska, D. Kasprzycki* (eds), Nieuczciwe praktyki rynkowe. Ocena regulacji, Kraków 2012

Kasprzyk R., Pietrzak B., Abstrakcyjny stosunek konkurencji, Pal. 1994, No 38 (11)

Katner W.J., Szczególne rodzaje sprzedaży poza przepisami Kodeksu cywilnego, w: *J. Rajski* (ed.), System Prawa Prywatnego. Prawo zobowiązań – część szczegółowa, t. 7, Warszawa 2018

Keirsblick B., The New European Law of Unfair Commercial Practices and Competition Law, Oxford– Portland–Oregon 2011

Keller E., Entwicklung und gegenwärtiger Stand des deutschen Lauterkeitsrechts, w: *H. Harte-Bavendamm, F. Henning-Bodewig* (eds), Gesetz gegen den unlauteren Wettbewerb (UWG) mit Preisangabenverordnung. Kommentar, München 2016

Kępiński J., Pobieranie innych niż marża handlowa opłat za przyjęcie towaru do sprzedaży po wyroku TK z 16.10.2014 r., MoP 2016, No 15

Kępiński J., Wzór przemysłowy i jego ochrona w prawie polskim i wspólnotowym, Warszawa 2010

Kępiński J., *Kępiński M.*, Umowy lawinowe i umowy do nich podobne, w: *J. Bart*, *J. Chwalba*, *R. Markiewicz*, *P. Wasilewski* (eds), Qui bene dubitat, bene sciet. Księga jubileuszowa dedykowana Profesor Ewie Nowińskiej, Warszawa 2018

Kępiński M., Problemy ogólne nowej ustawy o zwalczaniu nieuczciwej konkurencji, RPEIS 1994, No 2

Kępiński J., *Kępiński M.*, Przed art. 5, w: *J. Szwaja*, *J. Kępiński* (eds), Ustawa o zwalczaniu nieuczciwej konkurencji. Komentarz, Warszawa 2024

Kępiński M. (ed.), Rynek farmaceutyczny a prawo własności intelektualnej, Warszawa 2013

Kępiński M., Stosunek art. 3 ust. 1 ustawy o zwalczaniu nieuczciwej konkurencji do szczególnych deliktów nieuczciwej konkurencji, w: *J. Szwaja* (ed.), Dwadzieścia lat ustawy o zwalczaniu nieuczciwej konkurencji, MoP – Supplement 2014, No 6

Kępiński M. (ed.), System Prawa Prywatnego, t. 15, Prawo konkurencji, Warszawa 2014

Kępiński M., *Kępiński J.*, Nowa dyrektywa w sprawie ochrony tajemnic przedsiębiorstwa, w: *M. Bernatt*, *A. Jurkowska-Gomułka*, *M. Namysłowska*, *A. Piszcz* (eds), Wyzwania dla ochrony konkurencji i regulacji rynku. Księga pamiątkowa dedykowana Profesorowi Tadeuszowi Skocznemu, Warszawa 2017

Kępiński M., *Kępiński J.*, w: *J. Szwaja*, *J. Kępiński* (eds), Ustawa o zwalczaniu nieuczciwej konkurencji. Komentarz, Warszawa 2024

Kępiński M., *Kępiński J.*, Z historii prawa nieuczciwej konkurencji – międzywojenne orzecznictwo Sądu Najwyższego, w: *A. Matlak*, *S. Stanisławska-Kloc* (eds), Spory o własność intelektualną. Księga jubileuszowa dedykowana Profesorem Januszowi Barcie i Ryszardowi Markiewiczowi, Warszawa 2013

Kocot W., Pozakodeksowe umowy sprzedaży (szczególne umowy sprzedaży), w: *W.J. Katner* (ed.), System Prawa Prywatnego, t. 9, Prawo zobowiązań – umowy nienazwane, Warszawa 2018

Kopaczyńska-Pieczniak K., Czyn nieuczciwej konkurencji a nieuczciwa praktyka rynkowa, MoPH 2012, No 3

Korus K., Zwalczanie nieuczciwej konkurencji. Komentarz do zmian wprowadzonych ustawą z dnia 5 lipca 2002 r. o zmianie ustawy o zmianie nieuczciwej konkurencji, LEX/el. 2002

Köhler H., § 5a w: *H. Köhler, J. Bornkamm, J. Feddersen* (eds), Gesetz gegen den unlauteren Wettbewerb mit PAngV, UKlaG, DL-InfoV Munchen 2017

Köhler H., § 4 w: *H. Köhler, J. Bornkamm, J. Feddersen* (eds), Gesetz gegen den unlauteren Wettbewerb mit PAngV, UKlaG, DL-InfoV, BeckOnline 2015

Köhler H., Kopplungsangebote (einschließlich Zugaben) im geltenden und künftigen Wettbewerbsrecht, GRUR 2003

Köhler H., Kopplungsangebote neu bewertet. Zugleich Besprechung der "Plus Warenhandelsgesellschaft" – Entscheidung des EuGH, GRUR 2010

Kraus A., Zoll F., Polska ustawa o zwalczaniu nieuczciwej konkurencji z objaśnieniami dra Alfreda Krausa i dra Fryderyka Zolla, Poznań 1929

Kukiel-Kryńska A., Implementacja dyrektyw opartych na zasadzie harmonizacji pełnej na przykładzie dyrektywy o nieuczciwych praktykach rynkowych, MoP 2007, No 18

Kur A., Dreier T., European Intellectual Property Law. Text, Cases and Materials, Cheltenham–Northampton 2013

Lutz R., Veränderungen des Wettbewerbsrechts im Zuge der Richtlinie über unlautere Geschäftspraktiken, GRUR 2006

Łętowska E., Prawo umów konsumenckich, Warszawa 1999, 2002

Małobęcki I., Sprzedaż wiązana i pakietowa jako potencjalne naruszenie europejskiego prawa konkurencji – ekonomiczna i prawna analiza problemu, Warszawa 2013, www.uokik.gov.pl/download.php?plik=14380

Mayzel M., O zwalczaniu nieuczciwej konkurencji, PPH 1926, No 5

Mayzel M., O zwalczaniu nieuczciwej konkurencji (Dokończenie), PPH 1926, No 8

Mądry M., w: *R. Stankiewicz, M. Pieklak* (eds), Ustawa o refundacji leków, środków spożywczych specjalnego przeznaczenia żywieniowego oraz wyrobów medycznych. Komentarz, Warszawa 2014

Miąsik D., w: *T. Skoczny* (ed.), Ustawa o ochronie konkurencji i konsumentów. Komentarz, Warszawa 2014

Michalak A., Przeciwdziałanie nieuczciwym praktykom rynkowym. Komentarz, Warszawa 2008

Micklitz H.-W. (ed.), The Feasibility of a General Legislative Framework on Fair Trading, <http://ec.europa.eu/comm/consumers/cons_int/safe_shop/fair_bus_pract/green_pap_comm/studies/sur21_vol1_en.pdf> (dostęp: 13.7.2017 r., obecnie niedostępny)

Micklitz H-W., A General Framework Directive on Fair Trading, w: *H. Collins* (ed.), The Forthcoming EX Directive on Unfair Commercial Practices, Contract, Consumer and Competition Law Implications, The Hague– London–New York 2004

Micklitz H-W., Full Harmonisation of Unfair Commercial Practices Under Directive 2005/29, IIC 2009, No 4

Mokrysz-Olszyńska A., Rola kodeksów dobrych praktyk w ochronie konsumenta, w: *C. Banasiński* (ed.), Ochrona konkurencji i konsumentów w Polsce i Unii Europejskiej (studia prawno-ekonomiczne), Warszawa 2005

Mokrysz-Olszyńska A., Swoboda promocji a ochrona przed nieuczciwymi praktykami w projektach prawa Unii Europejskiej, PiP 2005, No 2

Mularski K., w: *M. Gutowski* (ed.), Kodeks cywilny. Komentarz do art. 450–1088, t. 2, Warszawa 2022

Namitkiewicz J., Uwagi nad polską ustawą o zwalczaniu nieuczciwej konkurencji, PPH 1926, No 6

Namysłowska M., Czarna lista nieuczciwych praktyk handlowych a granice prawa zwalczania nieuczciwej konkurencji w Unii Europejskiej, Analiza prawnoporównawcza, Warszawa 2014

Namysłowska M., Glosa do wyroku TS z 11.3.2010 r., C-522/08, LEX/el. 2010

Namysłowska M., Glosa do wyroku TS z 3.4.2014 r., C-515/12, EPS 2014, No 11

Namysłowska M., Kiedy przyznanie nagrody jest nieuczciwą praktyką handlową? – glosa do wyroku TS z 18.10.2012 r. w sprawie C-428/11 Purely Creative i in., EPS 2013, No 1

Namysłowska M., Nieuczciwe praktyki handlowe między przedsiębiorcami w prawie Unii Europejskiej, w: *T. Skoczny* (ed.), Prawo konkurencji. 25 lat, Pierwszy Polski Kongres Prawa Konkurencji, Warszawa 2016

Namysłowska M., Nowa ustawa o przeciwdziałaniu nieuczciwym praktykom rynkowym, MoP 2007, No 23, Legalis

Namysłowska M., O konieczności uchylenia ustawy z dnia 16 kwietnia 1993 r. o zwalczaniu nieuczciwej konkurencji, w: *J. Ożegalska-Trybalska, D. Kasprzycki* (eds), Aktualne wyzwania prawa własności intelektualnej i prawa konkurencji. Księga pamiątkowa dedykowana Profesorowi Michałowi du Vallowi, Warszawa 2015

Namysłowska M., Projekt reformy prawa zwalczania nieuczciwej konkurencji państw członkowskich UE – zagadnienia materialnoprawne, MoP 2004, No 3

Namysłowska M. (ed.), Reklama. Aspekty prawne, Warszawa 2012

Namysłowska M., Znaczenie czarnej listy nieuczciwych praktyk handlowych – uwagi na tle orzecznictwa, EPS 2010, No 8

Nestoruk I.B., Europejskie prawo o zwalczaniu nieuczciwej konkurencji? (Prezentacja projektu dyrektywy o nieuczciwych praktykach handlowych), Prace Instytutu Prawa Własności Intelektualnej UJ, ZNUJ 2005, z. 89

Nowińska E., w: *E. Nowińska, K. Szczepanowska-Kozłowska*, Ustawa o zwalczaniu nieuczciwej konkurencji. Komentarz, Warszawa 2018

Nowińska E., Ochrona wyłączności korzystania, w: *E. Nowińska, K. Szczepanowska-Kozłowska* (eds), System Prawa Handlowego, t. 3, Prawo własności przemysłowej, Warszawa 2015

Nowińska E., Zakaz nieuczciwych praktyk rynkowych (art. 3 u.p.n.p.r.) i klauzula generalna nieuczciwych praktyk rynkowych (art. 4 u.p.n.p.r.), w: *E. Nowińska, D. Kasprzycki* (eds), Nieuczciwe praktyki rynkowe. Ocena regulacji, Kraków 2012

Nowińska E., du Vall M., w: *A. Adamczak, A. Szewc* (eds), Konwencja paryska o ochronie własności przemysłowej. Komentarz, Warszawa 2008

Nowińska E., du Vall M., Ustawa o zwalczaniu nieuczciwej konkurencji. Komentarz, Warszawa 2013

Nowińska E., Kasprzycki D. (eds), Nieuczciwe praktyki rynkowe. Ocena regulacji, Kraków 2012

Nowińska E., Szczepanowska-Kozłowska (eds), System Prawa Handlowego, t. 3, Prawo własności przemysłowej, Warszawa 2015

Nowińska E., Szczepanowska-Kozłowska K., Ustawa o zwalczaniu nieuczciwej konkurencji. Komentarz, Warszawa 2022

Obergfell E.I., § 4 pkt 6 Koppelung von Gewinn und Erwerb, w: *O. Teplitzky, K-N. Peifer, M. Leistner* (eds), Gesetz gegen den unlauteren Wettbewerb, Großkommentar, Berlin–Boston 2013

Ohly A., w: *A. Ohly, O. Sosnitza* (eds), Gesetz gegen den unlauteren Wettbewerb mit Preisangabeverordnung, Kommentar, München 2023

Ohly A., Das neue UWG – Mehr Freiheit für den Wettbewerd?, GRUR 2004, z. 11

Ohly A., Die wettbewerbsrechtliche Beurteilung von Gesamptpreisangeboten, NJW 2003

Ohly A., Sosnitza O., UWG, Gesetz gegen den unlauteren Wettbewerb: mit Preisangabenverordnung, Kommentar, München 2023

Okoń Z., w: *E. Traple* (ed.), Prawo reklamy i promocji, Warszawa 2007

Okoń Z., Czyny nieuczciwej konkurencji w działalności promocyjnej, w: *E. Traple* (ed.), Prawo reklamy i promocji, Warszawa 2007

Panowicz-Lipska J. (ed.), System Prawa Prywatnego, t. 8, Prawo zobowiązań – część szczegółowa, Warszawa 2011

Peretz A., Z powodu ustawy o zwalczaniu nieuczciwej konkurencji (Głos kupca), PPH 1926, No 9

Picht P., Stuckel M., § 4 a Agressive geschäftliche Handlungen, w: *H. Harte-Bavendamm, F. Henning-Bodewig* (eds), Gesetz gegen den unlauteren Wettbewerb (UWG) mit Preisangabenverordnung. Kommentar-, München 2016

Piłka M., Ochrona przed nieuczciwą konkurencją – poradnik dla przedsiębiorców i konsumentów, Vademecum Rzeczpospolitej z 28.8.2002 r.

Podrecki P., Dyrektywa o nieuczciwych praktykach handlowych i jej implementacja do prawa polskiego w: *J. Barta, A. Matlak*, Zagadnienia prawa własności intelektualnej. Zeszyt 100. Prawo własności intelektualnej wczoraj, dziś i jutro Kraków 2007

Raglewski J., w: *M. Zdyb, M. Sieradzka* (eds), Ustawa o zwalczaniu nieuczciwej konkurencji. Komentarz, Warszawa 2016

Rajski J., Szczególne rodzaje sprzedaży premiowanej nagrodami a umowy gry, PPH 1995, No 1

Rasiewicz J., w: *M. Zdyb, M. Sieradzka* (eds), Ustawa o zwalczaniu nieuczciwej konkurencji. Komentarz, Warszawa 2016

Rączka G., Wprowadzenie do terminologii prawa reklamy, w: *M. Namysłowska* (ed.), Reklama. Aspekty prawne, Warszawa 2012

Safjan M, Bosek L. (eds), Konstytucja RP. Komentarz do art. 1–86, vol. 1, Warszawa 2016

Sieradzka M., w: *M. Zdyb, M. Sieradzka* (eds), Ustawa o zwalczaniu nieuczciwej konkurencji. Komentarz, Warszawa 2011, 2016

Sieradzka M., Glosa do wyroku TS z 11.3.2010 r., C-522/08, LEX/el. 2010

Sieradzka M., Glosa do wyroku TS z 3.4.2014 r., C-515/12, LEX/el. 2014

Sieradzka M., Oferta wiązana jako rodzaj praktyki handlowej – glosa do wyroku TS z 23.4.2009 r. w połączonych sprawach: C-261/07 i C-299/07 VTB-VAB NW v. Total Belgium NV oraz Galatea BVBA v. Sanoma Magazines Belgium NV, EPS 2010, No 8

Sieradzka M., Ustawa o przeciwdziałaniu nieuczciwym praktykom rynkowym. Komentarz, Warszawa 2008

Sieradzka M., Wzorzec przeciętnego konsumenta jako punkt odniesienia przy dokonywaniu oceny nieuczciwości praktyki rynkowej, Glosa do wyroku SN z 4.3.2014 r., III SK 34/13, Internetowy Kwartalnik Antymonopolowy i Regulacyjny 2014, No 6

Skoczny T. (ed.), Prawo konkurencji. 25 lat. Pierwszy Polski Kongres Prawa Konkurencji, Warszawa 2016

Skoczny T. (ed.), Ustawa o ochronie konkurencji i konsumentów. Komentarz, Warszawa 2014

Skubisz R., Cele i zakres zastosowania ustawy o zwalczaniu nieuczciwej konkurencji. Dylematy trudnego sąsiedztwa z ustawą o przeciwdziałaniu nieuczciwym praktykom rynkowym, w: *T. Skoczny* (ed.), Prawo konkurencji 25 lat. Pierwszy Polski Kongres Prawa Konkurencji, Warszawa 2016

Skubisz R., Klauzule generalne w prawie zwalczania nieuczciwej konkurencji, Annales Universitatis Mariae Curie-Skłodowska 2016, No 2, vol. LXIII, Sectio G

Sobczak A., Ochrona przed nieuczciwą konkurencją – poradnik dla przedsiębiorców i konsumentów, Vademecum Rzeczpospolitej z 28.8.2002 r.

Sołtysiński S., Gogulski S., w: *J. Szwaja, J. Kępiński* (eds), Ustawa o zwalczaniu nieuczciwej konkurencji. Komentarz, Warszawa 2024

Sosnitza O., w: *A. Ohly, O. Sosnitza* (eds), Gesetz gegen den unlauteren Wettbewerb mit Preisangabeverordnung, Kommentar, München 2023

Sosnitza O., § 2 Konkretes Wettbewerbsverhältnis, w: *A. Ohly, O. Sosnitza* (eds), UWG, Gesetz gegen den unlauteren Wettbewerb. Kommentar, München 2023

Sosnitza O., § 4a Aggressive geschäftliche Handlungen, w: *A. Ohly, O. Sosnitza* (eds), Gesetz gegen den unlauteren Wettbewerb mit Preisangabeverordnung, Kommentar, München 2023

Sroczyński J., *Mioduszewski M.*, w: *M. Zdyb, M. Sieradzka* (eds), Ustawa o zwalczaniu nieuczciwej konkurencji. Komentarz, Warszawa 2016

Stawicki A., w: *A. Stawicki, E. Stawicki* (eds), Ustawa o ochronie konkurencji i konsumentów. Komentarz, Warszawa 2016

Stawicki A., *Stawicki E.* (ed.), Ustawa o ochronie konkurencji i konsumentów, Warszawa 2011

Stefanicki R., Klauzula generalna w ZNKU, w: *M. Kępiński* (ed.), System Prawa Prywatnego, t. 15, Prawo konkurencji, Warszawa 2014

Stefanicki R., Nieuczciwe praktyki handlowe w świetle prawodawstwa Unii Europejskiej – dyrektywa 2005/29/WE, Warszawa 2007

Stefanicki R., Prawne granice swobody przedsiębiorcy w odniesieniu do reklamy "wartościowej", PS 2001, No 3

Stefanicki R., Prawo reklamy w świetle przepisów ustawy o zwalczaniu nieuczciwej konkurencji na tle prawnoporównawczym, Poznań 2003

Stefanicki R., Prawo uczciwej konkurencji a ochrona konsumentów w świetle ustawy o przeciwdziałaniu nieuczciwym praktykom rynkowym, SPP 2011, No 2

Stefanicki R., Ustawa o przeciwdziałaniu nieuczciwym praktykom rynkowym. Komentarz, Warszawa 2009

Stefanicki R., Wymogi staranności zawodowej przedsiębiorcy (w świetle dyrektywy o nieuczciwych praktykach handlowych), PiP 2010, No 4

Steinbeck A., Verkaufsförderungsmaßnahmen im Lauterkeitsrecht, w: *K-H. Fezer* (ed.), Lauterkeitsrecht. Kommentar zum Gesetz gegen den unlauteren Wettbewerb (UWG), Załącznik 2 do § 4a, München 2016

Strzelecki M., Klauzula generalna nieuczciwej praktyki rynkowej, PPH 2008, No 11

Strzelecki M., Nieuczciwe praktyki handlowe a ustawa o zwalczaniu nieuczciwej konkurencji, Internetowy Kwartalnik Antymonopolowy i Regulacyjny 2016, No 3

Stuyck J., The Unfair Commercial Practices Directive and its Consequences for the Regulation of Sales Promotion and the Law of Unfair Competition, w: *S. Weatherill, U. Bernitz* (eds), The Regulation of Unfair Commercial Practices under EC Directive 2005/29. New Rules and New Techniques, Oxford–Portland 2007

Surdacka A., Reklama wartościowa, PPH 1996, No 12

Szczepanowska-Kozłowska K.,w: *E. Nowińska, K. Szczepanowska-Kozłowska*, Ustawa o zwalczaniu nieuczciwej konkurencji. Komentarz, Warszawa 2022

Szczepanowska-Kozłowska K., Co przepis to wątpliwość, Rzeczpospolita z 17.10.2002 r.

Szpunar M., Pojęcie czynu nieuczciwej konkurencji – zagadnienia wybrane, w: *M. Pyziak-Szafnicka* (ed.), Odpowiedzialność cywilna. Księga pamiątkowa ku czci Profesora Adama Szpunara, Kraków 2004

Szwaja J., w: *J. Szwaja* (ed.), Ustawa o zwalczaniu nieuczciwej konkurencji. Komentarz, Warszawa 2006

Szwaja J., Kolejne nowelizacje ustawy o zwalczaniu nieuczciwej konkurencji (w latach 2003–2013), w: *J. Szwaja* (ed.), Dwadzieścia lat ustawy o zwalczaniu nieuczciwej konkurencji, MoP–dodatek 2014, No 6

Szwaja J., Ostatnie nowelizacje ustawy o zwalczaniu nieuczciwej konkurencji, part I, MoP 2002, No 24

Szwaja J., Ostatnie nowelizacje ustawy o zwalczaniu nieuczciwej konkurencji, part II, MoP 2003, No 1

Szwaja J. (ed.), Ustawa o zwalczaniu nieuczciwej konkurencji. Komentarz, Warszawa 2016

Szwaja J., Jasińska K., w: *J. Szwaja, J. Kępiński* (eds), Ustawa o zwalczaniu nieuczciwej konkurencji. Komentarz, Warszawa 2024

Szwaja J., Kubiak-Cyrul A., w: *J. Szwaja, J. Kępiński* (eds), Ustawa o zwalczaniu nieuczciwej konkurencji. Komentarz, Warszawa 2024

Szwaja J., Kubiak-Cyrul A., Wprowadzenie, w: *J. Szwaja, J. Kępiński* (eds), Ustawa o zwalczaniu nieuczciwej konkurencji. Komentarz, Warszawa 2024

Szwaja J., Tischner A., Dokąd zmierza prawo zwalczania nieuczciwej konkurencji?, w: *J. Barta, A. Matlak* (eds), Prawo własności intelektualnej wczoraj, dziś i jutro, Prace instytutu własności intelektualnej UJ, z. 100, Warszawa 2007

Szwaja J., Tischner A., Implementacja dyrektywy 2005/29/WE o zwalczaniu nieuczciwych praktyk handlowych do prawa polskiego, MoP 2007, No 20

Szwaja J., Tischner A., Legitymacja w sprawach zwalczania nieuczciwej konkurencji, w: *M. Kępiński* (ed.), System Prawa Prywatnego, t. 15, Prawo konkurencji, Warszawa 2014

Szwaja J., Tischner A., Odpowiedzialność cywilnoprawna za czyny nieuczciwej konkurencji, SPP 2009, No 2

Szwaja J., Tischner A., Odpowiedzialność cywilnoprawna za czyny nieuczciwej konkurencji, w: *M. Kępiński* (ed.), System Prawa Prywatnego, t. 15, Prawo konkurencji, Warszawa 2014

Szwaja J., Tischner A., System środków cywilnoprawnych, w: *M. Kępiński* (ed.), System Prawa Prywatnego, t. 15, Prawo konkurencji, Warszawa 2014

Szydło M., Wprowadzenie, w: *M. Zdyb, M. Sieradzka* (eds), Ustawa o zwalczaniu nieuczciwej konkurencji. Komentarz, Warszawa 2016

Szymański Ł., Kodeks dobrych praktyk na gruncie ustawy o przeciwdziałaniu nieuczciwym praktykom rynkowym z 23.8.2007 r. W kontekście ubezpieczeniowym, MoP 2015, No 5

Świerczyński M., w: *E. Traple* (ed.), Prawo reklamy i promocji, Warszawa 2007

Świerczyński M., Loterie promocyjne, w: *E. Traple* (ed.), Prawo reklamy i promocji, Warszawa 2007

Świerdza D., Sprzedaż premiowana w prawie polskim i prawie Unii Europejskiej w świetle orzecznictwa ETS, Problemy Współczesnego Prawa Międzynarodowego, Europejskiego i Porównawczego 2012, vol. X, A.D. MMXII

Targosz T., Odpowiedzialność cywilna – roszczenie o wydanie korzyści, odszkodowanie, ciężar dowodu, w: *E. Nowińska, D. Kasprzycki* (eds), Nieuczciwe praktyki rynkowe. Ocena regulacji, Kraków 2012

Targosz T., Ustawa o przeciwdziałaniu nieuczciwym praktykom rynkowym – model ochrony, zasady, zakres ochrony, implikacje dla systemu prawa konkurencji i konsumentów, w: *E. Nowińska, D. Kasprzycki* (eds), Nieuczciwe praktyki rynkowe. Ocena regulacji, Kraków 2012

Teplitzky O., Peifer K-N., Leistner M., Gesetz gegen den unlauteren Wettbewerb, Großkommentar, Berlin–Boston 2013

Timm-Wagner B., Die Umsetzung der Richtlinie über unlautere Geschäftspraktiken in Deutschland, GRUR 2013, z. 3

Tischner A., Cele i zakres zastosowania ZNKU, w: *M. Kępiński* (ed.), System Prawa Prywatnego, t. 15, Prawo konkurencji, Warszawa 2014

Tischner A., Miejsce implementacji dyrektywy 2005/29/WE do prawa polskiego, w: *E. Nowińska, D. Kasprzycki* (eds), Nieuczciwe praktyki rynkowe. Ocena regulacji, Kraków 2012

Tischner A., Model przeciętnego konsumenta w prawie europejskim, KPP 2006, No 1

Tischner A., Pojęcie "przeciętny konsument" w ustawie o przeciwdziałaniu nieuczciwym praktykom rynkowym na tle prawa i orzecznictwa Unii Europejskiej, w: *E. Nowińska, D. Kasprzycki* (ed.), Nieuczciwe praktyki rynkowe. Ocena regulacji, Kraków 2012

Traple E. (ed.), Prawo reklamy i promocji, Warszawa 2007

Travers D., Kopplungsangebote, Eine Studie zum Vertrags- und Lauterkeitsrecht, Frankfurt am Main 2015

Wadlow Ch., The Case for Reclaming European Unfair Competition Law from Europe's Consumer Lawyers, w: *S. Weatherill, U. Bernitz* (eds), The Regulation of Unfair Commercial Practices under EC Directive 2005/29. New Rules and New Techniques, Oxford–Portland 2007

Walaszek-Pyzioł A., Pyzioł W., Czyn nieuczciwej konkurencji (analiza pojęcia), PPH 1994, No 10

Weatherill S., Bernitz U. (eds), The Regulation of Unfair Commercial Practices under EC Directive 2005/29. New Rules and New Techniques, Oxford–Portland 2007

Wędrychowska-Karpińska A., Wiercińska-Krużewska A., w: *A. Stawicki, E. Stawicki* (eds), Ustawa o ochronie konkurencji i konsumentów. Komentarz, Warszawa 2011, 2016

Włodarska-Dziurzyńska K., Problematyka systemów konsorcyjnych (tzw. systemów argentyńskich), w: *E. Nowińska, D. Kasprzycki* (eds), Nieuczciwe praktyki rynkowe. Ocena regulacji, Kraków 2012

Wrona J., Ochrona przed nieuczciwą konkurencją – poradnik dla przedsiębiorców i konsumentów, Vademecum Rzeczpospolitej z 28.8.2002 r.

Wrona J., Promocje sprzedaży, w: *C. Banasiński* (ed.), Standardy wspólnotowe w polskim prawie ochrony konsumenta, Warszawa 2004

Wściubiak Ł., Dobre obyczaje w ustawie o przeciwdziałaniu nieuczciwym praktykom rynkowym, PPH 2007, No 11

Wyrwiński M., Kodeksy dobrych praktyk, w: *E. Nowińska, D. Kasprzycki* (eds), Nieuczciwe praktyki rynkowe. Ocena regulacji, Kraków 2012

Wyrwiński M., Odpowiedzialność cywilna – roszczenia o: zaniechanie, usunięcie skutków, złożenie oświadczenia, zasądzenie sumy pieniężnej na cel społeczny, w: *E. Nowińska, D. Kasprzycki* (eds), Nieuczciwe praktyki rynkowe. Ocena regulacji, Kraków 2012

Wyrwiński M., Pojęcie przedsiębiorcy, w: *E. Nowińska, D. Kasprzycki* (eds), Nieuczciwe praktyki rynkowe. Ocena regulacji, Kraków 2012

Zaradkiewicz K., w: *M. Safjan, L. Bosek* (eds), Konstytucja RP. Komentarz do art. 1–86, t. 1, Warszawa 2016

Zawada K., w: *J. Panowicz-Lipska* (ed.), System Prawa Prywatnego, t. 8, Prawo zobowiązań – część szczegółowa, Warszawa 2011

Zawada K., Majątkowy charakter roszczeń określonych w art. 18 ust. 1 pkt 1 i 3 ZNKU i wynikające stąd konsekwencje dotyczące opłat sądowych, ZNUJ PIPWIUJ 2007, z. 10

Zdyb M., w: *M. Zdyb, M. Sieradzka* (eds), Ustawa o zwalczaniu nieuczciwej konkurencji. Komentarz, Warszawa 2016

Zdyb M., Sieradzka M. (eds), Ustawa o zwalczaniu nieuczciwej konkurencji. Komentarz, Warszawa 2016

Zieliński M., Wykładnia prawa. Zasady, reguły, wskazówki, Warszawa 2012

Zientara A., Ostatnie zmiany ustawy o zwalczaniu nieuczciwej konkurencji, MoP 2011, No 6

Ius, Lex et Res Publica
Studies in Law, Philosophy and Political Cultures

Edited by
Barbara Janusz-Pohl

Vol. 1	Anna Jaron: Socio-Economic Constitutional Rights in Democratisation Processes. An Account of the Constitutional Dialogue Theory. 2012.
Vol. 2	Stanisław Filipowicz: Democracy – The Power of Illusion. 2013.
Vol. 3	Teresa Dukiet-Nagórska (ed.): The Postulates of Restorative Justice and the Continental Model of Criminal Law. As Illustrated by Polish Criminal Law 2014.
Vol. 4	Agnieszka Kupzok: Enforcement of Patents on Geographically Divisible Inventions. An Inquiry into the Standard of Substantive Patent Law Infringement in Cross-Border Constellations. 2015.
Vol. 5	Alicja Jagielska-Burduk / Wojciech Szafrański: Legal Issues in Cultural Heritage Management. A Polish Perspective. 2016.
Vol. 6	Maciej Mataczyński (ed.): The Takeover of Public Companies as a Mode of Exercising EU Treaty Freedoms. 2017.
Vol. 7	Maciej Barczewski (ed.): Value of Information. Intellectual Property, Privacy and Big Data. 2018.
Vol. 8	Pawel Smoleń, Marcin Burzec: Introduction to Polish Tax Law. 2018.
Vol. 9	Łukasz Pohl, Konrad Burdziak: Judicial Interpretation of the 1997 Criminal Code Provisions on Self-Defence. 2019.
Vol. 10	Adam Szot: Judicial Review of Administrative Discretion. The Influence of Court Decisions on Administrative Actions. 2019.
Vol. 11	Michał Peno / Konrad Burdziak (eds.): The Concept of Modern Law. Polish and Central European Tradition. 2019.
Vol. 12	Leszek Leszczyński / Bartosz Lińewski / Adam Szot (eds.): Potential of Precedent in the Statutory Legal Order. 2019.
Vol. 13	Łukasz Bolesta: In Search of a Model for the Legal Protection of a Whistleblower in the Workplace in Poland. A legal and comparative study. 2020.
Vol. 14	Paweł Chmielnicki / Adam Sulikowski (eds.): New Perspectives on Legislation. A Comparative Approach. 2020.
Vol. 15	Marcin Burzec / Beata Kucia-Guściora / Paweł Smoleś: Agricultural Activity in Poland: A Fiscal and Legal Study. 2020.
Vol. 16	Magdalena Półtorak / Ilona Topa (eds.): Women, Children and (Other) Vulnerable Groups. Standards of Protection and Challenges for International Law. 2021.
Vol. 17	Josef Albert Fox: Die polnische Verfassung vom 3. Mai 1791. Hintergründe der Entstehung und der Außerkraftsetzung. Stellung Polens im Zeitalter der Aufklärung. 2021.

Vol. 18 Barbara Janusz-Pohl (ed.): Juvenile Justice Systems: Poland-Brazil-Portugal. 2021.

Vol. 19 Leszek Leszczyński: General Reference Clauses in the Judicial Process. Context of Legislative Intentions Interpretative Discretion. 2021.

Vol. 20 Francisco J. Campos Zamora: Das Problem der Begründung richterlicher Entscheidungen. Eine Analyse auf der Grundlage der Theorie der juristischen Argumentation. 2021.

Vol. 21 Aneta Skorupa-Wulczyńska: Language Rights of the Citizen of the European Union. 2022.

Vol. 22 Mateusz Osiecki: International Legal Aspects of Aerial Terrorism. Methods of Law Enforcement in Aviation. 2022.

Vol. 23 Vladimír Sharp / Gabriela Blahoudková / Jakub Handrlica (eds.): Law, Pandemics and Ownership Restrictions. 2022.

Vol. 24 Piotr Kasprzyk / Anna Konert: Drones – Future of Aviation Law? Interference of Public Law in Private Law. 2023.

Vol. 25 Szymon Pawelec (ed.): Consensual Mechanisms in Criminal Proceedings – Integrative and Comparative Perspective. 2023.

Vol. 26 Dorota Pudzianowska: Statelessness in Public Law. 2023.

Vol. 27 Boguslaw Przywora / Aleksander Wróbel: Formalised Access to Pre-jurisdictional Free Legal Aid. 2023.

Vol. 28 Ewa Dawidziuk / Patricia Panero / Anny Tarwacka (eds.): Family, Law, and Society: from Roman Law to the Present Day. 2024.

Vol. 29 Marian Grzybowsk / Boguslaw Przywora / Aleksandra Syryt (eds.): Free Legal Aid, Theory, Legal Basis and Practice. European Standards. 2024.

Vol. 30 Karolina Gmerek: Trial as a Social Communication Occurrence. 2024.

Vol. 31 Pawel Wiliński (ed.): Effective Legal Remedies in Criminal Justice System. European Perspective. 2024.

Vol. 32 Jakub Hanc / Olga Sitarz / Anna Jaworska-Wieloch: On the (non)existence of the right to religious freedom of persons deprived of liberty. 2024.

Vol. 33 Marian Grzybowsk / Boguslaw Przywora / Aleksandra Syryt (eds.): Free Legal Aid – A Comparative Approach. 2024.

Vol. 34 Dominik Gajewski (ed.): Functioning of Administrative Judiciary in the Context of Economic Changes. 2024.

Vol. 35 Mikołajczyk, Barbara: Older Migrants – Vulnerable and Excluded. 2024.

Vol. 36 Świder, Maciej: The Exercise of the Right to a Fair Trial in the Era of the COVID-19 Pandemic. 2024.

Vol. 37 Tomasz Barankiewicz / Boguslaw Przywora (eds.): Public and Civil Service in Poland. 2024.

Vol. 38 Daniele Vicoli (ed.): Effective Justice 1. Effective Justice. International and Comparative Approaches. 2025.

Vol. 39 Barbara Janusz-Pohl (ed.): Effective Justice 2. Effective Justice. International and Comparative Approaches. 2025.

Vol. 40 Kinga Anna Gajda / Marta Pietras-Eichberger / Małgorzata Skawińska (eds.): Mediation as an Inclusive and Sustainable Method of Resolving Conflicts. 2025.

Vol. 41 Ewa Dawidziuk / Anna Tarwacka / Sławomir Kursa (eds.): Historical and Contemporary Issues of Democracy, Person and Human Rights. 2025.

Vol. 42 Jakub Kępiński: The Impact of Directive 2005/29/EC on Polish Law on combating unfair competition. 2025.

www.peterlang.com

www.ingramcontent.com/pod-product-compliance
Ingram Content Group UK Ltd.
Pitfield, Milton Keynes, MK11 3LW, UK
UKHW021831100926
8556IPUK00004B/270

9 783631 933480